SENIOR WOMEN'S ISSUES CORRESPONDENT
MARK YOUR CALENDA...
...EAU CHIEF DE HAVANA
...ROB CORDDRY
KRISTEN SCHAAL
...SS
...VE UP
PRODUCE PETE WITH STEVE CARELL
SENIOR ALTERNATIVE LIFESTYLES CORRESPONDENT
STEVE CARELL
...DENT
JON
LOOK...
...ERANGED MILLIONAIRE
...OHN HODGMAN
THIS JUST IN
AMERICA TO THE RESCUE
CARLOS DANGER
...ERESTING TO
...CCA
THE MANCHURIAN LUNATIC
TORTURE ANALYST
JOHN OLIVER
SENIOR MUSLIM CORR...
AASIF MAND...
EXTREME TAKEOVER: TEA PARTY EDITION
FOX: THE NEWS YOU WATCH WHEN NEWS ISN'T WHAT YOU WANT
CNN LEAVES IT THE...
OPERAT...
...AN CORRESPONDENT
...KLEPPER
WAR ON CHRISTMAS: S#@T'S GETTING WEIRD EDITION
H5: THE CLUCKENING
MITT HAP...
INDECISION 2000
SLIMMING DOWN WITH STEVE
SENIOR LIPIZZANER CORRESPONDENT
ROB CORDDRY
SENIO...
STE...
...BIA
MIDWEST MIDTERM MIDTACULAR
SENIOR FOREIGN-LOOKING CORRERSPONDENT
AASIF MANDVI
SENIOR ASIAN CORRESPONDENT
OLIVIA MUNN
...Y OF ROAST BEEF SANDWICHES
BEHIND THE IRON CLOSET
...HE AUDACITY OF GROPE
WILMORE-OLIVER INVESTIGATES
SCUMDOG MILLION-HAIRS
OBAMANIA
BEHIND THE IF...
...S GOT TORTURE
LET'S ALL STAND ON JOHN MCCAIN'S LAWN
BLIZZAPOCALYPSEGEDDON
TOPPINGTON VON MONOCLE
F**KFACE VON CLOWNSD...
...S
SENIOR DISASTEROLOGIST
ED HELMS
YOU'RE WELCOME
CHASING THE DRAGON WITH
ROB RIGGLE
INDIA JONES AND THE ELECTION OF DOC...
...E
...CHILDREN
SENIOR ESPIONAGE CORRESPONDENT
JASON JONES
OH, THE SPEW-HANNITY
SENIOR CASUAL RACISM CORRESPONDENT
MICHAEL CHE
...O'S WORLD
THE RUMBLE IN THE AIR-CONDITIONED AUDITORIUM
SENIOR WOM...
...TO
...CUE
FOIBLES OF THE RECONSTRUCTION
WORLD OF CLASS WARFARE
PUPPET MICHAEL STEELE
SAMAN...
SENIOR STATE SNACK CORRESPONDENT
JESSICA WILLIAMS
OPERATION DESERTER STORM
SENIOR SMOLDERING DRUG BOAT CORRESPO...
AL MADRIGAL
...M 2013
...ERO DARK
...00,000
THE NOTORIOUS AIG
ALIENS VS. SENATOR
SENIOR CONCEPTUAL ART CORRESPONDENT
STEPHEN COLBERT
SENIOR PET CORRESPONDENT
JOHN OLIVER
S...
RAPPERS OR REPUBLICANS WITH
WYATT CENAC
INDIGNATION! POPULIST UPRISING '09 THE ENRAGENING
STUPIDER ASCENDING
HURRICANE KATRINA: AFTER THE AFTERMATH
WHAAA?
OUT AT
FRA...
...INDIAN CORRESPONDENT
...AN MINHAJ
THE HUMAN DISSENTIPEDE
THE SEAT OF HEAT
THE SHILLING FIELDS
REFERENDUMOLOGIST
JASON JONES
THE AFROSPANICINDIOASIANATION OF AM...
SENIOR EXECUTIVE COMMANDER-IN-CHIEF WHO HAP...
LARRY WILMORE
...TLEFORD INTERVIEW
SHOWDOWN: IRAQ?
BUSH V. BUSH
INDECISION 1425
...OF MENACE
OH, FOR FOX SAKE
SENIOR ZIONIST BILLIONAIRE CORRESPONDENT
SAMANTHA BEE
WOMEN'S HEALTH WITH
VANCE DEGEN...
...E BEST F#%KING NEWS TEAM EVER
JON STEWART DELVES INTO YOUR BRIEFS
DIAGNOSIS: SCIENCE
...CCONNELLING
SENIOR ATROCITY-TRIAL CORRESPONDENT
DAN BAKKEDAHL
COALITION OF THE PIDDLING
...DEMOCALYPSE
GUANTANAMO BAYWATCH
ARBY'S: SEE? A LOT OF THINGS CAUSE DIARRHEA
RESIDENT EXPERT
JOHN HODGMAN
...ERICA
SENIOR ANONYMOUS CONGRESSIONAL GAY PUBLIC RESTROOM SEX CORRESPONDENT
INDECISION 2008
KLA...
...ANALYST
ROB CORDDRY
SENIOR FOCUS GROUP ANALYST
STACEY GRENROCK WOODS
CHIEF SPACE TRAVEL AND...
STEVE CARELL
...AMO CORRESPONDENT
...NTAL WATCH
...RIOR RACIS...
P9-CEH-433

THE
DAILYSHOW
(THE BOOK)

AN
ORAL HISTORY

As Told by Jon Stewart, the Correspondents, Staff and Guests

—

CHRIS SMITH
FOREWORD BY **JON STEWART**

GRAND CENTRAL
PUBLISHING

NEW YORK   BOSTON

Grand Central Publishing
Hachette Book Group
1290 Avenue of the Americas, New York, NY 10104
grandcentralpublishing.com
twitter.com/grandcentralpub

First Edition: November 2016

Grand Central Publishing is a division of Hachette Book Group, Inc. The Grand Central
Publishing name and logo is a trademark of Hachette Book Group, Inc.

The publisher is not responsible for websites (or their content)
that are not owned by the publisher.

The Hachette Speakers Bureau provides a wide range of authors for speaking events.
To find out more, go to www.hachettespeakersbureau.com or call (866) 376-6591.

Comedy Central's "The Daily Show with Jon Stewart" used with permission
by Comedy Central. © 2016 Viacom Media Networks. All Rights Reserved.
Comedy Central, all related titles, characters and logos are trademarks owned by
Viacom Media Networks, a division of Viacom International Inc.

Library of Congress Cataloging-in-Publication Data has been applied for.
Library of Congress Control Number: 2016952042

ISBNs: 978-1-4555-6538-2 (hardcover), 978-1-4555-6535-1 (ebook)

Printed in the United States of America

LSC-W

10 9 8 7 6 5 4 3 2 1

My wildest dream for *The Daily Show* when I started was, "This will be fun. Hopefully we'll do it well." Success for me would've been feeling like I figured it out. That I got to express the things I wanted to. It was never "I want this to be a cultural touchstone...but only for a very small portion of America." And I was hoping to stay on TV longer than nine months this time.

—Jon Stewart

Contents

Foreword by Jon Stewart

It was the summer of 1998 and I was riding a wave of dizzying show business success. I was a thirty-five-year-old New York City standup comic with a canceled talk show, an unproduced screenplay, a book of unpublished essays, and two upcoming roles in Independent Films critics would almost unanimously hail as "speaking parts." Life was good. People didn't randomly shout "on weed" at just any old jackass on the street. No. They shouted it at me. The "Enhancement Smoker" from *Half-Baked*. Did I have any "starring" roles lined up? Any so-called mainstream "successes"? or creative "focus"? or "ideas"? Maybe not. But between the time I hosted a show on MTV to the time Josh Hartnett jammed a pen in my eye in *The Faculty*, I bet there wasn't a Denny's in the entire country I couldn't walk into at three in the morning and not have someone want to get high with me.

So when my old MTV bosses, Doug Herzog and Eileen Katz, and my old talk show EP [executive producer], Madeleine Smithberg, called to talk about the soon-to-be-vacated hosting job at Comedy Central's *The Daily Show*, I was relatively cool on the idea. I actually was. My last foray in the real world of television hosting (fake hosting with Larry Sanders not withstanding) had ended with my face on a dartboard in the *New York Post* with the headline STEWART JOINS LATE NIGHT LOSERS. That'll leave a mark. So present lack of success didn't quite mitigate fear of future failure. My girlfriend at the time, and now wife, Tracey, felt differently. She knew I'd been a bit rudderless and creatively unmoored, and she thought this could be a chance to reengage a mind that, when unfocused, generally turned and kicked the living shit out of its owner. Tracey's good like that. She knows things that I don't yet know but will, and she waits patiently for me to know them, too, all while not displaying the I-know-things-you-don't-know-yet-but-will face.

It was a big decision. The kind you can only make while down the Jersey Shore over pie. So sitting at the big Horseshoe counter at Holiday Snack Bar, Long Beach Island, Tracey and I made a list of the Pros and Cons.

Pro: It's a job. For cash money.

Con: Got to get up early and wear a tie.

Pro: Only have to wear a tie for like twenty minutes a day.

Con: Wasn't sure the show was my sensibility.

Pro: Maybe it could be.

Con: If I screw this one up, the president of Show Business might kick me out, this time for good.

Pro: (*from Tracey*) It seemed like an incredible chance to make a funny, smart show about things I really cared about.

Con: The rightness of her position meant I couldn't have any more pie.

After the decision, the next sixteen and a half years are a bit of a blur. I know we enjoyed some incredible highs, endured some terrible tragedies, saw friends and colleagues come and go…I may have called the president "Dude" at one point and gotten a gospel choir to sing "Go fuck yourself" as a joyous refrain…

I don't miss the grind. I miss my friends. We may not have hit the mark with each bit, definitely left some laughs on the table, but damn, I'm proud of that place. We never forgot what a privilege it was to have a platform. I believe we treated the opportunity with the respect it deserved and we worked our asses off to get better at doing the show. And damn! The talent that I got to work with day in and out! And somewhere along the line the process of making that show became the mechanism by which I worked through my own emotions about the world. That's hard to replace. That morning meeting when we plotted the day. Writers, producers, correspondents…PAs and interns. Always interesting, often illuminating, sometimes challenging, occasionally heated, and once or twice ferocious. It was a process that forced us… me…to evolve. To grow and learn. To disappoint myself, only to have an opportunity for redemption the very next night. Not just on the show but in the hallways and offices. The people there made me be better. And every night we got to present the meal we'd made. There really was nothing like waking up in the middle of the night, feeling anxious and angry and hurt. Feeling like the institutions of our great nation were no longer functioning, that the entire political/media landscape was an incestuous circle jerk of inoperable self-interest, ignoring even the simplest of solutions for a status quo that cannot and should not hold...and coming in to work the next day to have that complex goulash of sadness and fear drained by having Justin [Chabot] build a giant wheel of dildos for that night's program.

This show was and will always be the honor of my professional life. I could never wrap my head around putting it or my experience there in any coherent context. Favorite memories? Moments? What were we trying to do? Did we help? hurt? It was too big a meal for me to even try to digest. I'm really grateful to Chris for taking on the challenge. In casting as wide a net as he could to bring as many voices as would speak to the task. I look forward to reading this book and finally finding out what it was really like to work at *The Daily Show*...just don't tell me how it ends...I get canceled, don't I...?

Dammit.

THE
DAILYSHOW
(THE BOOK)

Introduction to the Beginning

The daily show.

That's what was scribbled on the Comedy Central schedule grid, in the 11 p.m. slot, for months, as a placeholder, in 1995. What exactly would happen in that half hour of programming? No one really knew. Except that it would happen...daily.

Comedy Central itself was still a sketchy proposition at the time. In 1989, Time Warner, owner of HBO, had launched the Comedy Channel, the first cable channel devoted solely to comedy-based programming. Five months later Viacom, owner of MTV, had launched a competitor, Ha! The Comedy Channel featured a mix of quirky original shows and clips from standup comics; its signature creation was *Mystery Science Theater 3000*. Ha! countered with some low-budget original shows plus a wealth of reruns, including full episodes from *Saturday Night Live*'s middle years.

The Gulf War, beginning in August 1990, was a breakthrough for cable news, with CNN showing there was a large audience for round-the-clock coverage, even though the big three networks still dominated the nightly ratings. Further up the dial, Ha! and the Comedy Channel merged, reemerging as Comedy Central in April 1991. And in a bar in Manhattan, a comedian on a blind date had an insight that would eventually help connect those wildly disparate developments.

"I was at a sports bar, and all the TVs were turned to the war instead of sports," Lizz Winstead says. "CNN had replaced their fancy reporters with young people, and they were on roofs, and there was green, and there was a theme song and all this shit. And I just thought, 'Are they reporting on the war, or trying to sell me a war?' Then the guy I was with said, 'This is really cool,' and I was like, 'Oh my God, I might be on to something.'"

The blind date didn't lead anywhere, but Winstead's brainstorm eventually did. In 1995, Bill Maher announced that he and *Politically Incorrect* would be jumping from Comedy Central to ABC after the following year's elections. To replace *PI* at 11 p.m., Doug Herzog, Comedy Central's new president, wanted a topical show that would brand the network and appeal to young male viewers. The model he kept in mind was ESPN's *SportsCenter*.

To develop the show, Herzog recruited Madeleine Smithberg, who had been a producer at *Late Night with David Letterman*. The thirty-six-year-old New Yorker had also been in charge of a quirky talk show that ran on MTV in 1993 before being syndicated by Paramount, which then used it, for one season, as a replacement for the canceled *Arsenio Hall Show*.

Smithberg hired, as the head writer for the new Comedy Central show, a comedian who lived upstairs in her Chelsea apartment building—Lizz Winstead. Smithberg had hired Winstead to work on the old MTV show, and the pair had been talking to Comedy Central about a new idea, a satire of a failing cable network. Herzog steered Smithberg toward the nameless late-night show instead. She and Winstead, a thirty-four-year-old Minnesota native, worked through ideas for nearly a year, settling on a news parody format. "Madeleine was the brains and the structure," Winstead says. "She really knew how to run a show. And I was the person who knew a lot about politics and a lot about humor. I thought we should make the show itself a character. And we needed to differentiate ourselves from 'Weekend Update.' So we would operate like a newsroom, but be a comedy show."

Herzog's first choice to host the fledgling show was Craig Kilborn, who had built a following as a smart-ass talking head on *SportsCenter*. "He was sort of doing his bad version of Dennis Miller, who was a hot guy at the time," Herzog says. "Craig met with me, and Lizz, and Madeleine, and Eileen Katz [Comedy Central's head of programming at the time]. And I thought in the first five minutes that they were going to strangle him. The first thing Craig said was, 'Some of you guys worked at MTV?' And Eileen and I had come from there originally. 'Yes, why?'

"Craig goes, 'You know Downtown Julie Brown?' We go, 'Yeah, sure.' He goes, 'Because I love brown sugar.'

"That's how the meeting started. Craig actually managed to bring it all the way around, and by the time the meeting was over they were like, 'That's our guy.'"

Writers were hired—J. R. Havlan, Tom Johnson, Ray James, Kent Jones, and Guy Nicolucci—as were the first batch of "correspondents": A. Whitney Brown, Beth Littleford, and Brian Unger, plus Winstead. Lewis Black, a dyspeptic standup, came on as an Andy Rooney–type commentator who would deliver rants pegged to wacky news video clips. But as the program's debut date closed in, no one could come up with a suitable name. Until one day Smithberg called Herzog: "Why don't we just call it *The Daily Show*?"

It premiered on July 22, 1996, at 11:30 p.m. The format loosely tracked that of a conventional newscast: five or so opening minutes called "Headlines," read by Kilborn from the anchor desk, followed by "Other News," then usually a pretaped "field piece" with one of the correspondents, and finishing up with Kilborn interviewing an actor or a musician promoting their new movie or TV show or album.

Some segments played off the hard news of the day, like the presidential contest between Bob Dole and Bill Clinton. "There was more of a pop-culture-and-lifestyle component only because what we were satirizing—particularly local news—was doing a lot of that stuff," Winstead says. "We would make fun of the conventions of news. Like when TV reporters talk, how do you create drama in a story that doesn't exist? Brian Unger, who had been a producer at CBS News, invented what it means to be a *Daily Show* correspondent."

Yet the tone of Kilborn's *Daily Show* could be mean-spirited. A headline called "Operation Desert Shield Me from Impeachment" included a joke that investigators were having trouble analyzing the stain on Monica Lewinsky's dress because it was mixed with "liver-flavored Alpo." Field pieces often centered on true believers in UFOs and aliens.

The day-to-day creative process of the first few years of *The Daily Show* centered on Smithberg, Winstead, and the writing staff, which now included Paul Mecurio, Jim Earl, and Steve Rosenfield. "My first day on the job," Winstead says, "I have to pull the writers into my office and say, 'Guys, you can't have your mushroom dealer come up to the office.'" Kilborn came up with the signature "Five Questions" conceit for guest interviews, but otherwise largely read from the script.

In November 1996, after Bill Maher's exit, Comedy Central's executives moved *The Daily Show* to 11 p.m. in part to counterprogram the late local news—and in part because they knew their low-budget operation had no real hope of competing with the late-night mainstream comedy powerhouses. The war between David Letterman and Jay Leno to succeed Johnny Carson at the helm of *The Tonight Show* had been national front-page news in 1992 and 1993, and Comedy Central was available in fewer than half of American households. Leno took over the flagship NBC show, but Letterman's new *Late Show* on CBS was scoring high ratings, too. Each attracted around six million viewers per night. Kilborn's *Daily Show* would peak at a nightly average of 357,000.

Yet Kilborn's audience was growing and the show was generating critical buzz, helped by the addition of correspondents Mo Rocca and Stephen Colbert. Perhaps more important than the chatter was the fact that the *Daily Show* audience was indeed reaching the younger male viewers Herzog had targeted in the first place. The combination caught Letterman's eye, and in 1998 CBS offered Kilborn its 12:30 a.m. *Late Late Show* slot.

"He starts to get a little heat, we're starting to get a little attention with *The Daily Show*," Herzog says, "and then the next thing you know Kilborn goes and signs with CBS without even telling us."

Panic, followed by auditions: David Alan Grier, Michael McKean, Greg Proops, Bill Weir, and Mike Rowe came to the *Daily Show* studio and sat in the host's chair. Littleford and Colbert got tryouts, too. But Herzog and other Comedy Central executives wondered about a guy who had hosted the short-lived MTV talk show produced by Smithberg, a black-leather-jacket-wearing standup comic. He had lost out to Conan O'Brien as Letterman's NBC replacement; he had written a book of satirical essays; he had played Eve Harrington to Garry Shandling's Margo Channing on *The Larry Sanders Show*; and lately he'd had some supporting roles in Hollywood romcoms. Herzog didn't think the highly regarded, slightly adrift comedian would be interested in the *Daily Show* job. But hey, what did he have to lose in buying lunch for Jon Stewart?

1

This Just In

JON STEWART, The Daily Show *host, 1999–2015*

At the time, I was obviously making my mark in such films as *Wishful Thinking* and *Dancing with Architecture*, or *Dancing About*...Oh, no. They ended up calling it something else. *Playing by Heart*, I think it was.

JAMES DIXON, *manager for Jon Stewart, 1987–*

After *The Jon Stewart Show* was canceled by Paramount, he was...not burnt on being on TV, but he wanted to kind of wet his feet with film. We had this nice deal with Harvey Weinstein, and Jon was down in Tribeca and he's getting to kiss Angelina Jolie in films.

JON STEWART

Getting fired from Paramount was the real turning point for me. Because I thought that after appearing on *Letterman*, now I'm a made man. And the Paramount thing, I thought losing it meant I was an unmade man. I realized you still have to make your act better. The goal is to produce, the goal is to make things.

So I spent some time writing and performing on *The Larry Sanders Show*, and I learned a lot from Garry Shandling.

JUDD APATOW, *standup comic, writer, director*

Garry had the foresight to write about the talk show wars and this very subtle aspect of it, which is, you support a young comedian and slowly the network likes him more than it likes you, and then that younger guy, in ways that he understands and might not understand, slowly pushes you out of your job. Similar to what really happened with [Jay] Leno and Conan [O'Brien] and [Jimmy] Fallon. So there was a moment when Garry was considering continuing *The Larry Sanders Show*, and changing the name of it to *The John Stewart Show*, with an *H* so it wouldn't really be Jon. Everyone was excited about it for a while, but it went away.

JON STEWART

Probably my favorite Garry memory is his life being so bizarre to me. It was going to Warren Beatty's house with Garry and having dinner with Warren and Sean Penn in this beautiful mansion on Mulholland or wherever it was, and then heading down to the Chateau Marmont. And at this time, Warren Beatty's got to be fifty, sixty years old and Garry's not a spring chicken, and we're in the Chateau Marmont surrounded by fans, if you know what I mean.

I knew I didn't want to live in LA. Because everything is inflected with show business, and I found that to be suffocating. Even your Saturday basketball game over at Garry's house. It was a red carpet of people that you couldn't help but think, "Oh, wow. Look at me, I just got my shot blocked by that guy from *The Avengers*," or whatever it was. You always felt a little bit like you were on an audition, and I never liked that feeling.

JAMES DIXON

Worst-case scenario, he could always be a writer-producer on his own or on someone else's show. We didn't say, "Let's host a news parody show." Jon was always smart about the long play.

JON STEWART

The Daily Show wasn't necessarily on the radar. I think they called and said, "Hey man, would you be interested in talking about this?"—something along those lines, something as romantic as that.

JAMES DIXON

I definitely advocated for him to do it. I just said to him, "You can put this through your prism. You can make it smarter and different than what it's been." Now, I definitely didn't see the show becoming the political lightning rod that it evolved into.

J. R. HAVLAN, *writer, 1996–2014; member, original* **Daily Show** *staff*

I knew of him as a sort of leather-jacket-wearing, hipster young dude who was different from the personality that we had been working with, let alone created, for *The Daily Show*, for Craig, the newsman thing.

KENT JONES, *writer, 1996–2000; member, original* **Daily Show** *staff*

Oh, it was really positive, my reaction to Jon being hired. He was a name, and he had a good reputation. Hiring Jon is Comedy Central saying this is an important show to them.

LEWIS BLACK, *contributor, 1996–*

From the time I met Jon in the clubs, I liked him, he was funny. There was no bullshit to him. Hiring him for *The Daily Show* made sense. The only thing I found disturbing was that they auditioned everybody, and they didn't audition me. And you just do that out of etiquette. You don't have to hire me. I don't care. You don't have to put film in the camera. You just pretend that you're allowing me to do this.

DOUG HERZOG, *executive, MTV, 1984–1995; president, Comedy Central, 1995–1998; executive, Viacom, 2004–*

In the summer of '98 when we announced that Jon was going to take over *The Daily Show*, we had a little press conference in the lobby of the old Comedy Central offices. And Stephen Colbert showed up, as a member of the press representing *The Daily Show*, wanting to know why he didn't get the job.

STEPHEN COLBERT, *correspondent, 1997–2005*

"You told me he wasn't funny." That's what Jon said to Doug Herzog.

The Daily Show *offices and studio were in a still-rugged pocket of Hell's Kitchen, at 513 West Fifty-Fourth Street, between Tenth and Eleventh Avenues. The* Daily Show's *neighbors were abandoned warehouses, but the building itself was a cozy, three-story, redbrick townhouse. The production offices were upstairs, with the one-hundred-seat studio on the ground floor.*

JEN FLANZ, *from production assistant to executive producer, 1998–*

The area was rough in those days. I think Adrianne Frost got carjacked outside the Fifty-Fourth Street studio.

Jon's first day, he walked around and introduced himself. He was wearing a black leather jacket. I remember hearing rumors before he started: "He doesn't want to wear a suit." Our wardrobe girl at the time was upset. Jon did wear suits on the show. It was fine. But it was a big thing at the time.

MADELEINE SMITHBERG, The Daily Show *cocreator; executive* *producer, 1996–2003*

Because of the point of view that had been created by Craig Kilborn sitting in the chair, the writers' role had inflated. Yeah, they were spoiled rotten, because almost every show in late night is talent driven. They got too big for their britches.

STEW BAILEY, *from field producer to co–executive producer, 1996–* *2005; member, original* **Daily Show** *staff*

Madeleine had hired me as a segment producer on Jon's MTV pilot and then on the series, and then also on *The Daily Show* when she started with Kilborn. Jon came into *Daily Show* writing meetings originally and would listen. I think that he really wanted to make sure that he understood what the process was as opposed to coming in and immediately dictating terms.

JON STEWART

A couple of months before I officially started as host there was a meeting with the writers and producers. Let's call that "Jonny's surprise party." I knew that the people working on the Kilborn show were rightfully proud of it. It had done well. It was not the sensibility that I thought was right for me, and so when they approached me for the show, I was pretty clear about the direction I thought I wanted to take it. Seemed like everybody was on board with that, and so this was my first chance to meet with all the people who, I had been told, were so excited about that. *So* excited. They're so happy you're here.

And I walked in, and it was a room full of people who, as it turned out, were annoyed that I had an idea about where I wanted to go, who thought that I was going to MTV it up. I was told, "This isn't about bands. We do a real show here." I just sat there like, "Oh, fuck." It felt a little bit like, "Wow, none of this was in the brochure. The brochure said that this was oceanfront property."

JAMES DIXON

I had to talk Jon down. Not from a tree—from a skyscraper. Because they basically said to him, "Welcome aboard. This is how we do shit here. Grab a chair." It was bullshit. And Jon had to systematically mold the show piece by piece, person by person.

MATT LABOV, *publicist for Jon Stewart, 1994–2008*

The stakes for Jon were fairly high at that point, because he's not a super-young guy anymore, and he's had shots, and people easily disappear and go into the woodwork. He didn't get the Conan job on NBC, he didn't get the 12:30 job after Letterman. If this doesn't work on fucking cable, then where would Jon have ended up?

PAUL RUDD, *actor*

Technically I was Jon's first *Daily Show* guest interview. I went to the University of Kansas, and my roommate, Stewart Bailey, became a segment producer who was with the show from the very beginning. I'd been on Kilborn's *Daily Show*. When Jon replaced Craig, they wanted to do a test show so Jon could get used to the format. I was wearing my girlfriend's *Jon Stewart Show* MTV T-shirt.

Stewart made his debut on Monday, January 11, 1999. His first joke was that Kilborn was "on assignment in Kuala Lumpur." His first headline, "The Final Blow," was about the Senate impeachment trial of President Bill Clinton. His first guest was Michael J. Fox, then starring in ABC's City Hall sitcom Spin City. But Stewart looked, for the first months, very much the guest himself. Other than a new couch and desktop—and blue script pages for Stewart to scribble on portentously, replacing Kilborn's white paper—the set design was unchanged. The theme song, Bob Mould's "Dog on Fire," was the same. And Stewart's suits were so ill-fitting that they looked inherited from his much-taller predecessor.

J. R. HAVLAN

You watch his first shows, where he's wearing David Byrne's suit, you can see that it's the exact same format. He didn't want to change anything, at least at the beginning.

The first joke I wrote that Jon did on the air was on his first day. Popeye and Olive Oyl were getting married. We showed a picture of them, and you see

Popeye, with his huge forearms. The joke is, "As for the wedding night, Olive Oyl had only one request: no fisting." The crowd loved it. But when I go back and I look at the tape, I can almost see Jon falling to pieces inside his own head, like, "Maybe I should change things up here sooner than I was planning."

Recurring segments from the Kilborn days—like "Ad Nauseam," about dumb commercials—continued to appear regularly during Stewart's first year. And there were wince-inducing bits, including one with Stewart singing, "Homeless, homeless, man," to the tune of "Macho Man," in a piece about the destitute former lead singer of the Village People. There was also a headline taking crude potshots at flimsy Florida targets.

Jon Stewart: [*at anchor desk*] In what must have seemed like a good idea at the time, the Florida Department of State decided to celebrate the coming millennium with "Great Floridians 2000." The program stalled, however, when they only received two hundred nominees, including five governors, three athletes, and 156 misspellings of the name "Jimmy Buffett." The list then dwindles to ten bearded ladies, the inventor of the funnel cake, and a blind guy who can fart the theme to *M*A*S*H*.

Stewart did not arrive with a precise blueprint for where he wanted to take The Daily Show. *But he did have a clear idea of the sensibility he wanted to instill. One of Stewart's comedy heroes was George Carlin, who wove social criticism into his jokes and riffs about dirty words, organized religion, and hypocritical politicians. Stewart wanted to give his* Daily Show *a similarly substantive foundation—and, crucially, he wanted it to "punch up." He started shifting* The Daily Show's *sights to target powerful people and institutions, and he began changing the tone of the show from randomly coarse to deliberately barbed. Not that he was opposed to making a good dick joke now and then.*

ADAM CHODIKOFF, *from researcher to senior producer, 1996–*
It was pretty quick that things changed. One of Jon's lines was, "No more Carol Channing jokes"—the celebrity stuff. Instead of doing six headlines a show, we started doing three headlines a show, but they were more intense. They were longer and had more power and research to them, and more tape.

JUSTIN MELKMANN, *from segment producer to supervising producer,* *video department, 1997–*

During the Kilborn era, it was about "How can we seem like we've gone too far?" With Jon, we went from creating the news—creating funny spoof headlines—to making fun of the news. That was a big change.

JON STEWART

You can satirize news media conventions just by embodying the form in slightly exaggerated or subtle ways—for instance, the way that they do those camera turns. Making the story itself have purpose—that's when I felt we got something.

For me the key switch was relevance—turning the machine in a direction more toward politics, media, satire. The first two years, most of my energy was spent saying, "I understand that's a funny joke, but our point of view here is not that the lady who is selling the Barbie in that commercial is a whore. That joke runs counter to the idea that we are maybe looking at the underlying sexism involved in this product."

> **Jon Stewart:** [*at anchor desk*] Belly up to the Barbie! Some of Hollywood's biggest stars turned out to honor a hunk of molded petroleum, as Barbie turned forty, making her too old to play the girlfriend and too young to play the mother. Here's Brandy, singing the Barbie marching song, "Be Anything," with a choir of future divorcees. She looks just like Moesha!
> And here's Brandy talking!
> **Brandy:** [*in video clip*] "I love Barbie. She's so positive, she's very classy, and I'm just happy to be here, because that's the way I am."
> **Jon Stewart:** Yes, that's exactly right, Brandy, because class is all about telling people you're classy.

MO ROCCA, *correspondent, 1998–2003*

Shortly after Jon arrived, the whole staff piled into Madeleine's office. We had done a bit about Dana Plato dying, and Jon felt bad about delivering a joke when the end of her life had been so pathetic. He said he had resolved that the show needed to have a point of view and couldn't just be the kid at the back of the classroom throwing spitballs in all directions. I remember people trading the kind of glances that said, "Oh shit, this is going to be a disaster."

JON STEWART

To be fair to the writers who stayed from Kilborn's show, they had a successful thing going. They thought of it as a continuation of their show. I thought it was a new show. To me it wasn't edgy or provocative to just take napalm to a bush for no reason. You wanted it to be pointed, purposeful, intentional, surgical.

I felt like I walked in there with a very open "Okay, so this will be great," and it was "Hey, motherfucker, you came here to kill a baby."

KENT JONES

Well, I would not agree with that. I don't remember any of this being as hostile as it has been portrayed, I just don't.

J. R. HAVLAN

A month or two in, you could see flashes of pieces and jokes that have meaning, which has always been Jon's thing. That's what Jon instilled in everybody that came through there: "I'm not interested in the first thing off the top of your head. You're saying it before you've given thought to what it is you really want to say." That was the biggest learning process with working for Jon. It takes you away from being surface.

To change the culture of The Daily Show, *though, Stewart knew he needed committed allies as much as he needed people who could write funny and fast.*

CHRIS REGAN, *writer, 1999–2006*

I was thirty-one and I had been working as an advertising writer for Sony Music. It was a good job for someone trying to start a comedy career, because it was a company where they spent an awful lot of money, I had a big office, and I didn't do much in the way of actual work.

I got ahold of the fax number at *SNL* [*Saturday Night Live*] for Colin Quinn, when he was doing "Weekend Update." Every Friday, I would fax stuff to him, and he began to buy a decent chunk of jokes from me.

Jon took over *The Daily Show*, and he asked Colin Quinn if he knew of anyone who was writing decent topical stuff, and Colin gave him my name, which is awfully nice of him because I'd never met Colin.

I was called in by Madeleine Smithberg and Chris Kreski, who was the head writer at the time, and I had an interview with them. Jon came in only at the very end. He was eating Chinese food out of a Styrofoam tray. I think he had sweat clothes on: a gray sweatshirt and gray bottoms. He looked like an old-timey police cadet.

Jon just sat down on the couch, while he was eating, and he asked me one or two questions, and then said, "So, if we hire you here, are you going to be my guy?" And I wasn't quite sure what being "his guy" entailed, but I was very eager to get out of advertising, and I said sure, and then I was hired about a week later. I was Jon's first hire on the show.

JON STEWART

Six or eight weeks in, the writers called me into their office. They're like, "You can't change our jokes anymore." I didn't know what to say.

So after a weekend of pacing and smoking and having tremendous Lincoln-Douglas debates on the couch by myself, I went back in, and it was horrible. I basically told them all to fuck off. "You work for me. And if you don't like the direction, okay. I get that. Don't work here."

There were points where I thought, "I made the wrong decision. I've got to leave." But I don't give up very easily. It was open hostility, which is so enjoyable. It became that sense of "Okay, let's arm-wrestle." This will give you a hint of my personality of grudges.

CHRIS REGAN

It was tense. It was a weird experience to be involved in, because it was the first job I'd had in the industry, and I just kind of wanted to lay low and do my work. But there was a lot of conflict between Jon and the Kilborn writers. As time went on, it put into perspective the "Are you going to be my guy?" question Jon had asked me.

In those early days if felt like Madeleine and Chris Kreski had the final say over what went into the script. But that didn't last long, and some heads began to roll.

MADELEINE SMITHBERG

My professional and creative worlds collided, and it was not smooth. It was bumpy, and painful, and uncomfortable, and awkward, but it had to go through those convulsions. You had a show that was a real collaborative stew, and now it was just being taken apart and put back together and deconstructed and reemerging as *The Daily Show with Jon Stewart*. Instead of things being in this big free-form orbit, *boom*, suddenly we had a sun, and Jon Stewart was the sun.

JON STEWART

Well, I didn't really have a game plan. I knew what I didn't want. But then turning it into what you did want was the next scenario, and that was going to take time, and effort, and accomplices. What I needed most were accomplices.

BEN KARLIN, *from head writer to executive producer, 1999–2006*

I was living in Los Angeles, working with a bunch of guys from the *Onion*, selling pilots and doing punch-up on movies. We did a pilot for Fox called *Deadline Now*, at about the same time *The Daily Show* was launching. We kind of did the exact opposite. We didn't want to be winking at the audience. We wanted to play it straight and not really acknowledge we were a comedy show. We hired actors and went about trying to produce a news show that was very much in the spirit of the *Onion* newspaper. And frankly, we were quite scornful of the Kilborn *Daily Show*.

Our template host, when we'd come up with show ideas, was always Jon Stewart. We loved Jon Stewart. So when it was announced that Jon was taking over *The Daily Show*, our little comedy snob nerd group thought it was a bad move. For him. Comedy Central was still pretty second tier, and that might even be nice. And Jon was the Letterman heir apparent.

I got a call from my agent saying, "Listen, Jon is looking for a new head writer, loves the *Onion*, has heard that you're kind of the de facto leader of the *Onion* guys' group out in LA. Would you be willing to come out to New York and meet with them?"

I was twenty-seven. I had developed a lot of TV shows, I was the editor of the *Onion*, but I really hadn't worked on a TV show in a meaningful way, ever. You always feel like a fraud, unless you're a crazy person. But I really felt like, "This is bullshit—I'm totally not qualified for this."

JON STEWART

I really liked his sensibility. Ben seemed to be concerned with hypocrisy and the silly facades of politics. He seemed to know where the absurdity was, and that was an important change in focus for what we wanted to do. There's also a certain steeped-in-neurosis bathos that probably was a rhythm that we both clicked on. That similar Jewie Jewerman from Jewville.

The big thing was to find somebody who had thoughts, who cared, who had an opinion. Part of what the *Onion* is, and part of what Ben was steeped in, was the idea of deconstruction as your first step of re-creation. So Ben was a natural fit, although he had not had the TV experience.

BEN KARLIN

I was friendly with Bob Odenkirk and David Cross. They were kind of like the grand poobahs of the alternative comedy scene in LA—Sarah Silverman, Janeane Garofalo, Patton Oswalt. It was that whole wave of comics. Bob and David said *The Daily Show* sounded like a great opportunity. So I sublet my apartment, sold my Harley, found someone to take my dog for a while, and came to New York with three duffel bags.

JON STEWART

Ben walked into a buzzsaw.

BEN KARLIN

I'm not going to talk shit about anybody. But the staff had its allegiances, and the things that they liked to do, and the way they liked to do it. Now you've got this guy, Jon, who is a writer, who has a strong point of view.

LIZZ WINSTEAD, The Daily Show *cocreator; head writer, correspondent, 1996–1998*

As much as I loved the original writers, I created some little monsters. Once Jon realized he needed to take charge, you can't afford to have people who are not in the Jon Stewart business. And so there's a bit of Kool-Aid drinking that has to take place.

JEN FLANZ

It didn't necessarily feel like Jon was in charge right when he got there. When Ben came in, that felt like more of a shift in the universe.

Karlin arrived as head writer in April 1999 and quickly formed a complementary duo with Stewart. Karlin pushed for a higher quotient of righteous anger in the Daily Show's *jokes; Stewart had an innate sense of what would get big laughs.*

BEN KARLIN

We were very kindred spirits, with very similar points of view, and my critique of the show was very much in line with his problems with the show: Why are we going after these helpless targets? Maybe we should focus the power of this kind of big news show on things that are actually newsworthy, rather than just look through the paper for what seems funny. .

Clashes between Stewart, Karlin, and some of the holdover Kilborn writers would flare over the next year, with one confrontation—which became known inside the show as "the fuck-you meeting"—being leaked to the New York Post's *"Page Six" gossip column.*

JON STEWART

I think that was the meeting where I said, "You're not a group. You're not a unit. You're not 'the writers.' You're individual writers that have been hired, and you will be judged within that." It was just an attempt to reclaim some semblance of order. It was an absolute flat-out power struggle, but one that I felt blindsided by.

BEN KARLIN

At one point during the battle for the heart and soul of the show, one of the writers snuck into Madeleine's office and replaced some of the items on the board that tracks the stories we're doing with personal insults. Some of them were about me, some were about other people. It was the most juvenile thing in the world, and it only could have been two or three people.

Jon and I used to have this thing: crazy out, sane in. We wanted to try to build a show of smart, funny, reasonable people with a similar vision who were hard workers.

An enormous step in that direction was Karlin's first addition to the writing staff: a dizzyingly fast-thinking, cheerfully caustic twenty-seven-year-old who would become a major figure in the creative life of The Daily Show.

DAVID JAVERBAUM, *from writer to executive producer, 1999–2008*

I'd gone to Harvard and written for the *Lampoon* and Hasty Pudding, then I went to graduate school for musical theater composition, at NYU. It's arguably the most useless master's degree even by master's degree standards. I had a lot of creative things I was interested in, but I had no idea what I wanted to do. I was temping for three years at law firms and Merrill Lynch.

I knew Ben Karlin from a teen tour that we were on together, the thing where Jewish middle-class kids go around the country and pretend to rough it for six weeks. Ben, after college at Wisconsin, wound up working at the *Onion*, and he said, do you want to contribute? So I began writing a lot of *Onion* headlines and some articles, and I had the idea for the book, *Our Dumb Century*.

Then I spent a year at *Letterman* as a writer, and I hated that. Not the people, per se, but it all comes from the top down, and Letterman, even at that point, which was '98 to '99, was just a detached, aloof figure who would stay there for, like, thirteen hours a day for no reason. And I quit. I was making six figures. I'd never made the upper half of five before, but it just was not worth it. It was crushing my soul.

I was writing a musical. In the interim, Ben was hired as the head writer for *The Daily Show*, and once again, he called me and said are you interested in writing? So I owe Ben for both of those opportunities. I think I was Ben's first writing hire, in July 1999.

BEN KARLIN

D.J. has genius-like qualities, almost to the point where—it's not Asperger-y, because he's a funny, normal guy. But the way he can hold information, the speed with which his mind works, it's almost like he's got a broken brain that works really well in this way. I've known him since he was sixteen years old. He always was like this.

Usually in a writers' room, you know that this guy is my joke guy, that one is my story guy, that's my structure person. And D.J. has the ability to pitch individual jokes that are funny; he can come up with overarching structures that are funny; he can take over someone's script and make it better.

DAVID JAVERBAUM

I remember mainly Ben used to say, "Best idea wins." Well, that's nice, but what's the best idea? I mean, the best idea on *Benny Hill* is to run around in fast motion to "Yakety Sax." That's the best idea. So yes, best idea wins, but even more important than that is to create a culture where everybody agrees what the best idea is.

KENT JONES

Ben liked things that were more sophisticated. A little more wordy. His sensibility was more of a knowing kind of thing. It was more interpretive of the news. It's like, "Oh, here's the news and here's what this means."

DAVID JAVERBAUM

I think the personality of the *Onion*, abstractly speaking, is more despairing than Jon's. There's Horatian satire and Juvenalian satire, and I think Jon's is more Juvenalian, and the *Onion*'s is more Horatian. I think Jon offers the hope through his personality alone that we can do better, and the *Onion* doesn't. I personally probably side with the *Onion* more on that one. I don't believe there is hope in the biggest sense.

CHRIS REGAN

I would've liked to have seen D.J.'s feet less. We were officemates, and he was a real shorts-and-sandals-wearer to the office. D.J. was, like a lot of talented people, a bit of an odd duck. He might say the same thing about me, you know.

Changing the lineup of correspondents and contributors, the on-air faces of the show, was also crucial, if less contentious. Brown and Unger left when Kilborn did; Colbert, Rocca, Beth Littleford, Frank DeCaro, and Stacey Grenrock Woods stayed on. Stewart's first correspondent addition was Vance DeGeneres, who had a gift for the authoritative-but-vacant news reporter delivery. Then two major talents joined the correspondent team, almost by accident.

STEVE CARELL, *correspondent, 1999–2003*

I got a call from Stephen Colbert. He and I were on *The Dana Carvey Show* together in the spring of 1996, and one of the sketches that we did was called "Waiters Who Are Nauseated by Food." And Madeleine Smithberg, who had hired Stephen onto *The Daily Show*, saw that and asked who I was—asked Stephen—and then Stephen called me and said, "Would you be interested maybe in doing a field piece?" And then Madeleine called and followed up and asked if I'd do a field piece out here in Los Angeles. We were living out here at the time and I had a holding deal with ABC. So we were just watching a lot of the Game Show Network.

We decided to stage the field piece right underneath the HOLLYWOOD sign, up in the hills, and that I was going to do the walk-and-talk as I was essentially walking up the side of a mountain, and obviously play up the fact that I was really out of shape, that it was a very bad correspondent to have chosen for a walk-and-talk.

Apparently Madeleine Smithberg really liked that moment within the piece and thought that that was a good choice. They asked if I'd move out to New York and be a regular on *The Daily Show*.

No one was really familiar with this show. My agent didn't see it as a positive step in my career. Let's put it that way. They just saw it as a little nothing cable show. A job, but nothing that was going to amount to much. Jon had just become the host about six months before.

NANCY WALLS CARELL, *correspondent, 1999–2002*

We'd met Ben Karlin a couple years earlier. He was shooting a pilot, in Madison, Wisconsin, for an *Onion*-related TV show. They came down to Chicago and auditioned a lot of Second City people, including me. I don't think Steve auditioned for it. So we were up in Madison shooting this, and Steve and I were dating at the time, and he rode his motorcycle up to join us.

RORY ALBANESE, *from production assistant to executive producer, 1999–2013*

I remember Carell's first field piece, and all of us at the show saying, "Who is this guy? He's just, like, fat Brian Unger." I look back and think, "I can't believe that's what we were saying about Steve Carell. He's a comic genius."

NANCY WALLS CARELL

I had been on *Saturday Night Live* for one season, and then we had lived out in LA for about three years with mixed success, and I felt like it was a good move to come back to New York.

You know, *The Daily Show* was a pretty loose atmosphere back then. You would do a field piece and then you'd do a follow-up piece in the studio. So I went to Steve's first studio taping and met Madeleine and she kind of looked at me, she said, "Well, do you want to try it?" It was really that casual. That's how I began there as a *Daily Show* correspondent.

One of my first pieces, I think Deborah Norville had just gone to a prison in North Carolina and stayed for a night. So I went to a dog pound and got into a cage. I'm still living with the ramifications.

As the Carells found their place in the new Daily Show *order, some of the on-air holdovers were having a tougher time figuring out where they fit in Stewart's plans—or if they even wanted to fit in.*

RORY ALBANESE

Lewis Black's segment was so haphazard. It hadn't been brought under the new, larger *Daily Show* writing rulebook yet, because it was a holdover from the Kilborn era. The transitions in a "Back in Black" segment would be, "And then there's *this* idiot!"

> **Lewis Black:** [*sitting to Stewart's right, necktie askew, hands jabbing at the camera*] Welcome to '99! And if you're so delusional you think this year is gonna be better than last, get a grip! Just take a look down Mexico way, where the price of tortillas went up for the first time since syphilis was transmitted... Meanwhile, they're trying to shut down a Leonardo DiCaprio movie in Thailand. At least their hearts are in the right place. Anyway, environmentalists claim the production will damage the ecosystem on—now, get a load of this!—Phi Phi Island, located in the Krabi Province. Now, could you imagine? "Where do you live?" "Phi Phi Island, in the Krabi Province." "Where's that?" "Southwest of Bangkok." Hey, I'd be boycotting those names! And there's more: Here's the genius who's bringing Starbucks to China!

JON STEWART

Lewis had a sensibility that was political, but they were wasting his ability on footage of the Nazarene protest in the Philippines, just because that was the AP footage we could get. Everything we did was an attempt to move the show toward active pursuit, with a point of view about material we could get our hands on, instead of being passive and reactive.

RORY ALBANESE

I love Lew. Lew is the reason I'm a standup. But the segment didn't feel organic to the show anymore. Lew started showing up on the show less, and then they took the creative process out of his hands.

LEWIS BLACK

I take some of the blame for it, but there were two producers, who will remain nameless—yeah, D.J. and Karlin—who had no sense of why I was funny, none at all. I was not in their orbit of comedy, and they treated me like a piece of shit. They treated my words like a piece of shit.

BEN KARLIN

I don't know how close we came to cutting Lewis, to tell you the truth. It might've been very close. I'm not sentimental. I would've gotten rid of the "Top Ten List" on *Letterman* years ago. I was like, fuck that.

Lewis fell into the category of all these other little segments— "Ad Nauseam," "The Public Excess"—that were the property of the writers. The idea was, "No, we're doing a whole show that has to have a unified voice and everything needs to filter through an editorial control, and that editorial control, whether you like it or not, is Jon."

JON STEWART

There was no guarantee the network was going to go for this. We were moving away from what they wanted as well. I can remember hearing, "There should always be an entertainment portion of the show. That's what people like—they like the entertainment." We can all look back in hindsight and go, "Of course, it was inevitable they'd succeed." But it wasn't.

What Stewart and his Daily Show *colleagues could not have known was that they had arrived at the perfect moment, with the media and political worlds on the cusp of upheaval. When Stewart first sat behind the fake anchor desk, the anchors of the real news were still a trio of white male eminences: Tom Brokaw at NBC, Peter Jennings at ABC, and Dan Rather at CBS. But the network news hegemony had been rattled by the arrival of CNN, especially its coverage of the 1990 Gulf War. Now Fox News and MSNBC—both launched, coincidentally, within months of the* Daily Show's *1996 debut—were rapidly expanding their footprints on cable systems. Soon the Internet would flatten the traditional TV news industry. And a wised-up, postmodern generation of viewers was hungry for what* The Daily Show *would soon deliver.*

LEWIS BLACK

We'd come along at the right time and the right place. Jon ends up in a position on a show when the tipping point had been reached in terms of cable news, 120 hours of news a day coming out of five channels. So all of a sudden people have a visceral understanding of the way in which they're approached when they watch the news, by the newspeople.

The turn of the century was also a boom time for network newsmagazines. NBC was airing Dateline *five nights a week. ABC had* 20/20 *and* Primetime; *CBS had* 48 Hours. *Syndicated shows including* Inside Edition *added an even cheesier, tabloid flair to the genre.*

The TV newsmagazine formula—leaning heavily on sensationalized crime stories, breathless celebrity profiles, and consumer products scares—was ripe for parody. As were the self-serious anchor-reporter stars of TV newsmagazines: The style of The Daily Show's *correspondents drew special inspiration from the overinflated gravitas of* Dateline's *Stone Phillips.*

MADELEINE SMITHBERG

I always say that Stone Phillips deserves a "created by" credit for *The Daily Show,* because I was obsessed with the guy, and we studied him.

We studied his listening-face expressions. We studied the different ways he put his fist to his chin, the way that he furrowed his brow. We studied his walk-and-talk. We studied his attitude. We studied his self-aggrandizing, the way that he inserted himself into the story.

RORY ALBANESE

Colbert will tell you his character for years was just Stone Phillips.

BEN KARLIN

I had actually worked very briefly with Colbert. Robert Smigel was producing *The Dana Carvey Show*, and he wanted to buy some *Onion* stories and to do them with Colbert as the anchor. I flew in for the tapings of those episodes to see how they were using our material, and had a ships-passing-in-the-night moment with Colbert. Carell was also on that show.

JON STEWART

Carell, I knew very little about him. These guys didn't come from standup. I knew standups. I knew Dave Attell, I knew Lewis Black. I did not know Vance, Mo, Steve, Stephen.

In Karlin, Stewart had hired an invaluable off-camera ally. But he quickly recognized that he had inherited an indispensable on-camera coconspirator. Stephen Colbert had a subversive streak that was greatly abetted by the fact that he looked like a trustworthy middle-American insurance salesman.

STEPHEN COLBERT

It was a complete happy accident that I ended up at *The Daily Show*. I had been working for ABC Entertainment at *The Dana Carvey Show* in 1996. That show got canceled, my wife wasn't working, and we had a baby. I desperately needed a job. Someone from the entertainment division recommended to the news division that if they were looking for somebody who was funny but looked really straight, for a correspondent for *Good Morning America*, that they should consider me. They hired me. I did exactly two reports. Only one of which ever made it to air.

After those two reports, I pitched twenty stories in a row that got shot down. At the same time, my agent, James Dixon, who also represented Madeleine Smithberg, said, "You should meet with Madeleine. She's doing this other show and I bet that they would do those stories." They had me on for a trial basis, and for the next nine months I worked at *The Daily Show* occasionally, during Craig Kilborn's second year. But it was totally a day job. I never expected to stay because I did sketch comedy and I wrote, and I really didn't think that *The Daily Show* was going to go anyplace.

JON STEWART

The first bit Stephen did on the show after I arrived, I think it was something about baby back ribs. You could just feel, "This guy knows how to perform in a scene, is present, has an ease with language." The key then was, "What do we do with that?"

STEPHEN COLBERT

I don't really know why Jon and I worked together so well. It's hard to quantify, but it happened very early. When Jon first got there, he had a rough ride with some of the people who had worked with Craig. But I immediately knew he was a guy I should listen to. I saw how thoughtful he wanted to be about political comedy and how he invited us to have our own thoughts, invest the jokes with our own beliefs. And maybe he thought he could trust me.

BEN KARLIN

So much of the writing of *The Daily Show* actually comes down to brainstorming and coming up with the big-picture ideas. Once we started realizing what an incredible tool Carell and Colbert were, we said we've got to bring more of that into the studio. Let's not just see them once a week or once every two weeks in a field piece. Let's get both those guys on the show several times a week in one form or another. They're too talented.

One answer was "Even Stephven," pitting Colbert and Carell as warring pundits. The segments exaggerated the style of the superficial, vein-popping "debates" of cable and Sunday morning news shows, but also started making serious points about everything from the similarities between Islam and Christianity to government's responsibility for disaster relief.

> **Jon Stewart:** [*at anchor desk*] You know, scholars and historians may well debate Bill Clinton's presidency for centuries. But here to do it in two and a half minutes, our own Steve Carell and Stephen Colbert, with "Even Stephven."
> **Stephen Colbert:** [*to camera*] Have the Clinton years been good for America?
> **Steve Carell:** [*sitting two feet away*] Yes!
> **Stephen Colbert:** No!

Steve Carell: Yeeeessss! In 1992, our country was in a severe eco- nomic recession. Eight years of unprecedented prosperity later, America is richer and stronger than it has ever been. And the man responsible? William Jefferson Clinton.

Stephen Colbert: Oh, come off it, Steve. Alan Greenspan runs this economy. Not Bill Clinton. The only thing Bill Clinton has brought us these last eight years is moral turpitude and national shame.

Steve Carell: Two words, Stephen: Dow 10,000!

Stephen Colbert: Whitewater!

Steve Carell: Welfare reform!

Stephen Colbert: Monica-gate!

Steve Carell: Eight years of peace!

Stephen Colbert: Shut the fuck up! Shut up, *shut up*, SHUT UP! God, your voice is like a jackal picking at my brain! I hate you! I hate who you are and what you do and how you sound and what you say! You're like a cancer on my life! God!

Steve Carell: [*pauses*] Well, that was ugly and humiliating. Feel any better now?

Stephen Colbert: I'm sorry. I'm just tired and, uh, I'm upset about Clinton.

Steve Carell: Every time we fight, it's because of Clinton. Or the economy. Or NAFTA. I don't think the problem is out there. I think the problem is right here and I think we need to talk about it... I've been giving this some thought, and maybe we need to com- mentate with other people.

Stephen Colbert: Have you been working with CNN's Robert Novak?

Steve Carell: Bob appreciates me.

Stephen Colbert: I can *smell* him on you.

STEPHEN COLBERT

I was always interested in politics. I was always interested in the news. I didn't do political humor. Political humor to me meant "Hey, Ted Kennedy's drunk again!" Then Jon came in with a real desire to have a satirical point of view about the substance of the ideas, not just the actions of the people. What are they really talking about? What are they arguing about? What are the philosophical underpinnings of this argument going on in America right now? Part of the assignment when Jon came in was "You have to give this some thought—where do you stand here?" Because he wanted us to be able to write our own stuff and not be instructed. He wanted it to be from the bottom up, the process. He wanted us to come with our own sincere interests in the news, so each one of us had to find our own hook—what was the thing that interested us most about a campaign or a political argument or something of social significance?

I found out, through that invitation from Jon, that I had a political point of view. I wasn't just a consumer. I don't think I would have done that if Jon hadn't shown me a way to do it and still be joyful and inventive about it, rather than being finger-waggy.

There was a bumpy transformation taking place away from the studio, too— more slowly, but equally important to establishing the new direction of The Daily Show. *The field department does what the name implies: shoots segments out in the streets, fields, and offices of the real world, to parody the interview, investigative, and ambush segments of real TV journalists. But the name does not come close to conveying the spirit of the unit. The field department has always been, in the words of one of its longtime bosses, "the red-headed stepchild" of* The Daily Show—*the pirate squad of producers and correspondents who reveled in traveling from Homer, Alaska, to Uttar Pradesh, India, and operating beyond the direct observation of the home office and company lawyers. "The field department, we don't do things that are immoral," says Tim Greenberg, one of the department's top producers. "We only do things that might not be technically allowed, but that I think most reasonable people would say are okay."*

In the Kilborn era, field department pieces frequently featured obscure eccentrics—say, a man who pulled his own teeth and replaced them with driveway gravel. Those kind of bits didn't go away immediately under Stewart.

KAHANE CORN COOPERMAN, *from field producer to co–executive producer, 1996–2013*
I was managing the field department. There was a piece with Stacey Grenrock Woods as the correspondent, about a guy who had been a rock star in Ukraine and came here and was now a waiter in a hotel restaurant in Grand Rapids, Michigan. This piece may well have been in the works before Jon arrived. But it airs, and after the show you have a postmortem. And Jon

was not happy. He said, "Your targets are just wrong. They shouldn't be people on the fringe. Our targets need to be the people who have a voice, and that's politicians, and that's the media."

STACEY GRENROCK WOODS, *correspondent, 1998–2003*

I heard Jon was very unhappy with that piece, and I don't blame him at all. I didn't like it, either, but it was given to me. I think it ended up being a policy-changing piece.

Stewart was clear about how the tone of The Daily Show *needed to change. But he still gave the writers, producers, and correspondents plenty of creative room.*

STEVE CARELL

The correspondents had their own little thing going on with the field pieces. Jon left it up to us in terms of what sort of characters we were developing.

I saw my character as a former local news anchor who had been demoted to reporting on a nondescript cable news show and was a little bitter about it. Everyone to a certain degree had different variations on blowhard or idiot reporter. But I mean, let's face it—we didn't know what we were doing.

NANCY WALLS CARELL

No.

STEVE CARELL

None of us are correspondents. None of us have backgrounds in journalism.

NANCY WALLS CARELL

Mo was pretty knowledgeable, actually.

STEVE CARELL

It's a hard job description because you're not really a reporter. You're pretending to be one. You're not really in character but you kind of have to be. So you're improvising all day and you're pretending to be a correspondent, which none of us had any background in. So we were all sort of winging it. My character was a guy who took himself pretty seriously, but wasn't really up to the task, basically that.

STEPHEN COLBERT

There was a very specific way we were supposed to present ourselves when we set up field pieces: "I'm from *The Daily Show*." "What's *The Daily Show*?" "Well, it's an alternative news and entertainment program." "What channel is it on?" "Well, I don't know what channel it is where you live. Where we live it's Channel 29." Anything other than saying the words "Comedy Central." We were never allowed to lie, but let's not advertise we were on Comedy Central, because not being a famous show was really useful to us in the early days.

I was the first correspondent to be sued. After a piece ran, a guy claimed I claimed I was from CNN. I never said that. But if you make a man comedically look like Hitler and it turns out that he is a retired lawyer with a lot of time on his hands, you're going to get sued. That's the lesson for today, children.

STEVE CARELL

The field pieces with eccentrics and oddballs, those were uncomfortable. For all of us. I almost didn't...I won't say I almost didn't do the show, but I had some major reservations about doing it for exactly that reason, because I didn't like the idea of making fun of people only because they were eccentric or different, and...

NANCY WALLS CARELL

Duping them.

STEVE CARELL

Yeah. Shooting fish in a barrel is easy. When you go after someone who is intolerant or racist or has any sort of hateful nature, that's a different story. I think that's fair game. So part of what I tried to do with my character is put the impetus on myself, the comedic impetus, that I was the bigger idiot.

But I talked to Colbert about how to deal with it. His advice was that you just have to rectify it somehow, and be okay with it, and my way of doing it was to become more of the butt of the joke.

NANCY WALLS CARELL

Colbert just goes to confession.

STEVE CARELL

It's interesting, too, because all of those correspondents were incredibly kind people. With the possible exception of my wife, all extremely kind and generous. So it was really out of character for any of us to be in someone's face.

Not all of the great field-piece performances took place on camera.

STEW BAILEY

It turned out this always happened when you traveled with Stephen, but the first time I never saw it coming. When we check in at the hotel in Denver, they ask for his address. He says, "Sure. My name's Stephen Colbert. I live at 52 Poopiepop Lane." And they always would react, and they'd start to say, "Is that a..." And Stephen says, "Heard them all. Heard every one of them. Please don't make fun of it." So it was like a great antijoke. And they said, "Okay, so 52 Poopiepop Lane." And he says, "Neptune, Maine," and it's a made-up town. And the weird capper was, "And I'm going to need a zip code out of you," and he says, "I don't know my zip code."

STEPHEN COLBERT

Or I'd say, "We have three demands: I need a fifty-gallon drum of saffron oil, twenty feet of parachute cord, and a dwarf." It was about practicing being ridiculous.

STEW BAILEY

Another time we decided that we wanted to use a code expression that didn't mean anything and see how people responded to it.

The hotel clerk says, "So would you like a key to the minibar?" and Stephen looks at this woman and he says, "Okay. The squirrel is in the basket." And she says, "I'm sorry?" and he says, "You know what I mean. The squirrel is in the basket." And she says, "Sir, I really don't. I mean, I'm just asking if you want a minibar key." And he said, "You know where the squirrel is." And she said, "I'm going to just take that as a no."

The next morning, the wakeup call happens at 6:00 a.m., so Stephen answers the phone by saying once again, "The squirrel is in the basket." I've got to remember I'm traveling with a very strange person. And he's a supernice guy. It's not like he wants to make people uncomfortable, but he's just trying to get himself into comedy mode.

During his first year as host Stewart devoted far more energy to retooling the staff and the process inside the building. The show was becoming his own, even in small ways: Near the end of Stewart's first year, They Might Be Giants rerecorded the Daily Show *theme song. And then, in December 1999, the field department and Steve Carell, on an excursion to New Hampshire, created five minutes that changed the trajectory of the entire* Daily Show.

2

Indecision 2000—The Sunshine Wait

CINDY McCAIN, *wife of Senator John McCain*

All of a sudden there were these guys in these crazy jackets, popping up at campaign events, and nobody knew who they were. But they were funny.

MICHELE GANELESS, *vice president of programming, Comedy Central, 1996–2001; president, Comedy Central, 2004–2016*

The show sent correspondents up to New Hampshire beginning in 1999, before the primary. This was a big moment for *The Daily Show*, a big moment for the network. I remember that as the beginning of "Wow, we're sort of in this politics thing."

And the correspondents were totally flying by the seats of their pants.

STEW BAILEY

There was a Republican debate in New Hampshire, so we were going to do a piece from the spin room. And the spin room even then was acknowledged as the least newsworthy event of all time. Our premise was that it's essentially a parlor game, and if that's the case, let's really turn it into a parlor game. I had each of the correspondents asking questions from Trivial Pursuit to the candidates.

MO ROCCA

All of us were nervous as hell, and so I just went for it: "Senator McCain, who became the hottest pop star to come out of Iceland in the mid nineteen nineties?"

STEW BAILEY

Immediately our other correspondents start yelling, "Don't skirt the question, Senator! You have to answer!"

MO ROCCA

And McCain showed why he almost upended George W. Bush in that race, because he played along, making this silly face. I remember the CNN people looking at us like, "Okay, that was funny. But who are you guys?"

STEVE CARELL

When we went up to the first Republican debate we had our jackets with *The Daily Show* embroidered on them, and we're walking around with microphones. It was terrifying because people didn't know that we were fake. So we could get away with a lot of stuff. Bush looked at us like we were insane.

NANCY WALLS CARELL

The producers said, "Go over and get Tim Russert to talk to us," and Russert said, "I'll only go on camera if you give me your jacket." And I couldn't do it. And Russert didn't talk to us.

JON STEWART

When we went up to New Hampshire we were under the mistaken assumption that we had to integrate ourselves with the political media's process and become them to parody them. Turns out we didn't have to do that. We had thought, "Oh, you're a political reporter on television, which must mean something." Turns out it doesn't mean anything. All it means is that somebody pointed a camera at you and lit it. So that was a revelation, and not a positive one.

After that year we always talked about, "Did you get any on you?" Meaning, becoming like them. That was my problem with the New Hampshire bits that we did, is you could get it on you a little bit.

That trip provided a second breakthrough in defining the new Daily Show *tone—when Carell climbed into McCain's bus.*

STEW BAILEY

Remember, McCain that year was a huge deal. He won the New Hampshire primary. That was really his moment. And his big gimmick was his bus, the Straight Talk Express.

I was supervising in the field department. Our idea was that we were trying to get on the Straight Talk Express, but we couldn't. There was a secondary press bus. If you're in the rollover bus you just don't feel like you matter. So the premise was going to be if Steve Carell finally does get on the Straight Talk Express, that means we were at the table with all the big important players. To get on McCain's bus was a coup for us, it meant that somebody was going to allow us to bring our reindeer games into a legitimate political moment.

CINDY McCAIN

The actual press bus, which was completely different from ours, was really awful, in fact. Steve Carell was talking about, did we feed the press, or did we just lock them in the bus? They were pleading with me—is there any way I can get them on the main bus? They were a hoot to be around, so John invited them on the Straight Talk Express.

STEVE CARELL

You watch the finished piece and it feels like I'm chasing McCain for days. But we shot it in one day.

STEW BAILEY

We needed to then have Carell basically ask one question that is going to get us kicked off. The idea was going to be we had a brief moment of glory, we asked a question, and then we lost our privileges. If you watch the piece, he asks a bunch of innocuous questions. They're almost like those *Who Wants to Be a Millionaire* $100 questions—you can't get this wrong, no one's going to get hurt.

Then Carell asked a real question: "How do you explain that you are such an opponent of pork barrel politics, yet during your time heading the Commerce Committee, that committee set new records for unauthorized appropriations?"

Carell and Nick McKinney, the producer, had pulled the question out of *Time* magazine on the way there, driving to the shoot.

STEVE CARELL

Nick and I were both flying blind and he handed me that magazine story and said, "Ask him this." So I wrote it down and I just thought I'd really get McCain in a jovial mood, and the last thing he was expecting was anything even remotely serious. Then to ask him something that he actually might be asked on the campaign trail, he just...for a politician like that to be caught momentarily off guard, he just had sort of a quizzical look on his face.

> **Steve Carell:** [*on board the Straight Talk Express, reading from a legal pad as McCain grins*] Let's do a lightning round: your favorite book?
>
> **Senator John McCain:** *For Whom the Bell Tolls.*
>
> **Steve Carell:** Favorite movie?
>
> **Senator McCain:** *Viva Zapata!*
>
> **Steve Carell:** Charlton Heston?
>
> **Senator McCain:** Marlon Brando.
>
> **Steve Carell:** Close enough. If I were a tree, I would be a...
>
> **Senator McCain:** If I were a tree, I would be a root. [*pause*] What does that mean?
>
> **Steve Carell:** Senator, how do you reconcile that you were one of the most vocal critics of pork barrel politics, and yet while you were chairman of the Commerce Committee, that committee set a record for unauthorized appropriations?
>
> [*Four seconds of silence that feel like four hours*]
>
> **Steve Carell:** I was just kidding! I don't even know what that means!
>
> [*McCain looks at ceiling, shrugs in relief, awkwardly slaps hand to his own face*]
>
> [*Carell shuffles awkwardly down bus stairs and out the door, then stands on a highway median*]
>
> **Steve Carell:** Oh, they all laughed at my little question. But two things were abundantly clear. It was the wrong question to ask, and I was going to be walking.

STEW BAILEY

Just the fact that Steve Carell can get those words out of his mouth and that it sounded like something a smart person would say really threw McCain off. There was such a delay.

STEVE CARELL

It was really funny because all of McCain's handlers, you could feel the whole bus tense up. I thought McCain might just laugh it off, or probably give me some sort of joke response.

BEN KARLIN

I remember seeing it in the editing room. I remember Jon called me down, and seeing it and thinking, "Yeah, this is what we should be doing. This is the goal." It was one of Carell's most incredible moments. He asks McCain a question in a way that no journalists were talking to the candidates. And it was like, oh shit, we are able, in this weird, unintentional way, to add a level of insight to the process that doesn't exist. That was really, really exciting. It meets the standard of being funny, it meets the standard of being relevant.

STEVE CARELL

A show that can open the door to a discussion and then take a comedic detour, I think didn't feel important at the time. It just felt like a silly, fun moment.

JOHN McCAIN, *U.S. senator, Arizona, 1987–; Republican presidential nominee, 2008*

That was great. I still remember Steve Carell on the bus. I was certainly aware of Jon and the show early on, and knew they would try to have some fun with us. I wanted to be funny. I wanted these young people to know that I'm a guy with a sense of humor. I'm not some dull, dry, old senator.

BEN KARLIN

That moment, it was the beauty and the weakness of *The Daily Show*. You had this incredibly pregnant moment where you forced a politician to go off book, and it was uncomfortable, and it was honest. Then, because of our role as a comedy show, you have to take the air out of it, and it let McCain off the hook.

STEVE CARELL

Yeah, to press it—we really hadn't set ourselves up in that context to start going after him. It was making fun of a gotcha moment. And I think that's a lot of what we do on *The Daily Show* is making fun of journalistic tropes, and I think that was one of them.

BEN KARLIN

There's no joke unless you walk back from it. But we were living in this moment of the press starting to be not so interested in making politicians uncomfortable, and of having the candidates being able to tailor their appearances and their media in a way that didn't put them on the spot. It felt like we were able to slip one in.

The fact that it touched on something real, it opened the door. It went just a tiny bit deeper. You know, there was satire to it.

DAVID JAVERBAUM

That's the moment where you realize what's real and what's comedy can blur in these bizarre ways that are compelling and disturbing.

MO ROCCA

That was the first time we were in the *New York Times*—in a news analysis piece, not the TV column.

CINDY McCAIN

I still have those jackets, by the way. I talked them out of their big New Hampshire jackets. They were around John so much, and I finally said, "Look, these jackets are too good. I've got to get one from you, please." They gave them to me. It's a great souvenir.

MADELEINE SMITHBERG

The show got better. The year and a half leading up to the 2000 election was the most amazing time creatively. Have you ever seen *The Greatest Millennium*, our end-of-the-year special? That was the turning point. *The Greatest Millennium* was when *The Daily Show with Jon Stewart* became *The Daily Show with Jon Stewart*. It was so much fun, because of the absurdity that you can do a look back at a millennium in an hour.

BEN KARLIN

We tackled a very, very topical thing—Y2K—with a ferocity and with a real specific point of view. You saw a million shitty Y2K segments on every local news and national magazine show, but we were the only ones who did a really, really funny one. For me that was a turning point.

And then you're into the 2000 election, and then everything just came into focus.

The 2000 presidential primaries provided The Daily Show *with a bounty of comedic raw material: The pixie-size right-winger Gary Bauer, the flat-tax fantasies of Steve Forbes, the wooden wonkery of Bill Bradley. But the campaign also gave the show the substantive narrative framework that Stewart wanted and needed.*

What also allowed the show's increasingly confident satiric voice to stand out was the absence of real competition. Sure, Letterman and Leno took shots at the candidates, but that usually added up to a couple of jokes each night as part of a wide-ranging standup monologue. Over on SNL, the year started with Colin Quinn behind the "Weekend Update" desk and ended with Jimmy Fallon and Tina Fey. All three are gifted comics, but "Weekend Update" didn't have the time or the inclination to plumb the depths of, say, the paranoid stylings of Pat Buchanan.

JAMES PONIEWOZIK, *television critic*, Time, *1999–2015*, and the New York Times, *2015–*

At that time late-night political humor was pitched toward the middle. It was about foibles and politicians' particular characteristics and tics and failures—the Monica Lewinsky joke, the George Bush–is-kind-of-dumb joke. Leno would handle something like the O. J. Simpson case through the "Dancing Itos." It could be scathing and damaging and influence the public's perception of a candidate or a politician, but it wasn't really that much about engaging with the ideas of politics, the politics of politics. Before Jon Stewart came along.

J. R. HAVLAN

There was no competition. There were late-night monologues, but that's "setup, punch line," and you never go beyond that, and there's not much depth to those things, so there's not a lot of edge or risk.

BEN KARLIN

"Weekend Update," they wrote good jokes, but it was a very small part of a larger show that didn't really drive the success or watchability of *SNL*. I'm truly speculating here, but I think the way *The Daily Show* started getting a little bit of attention probably fostered a little more competition on their end—like, "Oh shit, we've got to maybe raise our game here, because this is now something that people are paying attention to." I wouldn't deign to say how aware or not aware they were of us. But I don't think we ever really looked at them as something that was analogous to what we were doing. And if you're doing *The Tonight Show*, and Enron's the front page of the news, you know what you do? Ignore it.

As Stewart and Karlin pushed the show steadily toward politics, many of the holdover elements of the Kilborn-era Daily Show *peeled away, accentuating the shift in tone. "The Beth Littleford Interview" had parodied Barbara Walters's celebrity confessionals by smearing Vaseline on the camera lens and smothering Littleford in fresh flowers as she quizzed Boy George about whether he'd "ever come face-to-face with a bearded clam."*

BETH LITTLEFORD, correspondent, 1996–2000

The way those interviews started was that we were in Las Vegas working on two field pieces, and we heard that John Wayne Bobbitt was staying at the hotel. We ended up doing a walk-and-talk that looked exactly like a Barbara Walters walk-and-talk, with me asking things like, "And how is your penis today?" My now ex-husband, Rob Fox, who was a *Daily Show* producer, wisely saw that footage and said, "Okay, this is something."

I got to shovel manure with Jesse "the Body" Ventura. I got to dance with Boy George, who told me that I'm pretty cute. A lot of those were really fun.

MO ROCCA

Beth was hilarious, but the show definitely did not, under Jon, have a camp sensibility to it.

BETH LITTLEFORD

I wanted to be on a network show and I wanted to be on a sitcom. I got put under contract from *Spin City* for about a hundred times more than I was making on *The Daily Show*, and the work was much less exhausting. I was in good standing, but I told Jon and Madeleine a year in advance that I was going to go.

I wasn't hugely supported by Jon, but I felt supported by the show. I remember when I left and had my little roast party, Jon saying, "Listen, I do like you." Because we had just never been close, and it seemed awkward even then.

*   *   *

Littleford left in the spring of 2000, just as the George W. Bush–Al Gore general election contest was starting to take shape and The Daily Show *was gearing up its first real political season. That summer, beginning with the guerrilla coverage of the Republican National Convention in Philadelphia and the Democratic National Convention in Los Angeles, Stewart and the correspondents became a cult hit. Then, after a long November election night,* The Daily Show *became indispensable viewing during the thirty-seven-day Florida recount fiasco. The epic and absurd standoff, with its hanging chads and Supreme Court contortions, seemed to have been designed by the comedy gods purely to showcase* The Daily Show's *approach. The slogan "Indecision 2000: Choose and Lose" was a good joke—and it became an even better, if grimmer, one when it became political reality.*

MICHELE GANELESS

We'd used the "Indecision" moniker for election coverage before, on *Politically Incorrect.* But in 2000 it really became meaningful.

ERIC DRYSDALE, *writer, 2000–2005*

I started at *The Daily Show* on the same day Allison Silverman did, February 21, 2000. They were staffing up to cover the election. I had been doing standup in this kind of nexus between what was then mainstream comedy and alternative comedy, as embodied by downtown places like the Luna Lounge and Surf Reality and Collective:Unconscious. I'd be on a bill and maybe Dave Chappelle or Janeane Garofalo would show up.

Was it clear at that point what Jon wanted the show to be? It was not. People talk about the 2000 election as being kind of the thing where the voice starts coalescing, but I actually think it was Elián González, that spring.

That's when there was a sense that we're following a story that's building. We're not just doing, like, a segment about somebody's long fingernails, we're actually learning about the characters in the story. Janet Reno was a character in the story, Elián was a character in the story. The media was a character in the story.

BEN KARLIN

I do remember covering that Elián González thing, and I remember there was a real philosophical divide between some of the writers, and myself, and

Jon, which was, does the inherent humor value of a story have to be the number one quality that makes it worthy for us to cover? And if there's something that doesn't have a lot of apparent comedic angles to it, isn't that a harder story to write about? And our attitude was—and I came from the *Onion*, which was making up stories—at the core of those stories were some real fundamental truths about the news and politics.

So I was like, "We have to come up with the funny take on this thing that doesn't necessarily seem funny. But there is humor, there is hypocrisy, there are people lying. In most of these cases, especially when you get into politics, there's people saying one thing but you know they believe something else."

ALLISON SILVERMAN, *writer, 2000–2001*

My big experience at *The Daily Show*, and later at *The Colbert Report*, was learning to react with great speed to find out the information, form your opinion on it, and then find a comedic take that expresses that opinion.

I was always the only woman in the writers' room. There were times when I really felt that viscerally, especially when I was reading a bunch of jokes and it had been a not-great day and I felt like I was somehow responsible for 51 percent of the world's population. It would've been great to have more women, I would've liked that. But I didn't feel like I was being alienated for being a woman or anything.

There would always be spasms of raw, spontaneous genius on The Daily Show. *But Stewart was intent on creating a structure that made room for the wild mercury moments to happen, a process that could reliably generate four nights of comedy a week with a minimum of backstage complications.*

Some of the times and details of The Daily Show*'s daily production schedule would change over the years, but the outline that was established by Smithberg in the Kilborn era endured for nearly two decades. During his first two years as host, though, Stewart made key alterations that eventually created a highly efficient comedy machine—but that initially threw off sparks.*

BEN KARLIN

The way it had worked with Kilborn, at noon, or 12:30, there was something called the joke read. The writers would read their jokes, out loud, basically because a lot of them have a performance background. We'd have a packet of jokes, and we'd circle the ones we liked. And then we'd assemble the headlines based on that. After a certain amount of time Jon was like, "This is ridiculous. The writers can just turn in the jokes, we'll read them and pick the ones we like."

It was taken as a repudiation of what they were doing, and that we were wrestling control away from them. And a lot of people were like, "Fuck you. Who are you to come in here and do this?" As we started shifting the show, and as we wanted to explore ideas a little deeper, we had to change the process.

JON STEWART

It's so important to remove preciousness and ownership. You have to invest everybody in the success of the show, and to let them feel good and confident about their contribution to it without becoming the sole proprietor of a joke. There has to be an understanding that that may be a great joke, but it might not serve the larger intention, or the narrative, of the show. You have to make sure that everybody feels invested without feeling that type of ownership.

Kilborn, as host, would arrive after the Daily Show *morning writers' meeting. Stewart arrived as it started, at 9:30 each morning, or not long after. It was a free-flowing discussion of stories in the news, possible segments, and available video clips that could be choreographed with jokes. After about an hour, Stewart and Karlin would assign segments to writers—sometimes working solo, sometimes in pairs. Scripts were due at noon. Then Stewart would meet with the executive producers in his office to read the drafts and assemble notes to be used in the revisions. Second drafts of scripts were due by 2:00.*

BEN KARLIN

I would compile the headlines. My job was to take all these individual jokes, find an order that made sense, find the connective tissue that made sense, and write little asides and little moments that made it feel like a cohesive script rather than just the individual jokes from ten individual writers.

People were very proprietary. Certain writers always worked with Lewis. Certain writers always worked with Frank DeCaro. They felt like it was their segment, and that Jon and myself shouldn't have any real say over them. And

Jon was like, "No. It's *The Daily Show with Jon Stewart*, and anything that's going on the air is going through me."

ALLISON SILVERMAN

Well, Ben hired me, so he obviously had a very sharp eye for talent. I think Ben is very funny. I think Ben has a really strong point of view about stuff, and a lot of times with the stories, he'd find where the outrage lies in this story, or, "This is the passion about this topic."

I felt like what Jon and Ben were looking for was something I was interested in writing, so I didn't really have much of a problem. But there was tension for sure, especially for people who had been there before Ben and Jon arrived.

STEW BAILEY

There was a drive to Jon on *The Daily Show* that he didn't have on his old MTV show. I think he was happy to have a show the first time around: "Hey, that's my name on the show." Not that he didn't work hard. But having had a show canceled, there was a responsibility to make this one work.

His attitude was, "I'm going for it on this one. I'm going to leave it all on the table." And Jon would come early, he would stay late. We would work on weekends. There wasn't any half-assing. He wouldn't let you off the hook.

ERIC DRYSDALE

During my first several weeks on the show there was definitely a lot of pot around. Maybe the first several months. I won't say which executive producer got me high on my first day before five in the afternoon, but yeah, it happened.

And it wasn't unusual to get some kind of afternoon assignment, be done at 4:00, and go home. That stopped happening very shortly. And I think that it was just Jon putting his foot down. It's fine to leave at 4:00, go up to the roof, and get high, having written two minutes on the guy with the longest fingernails in the world. But Jon had higher aspirations for all of us.

JAMES PONIEWOZIK

They realized in 2000 that actually engaging with elements in politics that people really cared about and got animated about was a more powerful fuel

for the show, as opposed to the show being what it was earlier, more sort of ·
a parody of newscasts. "Indecision 2000" is the point at which you see *The
Daily Show* moving from parody to satire.

LIZZ WINSTEAD

Instead of Jon playing a character—the news anchor, one of the derelicts
in a derelict world of media—Jon made a creative decision to take the show
in the direction of the correspondents presenting the idiocy, and then Jon is
the person who calls out the idiocy with the eloquence that the viewer wishes
they had. And he did it in a way that's not condescending, it's not smug. It's
funny, it's emotional, it's calling out bullshit. So Jon became the voice of the
audience.

JON STEWART

We learned there was only so much you could do with three white guys
and a green screen—and that was the show for a long time. For the 2000
campaign, we very much wanted to find somebody who could speak from
a position of authority, not a position of outside ridicule. This was all about
establishing various tributaries, so that you don't have to go to the same well.

Bob Dole was our opportunity. We hired him for, I think, six to eight
appearances. You had a guy who had run for president, and not in the distant
past, and this was our presidential campaign coverage. The idea was sort of
Statler and Waldorf, if Statler actually had been an actor for a long time, then
had lost his show and now he's up in the booth. And Dole turned out to have
a great wit. He knew how to deliver a good line, and he was open, and he was
not political. It gave us an authority that we shouldn't have had. Dole helped
us understand that this is a more intricate and interesting game.

MICHELE GANELESS

The next step was sending the show to the conventions. It was an investment for the network. It was huge.

BEN KARLIN

Well, for the Republican convention, in Philadelphia, we were staying in
the dorms at the University of Pennsylvania, because all the hotels were full.
It was summer camp and we're all putting on this show.

JON STEWART

Jackie McTigue, the show's security guy, was my roommate in the Penn dorm. The best guy in the world. Old school cop: "I was up at a gin joint in the Bronx…" He'd tuck me in every night: "You want a little nip before bed, kid?" And we'd have a nip and tell stories, and I fucking loved it. We had a ball.

MADELEINE SMITHBERG

We didn't have press credentials, but the Republicans would let us into the arena for forty-five minutes, so we'd run correspondents in and shoot for seven minutes at a time—go, go, go!

NANCY WALLS CARELL

They had me sidle up to the back of Wolf Blitzer and kind of repeat everything he was saying, but it was like a game of telephone. At that point I had never heard of Condoleezza Rice, so it was easy to mess her name up. Blitzer was playing along in that one. He was a really good sport.

> **Jon Stewart:** [at RNC anchor desk] We're going to check back in one more time with Nancy Walls, she's live at the First Union convention center. Nancy, we're in the home stretch here, you've been there all week, what's your analysis?
>
> **Nancy Walls:** [with graphic identifying her as SENIOR POLITICAL CHIEF CORRESPONDENT] My analysis? Oh. I thought you were going to be asking—[looks over right shoulder]—me about…my…analysis. [backs up out of frame]
>
> **Jon Stewart:** Nancy? Did we lose Nancy down there? Nancy?
>
> **Wolf Blitzer:** [looking off to left side of screen and confidently addressing a CNN camera] This convention has really energized a lot of these Republicans.
>
> **Nancy Walls:** [standing shoulder to shoulder with Blitzer and haltingly addressing Daily Show camera while too obviously trying to listen to Blitzer] Jon, here at this convention there's a lot of…energy in these Republicans.
>
> **Wolf Blitzer:** It's a new Republican Party. Because they're showing a new face of the Republican Party.
>
> **Nancy Walls:** These Republicans have many faces.

Wolf Blitzer: It's not the old Republican Party.

Nancy Walls: It's the old Republican Party.

Wolf Blitzer: Not the old Republican Party of Newt Gingrich, Tom DeLay, Dick Armey.

Nancy Walls: It's *not* the old Republican Party of...Tom Gingrich... Dick and his army.

Wolf Blitzer: This new Republican Party is the party of Colin Powell, Condoleezza Rice.

Nancy Walls: Conda—Consuela Gonzalez.

Wolf Blitzer: Minorities. There's even a gay Republican congressman from Arizona who addressed this convention.

Nancy Walls: And gay people. A lot of gay people, Jon.

Jon Stewart: Well, that's interesting, Nancy. Thank you.

Wolf Blitzer: For now, I'm Wolf Blitzer in Philadelphia.

Nancy Walls: I'm just—Wolf Blitzer.

Wolf Blitzer: Back to you, Bernie and Judy.

Nancy Walls: Back to you, Bernie.

MADELEINE SMITHBERG

On day two I said, "Why don't we just use our forty-five minutes putting a cameraman and a producer inside the arena and get lock-off [stock background footage], then we can use a green screen and do all the bits we want at our leisure and we can pretend that we're on the floor and nobody will ever know the difference?" And that changed *The Daily Show* forever, because now we could do two sketches with the correspondents in act one. And I will take full and 100 percent credit for that.

JON STEWART

This was a great stage, the conventions. We'd all been sitting around noodling in the studio, and then you went to the conventions and said, "Oh shit, we could really make a meal of this."

BEN KARLIN

There was a moment, a Carell-on-the-convention-floor moment, where he just played it in the pauses, the huge disbelief of where he was and what was happening. And it felt like: "This is the show. This is the show. You can totally feel it."

JON STEWART

If you notice in the 2000 coverage everything is done on a street, running. Everything looks like ambush journalism. I climbed a fence for one piece at the Republican convention. There was no other way to do it, and back then security was not as tight. It was a different era.

You look back and you realize you squandered a lot of opportunities. But there was a certain charm to it, and I remember at the time a grand excitement about it, because you couldn't believe "Peter Jennings is going to talk to me, holy shit!" At that point we still felt a certain deference. Which we were quickly relieved of.

As much fun—and as practically necessary—as the guerrilla pieces were, the Philadelphia excursion also included a semiscripted piece that was an important step in The Daily Show *finding a structure and a point of view with which to frame jokes.*

DAVID JAVERBAUM

The Shadow Convention was a group of very angry liberal people who were protesting very legitimate issues. I think it was my idea to say, "Well, why don't we just treat these people in a mock way, like they're a bunch of crazy idiots? You have to understand the unreliable narrator—the joke's on us because *we're* actually the assholes. We're making fun of society for treating them like assholes." That front became a thing that we often did.

> **Stephen Colbert:** [*at anchor desk with Jon Stewart*] I found one event that was happening a little bit aways from the hustle and bustle of the convention center called the Shadow Convention. Featuring such wacky characters as Senator John McCain and the Reverend Jesse Jackson. [*holds up poster*] You know, it was such a chuck-lefest that it prompted even the normally reserved Bob Novak to make this comment on CNN's *Capital Gang*:
>
> **Bob Novak:** [*in video clip, on CNN set overlooking Republican convention floor, voice dripping with disdain*] "What in the world John McCain was doing at that nutbag convention I don't know, but Arianna Huffington asked him to go and I guess he did!" [*fellow panelists guffaw*]
>
> **Stephen Colbert:** [*laughing both sympathetically and sarcastically*] You know, with a teaser like that, I just had to go check these crazy kids out.

[*Video clip begins, shows tables of literature*]

Stephen Colbert: [*voice-over*] "As an alternative to the main convention, the Shadow Convention deals with issues that are, to say the least, *not* mainstream!" [*shot of pamphlet reading, "Working to End Hunger"*] "But were the Shadow Conventioneers as funny as I'd been led to believe?"

Woman Wearing Shadow Convention Badge: "Right now, more than three million children are suffering from hunger."

Stephen Colbert: "That's *hilarious!*" [*woman, stunned, raises eyebrows*] "Some of their ideas are absolutely whack-job nut-case!" [*walks by display on high U.S. infant mortality rates while sucking on red, white, and blue popsicle*]

Different Woman Conventioneer: "Wealth is power, and the top 1 percent of the population has more money than the bottom 95 percent combined." [*Colbert blows kazoo*]

Stephen Colbert: [*voice-over, as video shows Republican delegates dancing in the aisles and wearing elephant headgear*] "So if you get tired of the substantive issues being debated by the Republicans, head on over to the Shadow Convention. But don't forget your rubber underwear, because you're gonna laugh 'til you pee!"

Jon Stewart: [*at anchor desk, looking bewildered*] Stephen, I have to say, it seemed like the Shadow Convention was the only thing here addressing real issues in a serious and meaningful way.

Stephen Colbert: [*smiling, cheery, and clueless*] Thanks Jon, it was a lot of fun to do!

ERIC DRYSDALE

Colbert would sit in the lounge with a bunch of writers around him and call the Dianetics hotline. And he's so good at remembering key words that he can pretend he knows what he's talking about, about Scientology for minutes and minutes and minutes. And he would have these very entertaining, very in-depth conversations with people about his norms and his, whatever it is, thetans.

JON STEWART

What we were also learning is that Colbert has a verbal equity that is second to none, and so, you could stuff ten pounds of shit into a two-pound sentence and he would Baryshnikov his way through it. Stephen has an agility, verbally, that's unmatched.

> **Jon Stewart:** [*at RNC anchor desk*] Now Stephen Colbert, our intrepid reporter, he's been down on the convention floor all week for us, filing wonderful reports. Stephen, let's go to him now. Stephen, now that the convention's over, can you tell me, what's your overall sense of the mood down on the convention floor? How did it feel to be there last night, during the speech?
>
> **Stephen Colbert:** [*with graphic identifying him as* SENIOR FLOOR CORRESPONDENT] Well, Jon, as a journalist, I have to maintain my objectivity, but I would say the feeling down here was one of pervasive and palpable evil. A thick, demonic stench that rolls over you and clings like hot black tar. A nightmare from which you cannot awaken. A nameless fear that lives in the dark spaces beyond your peripheral vision and drives you toward inhuman cruelties and unspeakable perversions. The delegates' bloated, pustulant bodies twisting from one obscene form to another. Giant spider shapes and ravenous wolf-headed creatures who feast on the flesh of the innocent and suck the marrow from the bones of the poor. And all of them driven like goats to the slaughter by their infernal masters on the podium, known by many names: Beelzebub, Baalzebul, Mammon, Abaddon, Feratis, Asmodeus, Satan, Lucifer, Nick, Old Scratch, the Ancient Enemy, and He Who Must Not Be Named. This is Hell, Jon, where the damned languish forever in a black flame that gives no heat, sheds no light, yet consumes the flesh forever and will not go out. Jon?

MO ROCCA

Comedy Central threw a party during the convention, and Jon walked in and was mobbed by reporters. I remember going, "Oh, this is a sea change."

DAVID JAVERBAUM

The best thing to come out of the 2000 Republican National Convention? I met my wife in Philadelphia. She was working for the Comedy Central website. I was smitten immediately, and here we are fifteen years later, and we have a family and two kids.

J. R. HAVLAN

Philly, we were in dorms, and we were away from everything else, but in LA there was debauchery. Now I'm implicating everyone in my own drinking pattern during the LA convention.

NANCY WALLS CARELL

You know, I think I'm most proud of the stuff we did at the conventions, and that was so much on the fly. They'd say, "Get down there on the convention floor. You have five minutes." There was one where my producer wanted me to imitate a Jewish lady talking about, oh my God, now I forget his name. He was the vice presidential candidate. [Joe] Lieberman! And I was supposed to talk like a proud Jewish grandma. Jon called me in later and he said, "Have you ever actually met a Jewish person?" And they used the clip, I think, as a "Moment of Zen" because I sounded like a vampire. Like Dracula.

STEVE CARELL

It was one of Jon's favorite things.

NANCY WALLS CARELL

I was pretty white.

STEW BAILEY

We did a piece where the idea was that when Al Gore picked Joe Lieberman, the media was making a big deal about this being the first Jewish candidate on a major party ticket. They're acting like there aren't other Jewish people in government, in terms of the novelty of Lieberman, so let's just pretend we've never seen ethnic people in our life.

So we would find people who looked obviously ethnic in any possible way and chase them down saying, "Senator Lieberman! Senator Lieberman!" So it's a Sikh, it's a woman wearing traditional Indian garb, it's a Native American.

At one point Colbert says, "I've got something. You guys follow me." So we run like crazy. He taps this guy on the shoulder and the guy turns around and it's James Woods. Stephen acts like he's kind of disappointed and says, "Oh, I'm sorry. I thought you were James Woods." James Woods says, "I am. I am James Woods." And Stephen says "Yeah, nice try, buddy." Then Stephen walks off and the camera stays on James Woods, and he looks so confused.

Anytime you start one of these pieces, you've got to ground it in reality and then you can take it to Crazytown. When we're telling James Woods that he's a bad James Woods impersonator, I believe we've pulled into Crazytown.

BEN KARLIN

Philadelphia was a real triumph for us, and Los Angeles was really challenging. The reason why Los Angeles was a shit show was partially Madeleine's fault, as executive producer of the show. It was probably partially my fault for not organizing the writers better. Some of it was that Philadelphia was such a triumph that this felt like failure, even though it wasn't.

MADELEINE SMITHBERG

The problem with the Democratic convention was there was no evil. For the *Daily Show* to really function, you're calling out hypocrisy and bad behavior. Here it was teachers and the unions and legalized pot and no death penalty and increase the minimum wage. And you're just like, "Where's the fucking funny?" And because of the time difference and nothing happens before four at the convention, we were in a really fucked-up production schedule. It was a mess.

BEN KARLIN

Jon very rarely, for a guy in that position, very rarely lost his cool, and I think everyone including Jon lost their cool in Los Angeles.

MADELEINE SMITHBERG

Jon felt like the stories we had selected were lazy, and the last day of the convention his point was "Look at all the stories that we're not covering."

BEN KARLIN

Madeleine and I were in Jon's office and a script was thrown out of frustration. I would not say that Jon threw the script at her head. My recollection, and I can't stress enough how shaky my memory is, is that a script was thrown. If I was in a court of law, a script was thrown in frustration. Was it down on the ground, was it on the wall? From where I was standing in that room, I could not say that it was thrown at her.

JON STEWART

The LA convention was a disaster. Based on administrative stuff, and so I was upset with it. I was in a room with Madeleine and Ben, and I did slam a paper down on a desk. Not a desk she was sitting at. She was not in the vicinity of it, but I did slam something on a desk.

MADELEINE SMITHBERG

Jon threw a newspaper at my face, and then he apologized to me at the party that night.

JON STEWART

Nobody threw anything at her face.

Despite the squabbling, The Daily Show's 2000 *convention coverage left a vivid, positive impression, particularly within political and media circles.*

BOB KERREY, *U.S. senator, Nebraska, 1989–2001; candidate for 1992 Democratic presidential nomination*

The first time I appeared on the show was in 2000, at the Democratic convention in Los Angeles. I believed then and I believe now that when it comes to things going on in America, the most honest people are the comedians. Jon had quite the reputation of actually doing the work on issues. You didn't go on with Stewart and you didn't go on with Imus and later you didn't go on with Colbert unless you were prepared.

JON STEWART

The real revelation for the show, covering the 2000 campaign, was that before everything that happens publicly in politics there's a meeting—so what's that meeting? That's what's interesting. It always struck me as, "We're always covering the wrong thing. We're always covering the appearance, but we're never covering that meeting." When you watch that pack of cameras follow a presidential candidate, you go, "That's not interesting. What's interesting is to stand behind them and watch that," because then you learn a little bit about the process.

That's when the idea of deconstructing the process came to the fore of how we were going to make the show. Before, it was just we were making jokes. Some of them were insightful, some of them were not. The show came to exist in the space between what they're telling you in public and the meeting that they had where they decided to do it that way. Seeing that was the a-ha of "That's the show."

BEN KARLIN

There happened to have been a very big and interesting contrast in those candidates, Bush and Gore. It happened to really put on display, in a very stark way, how the nation was split ideologically. These weren't two technocrats. The personality difference, the style differences, the qualitative differences between Bush and Gore made for outstanding television.

It also made for an election night, on November 7, 2000, that was as tense and strange as it was funny. The Daily Show did a special live one-hour broadcast, complete with indecipherable but colorful maps just like the networks, and—very much unlike the networks—Colbert sitting at a low-tech "analysis desk" that featured a bank of red phones and consoles that looked like something out of a high school production of Star Trek. The opening of the show both set the tone for the next eight years of Daily Show satire and proved prescient about the political mood to come.

Jon Stewart: [*at Indecision 2000 anchor desk*] Senior analyst Stephen Colbert will be joining us all night in the studio, dissecting the results as they come in. Stephen? What do you have for us? What's the word?

Stephen Colbert: [*turning away from some important-looking monitors*] Well, Jon, of course this year is the closest race since 1960, when the young John Fitzgerald Kennedy battled it out with Richard Milhous Nixon, winning by the slightest of margins and ushering in an era of untold promise, hope, and enthusiasm. Of course, an assassin's bullet ended all that. Jon?

Jon Stewart: Uh, Stephen, are you seeing parallels with tonight's election? A country flush with prosperity, two young, energetic candidates, perhaps ready to lead us back to Camelot?

Stephen Colbert: No, I'm getting more of a 'Nam vibe—you know, unwinnable wars, an inescapable downward spiral, chaos in the streets, that sort of thing. But you know, the night's still early. Be here 'til eleven!

MADELEINE SMITHBERG

The cool thing was that we really built *The Daily Show* as a news-gathering organization. We had footage deals. We had feeds. We started collecting B-roll. So we plotted our live election night special much as you would if you were an actual news-gathering organization. But we have to have a joke for whatever happened in every state. We had it all laid out on blue cards and in between commercial breaks we would assess where we were. That night felt like I was the pilot of a 747 in horrible turbulence and thunder and lightning and the bathrooms were broken, but it was really fun.

ERIC DRYSDALE

I remember at about midnight, D.J. coming in, walking up and down the hallway saying, "They haven't called Florida yet, they haven't called Florida yet." And it was the first time I remember getting that feeling like, "Oh, this is terrible, and this is great," which is a feeling I had over and over for the next ten years: "It's a war—terrible! But it's great for the show!"

J. R. HAVLAN

Look, it's no secret that there's a relatively liberal staff at *The Daily Show*. There aren't a lot of Republicans, or really hardcore conservative thinkers, and I remember on election night when they called Florida for Gore, you could hear a scream through the building, "Al Gore's president, Al Gore's president!"

MADELEINE SMITHBERG

So we're on the air live and Florida fucking flips and that was the first step in what was going to become the most amazing opportunity-slash–biggest political fiasco in American history.

STEPHEN COLBERT

They were supposed to check in with me one last time at the end of the show. I had written one bit for if Bush won and one if Gore won. We had no contingency for a tie. And the producers said, "Go come up with something."

So I ran off into a corner and I wrote what I said to Jon on scraps of like four different pieces of paper. It was just random words with lines running from one word to the other, so you see me reading off multiple pieces of paper there. Jon and I just improvised the act with each other.

> **Jon Stewart:** [*at anchor desk*] Stephen Colbert, what do you make of this race?
>
> **Stephen Colbert:** [*at decision desk*] Well, Jon, one thing is clear at this point: It is neck and neck. It is a nail-biter. A photo finish, if you will. A clash of the titans and a real barn burner. It's not the beginning of the end but the end of the beginning. Because what we've got here are two men who hunt with the hares but run with the hounds. Who must be feeling some butterflies in the stomach. The heebie-jeebies, Jon. The collywobbles. As nervous as a couple of whores in church. 'Cause eventually the chickens will come home to roost and it'll all be over but the shoutin'. One of these men will back down. Back off. Back out. Buckle under. Bite the dust. Cave in. Cash your chips. Give up the ghost and go the way of all flesh. And once one of those candidates does yell, "Olly, olly, oxen free," it'll be game over. No fair changeys. Last one there... is a rotten egg. Jon?

STEPHEN COLBERT

What I said to Jon when we got off the air was, "This is the greatest job in television."

JON STEWART

After our election night show I went home and watched TV. Like everybody else, I was like, "Well, this is weird."

The great part was just the giant fuck-up network-wise. "Gore's the winner. Gore's not the winner. Bush is the winner. Bush is not the winner, nobody's the winner." The media declared two people president, and then declared no one president. We'd met the media in New Hampshire during the primary and understood now, "Oh, this vaunted institution, that's really just a nice coat of paint."

The famous Fox News election night story—the guy on the phone with Jeb and George is their cousin: "Hey man, what's up, you're the president. Oh, wait, fuck, hold on." That was the first time it occurred to me that we took it a little bit more seriously than the media did. We were serious people doing a very stupid thing, and they were unserious people doing a very serious thing, and that juxtaposition really landed.

Blogs barely existed when Stewart took over as host. He was ahead of the curve, turning The Daily Show *into an audiovisual aggregator and deconstructor of politics and the media in a way that would, by the late 2000s, become a staple of the web (minus much of the humor). The Florida recount, and the Supreme Court's intervention—chronicled under the recurring rubric "Courting Disaster"—provided a wealth of primary source material, to which* The Daily Show *added value both humorous and insightful. Stewart was leading his troops from fisting to fisking.*

DAVID JAVERBAUM

I think the first time we all got a sense of what the show could be was the month after the 2000 election, and that was a really crazy, fun month, during the recount. It was a comedy. The *news* was a comedy.

J. R. HAVLAN

We had to cover the recount for a half hour each night. The news reporters who had to cover it twenty-four hours a day and had nothing to say, those were the people who went crazy, and that's what we realized we could focus on. The coverage of the 2000 elections was the turning point in the percentage of how much we covered a news story and how much we covered how that news story was covered.

CHRIS REGAN

You could see the traditional media outlets struggling to cover this whole situation with some sort of dignity, and we weren't bound by that. The 2000 election was so bizarre that only a comedy news show was really prepared to cover it. We were the only one who could approach what was going on in Florida honestly.

DAVID JAVERBAUM

The whole time, during the recount, it was just this air of inevitability—that the Democrats are going to lose because they usually do, and Al Gore will find a way. It's always worth thinking of the effects that resulted from the cause of 537 votes. Think of the effect on the world of a bunch of grandmothers oversleeping in Florida. It's unbelievable.

JON STEWART

A bunch of old Jews thinking, "Of course I...wait, I voted for Buchanan?" If it's separated by five hundred votes, the truth is you're never really going to know, it's just too small.

DAVID JAVERBAUM

The last night, we did a bit about how close the Supreme Court vote was, and I contributed this idea, that not only was it a five-to-four vote, but that in Kennedy's brain, it was 51 to 49 percent, and I showed the brain scan. I thought that was fun. Because you're bringing the subject of neuroanatomy in a germane way to a discussion of politics. I have a lot of things that I'm interested in, and to have a culture at the show where that is recognized and not thought of as being too obscure was great.

STEPHEN COLBERT

The night Al Gore conceded, I did a little editorial about what the Bush Administration was going to be like.

> **Jon Stewart:** [at anchor desk] Stephen, it's looking as if George W. Bush—that's it, he's going to be the next president. What is this going to mean for our country?
>
> **Stephen Colbert:** [sitting to Stewart's right] This is how I see the next four years playing out. On Inauguration Day, George W. Bush will take the oath of office and assume the mantle of leader of the free world, restoring his father's fallen dynasty. And to ensure his legitimacy, Chief Justice [William] Rehnquist will anoint his brow with chrism. Doves will be released and lambs will be slaughtered. Bush will mount a golden chariot. Then, with his aged squire, Dick Cheney, holding a laurel wreath o'er his master's furrowed brow, the man who would be boy-king will take his destined throne. And, in a much-needed show of strength, he will drive his enemies before him like leaves before a storm. He will make whores of our

wives and slaves of our children. He will appoint a horse to the senate. He will have the oceans whipped for daring to turn their tides without his leave. And while gangs of willowy young boys rub his body with perfumes from Persia and the fat rendered from the corpses of the persecuted poor, all about the fevered crowds will stare worshipfully at their unknowing, unseeing, girlishly giggling idiot emperor's head.

End of day one. Now, day two—

Jon Stewart: Thank you very much.

STEPHEN COLBERT

That was the spooky one. It was weirdly accurate to what things felt like five years later.

The tainted ending to the 2000 presidential election clearly colored Stewart's delivery the next night, in a headline bit woven around clips of Bush's victory speech that teed up The Daily Show's *approach for what turned out to be the next eight years.*

George W. Bush: [*in video clip*] "I was not elected to serve one party."

Jon Stewart: You were not elected. Nevertheless, Bush continued:

George W. Bush: "I have something else to ask you, to ask every American. I ask for you to pray for this great nation."

Jon Stewart: We're waaay ahead of you.

BEN KARLIN

Bush, it will go down in history, it's unbelievable that guy was president. Unbelievable. I'm sure, I'm 100 percent sure, in one hundred years, in one thousand years if society's still standing, they're going to say, "That guy was president? Like, what?" I know that to be a fact.

RORY ALBANESE

Nobody who was twenty years old cared about politics before that. There was a very sort of disenfranchised vibe of "What's the difference, your vote doesn't count." And then all of a sudden this Bush-Gore thing went down, and people were so lost in, "What the fuck was going on?" and *The Daily Show* became this place that was helping people to churn through it.

ERIC DRYSDALE

I think that I'm proudest of the fact that when people go back and look at that 2000 election you won't be able to talk about it without talking about Jon and the show. Probably the same way that they talk about the Smothers Brothers and Vietnam.

MICHELE GANELESS

The average nightly audience grew 47 percent that year. It would keep growing steadily, but that was the biggest one-year gain ever for *The Daily Show*.

MATT LABOV

Jon never aspired to walk down a red carpet to get his photo taken. He never wanted to be a celebrity. But he would do what he needed to do to promote the show. Howard Stern was a big supporter of Jon's, and Jon would get up early to do Howard's show. The fact that Jon was a hometown guy really helped. He's from New Jersey, but he essentially grew up in New York. Girls had a crush on him. But he's a guy's guy, because he wasn't threatening. He always had some champions in the press. *Rolling Stone* was good to him, and *GQ*, and the *New York Times*. *60 Minutes* did a profile.

ADAM CHODIKOFF

The show won a Peabody Award for the 2000 campaign coverage. Jon started being on the covers of magazines. All of a sudden my parents' friends knew what *The Daily Show* was.

JON STEWART

Anytime you're a new show and somebody says to you, "You've won an award," as long as it's not the award for fastest exit, then you feel pretty good. But outside validation goes away really quickly. That's why, in some ways, I was glad that I had all those other experiences, failures and otherwise, before I got this. You just have to do your shit.

BEN KARLIN

It was shocking to us, the idea that the show was influential. That was the reaction? We just thought that the show was really hitting its creative stride. There was no "Now we're influence makers." To self-deprecating comedy people that is just a nightmare. We didn't think of ourselves as in any way important.

Listen, I knew the show was good and I thought we were doing excellent work. But I always felt the show was overpraised. I felt the media loved it because it was about them.

JON STEWART

In the early days of standup, if I did a show where I thought it went really badly I would be rocked to the foundation. "Oh, this isn't going to work, I'm not good at this, and it's just not going to be a viable…I'm not going to be able to feed myself." And then if you have a great show you'd be like, "Or maybe I'm Jonathan Winters, classic genius!" But as you go along you start to develop a baseline of confidence in who you are, and in your ability to sustain yourself. And that's what, hopefully, started to happen with the show as well.

As if the political season and the remaking of The Daily Show *weren't enough excitement for one year, in 2000 Stewart also married his girlfriend of four years, veterinary technician Tracey McShane, and agonized as his beloved Mets made a surprising run to the World Series, only to fall to the hated Yankees.*

RORY ALBANESE

Jon used to smoke during rehearsal. Marlboro Reds. He'd have his feet up on his desk, reading the script, deciding on jokes. It didn't even seem weird at the time.

JON STEWART

Tracey quit first, and so I thought, all right, well, then I should probably do that, right? Because, you know, now we're married. I was driving out to Long Island in 2000 and threw the cigarettes out the window. And I'll tell you what happened: The Mets went to the World Series. That's what happened as soon as I quit, and I was like, "Oh my God, I'm not going to have smokes during the World Series? This is a nightmare." So I truly did not enjoy having the Mets in the World Series in 2000.

I don't know if you know this, but I have a bit of a stress issue.

The Daily Show would never completely lose its taste for inventive silliness, as long as the ideas fit within the news parody framework. But the lull following the fractious 2000 campaign, as the Bush Administration set up shop in the White House, included some of the show's looniest moments.

STEW BAILEY

There was a recurring segment called "Slimming Down with Steve," and in one from early 2001, for reasons that I can't even imagine were relevant, Carell ends up taking a big spoon out of a tub of Crisco and puts it in his mouth.

BEN KARLIN

We were like, "Let's just get some whipped cream." Carell was so insistent on, "No, no, no, I don't want to fake it. I need to feel the discomfort." That was probably the single funniest thing that ever happened on the show, like when you're stoned and you can't stop laughing.

JEN FLANZ

Oh my God. I bought the Crisco.

STEW BAILEY

Carell tries to just sit there and be still with a bunch of lard in his mouth, but he can't because it's so gross. He's trying to move it around with his tongue. You can see the sweat forming on him, and it's like the Carol Burnett side of the show that nobody planned for. You're going to do structural damage to the building it's so funny.

STEVE CARELL

I just wanted to see Jon's face knowing that I was actually eating Crisco. I just thought that would be really funny. It wouldn't be the same if it was fake, you know?

JON STEWART

That's Steve. He's the Tom Cruise of comedy. He'll put himself into the stunts. In *Foxcatcher*, that's his real nose. He grew his nose weirdly longer and killed a man.

You almost had to be careful in what you wrote for Carell because the show didn't necessarily follow OSHA rules. So if he was putting himself in harm's way, I'm not sure we had the safety net in place to protect him.

STEVE CARELL

The piece where Stephen and I go out drinking—God. That was actually my idea.

STEPHEN COLBERT

His idea was, "Let's both go out and get as drunk as you possibly can and record while we do it." I said, "I've got an idea—how about *you* do and I don't." He goes, "All right." I said, "We'll turn it into a report."

STEVE CARELL

I was watching, every year, these local stations that have the intrepid reporter who decides to test the effects of alcohol on the human systems to show that one should not drink and drive during the holidays. And they take the sobriety test. I always thought that was so corny and kind of dumb. So I decided I wanted to do that, but actually do it and not act it and really drink all that stuff.

NANCY WALLS CARELL

It should be said you do not drink very often.

STEVE CARELL

I'm not a big drinker. So I really didn't know what I was getting into. Stephen did, but he didn't say anything. First we went to Times Square and played some video games, and then we ended up at a bar. I started with, I don't know, white wine and I ended up with Jägermeister, with a lot of gin and beer and vodka and all sorts of things in between. But that was all real. And I had my shirt off, and I was getting him to punch me in the chest. I was just yelling at him to punch me in the chest. The next morning I woke up and I thought, "Why does my chest hurt so much?" Later I thought, "Oh, he could have stopped my heart so easily."

What the camera didn't catch, because they ran out of tape before all hell broke loose and I was . . .

There was a lot of vomiting that evening.

NANCY WALLS CARELL

In Stephen's car.

STEVE CARELL

Stephen drove me home and he said, "Whatever you do, there's a bag here on the floor if you need to vomit. Please don't try to vomit out the window." And I said, "I'm fine. Don't worry." And the first chance I had I tried to vomit out the window, but the window was not rolled down and it was his wife's car. It was Evie's car. The vomit went inside the window mechanism. It was bad. It was bad. I still haven't lived that one down.

STEPHEN COLBERT

The vomit went into the door. So no, we never got it out of the car. And I'll never get it out of my mind, I'll tell you that.

NANCY WALLS CARELL

I was home and I was really pregnant at the time, too. Stephen delivered Steve back to our condo and Steve just went straight to bed.

STEVE CARELL

I could hear them downstairs laughing at me. Colbert and my lovely wife were downstairs just laughing.

STEPHEN COLBERT

Well, we eventually laughed. Nancy was pretty mad, and I think at me, because I had done this to him. You know, no one wants their husband brought home stinking drunk.

Stewart was changing the show's personnel, but he was also turning the look of The Daily Show *into a comedy tool. As the producers and writers banged out the script for each episode, researchers in the postproduction department were editing tape and the graphics department was piecing together "over-the-shoulders." At first the graphics that appeared over Stewart's right shoulder were static, unimaginative titles and photographs. But they soon became a second, supporting joke, full of word-play and sight gags, adding punch to what Stewart was reading from the prompter.*

DAVE BLOG, *from field producer to graphics producer, 1996–*

In 2002 we had one woman on one machine doing graphics. I'd been doing field pieces and she needed help. A lot of the over-the-shoulders had just been an explainer: Here's a picture of the president. Here's a picture of a Yugo. The technology has made a big difference, going from Paintbox, which was an early TV graphics system, to Photoshop. But as we saw that these things could get a big laugh, we wrote more of them and refined them, to the point where we had a photo of Charlie Rangel asleep on a beach chair, and we mocked it up so his hand was in cold water and then he wet himself. It was an animation over-the-shoulder.

Momentum built throughout the day. No one is quite sure when Stewart first instituted an intense rewriting session in the hour between rehearsal and taping. But those sixty minutes became the most distinctive element of the Daily Show *day.*

JON STEWART

I have a bathroom in my office. I put the suit on in there, right before rehearsal. Some would say five minutes too late.

RORY ALBANESE

The root of every *Daily Show* script, like the root of any good sitcom script or any story, is a narrative arc. This is another Jon Stewart–ism: "The jokes are easy. We've got a lot of funny people. We'll get the jokes. You know what's hard? Why the fuck are we talking about this, and what are we saying about it? What's the arc? What is the essay that we're structuring?"

Now if that skeleton is laid properly at nine in the morning in the first round of scripts, then we're just adding layers of fun and comedy on top of it. But the rehearsal, at four, is where you see everything on its feet.

We would rehearse act one, the headline. Jon would sort of spout notes out loud, in the studio: "We don't have enough of that. We should start look-ing for a montage where we have this or this." Then we'd do act two, which is usually a chat, with a correspondent. And the act-two writers would come up to the desk and Jon would give notes to them directly.

Jon would finish rehearsal, he'd make himself an iced espresso. The joke used to be that he would put in a splash of Nestlé Quik powder and he'd call it Selenium.

JON STEWART

Now, the Selenium was really a very part-time situation. It depended: Was I Fat Jonny or Skinny Jonny? Fat Jonny had to cut down on the Selenium. Skinny Jonny needed a boost.

BEN KARLIN

The craziest time of the day really was between rehearsal and taping. We'd go to a small, windowless room behind the set. It would be the two or three executive producers, the head writer, the script supervisor, and Jon.

Sometimes they did fine-tuning. Often the script that had been in the works all day would go through radical revision.

RORY ALBANESE

The rewrite room itself, regardless of *Daily Show* era, was the show at its best. Jon would always say, "You've got to keep your foot on the neck of the beast. The show is its own animal. The show lives and breathes. Our job is to contain it."

It's true. The show is going to happen. There's a hundred people making it happen a day. It's going to happen. Our job was to make sure that that dragon was a controlled beast that can spray fire where it needed to, otherwise it would just annihilate the whole audience because it wasn't directed properly. So the rewrite was really just Jon crystallizing the fire.

JON STEWART

You have to think of the whole process, each day of creating the show, in some ways as a refinery. The rewrite room, that's at the point now where the raw material aspect of it is gone. Now it's a relatively refined whiskey, and you're trying to just bring out the right notes that make sense to you and that you can work with.

RORY ALBANESE

Jon starts pacing around, talking it out, rewriting the script out loud. For the other people in the room, the trick is not interrupting the fucking dude when he's about to have an idea, which is hard. He'll read a sound bite and then you'll say, "Potato chips and cheese!" You'll try to get a joke and he goes, "Mmmm…" and you can see his face sink. He's never mad but the worst thing you could do in that room is disrupt his flow.

Every now and then the vibe would be brutal, because the rehearsal was bad and we're all tired and Jon is in a bad mood. He would come into the rewrite room and say, "This is going to blow."

KIRA KLANG HOPF, *from production assistant to script supervisor, 1996–; member, original* Daily Show *staff*

I started doing the script under Craig Kilborn, in 1996. But it was very different then. Craig didn't do much rewriting—a word tweak here or there—and we made changes either by hand on paper or on a desktop.

Jon cared about the material from the beginning, and he was involved in everything. The rewrite room really evolved in 2001 and 2002. We'd have a monitor so everybody could see the changes I was inputting. Later on, in 2006, Jon came back from hosting the Oscars, where they projected the script on the wall as they were rewriting, so we started doing that. It was definitely my idea to have two people on laptops, one typing the script changes as Jon rewrote it out loud and the other computer for fixing all the elements, while we used the headsets to call for new graphics or rolls.

RORY ALBANESE

The "rolls" are the tape clips. Jon says, "Move roll 112 before roll 108, drop this here, slide this here, I need two jokes off of that." Then we're farming out jokes to the writers' room upstairs, telling them, "Gang that, gang that." A gang is as many writers as are available, working together. It's all hands on deck. "Here's the sound bite, we need a joke." They all pile into somebody's office and then they just spout out a bunch of jokes, put them into one document, document gets printed. In the rewrite room, as we're going through the script we're getting gangs printed and handed in and I'm circling jokes for Jon.

BEN KARLIN

It's like any kind of creative game. You feed off each other's energy, you pitch off the pitch. When the clock is ticking, you're forced to really focus in on what you want. And as you're coming up with stuff, you're like, "Oh, shit, this is a visual medium." So me, or Jon, or anyone else who might've been in the room would be on the phone to the graphics department— "We need an over-the-shoulder during this." Or to studio production: "Okay, we need a quick clip of this, we need to cut away to a full frame of this." It was the closest thing to *Broadcast News*, the comedy version of that, except all in a smelly room with Chicken Korma congealing in the corner.

JON STEWART

At one point, the rewrite room was filled with Rolos and Three Muske-teers, anything we could get our hands on that was sugar. Then I had a doc-tor's appointment where he was like, "What have you done!?" So we decided, let's switch out to something a little healthier, and it was a plate of every con-ceivable dipping vegetable and two barrels of hummus. Nobody ate any of it, but it was there for, like, three years.

KIRA KLANG HOPF

I got pretty good at translating Jon. He'd be staring at the script on the wall and saying, really fast, "The thing, take the thing, move it above the thing, the thing, the thing, thing, thing." Well, that was after we spent the first fifteen minutes every day talking about why fruit makes you burp.

BEN KARLIN

Kira, if there's a medal or career achievement award, she won it several years consecutively. She had to have that weird ear for "Okay, that's the word-ing that they want, what they said three iterations ago."

RORY ALBANESE

Kira was cleaning up all of the elements in real time, as Jon and the rest of us called out jokes. It was full-speed, badass kind of shit.

You know, not in the realm of helping children, but as far as making a nightly cable parody show, this is as badass as it gets. The jokes for, say, roll 102 come in from the gang upstairs, but by now Jon's further down in the script. So we are reading the gangs, laughing our asses off, circling the ones we like. Then we give them to Jon. The goal of that rewrite room is for the words on that screen to match the words that Jon Stewart wants to say. Not necessarily what we think is the funniest joke, meaning the other two or three of us in the room. At the end of the day the dude in the chair takes all the glory and all of the shit.

KIRA KLANG HOPF

In rewrite, D.J.'s style was very giggly and goofy, making silly insults. Ben was very passionate and smart and he'd really challenge Jon, stand up to him if he felt he needed to on a joke.

BEN KARLIN

There were days, and this continued on well into the later years of the show, where sometimes we'd rewrite more than half the show between rehearsal and taping. Then you're feverish. The audience has been loaded in, and you can hear the warmup comedian through the wall. You could hear the crowd in the studio, and we're halfway into rewriting the first act—it's like, "What the fuck are we going to do?" Jon's an intuitive live performer, and if he's got a super-bummed-out audience, because they were waiting outside on a January night and now we're an hour late, it's going to be that much harder. The whole thing is this incredibly delicate kind of organism and you're just trying to get it to function healthily.

RORY ALBANESE

For Jon the jokes had to be in conversational language, but powerful conversational language. That's where I really learned how to write. He used to say things like, "Specificity is key." In other words, if you're making a joke about, "Why don't you have another ice cream cone?" if you say, "Why don't you have another tub of rum raisin?" it gets funnier because now you're specific in the flavor. He'd go, "What do I preach?" I'd go, "Specificity."

BEN KARLIN

The writers did unbelievable work, pretty consistently, so there was always a foundation of stuff to work off of. I just would never want to, in any way, propel any kind of myth that Jon and I were holed up, kind of saving the show from lesser minds or anything like that. The times that Jon and I rewrote the show were mainly in panic triage mode after a speedy rehearsal. Maybe one out of four shows during certain times—maybe on a bad week two out of four shows—we'd do that. When we're in a really good groove, it would be like once every couple weeks we'd have to do that.

JASON ROSS, *writer, 2002–2013*

My first couple of years, I felt extremely lucky to be at the show. Around my fourth year, I started running into this frustration with the process, just the fact that as a staff writer I was so divorced from the actual on-TV version, and I would kind of whisper to other writers, "My God, do you ever feel this way?" They'd say, "Yeah, I do, but you can't argue with the result." At one point, someone told me, "I always think that my script is better than the final, but then I watch the show, and I realize I'm wrong almost 100 percent of the time." That was the most frustrating thing. The show just kept getting better and better.

Learning to accept that rewriting process—it's a journey that you have to go through, because you do feel some ownership. And even if it ends up being a great piece, you see things changing and it can be so painful. That's actually the one thing I envy about *SNL* writers—they get to direct their own pieces when they get approved. We never got that. It was always taken out of our hands. The creative director of *The Daily Show* was Jon Stewart.

RORY ALBANESE

Here's the beauty of it: You never had to worry because even if it was a shitty environment Jon would always power through. If the rehearsal or the rewrite had gone badly, right before the show I would be like, "Hey, man, I'm really sorry." Jon goes, "What am I?" I go, "A professional." He goes, "Yep, I'm a professional."

ADAM LOWITT, *from intern to executive producer, 2002–*

One of Jon's rituals was he'd walk into a room and say, "I'm open!" and we'd throw him a football. And Jon threw a football before the show every day, just to sort of get the blood flowing, before going onstage.

JON STEWART

The truth of the matter is the entire day was built toward superstition and ritual. Not in the sense of, I touch this three times, and then I move on, but in terms of the structure of our day. And they used to laugh at me about it, that if I came into a room and someone was sitting in my chair, I'd be like, "What do we do? I can't speak."

RORY ALBANESE

He'd throw the football, turn the corner, go out there into the studio, charm the shit out of an audience, sit down and charm the shit out of America. Then after taping we'd go back to the postmortem, and Jon would say, "Now what the fuck happened?"

Stewart's energies were initially focused on The Daily Show*'s writers and performers. But early on he made two off-camera hires who significantly altered the look and feel of the show because they came from the straight-news world. The first was director Chuck O'Neil, who quit a job at ABC.*

CHUCK O'NEIL, *director, 2000–*

My wife, Michele, was familiar with Jon, and she thought he was going to be something big. Because I said, "Why would I leave the network?" And she said, "Yeah, but you're miserable at the network. Why don't you go have fun somewhere?" It turned out to be the job of a lifetime.

I really wanted to make the *Daily Show* set and graphics look like *World News Tonight*. It would give much more gravity to the jokes, if we made it look serious. And when I came in they used to stop between acts, and the warmup guy would go back out and talk to the studio audience while Jon talked to the producers. I came from a live TV background where everything was done spur-of-the-moment and you've got to keep driving the pace. I told them we've got to get rid of the warmup guy and get to the next act as quickly as possible to keep the audience engaged. And Jon, by allowing slips and flubs to happen on air and not reshoot, helped give it that live feel as well.

CRAIG SPINNEY, *stage manager, 1996–*

Jonny One-Take! There were no reshoots with Jon. Though every so often some machine would break and I'd need to interrupt taping— "Sorry, Jon, we need to bust. We have a small technical malfunction." And he'd say, "I told you never to call me that in front of the audience."

*   *   *

The longer-term project was revamping the field department. In 2001, Stewart hired Jim Margolis, a veteran producer from 60 Minutes, and continued shifting the subject matter away from eccentrics. The changes eventually paid off in some of The Daily Show's *most memorable and controversial pieces.*

JIM MARGOLIS, from field producer to co–executive producer, 2001–2012

When I made my decision that I was leaving *60 Minutes* to go to *The Daily Show*, I went to tell Don Hewitt. Don looked at me and he said, "That's fantastic. What show is that? I'm happy for you kid, whatever." It was, yes, kind of a crazy decision to make and one that I never regretted.

JON STEWART

We were trying to move the field pieces from abject cruelty to something a little bit more relevant. The field is such an unusual place. You had these brilliant improv actors. But the field is improvising a scene with a partner that does not know they're in a scene with you, and doesn't realize that it's an improv.

The thing about Colbert and Carell, they were brilliant at incorporating these other individuals into the scene so that they weren't just roasting this person. They were taking a walk with them. You don't know where this is going, and then all of a sudden you end up at Hilariousville.

JIM MARGOLIS

These field pieces were parodies of this thing I was actually doing at *60 Minutes*, so I knew how to do it. The shock to the system was the budget and pace. You had one day to shoot the whole thing, in three different locations, and you had one camera.

The one-camera thing was particularly brutal. You need to get the subject on camera answering the question, and then it takes twenty minutes to flip everything around and shoot the correspondent asking the question again. Stephen Colbert's technique was to go outside, because he didn't want to have to interact with these people when the camera wasn't on. And people would change their minds or realize what they'd said. The one-camera thing went on well into 2006, just in time for me to stop doing those pieces because I was promoted to run the field department. Then Comedy Central finally had enough money to give two cameras to everybody.

During the spring and summer of 2001, as the Bush Administration was beginning to take shape, with "compassionate conservatism" still a major theme and Vice President Dick Cheney's large role still underestimated, The Daily Show *was still an uneven mix between lighter segments such as "Out at the Movies with Frank DeCaro" and wonkier headline bits like "Rich Man, Richer Man" that explored how the Bush tax cuts would screw working families—complete with a* USA Today*-style illustration of screws and butts.*

BEN KARLIN

Jon and I would have these late-night talks, after the show. I was a little more impatient than Jon, I was a little more of an angry young man, and I wanted to change everything instantly. Jon basically said, "If someone's pitching a Michael Jackson story, it may just make your stomach turn, you may hate it. But if Michael Jackson is in the news, we'll do the Michael Jackson story. Listen, the ship of state doesn't turn quickly, you know? But we're going to get there."

JAMES PONIEWOZIK

However great Letterman was at that time, Leno was the guy who led in the ratings, and his philosophy was always the big tent—as much as possible, you don't do stuff that alienates people.

What Stewart was doing was discovering and applying the programming philosophy difference between cable and broadcast networks that would define TV in the twenty-first century. The old network model was, you give people as few reasons as possible to change the channel. And cable, you're appealing more to passionate niches and trying to give people a reason to change the channel *to* you. To me, as a viewer and critic, *The Daily Show* was not necessarily refreshing so much because I agreed with its politics—in those early years around 2000, I'm not sure that the show's politics were as explicit as they later became. But I thought it was really refreshing to watch a late-night satire that had a point of view and wasn't timid about it, and would just call bullshit on things that seemed to be bullshit.

*   *   *

The outlandish 2000 election and Bush's victory had come along at the per-fect time, helping Stewart, the correspondents, and the writers sharpen The Daily Show's *tone of bemused mockery. The next world-changing events would have just as big an effect—and a late-night, basic cable comedy show would become an unlikely outlet for mourning, an antidote to anxiety, and gradually a center of principled, patriotic dissent.*

3

America Freaks Out

JON STEWART

I don't remember the show we did on the tenth at all. We had come back from a two-week break, so I would assume I had a pretty good tan going. But it was as unremarkable a show as you could possibly imagine. There is no significance other than the fact that we didn't know what was about to happen.

BEN KARLIN

I was friends with the guys from the band They Might Be Giants, who had done some music for us. On Monday, September 10, they had a record release party for their new album, which was dropping on the eleventh. So, the night of the tenth, I was out pretty late at a party down at the Bowery Ballroom. The next thing you know, you're taking a cab home and it's 4:30 in the morning and you just had a steak. That's what happens when you're thirty and single.

I was getting into work at the regular time the next morning. I'd stopped at the café that was right across the street from the studio. The woman working there, a Middle Eastern woman, is listening to the radio, and says, "A plane crashed into the World Trade Center." At the time, you're just like, "Oh, shit, that's really weird."

JON STEWART

We were living on West Eleventh Street. I heard the first plane hit while I was in bed. It felt like a bomb. It rattled the place pretty good. I flipped on the TV.

LEWIS BLACK

I woke up with a girl I was seeing. And I was on my way to the shrink. I lived on Forty-Second, the very west end, on Twelfth Avenue, the building on the left. After years I'd been finally able to get a nice apartment. I had a view to the south of lower Manhattan. We'd turned on the TV and the girl I was with said, "Oh my God, look at the Twin Towers." And one of them was smoking. Then the second tower was hit, and it was like I had a stroke.

I didn't go to see my shrink.

CHRIS REGAN

I lived two blocks from the studio, I didn't have to work until 9:30, so I was getting ready at 9:08, and I remember listening to Howard Stern talking about kissing Pam Anderson. And then he announced that a small plane hit the World Trade Center. They talked about that for a second, then they went back to theorizing if Howard could do Pam Anderson or not. And it wasn't until I got into work, where we had a TV monitor, downstairs, where a lot of the PAs [production assistants] sat, that I saw this smoke coming from the World Trade Center. Then we watched a lot of it from Ben's office.

BEN KARLIN

I'm in my office, writers are slowly gathering. This is 9:30. The morning writers' meeting starts at 9:30. We're watching a kind of locked-off shot of the smoke coming out of both the towers, on the big screen, in my office. There was no banner underneath the news before this.

I do remember standing there with Adam Chodikoff, and I think maybe D.J., watching the towers collapse, and I just broke down in tears and started crying hysterically.

DAVID JAVERBAUM

When one of the towers came down, I was with Ben, and Ben started crying. I thought that was very emotionally impressive, because most people were just too stunned to access their grief that quickly.

RORY ALBANESE

These dudes were on my train coming out of the World Trade covered in dust. It was a mess. There was something very safe about us all being together at *The Daily Show.*

Jon was there. I believe Jon was there. I'm trying to think. Yeah. I think Jon was in the office that day.

JON STEWART

I did not go to the office. We had helped Tracey's brother, Chris, move into the city the previous weekend. He lived about three blocks from us, so we went to go get Chris. We were out on the street when we saw the tower collapse. That's when just everything started spinning.

ALISON CAMILLO, *from intern to coordinating field producer,*
1998–2016

Jo Honig, who was a field producer then, came in covered in the dust. She lived down by Chambers Street and rode her bike to work. She had Fred, her dog, with her, and he was covered in soot. I was sobbing.

CHRIS REGAN

Ben announced there weren't going to be any shows, and D.J., my writing partner, said, "Well, Chris and I can stay and finish up 'We Love Showbiz,'" which was this *Entertainment Tonight* parody. And I snapped at D.J., saying, "No fucking way are we going to do that."

HILLARY KUN, *co-executive producer, guest booker, 2001–2016*

I had just moved back from LA and started work the previous week. My first show guest was going to be Tracey Ullman, on September 11. When I got into the office that morning I contacted her publicist, to say, "Hey, just letting you know, we are cancelling the show for tonight." And they said, "Oh, Tracey got out of New York. She started driving cross-country. She's long gone."

CHRIS REGAN

I went to a liquor store that was open early and stocked up. My apartment was the smallest one-bedroom, a fourth-floor walk-up, and about a dozen, dozen and a half people from the show came.

I had just gotten a DVD of *The Big Lebowski*, and I announced that I wanted to watch something that hearkened back to a gentler war, the 1990 Gulf War. We would stop it every twenty minutes or so and turn on the news to see if anything else had blown up. Yeah, I really spent 9/11 getting drunk, in my apartment, with a lot of my coworkers.

JON STEWART

Can I tell you the craziest thing? Tracey and I were walking that afternoon of 9/11, or it might have been the next day, in just the quiet of it. We didn't really know where we were going, just walking, and we walked by a building and there was a little street mouse, I don't even think it was a rat, a little street mouse. All of a sudden a dude—I guess it was the super in the building, we hadn't seen him—fucking clubbed it right in front of us. I remember us just both bursting into tears, and we just kind of like…I just remember us bursting into tears on a constant basis, as everybody was. The smell is the thing that I'll never forget, just that was…

I try not to remember, to be honest with you. I mean, I'm still not good at it, like I still can't particularly talk about certain things, and I just can't do it, you know.

ROB RIGGLE, *correspondent, 2006–2008*

At the time I was part of a Marine Corps reserve unit, MTU 17. The only Marine Corps reserve unit stationed in Manhattan. The next morning, September 12, we went down to Ground Zero and started moving rubble by hand. We didn't know how many people were under the rubble. Twelve hours on, twelve hours off, for six days. It was no longer search and rescue, it was search and recovery at that point.

BEN KARLIN

It was a few days, I think, before we gathered to talk about how the fuck we were going to move on.

JON STEWART

I'm talking to Ben and Stew, and the writers, just trying to figure it out. "Do we even have a show? Is there a show to do here, or do we just…do we tap-dance?" I thought it was going to go variety show.

JIM MARGOLIS

I'd quit a job at *60 Minutes* to work at *The Daily Show*, and I couldn't have been there more than ten days before 9/11 happened. There was actually a question whether the format should be changed to be a parody of a morning show, and I thought, "What the fuck have I done?"

STEVE CARELL

I remember Stephen and I sitting with Jon those days after, trying to figure out what to do, what to write, and how to even put on any show. It all just seemed...so irrelevant and small.

STEW BAILEY

There was a creative meeting before we went back on air where Stephen Colbert, and Steve Carell, and Jon, and Madeleine, and some others were all in Madeleine's office and we had looked at the board that we had programmed for what segments were going to be on, before 9/11. Everybody uses those colored cardboard things with the pushpins. It'll be eight thousand years from now and that's how late-night shows will be programmed. Anyway, we looked at the board and we just realized this didn't make sense to us anymore.

We were all so numb. I remember Stephen Colbert said, "I am legitimately asking if a pie in the face is still funny. I'm asking because I don't know." He was not joking.

DAVID JAVERBAUM

Our first instinct was, "Let's write a bunch of things that are so light and silly. Anything contiguous to the attack, we just can't touch."

CHRIS REGAN

Graydon Carter had gone on about the death of irony and all this other crap. I remember I worked on a piece with Carell, which was a *Crocodile Hunter* parody, where he was in a safari outfit at the desk. We just weren't talking about the big smoking elephant in the room. It was just a terrifying time to write comedy. Not the worst problem to have in New York, but still, it was a very strange time to try to be funny.

ALISON CAMILLO

I remember Madeleine said, "I don't even know if we have a show anymore."

KIRA KLANG HOPF

Jon knew we still had a show. He said, "This now is more important than ever." On that Thursday, when we came back to work, he came around to everyone's office and talked: "What should we do?" He wanted to make sure everyone was on board. He didn't want to go back on the air and be a dick.

JON STEWART

Comedians process our emotions through this peculiar refinery of whatever puns you could come up with that day. You remove that, and it's as though there's a narcotic on the digestive system. You're blocked, it's building up, and you don't know what to do.

I knew that for me, personally, I would have to express...I would have to use the process that I've used to process pain, and discontent, and happiness, and everything else, but in a way that was somewhat anathema to how I would normally approach it. It just had to be direct and I was going to have to do it without my crutches.

It's very hard for me to write without knowing, "Okay, I'm going to get to perform it now." I generally can't take myself to a place without knowing what the finish line is. It has to be timed right, because otherwise I will lose my inertia. If I don't time it right it'll be there and then it'll be gone, and I'll fuck it up, I'll ruin it by overwriting it.

That day, September 20, when we were doing our first show after 9/11, was basically me in my office just pacing and jotting stuff down.

JEN FLANZ

Nobody really knew what Jon was going to say.

JON STEWART

I wrote the 9/11 monologue on a paper plate. I ate a lot of pizza, so my office had a lot of paper plates in it, from a pizza place. Not the Chinet kind, either. The shitty paper kind.

On September 20, 2001, Stewart spoke directly into the camera for nearly nine minutes, tears welling in his eyes, tapping the anchor desk hard with a plastic pen when he needed to pause and compose himself, the studio audience silent except for several brief moments of nervous laughter.

Jon Stewart: Good evening, and uh, welcome to *The Daily Show*. Uh, we are back. Uh, this is our first show since the tragedy in New

York City and uh, uh, there's no other way to start this show other than to ask you at home the question that we asked the audience here tonight, and that we've asked everybody that we know here in New York since September 11, and that is, "Are you okay?" And that we pray that you are and that your family is...

I know we're late. I'm sure we're getting in right under the wire before the cast of *Survivor* offers their insight into what to do in these situations. They said to get back to work, and there were no jobs available for a man in the fetal position under his desk crying. Which I gladly would have taken. So I come back here and— tonight's show is not obviously a regular show...

A lot of folks have asked me, "What are you going to do when you get back? What are you going to say? I mean, geez, what a terrible thing to have to do." I don't see it as a burden at all. I see it as a privilege. I see it as a privilege and everyone here does see it that way.

The show in general, we feel like is a privilege. Just even, even the idea that we can sit in the back of the country and make wise- cracks, which is really what we do. We sit in the back and we—we throw spitballs, and uh—but never forgetting the fact that is a lux- ury in this country that it—that allows us to do that. This is a coun- try that allows for open satire, and I know that sounds basic and it sounds as though it goes without saying—but that's really what this whole situation is about. It's the difference between closed and open. It's the difference between free and and and and bur- dened and we don't take that for granted here by any stretch of the imagination. And our show has changed. I don't—I don't doubt that. What it's become, I don't know. "Subliminable" is not a punch line anymore. One day it will become that again, and, and Lord willing, it will become that again because that means we have ridden out the storm.

But the main reason that, that I wanted to speak tonight is, is not to tell you what the show is going to be. Not to tell you about all the incredibly brave people that are here in New York and in Washing- ton and around the country. Uh, but but we've had an unenduring pain here—an unendurable pain. And I just—I wanted to tell you why I grieve, but why I don't despair... [*tears up*] I'm sorry. Luckily we can edit this...

And the reason I don't despair is because this attack happened. It's not a dream. But the aftermath of it, the recovery, is a dream realized. And that is Martin Luther King's dream. Whatever barriers we've put up are gone even if it's just momentary. And we're judging people by not the color of their skin but the content of their character. And you know, all this talk about, "These guys are criminal masterminds. They've—they've gotten together and their extraordinary guile... and their wit and their skill." It's a lie. Any fool can blow something up. Any fool can destroy. But to see these guys, these firefighters, these policemen and people from all over the country, literally, with buckets, rebuilding. That, that—that is—that's extraordinary. That's why we've already won. It's light. It's democracy. We've already won. They can't shut that down. They live in chaos and chaos... it can't sustain itself. It never could. It's too easy and it's too unsatisfying.

The view from my apartment was the World Trade Center, and now it's gone. And they attacked it. This symbol of American ingenuity and strength and labor and imagination and commerce, and it is gone. But you know what the view is now? The Statue of Liberty. The view from the south of Manhattan is now the Statue of Liberty. You can't beat that.

So we're going to take a break and I'm going to stop slobbering on myself and on the desk and, uh, we're going to get back to this. It's gonna be fun and funny and it's going to be the same as it was and I thank you. We'll be right back.

RORY ALBANESE

I do remember thinking, "Fuck, dude, that's pretty heavy for a comedy show."

J. R. HAVLAN

Yeah. I wrote that. Every word of it. I had *crying* in parentheses and everything: "Really give them the waterworks here, Jon. I think they're going to fall for it."

I remember being a little surprised just because—the first time you see somebody that you know, who's an adult, crying over something, is a revelation. The one thing I remember is him talking about how the view from his apartment was of the World Trade Center, and now that that's gone, the view from his apartment was the Statue of Liberty. And thinking, "I have to believe you, but that's pretty convenient." Then thinking, "Pretty fancy view you got, Mr. Jon Stewart." And I remember, also, feeling bad that I questioned whether or not that was true.

ELLIOTT KALAN, *from intern to head writer, 2002–2015*

I remember so well Jon's first show back after September 11 and how much that meant to me at the time. I was a junior at NYU and watched it in my dorm room near Union Square. That episode didn't make anything okay at all, but at least someone was saying the type of thing I wanted the president or the mayor to say.

I remember Jon bringing his dog out at the end, and it being like a really silly thing to do but a really beautiful way to say there's a whole other world of existence that has nothing to do with this political violence.

JON STEWART

I think the end of it was just me holding up our dog, Monkey. And then we all kind of looked at each other like, "Now what?"

Afterward I had to walk away from the desk, and I went into the back room and I just bawled. I was just...I was done. It had been an incredibly emotional experience. We all knew people who had been down there and had lost people. It was just the act of getting it out, but it's not like that was the healing, that was just the...it honestly felt like that was, "Great, I've now vomited it up, but I'm still nauseous, and exhausted." That first show was not a statement of what we were going to do. It was a necessary draining of an abscess to even become ambulatory.

STEW BAILEY

We didn't do another show until September 24, I think. The challenge over the next few weeks was to acknowledge what had happened and do it in a way that didn't seem insensitive. How do you fight something so powerfully scary?

There was a great piece Lauren Weedman did, which was "New York City's Back in Business." It was Lauren saying, "Here are the ways that New

York City is luring back tourists." One of them was, "Now New York City offers personal piggyback rides across Central Park by some of New York's biggest celebrities." And you widen out, and Lauren is sitting piggyback on top of Paul Rudd, and Paul Rudd turns to the screen and says, "No fatties!" and he keeps running her across.

PAUL RUDD

I think the studio audience laughed over my line, because a couple of days later I was walking down the street and a woman said, "Hey, can I get a ride on your back through Central Park?" laughing. I was surprised she knew the bit, and I laughed and said—continuing with the bit— "No fatties!" And I realized, oh, that was not the right thing to say. She looked at me with the biggest fuck-you look. I don't think she had heard that part on the show.

DAVID JAVERBAUM

Slowly we found our way, and that is 100 percent attributable to the leadership and the moral fiber of Jon. I think also our own expectation, and the audience's, about what comedy meant changed—to the point where we would eventually do seven minutes on Abu Ghraib.

You know you're not going to get big, hearty belly laughs about Abu Ghraib, but that was okay. As long as you could point out an irony and make it so it's not too clappy. That's a shorthand for, "Well, you made a point," and the audience claps its approval. But you're not funny, and ultimately the goal is to make it funny.

JON STEWART

Oddly enough, the thing that snapped us out of it were the anthrax attacks. Somehow, that just made it funny. I don't know why, but as soon as we started getting hit by anthrax it was like, "Oh, okay. Let's embrace this. Let's embrace the fear that we all feel now." It was sort of like when I was in my drinking days, when shit would go wrong, and I'd be feeling lousy about life, I would have to steer into it. So that meant Tom Waits and booze at three in the morning, sitting alone until "The Piano Has Been Drinking" is fucking hilarious, because you're so pathetic. The combination of the grief, the sadness, the uncertainty, coupled with somebody's sending anthrax to all these reporters... "Okay, it's gone to a level of farce, and farce I can deal with." So we turned into it.

Jon Stewart: [*at anchor desk*] The media, of course, must walk a fine line covering this story. With more we turn to Steve Carell in the *Daily Show* news center. Steve?

Steve Carell: [*standing in front of a bank of TV monitors*] Jon, this is in many ways an unprecedented situation for us.

[*A blue band with white letters—the "crawl," or "chyron" in TV lingo— scrolls across the screen, at Carell's waist level*]

Crawl: MAJORITY LEADER DASCHLE RECEIVES LETTER CONTAINING ANTHRAX.

Steve Carell: On the one hand, we must alert the country to the latest events.

Crawl: AL QAEDA VOWS NEW ATTACKS.

Steve Carell: And on the other hand, we musn't cause undue alarm.

Crawl: FBI WARNS SOMETHING BAD TO HAPPEN SOMEWHERE SOMETIME.

Steve Carell: Scaremongering isn't the way to go.

Crawl: WHITE POWDER FOUND ON DONUT IN ST. LOUIS.

Steve Carell: So far the media has in fact shown restraint.

Crawl: STORMS BATTER NEW ENGLAND—LINK TO TERRORISM STILL UNDETERMINED.

Steve Carell: And I must stress this—there is absolutely no need to panic.

Crawl: [*picking up speed as it moves left to right*] CIA: THAT GUY SITTING ACROSS FROM YOU ON THE BUS LOOKS A LITTLE SHIFTY.

Steve Carell: Patience, diligence, and above all, responsibility.

Crawl: A FRIEND OF THIS GUY I KNOW CONFIRMS HIS GIRLFRIEND TOLD HIM "THEY'RE PLANNING SOMETHING IN A MALL OR SOMETHING."

Steve Carell: Jon, we have a job to do here, but we also need perspective.

Crawl: [*accelerating*] OH, F—! WHAT WAS THAT SOUND? SERIOUSLY, DID YOU HEAR A SOUND?

Steve Carell: And in keeping that perspective—

Crawl: "THE HORROR, THE HORROR"—KURTZ. POLL: 91% OF AMERICANS "WANT MOMMY."

Steve Carell: Okay, that was—no, no, no, that was unacceptable. Jon, would you excuse me for a minute? [*walks out of frame*]

Crawl: CHICKEN LITTLE: "THE SKY IS FALLING! THE SKY IS FALLING!" OH GOD, OH GOD.

[*Carell confronts technician typing the crawl, beats him up as screen goes snowy*]

Jon Stewart: We're having some technical difficulties with the crawl. Ah, Steve Carell is back!

Steve Carell: Sorry about that, Jon. As I was saying, we journalists have to make sure that our worst instincts are curbed in the sake of national interest.

Crawl: EVERYTHING IS GOING TO BE JUST WONDERFUL WITH LOLLIPOPS AND RAINBOWS AND HAPPY FEELINGS FOR EVERYONE.

Steve Carell: It's a unique challenge, but one I think the greatest free press in the world can easily attain.

Crawl: BUNNIES ARE CUTE, CUDDLY, AND COMFORTING.

Steve Carell: Jon?

JON STEWART

Before that the show was just silly; we didn't know what we were doing. And then the networks, bless their soul, steered into fear, and that was a great motivator for us. That was a gift. Now we can just make fun of them. That's when the tickers came out.

More and more, the show didn't just react to daily events, but dug around inside them. The guest list—which had been heavy on movie-promoting actors like Jenny McCarthy and Jason Biggs—now regularly included people who could analyze the war and its fallout, from diplomats (Richard Holbrooke) to civil rights experts (Nadine Strossen) to, eventually, former marines (Anthony Swofford). And the shift toward media criticism picked up speed, in running segments like "Operation Enduring Coverage" and "Operation Self-Congratulation."

RORY ALBANESE

What was starting to happen was, post-9/11 and post–Bush/Gore, which is when *The Daily Show* gets good, the media is different now. The media took a turn to lunacy. One of our favorites was you've got the reporter saying something serious and then one of the crawls below him was BEYONCÉ COINS THE TERM "BOOTYLICIOUS" FOR $14 MILLION. Meanwhile the reporter is talking about health care reform or Afghan refugees.

JON STEWART

It was "We're all going to die!" twenty-four hours a day. The networks are built for 9/11. A twenty-four-hour news network with that kind of reach and that kind of manpower is really only built for one thing, and that is catastrophe on an inhuman scale. They performed admirably. Unfortunately, they don't really know when to turn that off, and so, in their mind, "Hey, everybody's watching us, but if we stop this they might not. How are we going to keep this up? I know, let's just keep a running ticker tape at the bottom of the thing."

Though we did have an anthrax scare at the show and the whole building had to clear out. We had to bring in a biohazard team. Beth Shorr, my assistant, ended up in a Silkwood shower in some kind of decontamination unit. We had to switch procedures with the mail. By the way, it turned out not to be anthrax.

Yeah, we taped that day. We didn't tape, the terrorists win. And it was one of the secondary anthrax moments. Because we were on basic cable, it took a little time for them to get to us.

One bright spot as 2001 neared an end was The Daily Show's *first two Emmy Award nominations, for best comedy show and best comedy writing.*

CHRIS REGAN

Because of 9/11 they postponed the Emmys that year, and then they rescheduled it for November, and then Jon just said, "The heck with it, we're going to party here," so none of us were in LA for the awards. Comedy Central got us part of a bar on Fifty-Fourth Street. I think it was Iguana. We had one TV to watch it on. We had to watch the Emmys with subtitles. Wayne Brady was giving out the Emmy, and at one point the subtitle said, in parentheses, "Gibberish." Then we saw, "and the award goes to the gang at *The Daily Show*," in subtitles. None of us actually heard it announced. The show's first Emmy.

Right after that, a former writer ran in with his head bleeding because he'd gotten into a fight in the bar across the street. So, it was crazy, actually.

In Washington, the political response to 9/11 was escalating rapidly and ominously. First came the rush to pass the Patriot Act, whose name was a flimsy euphemism for increased government wiretapping and surveillance. Then neoconservatives pushed to turn the Global War on Terror into an actual shooting war. There were plenty of openings for humor along the way—when Bush, for instance, apologized for the negative connotations of calling the impending offensive a "crusade." But as the politically motivated fearmongering grew, The Daily Show *started to shed its apprehension about criticizing how the White House was exploiting the raw aftermath of the terrorist attacks.*

LEWIS BLACK

The thought occurred to me on 9/11—and it's a terrible thought, but I can guarantee you 90 percent of the United States had this thought at some point: "Wow, this really fucks up my day."

But the second thought I had was that our government's response is going to be really fucked up and they are going to do something awful. This is going to give them an excuse to do something really awful. And I'm never right. But it unfolded like a great tragedy.

I did not know anybody who died there, okay? So, obviously that is a certain filter. My reaction was mostly in terms of what the government was going to do in the name of the people who died—and it was wrong. And that's a lot of what *The Daily Show* became about for the next few years. Comedy was the correct response.

4

Check Your Soul at the Door

President Bush had urged the nation to fight terrorism by... going shopping. Donald Rumsfeld, the secretary of defense, tried to explain away the failure to find Iraqi weapons of mass destruction—which had been the supposed justification for the war—with an abstruse pronouncement about "known unknowns." A series of jingoistic, made-for-TV slogans—"Operation Iraqi Freedom," "Operation Enduring Freedom," "Operation Anaconda"—were trotted out to market an increasingly dubious military adventure. Refracting the lies and absurdities through comedy, The Daily Show's tone mixed more indignation into the wisecracks.

Jon Stewart: [*at anchor desk, after being interrupted midsentence by blaring trumpets as big black letters reading* BREAKING NEWS *fill the screen. From Moscow, Steve Carell reports on a press conference by Attorney General John Ashcroft to—belatedly—announce the arrest of an Al Qaeda operative, just as congressional hearings were investigating U.S. intelligence failures*] Steve, I'm worried that whenever the dialogue about the war on terrorism gets difficult politically, these scary stories start surfacing, and the media jumps right on board. Watching the news today, you'd think terrorists had actually built this dirty bomb and were caught today trying to detonate it. But the story's a month old! So let's go back to talk about what our government and security agencies did and are doing to prevent—

Steve Carell: [*imitating the portentous trumpets*] Ba, ba, ba ba baaa! Iraq! Jon?

Jon Stewart: Iraq, what? What are you even—

Steve Carell: Is Iraq behind the dirty bomb? Should we overthrow weapons of mass destruction? Saddam!

Jon Stewart: Steve, you're just fanning the flames of fear. You might as well be shouting "smallpox" in a crowded theater.

[*Trumpets blare.* BREAKING NEWS *logo fills the screen*]

Stephen Colbert: [*sitting behind Stewart in the studio*] I'm Stephen Colbert from the breaking news desk! Cable television anchors are reporting a potential smallpox epidemic breaking out in theaters here in the United States! This is a nightmare scenario, a biological doomsday from which there can be no escape!

BEN KARLIN

It was so obvious, the snow job that was being pulled, and it was so heartbreaking. We felt, from the beginning, that the people who were being unpatriotic were the people who were lying about vials of anthrax and weapons of mass destruction. You just knew it was bullshit. And once the show decided that we were going to talk about the most important things that are going on in the world, you always had two ways to go: the story itself or the coverage of the story. But it was only over time that we started to realize how it could work.

By early 2002, The Daily Show's nightly average audience had more than doubled from the Kilborn years, from 350,000 to more than 800,000.

STEPHEN COLBERT

We knew that people liked what we were doing, but we were still a little show. Then I went someplace in Florida to do a piece where there were college students, and I could barely walk. I remember turning to the producer and going, "What's happening?" I had to hide because people were storming me as a correspondent on *The Daily Show.* That was really shocking to me and I thought, "I wonder if they know we were joking?"

Another sign was that Stewart became a hot show business property. Fox came calling in 2003, offering a primetime or late night show; years later, NBC wanted to make Stewart the "permanent guest host" for Jay Leno. But the closest Stewart came to leaving The Daily Show was in 2002. ABC had pursued David Letterman, who eventually decided to stay at CBS. ABC's next target to host a show after Nightline *was Stewart, who was highly interested. Then, as a deal seemed likely, Lloyd Braun, ABC's president, quietly became intrigued with Jimmy Kimmel. Making the situation more complicated was that Dixon represented both Stewart and Kimmel.*

JAMES DIXON

Lloyd Braun came to us, and Jon definitely thought about it. They made a fucking offer. The offer was basically what Jon was making doing *The Daily Show*. ABC said, "We can't pay this guy or any guy who isn't already like Letterman that kind of money. This is big-league. We're giving him a major opportunity."

Jon and I never viewed it like that at all. If you're going to cheap out on Jon, you're not going to get Jon. So when it became obvious that it was like, "Hey, cable boy, this is the big leagues," I said what I needed to probably get it done. That killed it right there. That doesn't mean that even if they gave me the money that we were looking for that Jon would have said yes. It wasn't like Jon was pining for the ABC job. The first meeting with Jimmy was after it became obvious that Jon was not happening. Lloyd never met with Jimmy behind my back.

By the way, I love Lloyd Braun. He's one of my best friends in the business.

In May 2002, ABC hired the lesser-known Kimmel to replace Bill Maher and Politically Incorrect *at midnight. Stewart stayed at* The Daily Show—*a turn of events that disappointed him at the time, but proved the right fit for both Kimmel and Stewart.*

JAMES DIXON

Jon always said, "I don't need to be on a broadcast network to validate myself. I'll do what I do for basic cable, and if I do it well it won't matter where I do it from. That will be my legacy."

The fallout from 9/11 was providing plenty of bleak grist for The Daily Show. *What had been billed as a quick and tidy punishment of Al Qaeda and the Taliban was turning into an extended, costly mess, with Osama bin Laden eluding American troops and Afghanistan descending into civil war.* The Daily Show *responded by becoming one of the rare media voices that was openly skeptical of Bush— pointing out how the president was shifting attention away from the Afghanistan fiasco by supervillainizing Saddam Hussein, in segments like, "Showdown:*

Iraq? Wal-mart of Evil." The show geared up for the invasion itself by hiring two new correspondents with the edge and range to file mordantly funny "battlefield" reports. And with the Republicans surging in the polls and on the verge of seizing a majority in both the House and the Senate, The Daily Show, *as part of "Indecision 2002," made its first midterm road trip, this one to Washington, DC.*

ELLIOTT KALAN

In the fall of 2002 I was an intern. There was a lot of energy in the place. It felt like being on a TV show in the movies, and it felt very low-rent in some ways. Things were a lot less structured than they would become later. It was a fun, creative place to be. Every Thursday night most of the staff would go drink and hang out.

STEVE CARELL

As Nancy said, it was so loose back then. People would just come in and say, "You want to do this?" And I'd say, "Sure." I don't remember who came to me with "Produce Pete."

CHRIS REGAN

Where did "Produce Pete" come from? Just boredom. It was a time where we were really beginning to shift into constant news coverage, and I just wanted to do something else. I stayed late one night, and there was a guy in New York who used to appear on, I think, the NBC *Saturday Today* show, and his name was Produce Pete. I think he was a guy from Staten Island, and they would do these ten-minute segments talking about what was in season. I'm thinking to myself, "Do you think this guy was a journalist once?"

I'm thinking about the career path one takes to become a produce expert on a news show, so I just banged out one segment. They all eventually melted down into him being a loser, and it was never about the produce. It was always about Produce Pete and living in a men's residence and people he tormented.

STEVE CARELL

And then the more "Produce Pete"s we did, the more his character kind of came to life as this extremely depressed guy who was probably living in his parents' basement. You know, just the layers of sadness underneath this ostensibly very light lifestyle segment.

STEVE BODOW, *from writer to executive producer, 2002–*

Carell and Colbert were similar in some ways. They did improv together in Chicago, and they shared that ability to react in the moment in funny but still real ways. They had both worked for other pretty good people. They had both worked with Dana Carvey's show. That was a writing room of fucking legend—Charlie Kaufman, Louis C.K., Robert Smigel. But a good distinction between them, at *The Daily Show*, is vulnerability versus invulnerability. Carell's characters would be buying their own bullshit ultimately less than Stephen's, who were just a bulletproof fucking wall of believing their own bullshit.

CHRIS REGAN

Carell would just take his time and let these pauses hang in the air, and it was completely different from anything else we had done on the show.

"Produce Pete" Steve Carell: [*wearing a lei and a grocer's apron, standing behind a table piled with fruit*] Aloha, friends! Today I, "Produce Pete" Steve Carell, am or will have discussed pineapple. This beloved fruit is a favorite July Fourth picnic refresher that is wonderful served whole or sliced and cooked on the grill with ham steaks. Who doesn't love ham in the summer?

Pineapples began to spread around the world in the 1700s when explorers brought them along on voyages to prevent scurvy. Incidentally, I once contracted scurvy years ago. It's not fun. My gums bled, my teeth fell out, and I was covered in these awful purple deep-tissue bruises. I wasn't a sailor, of course, but I guess you could say I was, um, I don't know, adrift? Out to sea? Living in a men's residence in Chicago. Young man overboard. Really wasn't, uh, taking the best care of myself back then. Shiver me timbers! [*forced chuckle*] Anyhow.

Look for a pineapple that's firm, never spongy, and has no bruises or soft spots. Like the kind I had when I had scurvy. Remember [*reads nonsense Hawaiian words from index cards*], which means, "Me likey shaky hiney for old men."

You know, I don't know who's messing with the cards, but I don't think that's funny. 'Cause it was a matter of survival, okay? [*glares off camera*] Like you guys never had sex for cash or drugs. Hypocrites. Are we still on?

CHRIS REGAN

I wrote a bunch of them. Eventually, I think they got a little tired with my approach, and Eric Drysdale and I cowrote two or three of them, and then Steve went off to Hollywood and never came back.

NANCY WALLS CARELL

We moved to LA in August of '02. Our daughter was one at that point, and it was just time.

STEVE CARELL

I was doing this birdwatching field piece. It was a twenty-four-hour bird-watching competition so we decided to cover it for twenty-four hours. It was like three or four in the morning, and we were in the middle of a swamp in New Jersey being attacked by swarms of mosquitoes and bats, and I thought, "I think I'm done."

I left *The Daily Show* with nothing specific to go to. I didn't have a job.

JUDD APATOW

When Steve Carell came in to read for *Anchorman*, he was hysterical doing Brick Tamland. And then afterward Adam McKay, Will Ferrell, and myself were talking and we all paused. Steve was so amazing on *The Daily Show* as a correspondent, and then he had played an anchorman in *Bruce Almighty*. So we were considering whether or not that would rule Steve out: "Oh, he's played around with the news too often." And a couple of weeks later we said, "Are we insane? This is the funniest man ever."

STEVE CARELL

I did a couple *Daily Show* pieces after we moved to LA, I kind of kept my toe in a little bit.

NANCY WALLS CARELL

I think from the beginning it felt like Jon was going to create something special. But I have to say, though, I didn't have the impression that "Oh, this is going to turn into something that's going to appeal to the masses of America." It just seems that people like Jon who are that smart and funny, that doesn't then go out to the masses. You have your niche audience for something like that. But that's not what happened, which is amazing.

STEVE CARELL

I didn't think that a book would be written about this show.

NANCY WALLS CARELL

No. It's not a coincidence that the show really took off after we left.

STEVE CARELL

We figured we had to do it for the good of the show. And I'd grown tired of carrying Colbert.

The exit of Mr. and Mrs. Carell was a loss, but it was the first high-profile example of what would become a pattern. As The Daily Show *became a launching pad for comedy careers, Stewart didn't fight to hold on to talented people indefinitely. He treated the defections as an opportunity to find new weapons. The show's growing popularity ensured there would be eager applicants coming out of the comedy clubs and casting agencies. But* The Daily Show's *success would in some ways also be constricting, at least at first.*

RORY ALBANESE

Colbert was the master of false authority. The problem came when you'd go out to do auditions for new contributors and correspondents. I'd be having a casual conversation and it'd be superfunny. Then I'd say, "Let's run it," and do the real audition. So often they'd be like, "Four dead today…" I'd go, "Stop affecting your voice! Just talk the way we were just talking." They had practiced Colbert.

CHRIS REGAN

The Daily Show is full of people who did one field piece and were never seen on the show again. There was Jerry Minor, there was Adrianne Frost.

STEW BAILEY

When we looked at tape of Rob Corddry and Ed Helms, the code name for Corddry was "Tufty," because he had a small tuft of hair right on the top of his forehead that he did not shave. The fact that we wouldn't even use his name when talking about hiring him just shows you what awful people we are.

We were only looking to add one person, but Corddry and Helms were both so funny we just decided to add them both.

CHRIS REGAN

Corddry and Helms were kind of the new breed. Corddry was a very smart guy, and a very funny guy, and also a really nice guy, and those three qualities rarely join hands. Helms was unlike anyone we'd had as a correspondent, really unafraid to make himself look unattractive. There was one field piece where he's having moles cut off his face. There was another where he's in a Speedo for half of it.

ED HELMS, *correspondent, 2002–2006*

It was just something that came up in the news about Cape May, New Jersey, reversing a ban on Speedos that they'd had since I think it was the '70s. Stew Bailey liked it and assigned it to me, and the field producer was Glenn Clements. The only thing I'll take credit for in creating that piece was fervent opposition to the dog licking my balls. I lost that argument.

ROB CORDDRY, *correspondent, 2002–2006*

I'd graduated from college, UMass Amherst, and been performing in a Shakespeare company, but then I joined Upright Citizens Brigade. Not long after that Amy Poehler and Rob Riggle, who were also at UCB, got cast at *Saturday Night Live* and so other casting agents started mining UCB, and *The Daily Show* came down. I think Ben Karlin saw me, and then I auditioned with Jon. It was a piece about an icicle as the perfect murder weapon. I made him laugh, which is not as hard as it looks.

ED HELMS

Well, let's see. I was living in New York City, really trying to make a career as a comedian, and I had managed to sort of wedge my way into the commercial voice-over scene.

I got involved with Upright Citizens Brigade, and it became this kind of mash-up of improv and standup. My end goal at that point was *Saturday Night Live.* I'd always been a fan of *The Daily Show*, even from Craig Kilborn. That started when I was, I think, in college. I went to Oberlin, obviously kind of politically oriented. When Jon took over, the show felt much more editorial, and I loved it.

In 2002, I went to a huge cattle-call *Daily Show* audition, three hundred people. Got a haircut, put incredible amounts of product in my hair. I looked like a Ken doll. They hand me a script. I recognized the segment, and I did it exactly how I knew that Stephen had done it. The callback was at the *Daily Show* studio, and there were five of us called back. It was Rob Corddry, Jessica St. Clair, who's a dear friend, and a couple of other great comedians that I knew.

Later I get the call, "You got a segment." I'm not staff, I'm not hired, but I got a segment. That was a very common way to initiate a correspondent at the time. You get a chance to give it a go, and see how it works. Was it nerve-wracking? Not really. My recollection is, especially looking back now, I was bizarrely confident.

The mole removal, that was right on the heels of Katie Couric's—did she get a colonoscopy? I think she did. We were prepping it when I was on probation, before I got hired. I think that's when the powers that be thought, "Maybe Ed can stick around a little while." Jon loved that one. And I got a mole removed for free.

ROB CORDDRY

Ed immediately started getting all these field pieces, and I was sitting in the office for two weeks with no assignments, thinking I'd done something wrong. So I spent the time just studying tape of Colbert and Carell.

STEW BAILEY

Corddry's first field piece was a rough one. There was a new Spider-Man movie out, so the piece was to try and take that local news aspect of "Could this really happen? Could a radioactive spider bite you, and if so, what happens?" and blow it up into "What would happen if you really tried to be Spider-Man?"

ROB CORDDRY

They put me in a pink leotard and had me walk around midtown. It started a trend of making me wear ridiculous costumes and parading me around Manhattan.

ELLIOTT KALAN

We were shooting a piece where for some reason Rob Corddry had to walk down the street in a Klan outfit. Then he walked into a Dunkin' Donuts where we were waiting for him, and he's like, "I can't do this bit. I can see the way people are looking at me. It's too raw."

So we rewrote it. He walked down dressed as Hitler, and then it was totally fine. For some reason Hitler was not real enough, and people on the street could react with "What?" as opposed to anger. And it impressed me that Rob was that in tune with both how people would react on the street and how an audience would react to it.

ROB CORDDRY

Dressing up as Hitler was the worst. I was out there and realized this could get ugly. I remember coming back to the studio for editing and Jon had some idea for another bit, and he says, "Aw, c'mon, get back in the Hitler costume." He was almost begging. It was the one time I said no to him.

Colbert gave me two invaluable pieces of advice for doing field pieces. The first was, "Check your soul at the door."

ED HELMS

What's funny about that is that it's a little bit pissy and a little bit silly, but it speaks to something very real, which is when you're doing those field segment shoots, and in the middle of an interview, your instinct is to be kind and gracious to somebody. You really have to squash that instinct and stick to the game plan, which often leads to a significant discomfort on the part of your interview subject and yourself. But it's all in the service of irony, which hopefully is also funny.

And what I found out at Jon's last show was that "Check your soul at the door" was a kind of mantra that Colbert had told many correspondents, when they were starting out. As I was sharing that anecdote with somebody else, they were like, "He told me the same thing." It was fun to find out this Colbert nugget of wisdom that really trickled through a lot of us.

STEPHEN COLBERT

It's not actually that way. What I would say is, "What you're going to want to do is get a nice hanger—like a wooden hanger, something with padded shoulders. Take your soul off and hang it on the hanger. Don't fold it up or leave it crumpled on the floor or put it on a wire hanger. Put it on a nice hanger, because you care about your soul. Don't forget where you put it. Then go out on the road and do these interviews. Your soul will be part of this decision. It's not like you do it in a soulless way, but when you're in the field you're in a character of a correspondent who has no interest other than getting what he needs out of the person he's interviewing. Your relationship with the people you're going to be talking to is purely parasitic. You are going to suck them dry like a lamprey until their brain and their soul is as dry as a crouton and you get everything you can out of this interview. Don't get that on you, because that behavior has got to be cold-blooded. When you're doing it you might get it on you—the badness of what you're doing on you—and you don't want to get that on your soul. You can get it out, but you've got to dry-clean it, and your soul gets shiny after you dry-clean it too many times. Just for the life of your soul, take it off before you go, and then when you come back to New York put your soul back on when you watch the footage. Because then you have the opportunity to exercise your ethics over what you did in the field and not put on the air what you think is unethical or is not comedy or is not fair to the subject.

"But when you're out there you have to be able to immediately seize on an opportunity carnivorously, because you're not there for just discovery. You're there to get what you need to get. You're a Spartan. You come back with your shield or on it." I used to say, "Come back with your funny or on it, because you've got one responsibility, which is to come back with a story that you intend to tell no matter what the truth is. If you discover something better, you can do that story, but remember, you've made a promise to Jon and the other producers that you will go get this story come hell or high water. Then when you come back you can make the case that that is not the story, or this is better, or this person isn't a worthy target or whatever, and Jon always listens."

The end product always had ethics and always had soul in it, because Jon is not a soulless person. Ultimately, he's a very moral person, and ultimately the piece was always filtered through his judgment, but you were allowed to inform him. If you said, "I don't like this," it wouldn't go on the air. But when you're in the field you can't be second-guessing like that. You've got to be athletic. You can't think about your backhand. You've just got to hit the ball. So that's why I would say, "Take your soul off before you go." Not because it's a soulless business, but when you're in character in the field, you've got to stay in character for what may be a ten-hour shoot day. Your soul will go, "They seem like nice people, stop making fun of Bigfoot." No—you're *there* to make fun of Bigfoot.

ROB CORDDRY

Colbert's second piece of advice was, "When you're traveling, make sure you spend all of your per diem."

JIM MARGOLIS

Which was nothing, by the way. It was thirty-eight dollars.

ROB CORDDRY

In my case, that became, "Make sure you *drink* the per diem." What people don't realize when they watch a four-minute *Daily Show* field segment is that it often meant sixteen hours of shooting. So we would spend the whole day working our asses off, and then the field producer and I would get ripped. It was just so much fun. Some of the coldest beer I ever drank.

STEPHEN COLBERT

Yeah. Drink it away. Drink it all away.

When you come back you don't need the meal money because they have free cereal at *The Daily Show*. You can eat the free cereal in the break room and you're fine.

ED HELMS

Corddry and I shared an office for many years.

ROB CORDDRY

I don't remember the days before Ed brought his guitar into our office. I remember every day after that, though.

ED HELMS

Is he saying he was annoyed by this, or charmed by it? I thought we had a great time.

ROB CORDDRY

What Jon said at the finale wasn't a joke—Ed loves to sing. And when he's singing, Ed's eyes say, "*You* can't sing like that."

JEN FLANZ

If we went on the road, as a warmup thing, the correspondents would go out and sing the national anthem to the studio audience. Stephen and Steve, Nancy, Vance, and Mo could all sing, and they would sing the national anthem for the audience. Not goofing around. Ed could sing, and Rob could kind of sing. The audience loved it. Oh my God. An in-studio audience only ever saw it, because we never did it on the show.

ED HELMS

Matter of fact, I have recording of a rehearsal that we did in my office at one point, when Mo Rocca was still on the show.

You're waiting for the show to start, that half hour, and doing bits and jokes, and I think maybe we just started singing because Stephen knew the bass line of "The Star-Spangled Banner." He knew this really beautiful bass line that I think he'd sung in a chorale at some point. I knew a harmony line, and Mo would sing the melody.

It was not a gag version. It was completely straight, and I would even say it was beautiful and transcendent. It always got a laugh when Stephen hit this low note. But it was really good.

The show's segments were genuinely patriotic, too—but in a sardonic, increasingly trenchant way. Sure, Stewart played and replayed Bush's verbal stumbles ("Fool me once, shame on...shame on you. But fool me—we can't get fooled again"). But as the country was moving toward another major military action, the show was moving away from easy laughs toward more pointed, issue-based gags, like "So You're Living in a Police State," with Colbert talking to a surveillance camera as he peed into a toilet: "The curtailing of your civil liberties doesn't have to be oppressive—it can be fun-pressive!"

And in the run-up to the Iraq invasion the media was becoming a more frequent target. The correspondents passed along the show's one flak jacket to report "from" Baghdad or Kabul, and the garment seemed to bring out a delightfully overconfident pugnacity in Corddry as he mocked the war zone macho of blow-hards like Fox's Geraldo Rivera.

BEN KARLIN

Rob in particular had a real kind of sinister gravity to his performing style that played very nicely with Jon, because Jon was able to become a wide-eyed naif. Ed played a little more into the Carell boob character, a little more clueless, so Jon had to pretend to inform him about things.

JON STEWART

Helms, in some ways, was almost more subversive because he snuck up on you. Rob was a physical presence, and more of a sketch performer.

JIM MARGOLIS

As a measure of how much things have changed, before about 2004, when we were traveling with Carell or Colbert they were always being mistaken for one another. I was with Carell once and someone came up and called him Stephen Colbert, and said how much she liked him and asked him to sign something, so he signed it "Steve Colbert Carell." This also happened to me with Stephen Colbert—this woman was convinced he was Steve Carell. This might've been right after *40-Year-Old Virgin* came out, and so Stephen signed something, "I crave cock, Steve Carell."

STEW BAILEY

People on the show were getting recognized more, though. We went to Washington, DC, for the 2002 midterms. One night we were all in the same hotel bar, and this woman was going up to the people she'd seen on TV, the correspondents, and sort of presenting herself with this "Wink, wink, I have a room upstairs" kind of thing.

She ended up not getting on-camera talent to go up to her room, but she picks this good-looking guy on the staff, and then they go away for thirty minutes. And she doesn't come back down but he does, and he orders a drink. We are all waiting: "And, and, what happened?" He says, "I just learned what a Rusty Trombone is." And he explains as though he's just literally had a sex education class. I don't know if you want this for the book. You might want to end at "Rusty Trombone," because it's going to get dirtier.

*   *   *

And this is, of course, a book for the whole family. So: The Daily Show's first trip to DC came at an unsettled moment, both outside and inside the show. The impending war made for a foreboding mood, but Bush was still riding the patriotic wave, and those four episodes were an indication that the show's point of view and tone were still very much evolving. Stewart's questioning of Torie Clarke, the Bush Administration's Pentagon spokeswoman, about preparations for the invasion of Iraq was strikingly deferential. The Washington trip also became the final straw in the strained relationship between Smithberg and Stewart.

JON STEWART

Madeleine and I had worked together well on the MTV show. With *The Daily Show*, I think she had built something she felt ownership over, and I probably underestimated that proprietary feeling. That was not openly expressed in the beginning, but it became clear to me that there was a resentment.

MADELEINE SMITHBERG

Of course. *The Daily Show* was my baby and I said to Jon many times, "Look, you control the content. Let me control the experience of life here." I just wanted to own the vibe.

Smithberg, by all accounts, could be a great deal of fun. But her melodramatic style could make her an unpredictable boss when Stewart needed his executive producer to be a stabilizing force. Daily Show *lore from those years includes Smithberg making personnel decrees in barrooms and making out with an intern.*

MADELEINE SMITHBERG

No, it wasn't an intern. It was a PA. It was Rory Albanese and it was a Comedy Central Christmas party. I was married at the time. He initiated it, but no, it wasn't a mistake—it was awesome. It was really fun. It was at the point that maybe I should have known that my marriage wasn't that great.

I definitely had a good time. Everybody did. And everything that I said at a party happened. Everybody that I promoted got promoted.

RORY ALBANESE

I was mortified at the time. I was twenty-two, and I'd worked at the show six months. I'm nervous I'm even around the bosses at a party. This woman leaned over and tried to make out with me in front of people. I wasn't wanting to do that, or expecting it.

I had no bad blood toward her, and still don't. She was very good to me as a person, but as far as creating a culture of drinking and going out and a party culture, she was bad at that. She was cool as shit when you are twenty-two and twenty-three and the EP is putting her credit card down. But there was definitely an immaturity in the management of the show in those days.

It was a different time, too. People smoked in their office. It was a component of that—Madeleine taking everyone out drinking matched the tone of the times in the industry, and this was cable. Nobody was watching cable.

As Stewart asserted more control over The Daily Show's *process and content, Smithberg's estrangement grew. The more sympathetic accounts from colleagues say Smithberg's and Stewart's visions of the show diverged. Other staffers say Smithberg was lax in her duties as executive producer. What started as professional differences became personal as well. "Jon eventually cut her out of the loop," one* Daily Show *veteran says. "But Madeleine earned it with her behavior."*

BEN KARLIN

Especially during that first year, it felt like it was us against everyone. And there was a lot of politics and personal drama that we inherited in that workplace. And Madeleine, who was a real good friend of mine and who I loved, she kind of was okay operating in that environment. It just kind of fit her personality a little better. And Jon and I thought it was chaos, and we were really uncomfortable with it. I think we just always said like, "The job is hard enough, and to add in all this kind of crazy-making just makes it so much harder."

DAVID JAVERBAUM

Madeleine's hilarious. But Madeleine's a crazy person. She wasn't showing up for meetings. She wasn't doing anything with the show.

MADELEINE SMITHBERG

That's complete and total bullshit. Whoever is saying that is a really awful, ungrateful fuck. What happened with Jon and I had nothing to do with my skills as an executive producer. I brought humanity to the process, and joy. I made it fun. We were doing comedy. If I wanted to save lives, I would have become an oncologist.

DAVID JAVERBAUM

We went to Washington for 2002 for the midterm elections, and she was just such a trainwreck. She was just a difficult person.

JEN FLANZ

That DC trip felt like a real breaking point. It was a technical shit show. I don't know that it was Madeleine's fault. I think it brought out tensions, but I don't think she could've fixed any of those technical problems. And Jon and Madeleine's split had been a year and a half in the works.

Returning to New York did not solve the underlying problems, so at the end of 2002, Stewart replaced Smithberg with Karlin, and Javerbaum moved up to become head writer.

MADELEINE SMITHBERG

We kind of spun it, my leaving. It was true that I wanted to be more present in my son's life. I was missing everything, and I didn't feel like it was worthwhile, especially since all the joy had been surgically removed from what had been the most joyful, creative, incredible professional experience anyone on the planet will ever have.

What Jon did with the raw materials and this sort of teenage show was to take it on a ride that nobody in the building on that awkward, horrible, uncomfortable Day One could ever have foreseen. The show could not have been more fucking successful and I could not be happier. I created the fucking thing. My name is on it every night, and yet there's this sort of personal hurt and disappointment and really confusion as to how I ended up in that situation.

Thanks for dredging all this up, by the way!

KAHANE CORN COOPERMAN

There are a lot of great things about Madeleine that shouldn't be discounted. She's a very visceral, alive person. *The Daily Show*'s respect for people's family priorities started with her, and Jon continued it. I was able to raise children while having a fair amount of responsibility at the show. That's huge.

JAMES DIXON

Madeleine is a very, very creative person. A lot of what still remains at *The Daily Show*—the senior whatever correspondent—that was all Madeleine. Whipping a staff into shape just wasn't her strength. Jon gave her a long lead to try to figure it out, because he was appreciative. She created the show. He wasn't looking to fucking get rid of her. He wasn't.

ELLIOTT KALAN

Once Madeleine was out [in December 2002], it felt like the door was shut on those Kilborn transitions. The writers had almost all been turned over, and the new group was much more in line with what Jon wanted. They were less old-school, standup gag writers and much more conceptual writers.

JON STEWART

After Ben brought in D.J. we were just looking for a different type of individual, so that's when the writing staff really began to gel. People like Tim Carvell and Steve Bodow and Rachel Axler and Eric Drysdale started to come on board, and changed the tenor of everything really nicely.

STEVE BODOW

I'd gone to Yale, where I'd helped found an improv group. Then I'd spent a number of years in New York splitting my time between being a magazine writer and a theater director with Elevator Repair Service, and had moderate success with both things. But it was August 2001, and I was thirty-four years old, and I was feeling kind of restless. I was thinking TV might be interesting. The one show that I could see myself really joining was this *Daily Show* thing. Then September 11 happened and the magazine business really cratered. I started to try and more actively look, how can I work my way into *The Daily Show*? And then I found out that Jon Bines, who had been the roommate of some of my theater buddies years ago, was a writer at *The Daily Show*, so I got in touch with him.

Bines told me writers don't tend to leave very often. Then, just a few weeks later, he called and said, "So, they actually just fired somebody and they're looking for one or two people." If I'd contacted him a month later, none of this happens.

The process for finding and hiring writers would become more formalized over the years, as the show became a hit and was inundated with applicants, but the basics stayed the same. In the first round, aspiring writers submitted a "packet" of segment scripts about subjects of their own choosing, to be read by a couple of current Daily Show *writers and producers. Candidates who advanced to the next round were given twenty-four hours to submit a second packet, this time on an assigned subject—a topic in the news at that moment—plus background research assembled by the show's segment producers. If the writer did well, he or she would be invited to the* Daily Show *offices for an interview with the head writer and, eventually, Stewart.*

JONATHAN BINES, *writer, 2001–2002*

The hiring was mostly based on your writing. The interviews were to make sure you weren't the wrong kind of psychopath.

STEVE BODOW

I was definitely nervous after I was hired. I wasn't very good at it at all, and I started to choke a bit, too.

At one point, in December 2002, I went to Ben to ask for advice. He said he was glad I asked, because he wanted to have a talk with me. Not to fire me, but to put me on notice: This might not be working. The helpful thing that he said was, "You have to realize you got the job, so don't worry about proving that you *should* have the job. Just do the job." The second note, which I really took to heart, was, "Write about stuff you care about. Show us some passion."

Then right around that time we were going to war in Iraq. And that really worked out great for me because I had a lot of ideas. The war was the best thing that ever happened to me professionally. We're disgusting that way. We're not good people.

Mixed motives and morality aside, The Daily Show *locked on to the Bush Administration's campaign to build public support for the invasion of Iraq and the overthrow of Saddam Hussein, examining the propaganda efforts with a rigor lacking in much of the mainstream media. When the White House effort paid off with congressional approval for Operation Iraqi Freedom, the fake gravitas of The Daily Show's correspondents took on real substance. Stewart and the writers still prioritized laughs in every segment, but the tone and subtext of the setups to those punch lines grew darker.*

5

Mess O'Potamia

JON STEWART

On the eve of the Iraq War, in March 2003, we did a segment where we went to Carell reporting from Baghdad and I said, "Oh you know, the bombing has begun." And Steve just does this little burn: "Oh." And the whole bit was, "You didn't know that? None of the other reporters had told you that?" The next thing is Carell with a suitcase, and then the next thing is him in a cab, and he ultimately ends up in the studio. There are very few lines. It's just Carell. He has an ability in silence that's unmatched.

STEVE BODOW

In addition to the policy of the war itself, the show's maybe greater dissatisfaction, especially in the lead-up to the war, was how it was covered or not covered by the media—a now familiar story of how unquestioning the coverage was, not just at Fox, but everywhere.

ELLIOTT KALAN

It was appalling to see the administration misleading people so blatantly and ham-handedly, and with so little resistance. Bush, in the 2003 State of the Union, is talking about Iraq buying yellowcake, and this is being swallowed by senators and the media and by people I knew. At *The Daily Show*, it wasn't like, "Okay—we're gonna bring down the Bush Administration today!" But there was definitely a sense that we can't just let them say that stuff and not comment on it. And among the guys like me who were, at the time, ordering the *Daily Show* office supplies, I didn't care how many pens I had to stock, I was gonna do my part!

JON STEWART

Normally the election cycle dictated where your mind was. But now the Iraq War was an ongoing world event, and it was shaping everything about where the show was going. You were dealing with a president who was saying, "This is the cataclysmic battle between good and evil. It's catastrophic. This will define who we are as a nation, as a people, as a world. So don't worry about it. Go shopping. I got it."

You had all these contradictions, and the show always did best when it existed in the space between what was presented as public policy and the strategizing that went into creating it. That was the defining thread of the show, that sense that we were being sold something.

BEN KARLIN

The election in 2000 was the first crack in my kind of loss of innocence, and the invasion of Iraq was the complete dissolution of my faith in the country. It was just devastating to me.

STEPHEN COLBERT

Ben's a great writer, really funny, a great structuralist, a great ear for style. I think that came from editing the *Onion*. Massively talented guy who could work both verbally and visually.

ELLIOTT KALAN

Ben's *Onion* skills helped the show a lot. How is a field piece in the news really made? How is a headline really reported? What do their graphics really look like? How can we mimic the form of these things as much as possible, so that there are more ways to do a joke than just telling a joke, and so we can really comment more on how the news does things? He focused on "This is how a specific network does a specific thing." Like Fox News: Everything's a news alert. Nothing is ever just a story. How do we do something with that rather than just a broad joke about those Fox guys, they're crazy, they're assholes?

Where Kilborn's show had parodied news media phoniness, Stewart's show was rapidly becoming a commentary on the phoniness and shortcomings of the news media and politicians, wrapped in a parody newscast.

The war was a new test. Could The Daily Show *be indignant—and funny— without being self-righteous? In April 2003, the war, the show's new way of thinking about politics, and the people Stewart had been putting in place came together to create a giant step forward in* The Daily Show's *storytelling methods.*

ADAM LOWITT

"Bush v. Bush," that was a big moment for the evolution of the show.

STEVE BODOW

Sometime early in 2003, President Bush was giving a speech about bringing democracy to Iraq and building up a new country from the ashes of the Hussein regime. Somebody—probably Jon, because he's got the head for this—said, "Well, Bush is saying this now, but he said something very opposite that just a few years ago, when he was running for president."

I thought, "Oh, I wonder if there are other such things where there's that juxtaposition. It would be interesting if we could go back and get those tapes from 2000. Can we do that?"

BEN KARLIN

We were hearing and seeing Bush Administration people say things that directly countermanded things that they or their surrogates had said before. If we, as basically stoner comedy people, could remember it, how was it possible that the actual media couldn't remember it, or didn't care, or didn't think it was important? People were so caught up in this cycle of new news that they had completely lost the fact that these politicians are all over the place.

STEVE BODOW

At the time, all we kept were tapes of major moments like the presidential debates, convention speeches.

ERIC DRYSDALE

And we had Adam Chodikoff to remember it all.

STEVE BODOW

Eric was my officemate. He got put on it, too, and a tape producer, Ari Fishman. Chods was involved, because he's the king of savant memory. We started compiling a bunch of research, mostly through Nexis, in ways we take for granted today.

So, here's the thing Bush said recently. What could we look for him saying that would be in opposition to that from, say, 1999, 2000? When he'd been out on the campaign trail, he was more or less an isolationist—even in 2001, once he was actually president but not going into this war yet. Over the course of a solid couple weeks we started to put together a bulletin board, with index cards to write all this stuff out, like something out of *Homeland*.

I had a stack of cards, six inches high, of all these things Bush had said and what might've juxtaposed well against that, and when it was from. There were yellow cards, and blue cards, and red cards, and green cards. It was important to have a lot of different color cards.

The older tape we found turned out to be from Bush debate performances in the 2000 campaign. We thought, "Oh, maybe we can frame this thing as a debate, if we can get the right pieces of tape that are shot the right way. We could set it up where Jon moderates a debate between Bush then and Bush now."

JUSTIN MELKMANN

We had two mountains of VHS tapes. It took about two weeks to assemble.

STEVE BODOW

We got it down to about six or seven exchanges, and it became a piece that was more about its construction and concept than it was about the jokes. Putting the piece together in the right way was the joke of it. Then Jon figured out how he was going to perform it, taking on that debate moderator persona.

We put the segment out there in April 2003, "Bush v. Bush." And I think everyone felt it: "That was a cool fucking thing."

> **Jon Stewart:** [*at anchor desk*] Now, since the beginning of all this weapons of mass-destruction, regime-change, pockets-of-resistance, targets-of-opportunity business, it's been difficult to have an honest discussion about the direction President Bush has taken this country. In fact, when you combine the new mandate that criticizing the commander in chief is off-limits in wartime with last year's official disbanding of the Democratic Party—well, we're left at an all-time low in the good old-fashioned honest debate

category. Well, I know you're thinking, "Jon, every time I want to have a calm, honest discussion about these kinds of issues, I'm shouted down and harassed by the Dixie Chicks and their ilk."

Well, tonight it all changes.

We're going to have an honest, open debate between the president of the United States, and the one man we believe has the insight and the cojones to stand up to him. But first, joining us tonight, George Bush, forty-third president of the United States. Welcome, Mr. President.

President George W. Bush: [*in video clip, standing behind a podium for a White House press conference*] "Good evening, I'm pleased to take your questions tonight."

Jon Stewart: Well, thank you very much sir, I'm pleased to ask them. Taking the other side, joining us from the year 2000, Texas governor and presidential candidate George W. Bush.

Governor George W. Bush: [*in video clip, in front of the Statue of Liberty*] "Good evening."

Jon Stewart: Mr. President, you won the coin toss, the first question will go to you. Why is the United States of America using its power to change governments in foreign countries?

President Bush: "We must stand up for our security and for the permanent rights and the hopes of mankind. The United States of America will make that stand."

Jon Stewart: Well, certainly that represents a bold new doctrine in foreign policy, Mr. President. Governor Bush, do you agree with that?

Governor Bush: "Yeah, I'm not so sure the role of the United States is to go around the world and say, 'This is the way it's gotta be!'"

Jon Stewart: Hmmm. All right. Well, that's interesting. That's a difference of opinion, and certainly that's what this country is about. Mr. President, let me just get specific, why are we in Iraq?

President Bush: "We will be changing the regime of Iraq for the good of the Iraqi people."

Jon Stewart: Well, Governor, then I'd like to hear your response on that.

Governor Bush: "If we're an arrogant nation, they'll resent us. I think one way for us to end up being viewed as the ugly American is for us to go around the world saying, 'We do it this way. So should you.'"

Jon Stewart: Well, that's an excellent point. I don't think you can argue with that. Mr. President, is the idea to just build a new country that we like better?

President Bush: "We will tear down the apparatus of terror. And we will help you to build a new Iraq that is prosperous and free."

Governor Bush: "I don't think our troops should be used for what is called nation building."

Jon Stewart: [*as a split screen shows a smirking Governor Bush staring at a peeved President Bush*] Well, that's fair enough, Governor. You're entitled to that. But then, Governor, answer this: How do you propose we nation-build? Would you use diplomacy?

Governor Bush: "Let me say this to you: I wouldn't use force. I wouldn't use force."

Jon Stewart: Mr. President, clearly you're skeptical of the governor. Governor, in your time in Texas, what have you done to demonstrate your willingness to be tough?

Governor Bush: "Well, I've been standing up to big Hollywood, big trial lawyers. What was the question? It was about emergencies, wasn't it?"

Jon Stewart: No, no it wasn't. Getting back to Iraq, Mr. President, you're as familiar with the governor's record in Texas as anybody. Are you willing, Mr. President, to trust Governor Bush with our foreign policy?

President Bush: "I'm not willing to take that chance again, Jon."

Jon Stewart: Strong words from two very different men.

STEVE BODOW

"Bush v. Bush" is a Rosetta Stone piece, the first time we put together pieces of tape to show that kind of hypocrisy. And it was the beginning of using our institutional memory as a major asset to the show. You could get people in a room and someone notices this thing, and somebody else is going to remember, "Wait, didn't he say..." We began to understand that collaboration and finding contradictions is a big part of what we can do.

We applied that process to all these other politicians, to media outlets, to pundits. And then the technology, coincidentally, was evolving to help enable us to do more and more of that.

BEN KARLIN

It felt like we were crazy. How could we be the only people who were recognizing this ridiculous disparity? It became one of the signature things for the show to find these quotes and have people contradicting their own words, but in the early stages it felt pretty novel to do something like that so vividly with one person.

ADAM LOWITT

It's funny, because *The Daily Show* became famous for using video clips, but in those days it used to be: "President Bush is speaking—are we recording that?" "No, I forgot. Fuck it. Hopefully they'll re-air it somewhere."

There were companies, like Multivision, that recorded everything. We would pray that they had the clip, wait for them to dub it off, and send myself or another intern or a PA to pick up the tape, run back, hopefully in time for rehearsal.

RORY ALBANESE

It was [production manager] Pam DePace who said, "You know, this thing TiVo—we should get one for the show."

ERIC DRYSDALE

Within no time there were sixteen TiVos running at all times.

It wasn't hard to acquire one image that became a recurring part of The Daily Show's *war coverage for the next two years: Bush, in May 2003, standing on the deck of an aircraft carrier in front of a giant banner reading* MISSION ACCOMPLISHED. *Stewart used that clip to great effect as the Iraq invasion devolved into an extended occupation, to help make the point that much of the mainstream media had lost interest.*

"What could it be? All that fanfare!" he asked after a montage of blaring "breaking news" alerts. "They finally found those weapons of mass destruction we've heard so much about?" No—the breathless hype was devoted to the indictment of Martha Stewart on insider trading charges. The clip that sealed the bitter joke was a commentator on Fox News saying, "After terrorism, this is the number two priority for the Justice Department." Stewart rubbed his eyes in exaggerated but sincerely pained disbelief.

That piece was a small but prime example of how The Daily Show *was gradually becoming, in Stewart's phrase, "more essayistic." Instead of a series of rapid-fire headlines and jokes, segments were starting to focus on a single topic or event for four or five minutes. Lewis Black could still veer, splenetically and refreshingly, from, say, the Loch Ness monster to P. Diddy, but the show's tighter focus was apparent in "Back in Black" as well.*

Lewis Black: These are dark days for President Bush. The State of the Union controversy won't go away. Iraq is getting more and more expensive and more and more deadly. And he has the worst record of job creation since Herbert Hoover. So it's no wonder Bush's approval has plummeted all the way down to...59 percent! Fifty-nine percent? Who's judging this guy, Paula Abdul?... When Ari Fleischer marked his final day as press secretary last week, a soldier sprayed him with a fire hose. Now, they *say* it was a playful prank. But I like to think they were hosing the bullshit off of him! Jon?

LEWIS BLACK

I decided I needed the show because it's a two-minute ad that reminds people every few weeks that "Yeah, there's Lewis Black." I talked it out with my shrink and I realized, "Okay, so they have no interest in my standup. Now they're going to pay me to be an actor." Once I got to that, I was set. So I acted for two years. They gave me the script and I did it like "Lewis Black" would do it, you know?

I've known for a long time the reason I didn't get further than I could have gotten was because I had an attitude problem. By the time I *didn't* have an attitude problem, nobody believed me anymore.

The tragic and the ludicrous took turns in 2003: the explosion of the space shuttle Columbia, *the massive East Coast blackout, the election of California governor Arnold Schwarzenegger, the too-good-to-be-true rescue of Army private Jessica Lynch. As Bush deepened the country's involvement in Iraq and Afghanistan, and Saddam Hussein was captured,* The Daily Show *was entering one of its strongest stretches, but still in need of different dimensions in the cast and the writing staff.*

DAVID JAVERBAUM

I spent three and a half years as writer, four years as head writer, three and a half years as EP, and for me personally, the meat of that sandwich, the head writer job, those four years from 2003 to 2007 were just spectacular. We had an amazing staff. Tim Carvell—that was an easy call, to hire him. That was the funniest packet I've ever seen. I was very happy about Rachel Axler because she was a judgment call for me, but she's a playwright, which appeals to me, and she's great.

The show was really cooking on all cylinders, and that was the Iraq War period.

The real news shows had Christiane Amanpour and Ashleigh Banfield in the war zone, donning headscarves or dyeing their hair to blend in with the locals. Littleford and Walls had left The Daily Show; *Grenrock Woods was living in Los Angeles and appearing infrequently. Rachael Harris and Lauren Weedman departed after brief runs. The* Daily Show *needed a strong female correspondent who would be a regular in the lineup.*

BEN KARLIN

We went out and did an open call, basically, in Toronto. We did a night in the clubs where we went and saw a bunch of people, and then we did a day of auditions. We had all the top Toronto comedy people call people they thought were good, and we did a day in some horrible casting agency or hotel room.

SAMANTHA BEE, *correspondent, 2003–2015*

I had been doing sketch comedy in Toronto for a long time in an all-female sketch troupe called the Atomic Fireballs. Which meant performing in the back of a bar, rolling around on the floor in vomit for no pay, basically. Catherine O'Hara was a hero to me. Carol Burnett, of course. But by 2003 I felt I needed to have a more structured life, and I was leaving show business. I was working at an ad agency in the printing department.

Then my agent at the time called me and she said, "There's a show, they're having auditions on a Saturday." Going in for an audition on a Saturday usually meant that it was really janky and it was just a nonprofessional organization. She says, "So some show, it's called *The Jon Daly Show* or something like that. I don't really know anything about it." And I said, "Hold on a second. Are you talking about *The Daily Show*?" She says, "I guess so. I don't watch it. I don't have a clue."

It was my favorite show.

I trained for the audition like I was training for an Olympic event. Started eating salmon every day. I'm not kidding. I exercised, went for runs. Learned the scripts they sent backward and forward. After the audition I felt I'd left it on the floor, I did what I intended to do. Now I'll retire from acting and pursue something else. This was a really nice end point to my career.

My understanding is that they had a really hard time finding women, for various reasons that I don't really actually know. It generally is probably the show's hatred of women.

I went back to the ad agency job. A few weeks later I was at my desk and I answered the phone. It's my agent, and she says, "You're not going to believe this, but they've just hired you." I left the ad agency with an absolute insane paper clusterfuck, which they're probably still trying to unwind. There were definitely billboards that did not go up because of me.

Jason [Jones, her husband] and I moved to New York on July Fourth. Yeah, it was very symbolic.

I can't stress enough, when we came from Canada we knew nothing. We had a U-Haul full of stuff and thought, "It's normal to spend eighty dollars on a motel room." But eighty dollars in New York City means there's going to be a murder down the hall from you, maybe two. You're going to hear gunfire, and someone might go through all of your personal stuff. Our motel was at the mouth of the Holland Tunnel, on Tonnelle Avenue in Jersey City. It was just terrifying. Jason says, "It'll be fine." And it was quite the opposite. I slept in my clothes.

BEN KARLIN

Sam came in with a pretty impressive skill set as a performer, but I think it probably took a while for her to kind of find her groove.

Plus *The Daily Show* hates women, so there was that ax to bear.

SAMANTHA BEE

The Daily Show is a very independent-study type of workplace, because it is operating at such a fast pace. Nobody really has time to hold your hand. I didn't know that there was a complimentary lunch for months. I brought my own lunch. Eventually I started seeing people with plates of food. And they were like, "Jesus Christ, why don't you ask questions?" I said, "You know why? Because I'm really happy here. I don't also need a lunch on top of this." Oh my God, what a dork.

STEW BAILEY

What Samantha did, her run at the show is legendary. But that's the kind of person we wanted, who knows what this show is, really wants to be here, and has a background that makes her skilled. What we learned is that anyone who's using *The Daily Show* as a stepping-stone to get a sitcom, they probably weren't going to be invested. This isn't just an acting job.

SAMANTHA BEE

Stephen, and Rob, and Ed had offices up in the writers' wing, so I ended up embedding myself with the field producers. That's where I found my voice, really. And it was just lucky happenstance. I mean, the studio stuff is fine. But I really preferred the independence of the field, and the ability to get my own jokes on the air in a way that just didn't exist for me in the studio stuff at the time. I got more material of my own on the air than almost anyone because I was in the field. It was the show, but through me.

Not that it started out very well. They really only hire you for twelve weeks at a time, and I thought I was going to get fired immediately.

There was a field producer whose name is Jim Margolis. I love Jim. Like, I *love* Jim. He is surly, in the best possible way. But I didn't understand it when I first got here.

Jim had written a pitch for a story. It was a very flimsy story about the TSA, and it was meant for Stephen. But Stephen didn't really like this one, so it got assigned to me. Jim was so angry, because he hates new people and we had to travel to Sioux Falls, South Dakota, together. He very, very consciously did not sit next to me on the plane. We had to change planes and he totally abandoned me. I was so hurt, so mad that I wasn't Stephen.

So we shot the piece. Jim yelled at me in front of people many times, because I really didn't know what I was doing. The piece was fine. It wasn't good. I would never suggest watching it. Please don't. But we accomplished it, and I think Jim saw that I wasn't a complete washout. And then we went out many times together after that.

JIM MARGOLIS

Sam was so good and so funny. Just fearless.

Mainstream TV journalism sometimes covered the first years of the Iraq War almost as if it were a sporting event. Reporters selected by the Defense Department were allowed to "embed" with troops invading Iraq. The reports, especially on Fox, could devolve into cheerleading. Later, as the invasion soured and reporters dared question the triumphant narrative that U.S. soldiers would be, in the words of Vice President Dick Cheney, "greeted as liberators," they were denounced as unpatriotic by the president's operatives. With cognitive dissonance becoming the prevailing national mood, The Daily Show, *under cover of satire, went straight at the depressing dynamic.*

Jon Stewart: [*at anchor desk*] For more now on the tricky issue of press freedom at a time of war, we turn now to *The Daily Show*'s Senior Senior Media Analyst, Mr. Stephen Colbert. You've studied [Marshall] McLuhan and many of the media moguls over time. Stephen, what should the media's role be in covering this war?

Stephen Colbert: Jon, very simply, the media's role should be the accurate and objective description of the hellacious ass-whomping we're handing the Iraqis.

Jon Stewart: Now, if I may step in right there. "Hellacious ass-whomping"—that phrase to me sounds subjective.

Stephen Colbert: Are you saying it's not an ass-whomping, Jon? I suppose you could call it an ass-kicking, or even an ass-handing-to. Unless, of course, you love Hitler.

Jon Stewart: I don't love Hitler.

Stephen Colbert: Spoken like a true Hitler lover.

Jon Stewart: Stephen, even some American generals have said that the Iraqis have put up a lot more resistance than they expected.

Stephen Colbert: The first rule of journalism, Jon: Know your sources. Sounds like these generals of yours may be a little light in the combat boots, if you know what I'm saying.

Jon Stewart: I don't think I know what you're saying.

Stephen Colbert: I'm saying they're queers, Jon. They're Hitler-loving queers. [*makes* Sieg Heil *salute that collapses into limp-wristed pansy gesture*]

Jon Stewart: I'm perplexed. My feeling is this, though, Stephen—is your position that there is no place for negative words or even thoughts in the media?

Stephen Colbert: Not at all, Jon. Doubts can happen to everyone, including me. But as a responsible journalist, I've taken my doubts, fears, moral compass, conscience, and all-pervading skepticism about the very nature of this war and simply placed them in this empty Altoid box. That is where they'll stay, safe and sound, until Iraq is liberated.

Jon Stewart: Stephen, isn't the media's responsibility in wartime to—

Stephen Colbert: That's my point, Jon! The media has no responsibility in wartime! The government's on top of it. The media can sit this one out... It was Thomas Jefferson himself who once said, "Everyone imposes his own system as far as his army can reach."

Jon Stewart: Stephen, Stalin said that. That was Stalin. Jefferson said he'd rather have a free press and no government than a government and no free press.

Stephen Colbert: Well, what do you expect from a slave-banging, Hitler-loving queer?

STEVE BODOW

At the time we were the only game in town for making fun of and critiquing this thing everyone was watching, the war. "Mess O'Potamia" started the roll that didn't stop—maybe because the war lasted such a long time and defined a whole era of politics and media, which were our two sweet spots. That's when the show took off.

BEN KARLIN

Who thought of "Mess O'Potamia"? It was always hard to attach provenance at *The Daily Show*, because so many things came up within a room. D.J. had such an unbelievable gift, almost an insane genius kind of way for wordplay. I wouldn't be surprised if it was him. But it also sounds very much like something Jon would come up with.

JON STEWART

The war was something incredibly visceral, and it was the first time where I had a sense of we, as a nation, had turned down an incredibly dangerous and wrong path and had committed fully to it. So there was a purposefulness to the show. It gave you a sense of drive. You just felt like screaming.

STEPHEN COLBERT

We forget now what it was like in the middle of the Bush Administration, to even do jokes about them.

JON STEWART

When we were first doing jokes about the war, the country was scared and wanted to believe that what had happened on September 11 had sobered our politics and our media. And what it did was it lent a weight and a consequence to criticism and dissent. Dissent was now seen as not just snarky, but unpatriotic. We had never gotten death threats before.

STEPHEN COLBERT

There was a demanded uniformity of opinion in what you could write or what you could say about the war. There was a reasonable and expected honoring and elevation of the sacrifice of the troops, but that turned into a shillelagh to hit anybody who dissented. We were a dumb little show, and we could still get under the radar at that time.

Steve Bodow said it to me best, which is, "I don't think we're anti-Bush, I think we're anti-bullshit." And there was just so much of it spread around to shore up what were transparently poor decisions. If there was an attitude at *The Daily Show*, it was that we were willing to say things that would get you in trouble by naming what was bullshit.

The Daily Show's *critiques of the Iraq War and the Bush Administration quickly made it a favorite of the left and of liberal Democrats. "Throughout the war, Mr. Stewart has turned his parodistic TV news show into a cultural force significantly larger than any mere satire of media idiocies," columnist Frank Rich wrote in the* New York Times. *"It does not take genius to make Geraldo look like a clown. (You can just show the actual video, as Mr. Stewart is wont to do.)*

But it does take a certain kind of brilliance to mine the comic absurdities in a continuing news story featuring such sobering phenomena as a grotesque tyrant, the wholesale loss of human life and a president even his political opponents are afraid to take on."

Bush's public approval rating had soared to 74 percent just after the start of the Iraq War, but as the invasion bogged down his numbers plummeted to near 50 percent. Democrats believed they had a real chance to win back the White House, and, in another change from 2000, they viewed The Daily Show *as a vital campaign stop.*

JAMES DIXON

I got a call from Senator John Edwards, before all the shit in his personal life, when he was still a future presidential candidate, saying that he wants to announce his candidacy for president on Jon's show. This is 2003. I got that call at home, by the way, in an age where you just didn't get business calls at home. He had somebody track me down.

STEW BAILEY

We weren't sure what to make of it. It was odd to be a player in the political realm. It sort of happened without us noticing it.

KIRA KLANG HOPF

I remember the first time Hillary Clinton was coming on. It was a huge get for *The Daily Show.* We were sitting in Ben Karlin's office that afternoon, reading an "Even Stephven" script, and all of a sudden the lights went out. August 14, 2003. The blackout. I was sitting next to Colbert. He was terrified.

ALISON CAMILLO

Really terrified. But Stephen is such a gadget dude—he went and got his hand-crank radio. He'd given them to all of us for Christmas after September 11.

Presidential candidates were eager to appear as guests. Polls claimed that TV viewers trusted Stewart as a news source just as much as NBC's Tom Brokaw and CBS's Dan Rather. Critics complained more loudly that The Daily Show *had a partisan agenda. And in 2003* The Daily Show *began a streak in which it would win at least one Emmy Award, and usually two, for thirteen straight years.*

All that acclaim and static was impossible to tune out completely. But Stewart and the staff, to a remarkable degree, stayed focused on the task of creating 160 or so shows each year. The pace and the grind required putting on blinders, but the approach and the internal culture flowed from Stewart's attitude.

JON STEWART

People said the show had an important voice in the discussion, that we were influential. I think they overestimate the tangible qualities of that place at the table.

We felt like we did a successful show on television, but you're actually not aware that people are paying attention to it. I will say this. There were moments we'd do a bit, and someone would come in and go, "Man, that thing was all over Facebook last night." You knew if you hit the Israel question or if you hit the war stuff, we'd get more phone calls. We'd get more letters. Threats would increase.

But the reality of the day-to-day was a bunch of people talking about things they cared about and turning it into comedy, having nothing to do with the outside reaction. I think our isolation helped with that. Location-wise, being where we were on Eleventh Avenue, you don't feel like you are in any business other than making the show. There was more difference in our world when they brought a sandwich shop to the area or not.

RORY ALBANESE

I'm not diminishing people's love of it, but we never walked around that building saying, "We're doing it, guys! Truth to power!" We were just coming in every day and like, "What's a fun thing to talk about on the show tonight?"

Athletes are allowed to be, "I'm the best, what's up?" Rappers, every one of their songs is like, "Who makes more money than me, bitch?" There's a weird thing in the entertainment business where you're not allowed to have that attitude, particularly in comedy. Comedy always seems to come from Borscht Belt roots: underdog, Jewish, nebbish, uhhh, I'm wheezy. A lot of Jon's shtick is, "I'm four foot two with asthma." Not really—he's actually a great athlete.

J. R. HAVLAN

There's just a really tiny pile of backstage dirt for the amount of time that we were there. I was actually always amazed by that. I think it came from one of Jon's best qualities, his ability to stay grounded. He had his moments, but in sixteen and a half years, to actually see a guy get visibly and audibly pissed off at the crew, or the staff—you know, I worked for Bill Maher for half a year and saw it more often than that.

ELLIOTT KALAN

Jon was not very tolerant of people being toxic in the workplace. There was a fair amount of party drinking, but the worst that happened would be, one particular person would take his penis out and put it on a table. The drug stories are pretty lame. The sex stories are pretty lame.

ADAM LOWITT

Did I fuck everyone? Sure. Do I have multiple kids in multiple states from multiple head writers? Possibly. Yeah.

ED HELMS

Colbert often fantasized about lighting shit on fire and running down the halls, whacking stuff with baseball bats, just to spice up the office vibe.

ELLIOTT KALAN

Our work ethic and the *SNL* work ethic were very different. For a long time the *SNL* philosophy was, "People have got to loosen up and get crazy and that's when the crazy ideas come out." Our feeling was, "It's so hard to make this show. Why would we make it more difficult by staying up late and doing drugs?"

The worst scandal is probably just that dogs were pooping in the office all the time. In the *SNL* book it's Belushi who is pooping in the office.

JON STEWART

We had the regulars and we had the satellite crew. Very much like Warhol's Factory, for dogs. Everyday regulars, probably five or six, but it could swell to ten to twelve.

* * *

The free-ranging dogs kept things light and homey. So did Stewart's dancing, which was likely to break out at any time.

ELISE TERRELL, from intern to supervising producer, 2003–

"Dancing" is a generous term, I would say, but there was a lot of heart in it, along with Jon's singing. It's dad dancing. He would dance around in meetings quite a bit, and there was this period of time that he would blast "Empire State of Mind" on the office PA system and make everyone stand up and dance at their cubicle. He just so clearly enjoyed being at work and doing what we were doing and the people that he was doing it with.

JEN FLANZ

I like getting everyone to do stuff together. We have a soccer team. I started *Daily Show* softball with Matt O'Brien. I love planning parties. We started doing summer fun day. That was Ben's idea. The first one, we got the staff on a bus, took them out to the North Fork of Long Island, did a wine tasting in the morning, and we went to this mansion that had a private beach and had a clambake. We threw a *Daily Show* prom in the audience holding area. That was our holiday party one year.

STEVE BODOW

Fundamentally Jon's a mensch, and he constructed the place to be run mensch-ily, with respect, as much as you can do that in a place where there has to be authority and decisions.

JUDY MCGRATH, executive, MTV, 1991–2003; chairwoman, MTV Networks, 2004–2011

Jon was fun, but a lot of people would have gotten the *Daily Show* slot and then immediately turned into, "I'm the best thing there ever was, and I don't need to do any work!" Jon was never that guy.

SAMANTHA BEE

Jon's a heroin addict, though. He injected us all with heroin. It's like *Minority Report* here. You can have that.

6

Indecision 2004—Crasstastic!

The political and media worlds had changed drastically in four years—and so had the stature of The Daily Show. *The 2000 campaign, conducted during robust economic times between Bush and Gore, two easily caricatured but seemingly competent, seemingly moderate candidates had given way to terrorism, recession, and the bitter clarity that the Iraq War had been launched to find weapons of mass destruction that didn't exist.*

Meanwhile, the major networks were wobbling from generational and technological pressure. Friends ended; Facebook *launched. Tom Brokaw left the* NBC Nightly News *after twenty-two years and was replaced by Brian Williams, as the energy and influence continued to shift from the middle-of-the-road anchors to the cable opinionators on the left and right—Chris Matthews and Joe Scarborough at MSNBC, and, at top-rated Fox News, Bill O'Reilly.*

In 2000 The Daily Show, *with Stewart as its rookie host, had been a scrappy, playful outsider. Now it was a cultural phenomenon, its audience tripling past one million per night, and it was becoming a sharp satirical machine. The jokes still came first, but more of them were about deeply serious issues:* Daily Show *segments highlighted the Bush Administration's evasion of responsibility for the Abu Ghraib prisoner abuse scandal, and how Republican campaign strategists were behind the wave of anti-gay-marriage referendums on the fall ballots.*

BEN KARLIN

The Bush Administration was so outrageous in the kind of false moral high ground that they took, and then to turn around and see this behavior with things like Abu Ghraib, with the White House backing away from it and saying, "It's a few bad apples." Whether you want to call it irony or whether you want to call it hypocrisy, it was so rich it was kind of impossible not to comment on it. And these are the people who the country reelected.

The Daily Show's *more precipitous disillusionment, though, was with the political media, particularly cable news. One vivid sign of the change came in New Hampshire. In 2000, this was where the unknown Carell had charmed his way onto McCain's Straight Talk Express. Back then, the conventional media viewed* The Daily Show *as a cute curiosity, and* The Daily Show *retained some respect for real reporters. In 2004, Stewart went to Manchester in January to host a "town hall," and big-name panelists were eager to be part of the show. But four years of close study had sulphurized Stewart's opinion of TV journalism.*

JOE KLEIN, *journalist,* **Time**

Jon invited me to be on a panel a couple of nights before the primary, with Tom Brokaw, Senator John Sununu, former senator Carol Moseley Braun, Bill Kristol, and the guy who was then the head of MSNBC, Erik Sorenson. Everybody thought it was going to be a lot of fun. I emerged unscathed, Brokaw did well, Kristol did okay, but Stewart fixed in on the guy from MSNBC and just brutalized him over cable news, that the coverage was superficial, stupid, and he had specific examples. And Jon was so smart and so quick, I think everybody was shocked by it.

Expectations, nonexistent the first time around, soared as the 2004 presidential campaign unfolded: Daily Show *fans and the mainstream media saw it as a leading voice of opposition to Bush and the Republicans. A* Newsweek *cover story decreed* The Daily Show *"the coolest pit stop on television." A* Rolling Stone *cover story went further: "The most trusted name in news."* 60 Minutes *profiled Stewart for the second time in three years. In August, Bill Clinton became the first president to appear as a guest. Conservative critics and media pundits, meanwhile, turned up their attacks, saying Stewart hid behind the job title "comedian" when he was really a Democratic propagandist and sanctimonious media scold.*

So Stewart doubled down on the workload (on top of becoming a father for the first time, in early July). The Daily Show *wouldn't just construct "Indecision 2004" segments four nights a week, air live coverage of the debates between Bush and John Kerry, and swarm the two conventions—Stewart and the staff would write* America (The Book), *a parody American history textbook, its 227 pages overstuffed with original humor and dense with actual educational nuggets. Plus one photo of nine naked Supreme Court justices.*

At the same time, one key Daily Show *cast member was growing eager to take on new challenges, while the newcomers were pushing for screen time. The combination of tumultuous world events and internal shifts spawned a great year of TV comedy, a brilliantly realized ink-and-paper version of the show, and one rivetingly awkward volcanic outburst. And 2004, even as it yielded another frustrating election night, sharpened Stewart's focus on infusing the show with a point of view.*

MICHELE GANELESS

With Jon and *The Daily Show*, the conventions were our event. That was our MTV movie awards, our VMAs. It became, from a business point of view, a way for sales and sponsors to come in and package it up. And 2004 was when that started to become a big thing.

JEN FLANZ

Getting credentials for the conventions—it's funny, it's gotten easier but in some ways it's gotten harder, because the Democratic and Republican parties started to be like, "We don't know if we want *The Daily Show* there."

Creative prep starts about two months in advance. We start picking the title, and building the graphic packages, and we start working on the biographical films—that year, Bush and Kerry. We have an advance team that goes out about a week before and starts setting everything up. I'm usually on that team.

LEWIS BLACK

Jen is the center of the wheel at *The Daily Show*. She also seems to be the one producer who understands the word "polite." She's like the show's Jewish mother, without the angst.

ED HELMS

Going to the conventions was just so thrilling. God, I was like a pig in shit. I loved being close to the action, and realizing if I went to a dinner party or something, I knew what I was talking about, because this was my job. I could tell you every candidate and ten bullet points about their platforms, then I could tell you a bunch of their staffers and who they were and what, and I might have even known some of them personally at that point. It just felt like we were close to the beating heart of politics at those conventions.

JIM MARGOLIS

The period that I'm proudest of was around the 2004 conventions. I did a piece with Corddry, his coming home to Boston for the Democratic convention. We started out stereotypical, like the networks do those convention city tourism pieces, and then got more real.

Rob Corddry: [*standing in front of Faneuil Hall*] From Beacon Hill to Back Bay, from burning witches to busing blacks, this city has something for everyone! [*pause; walks off camera, then leans his head back in frame*] Unless you're black.

There's so much history here. [*montage of famous attractions*] Like Faneuil Hall. Bunker Hill. The site of the Boston Tea Party. Of course everyone knows about this little piece of Boston history: [*stands outside nondescript hotel*] The Adams Inn! Where I treated Maureen Sullivan to my virginity. Room 223!

Of course, Boston isn't all about my personal sexual history. It's also about entertainment. Fenway Park! [*strolls through ballpark gate, sits in front row by field*] The world-famous Green Monster! Growing up, I had my own green monster. [*pause; face goes fearful*] Father Green.

Reliving painful childhood memories is sure to make you want to visit one of Boston's fine watering holes, [*walks into scruffy 21 Nickels Grille and Tap*] where old friends are always happy to see you.

Drunk Guy: [*shouting*] Remember the time we had a fight with Sig Ep up the street? You were *where*? Come on, Corddry! You were gay! [*Corddry gulps beer*] What the fuck is up with your hair? You look like Gorbachev, for chrissake! This bald bastard, that didn't fight, and didn't do shit in college, and now he's a pussy, and now he's on fucking national TV and here we are! That's bullshit. Fuck him!

Rob Corddry: [*trying to sound macho*] You remember Maureen Sullivan?

Second Drunk Guy: Whore!

ROB CORDDRY

Yeah, her name was Maureen, but not Sullivan. She said, "No fucking way can you use my real last name."

JIM MARGOLIS

Those moments where they're giving Rob a hard time for being basically a pussy—yeah, that was real. That was actually a visceral moment. So was when they started wrestling and broke a bunch of bar stools.

ROB CORDDRY

Those are my real buddies from UMass. They're Watertown, great guys, really funny, townies. We told them to get there at like 2:00 in the afternoon, and start drinking on us. We didn't get there until 5:00 and had some catching up to do. They actually got into a fight in the bar. It was standard for them. I've been thinking of pitching a reality show based on those guys.

My friend in the piece who's yelling "Come on, Corddry!"—that became sort of a minitrademark for me. Whenever I see Jon since that day, he yells, "Come on, Corddry!" Jon even said it at the final show.

JIM MARGOLIS

There was nothing more frustrating than directing Rob while he was drunk. Though I was a little drunk, too. And Rob's father was there. He was pretty sauced himself. But it was funny, and we brought his friends back for a few more pieces.

ROB CORDDRY

It was a great bar, 21 Nickels, but it's closed now. When *The Daily Show* won Emmys, the correspondents got certificates, not Emmy statues. I sent my certificate to the bar and they framed it.

The Daily Show's Democratic convention episodes beat all the other cable networks' coverage in the ratings. Two weeks later, as the scene shifted south, the growing audience was served just as much humor, but delivered with a decidedly sharper edge.

The Republican convention, staged in New York three years after the 9/11 attacks, was a four-day patriotic panderfest. Stewart and the team displayed how nimble The Daily Show *had become at lobbing jokes and throwing punches, walking the line between having fun with wide-eyed delegates and shredding the contrived symbolism of the Bush reelection effort.*

SAMANTHA BEE

The security at Madison Square Garden was crazy. I had a camera and a microphone and a producer, and we had a writer with us, Jason Ross. We would go out with fifteen jokes and we tried to get great responses from people. The first person I ever interviewed I think was Tucker Carlson.

Jason says, "Go up to Tucker and say, 'Who did you have to blow to get in here?'" I was like, "Okay." Jason says, "No, well, don't really."

And I was like, "No, it's good. It's a good question." And so I went up to Carlson and I say, "Hey, can I ask you a quick question? Who did you have to blow to get in here?" As much as I don't love the work that Tucker Carlson does, what a rude question. I mean, he was a professional person, and he didn't really need this smart-ass from Nowheresville coming up and shining a camera in his face, and being so rude.

And that was actually the moment when everything coalesced for me. I thought, "I totally get it. This is what I'm going to be good at. That was a great moment. I just need to have a million more moments like that, and I'll be completely indispensable."

Then right at the end of the convention there was a delegate from Montana. I said, "Hey, welcome to New York," and we had this really nice conversation. "Have you met any black people yet?" He says, "I haven't, but I would love to." "Do you have any black people in Montana?" and he said, "No. No, we don't." "You could get your picture taken with one."

It was sweet in a way, actually, a really sweet moment with this really nice man. He was just so honest and earnest. And so I felt really useful after that.

ED HELMS

I love journalism, real journalism. I think it's an exciting profession, and there were times even during *Daily Show* segments when I would think, "God, I wish I could just put the comedy aside and really dig in with this person." Being close to the politicians themselves, and actually being able to buttonhole them on the floor and ask them questions or even just, like, crack a joke in the men's room with Lindsey Graham or something, it was a huge thrill.

In the studio, Stewart highlighted the Republican appeal to patriotism and fear, a political marketing strategy that he was both appalled by and delighted to deconstruct.

Jon Stewart: [*at anchor desk*] For more, we're joined by *Daily Show* senior convention analyst Stephen Colbert. What did you make of last night's focus on September 11?

Stephen Colbert: [*sitting to Stewart's right*] Well, remember, Jon, 9/11 and its aftermath bring to mind a time of unprecedented national unity. When, from the crucible of an unthinkable tragedy, there arose a steely patriotism transcending ideology and partisanship. That stuff *kills* in the swing states. Those NASCAR dads suck it down in a feeding tube.

Jon Stewart: So you had no problem with it?

Stephen Colbert: Jon, I found it crasstastic! The message was delivered by the Republicans' most popular figures, John McCain and Rudolph Giuliani. Two men of bravery and leadership. Qualities the president would very much like associated with him.

Jon Stewart: Well, Stephen, let me ask you this: What is tonight's theme?

Stephen Colbert: Tonight, Jon, they took last night's theme—a Bush victory would bring closure to the 9/11 families—and built on it with a theme of compassion. We heard from widows, orphans, the enfeebled, the limbless. All raising their voice in support of the president—whose compassion, like the Olympics, triumphantly springs forth every four years. You see, it all goes with the overall theme for this convention: a time for unmitigated gall.

Jon Stewart: But Stephen, to be perfectly fair, aren't all political conventions manipulative?

Stephen Colbert: No, Jon, to call this convention "manipulative" is to call Marcel Marceau "a little quiet." These people are artists, operating at the peak of their abilities. For example, take Thursday night's theme: "Fuck you, what are you gonna do about it?"

Jon Stewart: That can't be right! Stephen, that sounds absolutely awful!

Stephen Colbert: Yeah, but... fuck us, what are we gonna do about it?

The four RNC shows set a Daily Show *record, averaging 1.4 million viewers per night, the most-watched week in the show's history to that point. At least one viewer was watching in South Carolina.*

JIM MARGOLIS

At the 2004 Republican convention, we're on the floor and this woman says to Stephen, "Who are you with?" And Stephen says, "NAMBLA." The thing aired, and Stephen gets a call from one of his sisters. "You know that woman you told you were with NAMBLA at the Republican convention? Our kids go to school together."

Sometimes the punch lines were born of brainstorming, sometimes booze. But the continual tightening of The Daily Show's *routine not only made space for the funny stuff to emerge, but it honed the points being made between the jokes. In the field department, for instance, this meant focusing on two new steps: the "take meeting" and the "elements meeting."*

JIM MARGOLIS

By 2004, that was when the field pieces really started to have a form in terms of what they were saying and doing that was distinct from just goofy, or oddball, or even just unworthy targets that filled many of the early pieces. Even if they weren't directly tied to the campaign or politics, the best ones often had a real issue at the center.

TIM GREENBERG, *from field producer to executive producer, 2006–*

It used to be you would just pitch story ideas, the producers would collect pitches, some would get approved and some wouldn't, and then you'd shoot. Now the producers cull the ones that we don't like, bring them in to Jon, and then he'll go through and approve usually about 30 to 50 percent.

They get assigned to segment producers, who start to try to book them— line up people who agree to be interviewed, and locations, finding out what is possible. Most of the pieces die because we can't get either the specific people involved to cooperate or anyone to cooperate on that topic.

Then a field producer rewrites the piece in their own voice. Usually it's about one page long. Then we go in for a take meeting.

STU MILLER, *from field producer to co-executive producer, 2003–2016*

The take is, "What's our point of view, and what's the larger point we are trying to make with this story?" Usually we're trying to tie it to something in the real world. You can eliminate a lot of pitches right off the bat where the take doesn't exist. Yeah, Newt Gingrich fell off the stage. That would be funny, but we don't have a take.

TIM GREENBERG

We used to say, how does it make it different than a Jeanne Moos piece? We have somebody now at the show who keeps pitching these sex robot stories and it's like, yeah, fine. CNN would cover this in exactly the same way, somewhat lasciviously, somewhat mocking the idea of sex robots. But unless we're not connecting to something bigger, then what's the point of *The Daily Show* doing it?

The take is usually about one page long. Sometimes the idea dies there, or Jon gives you notes on it. Essentially, now you're writing the piece. You spend three days, five days creating what we call the elements sheet.

Elements could be interviews, they could be videotape, they could be sound effects—the building blocks needed to tell a story.

TIM GREENBERG

You can read it and you'll see this is roughly how the piece will go based on preinterviews you've done with the subjects. Now we've written jokes off of those preinterviews. Much better than a one-line joke is a "run": Here's what this person says, here's the correspondent's response, here's what we figured the subject's response is going to be, here's the correspondent's response to that. If you get those, you have a piece.

You meet with Jon about the elements. It can die there for a different reason. If not, he'll give you many more notes, and then you shoot it.

Afterward, back in the Daily Show *offices, the producer and sometimes the correspondent would develop a script from the raw footage.*

TIM GREENBERG

Then the editor cuts it together. And if the editor is Mark Paone, he tells you what's wrong with it. And screams at you.

ROB CORDDRY

We always wanted to work with Mark. He's the best.

TIM GREENBERG

You do maybe a couple of screenings with the field producers. Then we screen it for Jon. Jon's notes are almost always that he's worried about the point. And then, at the end, "Okay, just make it funnier."

JIM MARGOLIS

Here's the frustrating thing. You would spend two weeks trying to make something work, and Jon would come in, and in twenty minutes he would fix it. It always made me angry how often he was right.

TIM GREENBERG

You'll usually do three screenings, and then finally it's ready to air. If you count pitches, that's six separate meetings.

JIM MARGOLIS

Jon was very demanding, and sometimes you just couldn't get what he wanted with real people. So you would spend hours trying to reengineer things.

STU MILLER

For six minutes on the air.

Certainly there were misfires, and there were plenty of field pieces whose highest aspiration was generating wild laughter (see: "Dirty Dancing," in which Colbert boogies to Van Halen and later, while slow-dancing, grabs a Democratic convention delegate's ass). But as Stewart continued turning more of The Daily Show's *energies toward relevance, a pair of 2004 field pieces stood out. They tackled two subjects that would become major American issues in the next decade, and recurring* Daily Show *themes: the hypocritical, divisive arguments over guns and gays.*

ED HELMS

We did a piece about gun laws in Arizona, and I got a little sassy with this bar owner. It's a biker bar, a big, huge, well-known, superscary biker bar in Phoenix, and I'm talking to the owner, who's a big, intimidating guy, and he doesn't think guns belong in bars. Really reasonable point of view. But because it's a *Daily Show* segment, I'm on the opposite side of reason. And I call him a pussy, and he doesn't like that at all.

And he knows it's a comedy show and we're supposed to be having fun, but there was a very primal reflex that kicked in for this guy. This is a guy who does not tolerate humiliation at the hands of a nerd in a suit with glasses. And it took him a second to pull back and remember the context. That was one of the sketchiest moments for me, for sure.

By the way, he was not opposed to bar *owners* having guns.

STEW BAILEY

The Central Park Zoo had a pair of gay penguins. And our angle was "We can't acknowledge that there are gay penguins because then it starts to have a ripple effect." Samantha is interviewing the director of the penguin section of the Central Park Zoo, and he's saying, "This happens in the penguin community, but it happens in a lot of other animal species. It's actually very common, and in fact it happens a lot in nature." I knew that he was going to say that, because we had done a preinterview. So the joke that I had written for Samantha was "Just because it happens in nature doesn't make it natural," as though she's that dumb.

And the zoo guy says in a snooty way, "Actually, I think by definition it does."

But the other half of the piece was even tougher. There were traditional family values groups that were instantly fighting the idea of "gay penguins," and Sam interviewed one of their spokesmen.

JIM MARGOLIS

I only saw Sam upset once. In the middle of the day, we had to have lunch with this guy, and he was so hateful.

SAMANTHA BEE

Oh, yeah. We had to sit and eat French fries with him at Tad's Steaks or something. That's an awful restaurant, and it was a terrible dining experience. I could barely get through my meal. I just thought he was a person putting terrible things into the world, floating disgusting ideas out there that were hurting people. He had a lot of theories about how gay people consume each other's fecal matter.

JIM MARGOLIS

Sam's the nicest person in the world. And she wanted to kill this guy. And then we have to go back to work with him—"All right, Sam, you're going to remark on how that penguin looks like he might be gay, but that one looks very hetero." It's a crazy job, and a testament to those performers, because they were able to wring so much comedy out of real people, who were not saying scripted lines.

SAMANTHA BEE

You had to be nice to the people you were interviewing. You needed them to continue talking to you. And you ended up spending like six or seven hours with someone who you really, truly, think is disgusting.

DR. PAUL CAMERON, chairman, Family Research Institute

I liked them, and I think they liked me, personally. I thought Samantha was a nice person. If you're a conservative, you expect to be drilled and mocked. I thought the piece was semidecent to me.

SAMANTHA BEE

The piece was great. I think we accomplished a lot. It was the first piece that I ever loved.

> **Jon Stewart:** [*at anchor desk*] This November, voters in many states will decide whether to ban marriage between people of the same sex. But would such laws still leave room for a loophole? Recently Samantha Bee discovered the real effects of gay marriage.
>
> **Samantha Bee:** [*in video, voice-over as we see frolicking penguins*] The effects of gay marriage are being felt across the country, in ways we could have never imagined just a few months ago. One of the most alarming developments is happening in New York City, at the Central Park Zoo.
>
> How many gay penguins did you have two weeks ago, before the gay marriage boom?

Dr. Dan Wharton: [*Central Park Zoo director, sitting in penguin house*] Well, I don't think gay marriage has anything to do with our penguins.

Samantha Bee: But according to Dr. Paul Cameron of the Family Research Institute, the gay penguins have everything to do with gay marriage.

Dr. Paul Cameron: There is no such thing as gay penguins. This is just propaganda. If you can believe that these are gay penguins, you're buying the gay agenda.

Samantha Bee: When children see these featherdusters, these flightless felchers, these chum guzzlers, what message does it send to them?

Dr. Paul Cameron: When you have gay penguins, you tell the kids this—you're saying to them, homosexual activity is everywhere! Even among penguins. You can even get homosexually married. It's all okay, whatever you want to do.

Are there such things as homosexual animals? Boy, I don't think so.

Samantha Bee: Then how do you explain Chip and Dale? [*clip of the confirmed bachelor chipmunks wrestling*]

Dr. Paul Cameron: Ummmm...Our children should not be taught such a silly thing as that there are, quote unquote, gay penguins or lesbian penguins.

Samantha Bee: Hey, I'm with you on the male penguin sex. Deviant and disgusting. But girl-on-girl penguin sex? That's hot.

JON STEWART

Sam's got a heart, as they say, as big as the great outdoors. Her ability to get in touch with that is I think what made her pieces stand out so much.

Looking foolish in a field piece, especially as the show's audience grew, left some interview subjects feeling embarrassed or angry, and they'd claim they were unaware that The Daily Show *was a comedy, or that their answers had been taken out of context.*

TIM GREENBERG

We don't take people out of context. We don't. Sometimes we will take an answer and condense. Sometimes we might even take an answer from a question and use it in a different part, but it's still what they were saying to basically the same question. The whole point is to sit with people who really believe the things that they believe and confront them with the contrary point of view in a humorous way, and then let them give us their perspective. Otherwise, why not just hire fucking actors?

JIM MARGOLIS

You would be surprised how much people like just having been on television. After the gay penguin segment, the homophobic guy came back for another piece. I never really could understand it.

DAVID JAVERBAUM

I think it's because in our culture, being on TV proves that you exist. It's existential. You are alive. There's evidence of your external existence above and beyond your own consciousness.

ED HELMS

Oftentimes, the people who understood *The Daily Show* best gave you targets, because they were arrogant. They would sit down for an interview, thinking, "I'm not going to play along with your bullshit. I'm just going to get my message across." And invariably, we've done more preparation than they have.

The other thing that they rarely understand—I'm sort of letting the genie out of the box—is that we have, like, two weeks to edit the material however we want when we get back. They lose all control once the interview's over. Anyway, that's one way of saying it. We generally get something close to what we want out of the interview. If not, we go back in the edit room and just hack it up so we get something funny.

A guerrilla approach had been necessary during the 2000 campaign. The 2004 version of "Indecision" was more calculated, because the producers and writers now thoroughly understood the talents of the individual correspondents and because Stewart had identified the issues he found worth satirizing. As the Kerry-Bush race stayed close, The Daily Show *kept coming back to the corrupting influence of money in politics, the obsolescence of media norms, and the Republicans' cynical use of cultural wedge issues.*

JON STEWART

Sam could do anything. Her skill set is very unusual because she could do the broader sketches, or a performance piece, but then she could also do the straight commentary.

> **Jon Stewart:** [*at anchor desk*] Throughout the year the public has been subjected to negative, marginally legal attack ads known as 527s. They're part of the miracle of democracy. And Samantha Bee shows you how to get involved.
>
> **Samantha Bee:** [*in video, smiling and striding through the glass doors of a law firm*] Starting a 527 group is a snap!
>
> The first thing you're gonna want to do is understand the law, because you're gonna be right on the edge of it. To do that, you'll need an election law specialist like attorney Cleta Mitchell, who can explain the legal restrictions on what your 527 group can say.
>
> **Cleta Mitchell:** You can say, "Candidate X is a scumbag." You cannot say, "Vote against candidate X." You cannot say, "Vote for candidate Y." As long as you stop short of that, you can say pretty much anything you want to say.
>
> **Samantha Bee:** Can I legally say, "If you like pussies, vote for George Bush"?
>
> **Cleta Mitchell:** If you like what?
>
> **Samantha Bee:** Pussies.
>
> **Cleta Mitchell:** No. No. You can't say that. It's not the "pussy" part. It's the "vote" part.
>
> **Samantha Bee:** What about "John Kerry went to Vietnam—but he went for the whores and the drugs"?
>
> **Cleta Mitchell:** You can say that. Sure.

JON STEWART

Corddry, you could see he would aggressively inhabit characters.

> **Jon Stewart:** [*at anchor desk*] With more on the Swift Boat controversy, I'm joined by our senior political analyst, Rob Corddry.
>
> Here's what puzzles me most, Rob. John Kerry's record in Vietnam is pretty much right there in the official records of the U.S. military, and haven't been disputed for thirty-five years.

Rob Corddry: [*in "Vietnam," standing in front of photo of lush rice paddy*] That's right, Jon. And that's certainly the spin you'll hear coming from the Kerry campaign over the next few days.

Jon Stewart: That's not a spin thing. That's a fact. That's established.

Rob Corddry: Exactly, Jon! And that established, incontrovertible fact is one side of the story.

Jon Stewart: That should be the *end* of the story. You've seen the records, haven't you? What's your opinion?

Rob Corddry: [*sarcastic*] I'm sorry—my opinion? I don't have— [*makes air quotes with his fingers*]—o-pin-ions. I'm a reporter, Jon. My job is to spend half the time repeating what one side says, and half the time repeating the other. A little thing called objectivity. You might want to look it up someday.

Jon Stewart: Doesn't "objectivity" mean objectively weighing the evidence and calling out what's credible and what isn't credible?

Rob Corddry: Woah! Well, well, *well*, sounds like someone wants the media to act as a filter! [*in haughty, girlish voice*] "Oh, this allegation is spurious! Upon investigation this claim lacks any basis in reality!" [*pinches own nipples in mock excitement*] Listen! Listen, buddy! It's not my job to stand between the people talking to me and the people listening to me!

DAVID JAVERBAUM

Corddry, he's much more of a punchy personality, and you write for that. Whereas Ed Helms, I think of him as this Jimmy Stewart kind of all-American man of the people.

JON STEWART

Ed was very laid-back, and all of a sudden, he would drop the hammer.

Ed Helms: [*somber voice-over*] Last year, Massachusetts became the first state to allow gay marriage. And critics feared the worst.

Senator Rick Santorum: [*in video clip from Senate floor speech*] "The breakdown of the family, children being born out of wedlock, and communities and cultures in decay."

Ed Helms: Now, just one year later, Massachusetts family activist Brian Camenker believes those fears have become reality.

Brian Camenker: The gay marriage issue is destructive on many levels. You have to deal with it in the public square, you have to deal with it in the public schools.

Ed Helms: [*deadpan*] So the quality of life is decreased?

Brian Camenker: Yeah.

Ed Helms: Homelessness has gone up?

Brian Camenker: I could, you know—

Ed Helms: Crime rates?

Brian Camenker: [*puzzled*] Crime rates?

Ed Helms: Air quality?

Brian Camenker: [*pauses, stares*] I mean, let me put it this way. I could sit here and I could probably find some way of connecting the dots from gay marriage to all of these if I had enough time and I did some research.

Ed Helms: Yeah! Why take time to do the research when saying it is so much faster? Besides, the statistics are clear-cut. Now that gay marriage is legal, Massachusetts ranks dead last in illiteracy. Forty-eighth in per capita poverty. And a pathetic forty-ninth in total divorces.

BRIAN CAMENKER, *president, MassResistance*

I'd never watched *The Daily Show*. I thought, "It's on at 10:30 at night—nobody will ever watch that." I had no idea what I was getting into. For the interview, they have the cameras looking at me, and Helms reads me a bunch of questions, and I answer them. Then they move the cameras in back of me, so they're facing him. And he asks different questions from the ones he asked me. It wasn't really fair. The interesting thing was, the final piece, they were reasonably fair, given the fact that the whole thing was a setup.

GLENN CLEMENTS, *field producer, 2005–2008*

That's not what happened. Sorry. There's a list of questions we go in with, we flip the camera around, and it's the same list when we do it on the B side. We never did that. I want to be absolutely clear about this. We didn't lie or deceive anyone. I remember him distinctly saying, "Everyone in the world is telling me not to do this, but I think I'm pretty smart, and I think I'm gonna do okay." And he just said all these awful things, which we used.

ED HELMS

The Daily Show at its best, and certainly the field department at its best, it wasn't just finding hypocrisy. It was exposing cynicism. A lot of what was perceived as a kind of an agenda-driven attack on some of the cable channels, like Fox News, was really more about us saying, "What they did in this situation is actually incredibly cynical and manipulative." Whether or not we agree with the politics, we should at least understand the kind of Goebbels-style information control that's happening.

The priority was holding people and institutions accountable for things that were preposterous, and things that most of the mainstream media just sort of take for granted.

Or, to put it another way: Applying common sense was often the funniest tactic possible. Certainly that was true when it came to the Iraq War, and how the Bush Administration was tying language and logic in knots. Stewart sometimes found it hard to out-absurd reality: Reading Rajiv Chandrasekaran's book Imperial Life in the Emerald City, *he learned that Bush operatives so prized political loyalty that they put an antiabortion advocate in charge of rebuilding Iraq's health-care system, firing a physician who specialized in disaster zones.*

When he couldn't top the preposterous, the tone of Stewart's satire became more direct, more disappointed, and often more powerful.

Jon Stewart: [*at anchor desk*] We begin tonight with the story dominating the world's headlines. The situation in Iraq, which we had been calling "Mess O'Potamia," but as of this week has officially grown into a "Giant Mess O'Potamia."

The stories and photographs of Iraqi prisoners being beaten with broom handles, threatened with pistols, and doused in acid poured from broken chemical lights are very difficult for all of us to wrap our heads around. Clearly, this is a time for our leadership, starting with our defense secretary, to speak clearly and honestly to the American people about these egregious instances of torture.

Donald Rumsfeld: [*in press conference clip*] "I think that—I'm not a lawyer. My impression is that what has been charged thus far is abuse. Which I believe, technically, is different from torture. And therefore I'm not going to address the 'torture' word."

Jon Stewart: You know, I'm also not a lawyer. So I don't know technically if you're human. But as a fake newsperson, I can tell you, what we've been reading about in the papers, the pictures we've been seeing—it's fucking torture.

However you choose to characterize what took place—torture, abuse, or, to use deputy defense secretary Paul Wolfowitz's term, "freedom tickling"—the real tragedy is the damage it has done to our standing in the Middle East. So just how is this playing with Muhammad Q. Public?

Iraqi Citizen: [*in video clip*] "I'm going to answer this question with another question: How would the Americans feel if this happened to them by Iraqis in America?"

Jon Stewart: We would bomb you. It's kind of our first response.

Clearly the best first step toward soothing Arab anger would be for the president to appear on Arab TV. Which he did yesterday, giving two separate interviews, one of them with Alhurra, the U.S. government–sponsored satellite network.

President George W. Bush: [*in video clip*] "What took place in that prison does not represent the America that I know. The America I know is a compassionate country. That believes in freedom. The America I know cares about every individual."

Jon Stewart: In fact, I would really love for you to meet that America someday. The one that you've seen, the bombing one—yeah, he's kind of a prick. But the other America—*very* sweet!

JON STEWART

You have a friend who is an alcoholic, and he goes, "Hey, you know what we should do tonight? Cinco de Mayo, man! Let's head out to that bar!" You say, "You're not supposed to drink." "Yeah, I know, I just think it would be a good idea."

You can feel nothing but pride in that person and still want to say to them, "I think being around people wearing ammunition belts filled with tequila, I think that's going to be a bad thing for you." What became infuriating when expressing that concern about the war, on the show, was the attempt to shut us up by accusing us of not being patriotic.

That's when confusion turned to anger. And that fueled a lot of the show, that sense that if we disagreed with what the government was doing because we thought it was disastrous, it would be viewed as somehow not supporting America. The whole bullshit to me was how ridiculously symbolic everybody else's patriotism within that was, as though by putting on a flag pin and a little bit of Sousa, that means you love the country. To me, that's what informed so much of what we were doing during that time.

One of Stewart's core methods for keeping The Daily Show *fresh—and to keep himself from getting bored—was to continually find new creative challenges. So covering the presidential campaign and the Iraq War wasn't enough: Stewart and the* Daily Show's *writers would research and reinterpret two hundred years of American history for pointed laughs in print. Work on* America (The Book) *had started in 2003, with two hundred years of history divided among the eleven staff writers, plus Stewart and Karlin and Javerbaum. Now the Spring 2004 book deadline was closing in.*

BEN KARLIN

Why do a book? Hubris, I guess. I was probably thirty-two, thirty-three years old. I wasn't married. I didn't have kids. I just felt infallible at that point, there was nothing I couldn't take on. It was part of that arrogance of youth, the last vestiges of it, I guess.

DAVID JAVERBAUM

We were overwhelmed.

BEN KARLIN

We basically did it on nights and weekends.

DAVID JAVERBAUM

We spent the entire last week writing a quarter of it. There's a lot of jokes in there that I like. There's a picture of Hitler in the Western Europe section, and the caption says, "In many countries, people say, 'I've never seen things as bad as they are now.' That does not happen in Germany."

JON STEWART

So many of the political books that come out are polemics—how virulently can you attack your opponent? We thought, "Let's take a step back, take an overview of the system." A textbook is the least emotional form you could use and still maintain the pretension of sort of academia or news. So the book has the same sort of voice of the show without the restrictions.

BEN KARLIN

You get a little punch-drunk because it's so many jokes and it's so dense. We were doing a mix-and-match chart for Scandinavia geographical locations and the event that it's famous for. So it was "Stockholm" in one column and "syndrome" in another. Every one had an actual analog in a real world topical event, except for Helsinki. We were stuck, it was probably two o'clock in the morning, and one of us, D.J. or me, said, "Rendinki." We probably laughed for twenty minutes straight on "Helsinki rendinki," you know? It was just ridiculous. When I think back about the book that's the moment I think about, that joy of being there, late at night, in a room, just pure writing, in a moment.

DAVID JAVERBAUM

We worked really, really hard on it. All the writers, but especially Jon and Ben and I, and while not skimping on the show. Ben did an amazing job producing that book.

BEN KARLIN

America was probably one of the things I'm most proud of, of everything we did. It was topical. It was timely. It felt like it would withstand the test of time. We had one of the best designers in the world, Paula Scher. We had no idea how big it was going to be, but we knew the book was going to be good.

DAVID JAVERBAUM

I remember coming home, I guess probably September or October '04, and my wife was waiting outside, pregnant, and said, "David, you cowrote the number one book on the *Times* best seller list." We were number one for fifteen weeks as a comedy book.

CHRIS REGAN

We did a signing for *America* on Union Square, in the Barnes and Noble there, and it was a mob scene. Over a thousand people. There was a Q&A portion, and a woman came up, with tears in her eyes, and begged us to stop making fun of John Kerry because we were too important to the country, and he was too important to the country, that we should never be at odds, and we needed to be on his side 100 percent. I could see, at that point, it's like, "Oh boy, we're not just a bunch of kids in the back of the classroom lobbing spitballs anymore."

And then Stewart, without much planning, seized the spotlight and made it even brighter by dropping the jokes and the subtext to directly attack one of the political media's more risible formats: the cable-news bipartisan yellfest.

BEN KARLIN

The more the news media got delighted and tickled at how they were being sent up, the more gross it felt. It felt like, "Fuck you, we don't like you. We think you're doing a bad job. We don't want to be your friends. We're not taking a pose because we figured out it connects with viewers. This show is an expression of what we think of the media, and if you really looked at it, you might not be so tickled. You might actually think, 'Oh shit, maybe we should change some of the ways that we do things because we're so easily decoded.'"

That's a crass version of what happened on *Crossfire*.

We were in DC, riding high. We did a big bookstore event, a thousand-plus people. An in-store, a signing, for *America (The Book)*. We were kind of giddy off of that. And we had booked the *Crossfire* appearance.

CHRIS REGAN

I remember being in the room before Jon went over to *Crossfire*. It became a really, really big turning point, but at the time it really seemed, if anything, like a last-minute "How do I spice this up?"

JON STEWART

The only time I ever really got in trouble is when I was out promoting, because normally you're not outside of your studio, and so the machine that digests conflict does not have access to you. We were out promoting *America*, and I think had been at a book signing that morning in DC. We used to talk sometimes in the writers' meeting, "Wouldn't it be funny if I went on *Crossfire*?" given how much I hated the show. "Wouldn't that be hilarious?"

Turns out it really wasn't. Turns out it wasn't as hilarious as it would be in theory.

STEVE BODOW

Ben and Jon would whip each other up. They shared a lot of interests and frustrations.

BEN KARLIN

I just remember being in the car, on the way to the studio, and talking with Jon. "This is the moment. What are we going to do with it?" We were debating how to get into it, and Jon is an incredibly thoughtful person and really takes pride in being able to deliver what he wants to say in a coherent and funny way. The whole conversation on the way to the CNN studio was about how to do that—and how not to be sucked into being a little toy that they bring on for comic relief.

JON STEWART

The idea wasn't necessarily to burn the place down. The idea was to go on and say, "Just to let you guys know, I do hate your program." But combine low blood sugar with a show that you truly did not like, and with a guy that I thought was instigating in an incredibly purposefully ignorant way—that instigation is what probably caused it to go into that area.

TUCKER CARLSON, *journalist;* Crossfire *cohost, 2001–2005*

I'd never seen *The Daily Show*, though I knew Jon because in 2000 he was always around CNN doing *Larry King*, and we'd both be outside smoking cigarettes. I thought he was kind of a sparkling conversationalist, intense and genuinely interested in politics—not well-informed, but sincere about it, and pretty funny. So I didn't have any inkling that he was going to try to make a statement on our show.

BEN KARLIN

I remember being in the green room with one of the producers, watching Jon with Paul Begala and Tucker Carlson. When it started going south, it got real quiet in the green room. Jon started to slowly sag toward the floor a little bit, and I could tell that it was not going the way Jon wanted it to go. But you're in the moment, and then a conversation takes on a life of its own.

Jon Stewart: [*on* Crossfire *set, seated between hosts Paul Begala and Tucker Carlson*] I made a special effort to come on the show today, because I have privately, amongst my friends and also in occasional newspapers and television shows, mentioned this show as being bad.

Paul Begala: We have noticed.

Jon Stewart: And I wanted to—I felt that that wasn't fair and I should come here and tell you that I don't—it's not so much that it's bad, as it's hurting America...Stop, stop, stop, stop hurting America...See, the thing is, we need your help. Right now, you're helping the politicians and the corporations...

Paul Begala: We're thirty minutes in a twenty-four-hour day where we have each side on, as best we can get them, and have them fight it out.

Jon Stewart: No, no, no, no, that would be great. To do a debate would be great. But that's like saying pro wrestling is a show about athletic competition...You're doing theater, when you should be doing debate... What you do is partisan hackery. And I will tell you why I know it.

Tucker Carlson: You had John Kerry on your show and you sniff his throne and you're accusing *us* of partisan hackery?

Jon Stewart: Absolutely.

Tucker Carlson: You've got to be kidding me. He comes on and you—

Jon Stewart: You're on CNN! The show that leads into me is puppets making crank phone calls.

Tucker Carlson: You need to get a job at a journalism school, I think.

Jon Stewart: You need to go to one.

The thing that I want to say is, when you have people on for just knee-jerk, reactionary talk—

Tucker Carlson: Wait. I thought you were going to be funny. Come on. Be funny.

Jon Stewart: No. No. I'm not going to be your monkey.

Tucker Carlson: I do think you're more fun on your show. Just my opinion.

Jon Stewart: You know what's interesting, though? You're as big a dick on your show as you are on any show.

TUCKER CARLSON

I *am* a dick. I think that's fair. I'm a total prick. I don't think I'm a dick in my personal relationships, but I was hosting a debate show. So, yeah that didn't bother me.

MICHELE GANELESS

When Tucker Carlson challenged Jon, saying, "You're not any better than us," and Jon says, "I'm on a show where *Crank Yankers* is my lead-in!"—I remember that very clearly. It was a moment that Jon became this figure.

TUCKER CARLSON

I could never fully understand, even years later, his argument against the show. If his argument was the show is sort of mediocre, I was in full agreement with that. But if the argument was, "You suck up to politicians," well, that's the only sin I've never committed. And I have to say, I found it ironic at the time because I was annoyed by the fact that he didn't use these awesome opportunities he had to ask real questions. It was pure projection. He had just fellated John Kerry on his show and really kind of let his viewers down, and you're saying I'm a suck-up?

Jon was never brave enough, really, to challenge the unthinking assumptions that his audience had, and that made them feel morally superior to everybody else. He never had any balls.

BEN KARLIN

Carlson was so out of his league. But the reaction to it was truly mind-blowing. What we thought was a low point—maybe we'd gotten a little full of ourselves—the fact that people had the exact opposite reaction was genuinely shocking. To this day, if I was trying to list a bunch of amazing things that we did, I wouldn't remotely put *Crossfire* in the top of anything. I guess because Jon had the capital to spend, the reaction wasn't "Shut up and be funny." It was "Thank you for saying that."

JOHN HODGMAN, *contributor, 2006–2015*

I remember the moment, and this is obviously long before I was ever on the show. I was sitting there working on something on my dining room table. Jon was on *Crossfire* just eviscerating Paul Begala and Tucker Carlson. I had the TV on specifically so I could find something to distract me from actually working, but in this case it was really worth it. Jon is saying, "You guys are doing theater, and it's bad for America."

And Tucker telling him to tell a joke, and Jon saying, "I'm not your dancing monkey," was just this one-two punch of principle that I think defined what attracted people to Jon, and it was a principle that Jon was figuring out for himself at that time.

TUCKER CARLSON ,

I had to go host a dinner after the taping, but my assistant called and said Jon wouldn't leave. He was backstage for an hour and a half waxing on about his political views to Paul Begala.

JON STEWART

Well, I wanted him to know that there was a foundation behind what had just happened. That it wasn't a random act of sabotage or anarchy. I didn't just come in and go, "Hey, do you mind if I take a shit on your drink table?" There was actually a thought behind it that was interesting to me about what political debate was and what television could be, and what news shows were.

And that was the day TV news got better.

Clips of Stewart's Crossfire *appearance became an Internet hit, even though video-file sharing was still cumbersome—a combination that helped spur the creation of YouTube. Well, along with huge demand for video of Janet Jackson's Super Bowl "wardrobe malfunction."*

ELLIOTT KALAN

When Jon went on *Crossfire* I was a PA at the time. I remember watching that in the office and thinking, "Well, the show's been going good for a while, but this is when we stop being popular. Jon's gone too far here." But he hadn't. I constantly thought that we were on the crest of the wave when in actuality there was a lot more yet to come.

Including the cancellation of Crossfire. *Four months after Stewart's combative appearance, CNN president Jonathan Klein shuttered the show, saying, "I agree wholeheartedly with Jon Stewart's overall premise." The Daily Show didn't really need or want the help, but CNN's reaction made Stewart even more of a force inside the Beltway.*

BOB KERREY

In 2004 I was on the 9/11 commission, investigating the attack on the World Trade Center. Shortly before we went to the White House to interview President Bush and Vice President Cheney I was on *The Daily Show*, and talked about how the administration had been uncooperative. The next day, on the Senate floor, I got a note from Senator Roy Blunt, claiming it was undignified to talk about the commission's work on a comedy show. I was smiling when I got the note. It's part of being a Republican senator. Defending your guys. But I would say Jon Stewart is at least as dignified as all one hundred members of the United States Senate. And I have a high regard for the Senate.

It was proof of *The Daily Show*'s relevance. And I wouldn't even say it's backhanded proof. I mean, Blunt doubled up his fist and took a shot. He was worried that if they didn't respond, that whatever I said might have more credibility and might damage President Bush and Vice President Cheney.

Jon had a lot of impact in Washington. Especially with the introduction of YouTube and the ubiquitous deployment in Washington of social media. I don't think politicians worried that they were going to get thrown out of office because they did something to displease Jon Stewart. But I do think that he affected the debate.

JON STEWART

There were two times when it really hit me that, "Oh, people are paying more attention to the show than I thought," and it got in my head a little bit.

The first was after we won Emmys in 2002, and it felt like we had to live up to them. The second was the reaction to the *Crossfire* thing. People were not necessarily accustomed to having something amplified through social media. That was a really strange feeling.

You just have to remember, "Oh, right. I have to make my decisions exactly the same way," which means that we're going to put in this ridiculously absurd scatological joke without the concern that it will be looked down upon by those who have bestowed upon us this title. You had to let yourselves just be free.

One aspect of the outside world that Stewart allowed to shape the show— indeed, an element that he actively sought out in greater, firsthand detail—was the experiences of American soldiers. Because even as the campaign horse race was gobbling up media attention, the grisly toll of Operation Iraqi Freedom was soaring, with 849 U.S. men and women killed and more than 8,000 wounded in 2004.

JON STEWART

We tried to be thoughtful because of the material that we were working on, not because of the reach of the platform. It's one of the reasons why, after the Iraq War started, I started going to the VA hospital. I wanted to know what I was talking about. I wanted to know the people involved in this. But that's what had the impact, not "Your show is in the political conversation." The subject matter dictated the approach much more than the external effect, or not effect. I was talking about the war on the show. We were making satire, and I wanted to know what those guys who fought the war thought.

So I went to Walter Reed [Army Medical Center] and Bethesda [Naval Hospital]. That started relatively early on after the Iraq War started, 2004 maybe. There was a woman named Elaine Rogers who ran the Washington USO. I'm going to be making jokes about the war every day, and I want to have a sense of what it is that I'm talking about from different perspectives.

JASON REICH, *from writers' assistant to writer, 1999–2007*

If you didn't have a point of view or an intent in your first draft of a *Daily Show* script, Jon was pretty good at making you think about "What is the real irony here? What do we really want to say with this piece?" For me, personally, it was always a bit of a triumph when you came up with a dumb, goofy sight gag and Jon wanted to do it. Like during the 2004 campaign, one of the candidates, Wesley Clark, said that *Journey's Greatest Hits* was his favorite album. So we wrote a bit where we played the clip of Clark and then Jon said, "Okay, now we're going to check out Wesley Clark's campaign rally," and it was two of our interns slow-dancing under a disco ball to "Open Arms," like it was their prom. It sounds so stupid when I say it, but...

JAMES PONIEWOZIK

The tone of *The Daily Show* could be sarcastic and adversarial, but it generally wasn't cynical or snarky. The show cared about stuff and it didn't simply give up. It didn't have the point of view that the world is just fucked up and it's unsalvageable, so LOL, nothing matters and we might as well laugh about it, you know? The humor was always from a point of view that held out a hope that the world could be improved, and I think that tone was essential to its success.

KAHANE CORN COOPERMAN

My husband worked as a producer at *Dateline* for nine years while I was at *The Daily Show*. When he left NBC, in 2005, he said to me, "When I first started at *Dateline*, we were the news and you guys were the jokes. And then by the time I left, you guys were the news and we were the joke."

Through the mid-2000s, as the Internet and cable TV eviscerated the business model of major network news divisions, politicians eagerly exploited the media chaos, and the peddling of truthiness and outright dishonesty ran rampant. The Daily Show's *main mission remained comedy. But Stewart became more determined to fill the media-credibility void, shifting* The Daily Show's *emphasis even more toward holding politicians and the press accountable.*

Often those reality checks came in small doses. For instance, during the 2004 campaign, The Daily Show *played a clip of Bush jabbing Kerry on taxes by saying, "The rich hire lawyers and accountants for a reason, to stick you with the tab." Stewart then said, "Let me get this straight: Don't tax the rich because they'll get out of it? So your policy is, tax the hardworking people, because they're dumb-asses and they'll never figure it out?"*

When it came to Fox News, Stewart had a queasy respect for Roger Ailes's

creation, for how entertainingly and relentlessly it could deliver a partisan narra-
tive dressed up to look like news programming. Fox's right-wing truth-bending,
however, drove The Daily Show *crazy.*

BEN KARLIN

You could say, "Yeah, Fox was really good at what they were doing," I
guess in the same way that you can admire cancer, because it's a really effective
killer. But Fox wasn't good for anybody. It wasn't even good for their cause.

Bill O'Reilly had twice been a Daily Show *guest, and in September 2004,*
Stewart returned the favor by making his first visit to The O'Reilly Factor. *"You*
know what's really frightening?" O'Reilly told him. "You actually have an influ-
ence on this presidential election. That is scary, but it's true. You've got stoned
slackers watching your dopey show every night and they can vote."

Stewart took the line as it seemed to be intended, as a joke—mostly. And
The Daily Show's *tone toward Fox was often still playfully mocking—never*
more so than when the words of Sean Hannity or Ann Coulter were read by a
panel of children in a segment called "Great Moments in Punditry." But The
Daily Show *was devoting an increasing amount of time to dismantling Fox's*
skewed point-of-view, and doing it with a harder edge.

> **Jon Stewart:** [*at anchor desk*] The Republicans see the economy
> one way. The Democrats seem to see it another. I wish there was
> somebody to tell us who was right.
>
> **Chris Wallace:** [*host of* Fox News Sunday, *in video clip, sitting across
> from Republican New Hampshire senator John Sununu*] "There are
> a lot of charges flying back and forth right now, and it's frankly
> hard for the layman to understand what's right and what's wrong.
> So let's try to have a truth squad, if we can here."
>
> **Jon Stewart:** Oh, a truth squad! Oh, oh, oh my God, I think my nip-
> ples are hard. A truth squad! A nonpartisan exploration of what's
> real, of who's telling the truth! Please, have at it.
>
> **Chris Wallace:** "So let's try to have a truth squad, if we can here.
> Senator Sununu, tell me the three worst things about John Kerry's
> economic policies."

Jon Stewart: [*after long, dumbfounded pause*] You know, it's questions like that that almost make a man lose his faith in Fox News truth squads.

JIMMY DONN, *from production assistant to producer, 2003–*

One of the main, early things that Jon would pick up on was, "Fox is saying that their opinion people only say this stuff during these opinion hours. No—in the news hours, they echoed the thing that Hannity said last night." And we'd find the clips to illustrate that.

JAMES PONIEWOZIK

It's now pretty much widely accepted in the media that Fox News is a conservative news outlet. But I'm old enough to remember when that was a controversial thing to actually come out and say at a mainstream organization, because Fox's party line was, "No, we have conservative commentators, but we play it down the line when it comes to our news reports."

The Daily Show did a lot to change that narrative and change that perception in the larger consciousness. They would do video essays and compilations to show how interviews and statements made during Fox News's straight news programs would feed into the controversies that Fox's conservative commentators would then argue about in prime time, or conversely, inflammatory statements that Fox's conservative commentators and their guests would make in prime time would become the "People are saying such and such" fodder for their straight news shows during the day. It was a great critique, often using Fox against itself. And no one disputes that Fox is conservative anymore.

In 2004, Stewart's viewership was double that of MSNBC's Hardball, *but it wasn't just the raw numbers that gave* The Daily Show *influence. A large portion of its audience was young, male, and politically aware—a demographic that politicians found hard to reach.*

JUDY MCGRATH

Let's face it, cable doesn't deliver the biggest absolute number of eyeballs on a good day. But is the show going to be influential? Is it going to be noticeable? Are people going to talk about it? I mean, that's what I wanted from Jon and *The Daily Show*: cultural heat. Comedy Central wasn't as loud a brand as MTV or Nickelodeon. Jon kind of dragged the network up with him, frankly.

*And for all the growing acclaim and ratings—they would climb 14 percent during 2004—*The Daily Show *remained a remarkably unpretentious, low-budget operation. Correspondents wore their own suits. Props were improvised.*

ELLIOTT KALAN

The guest entrance was this low-ceilinged hallway with a broken coat rack and a fly strip hanging from the ceiling, which was stained acoustic tiles. The show's gift bag for guests back then used to have a big bottle of vodka in it. Christopher Hitchens was on the show and he was there with some college students, girls that I guess were students of his, and he walks in and just immediately opens up the vodka and starts pouring it.

To Stewart, the value of The Daily Show's *success wasn't political influence, but the leverage to add news weapons, in the form of talent and technology.*

JON STEWART

As long as we were selling enough beer we knew we'd stay on the air. The thing I always said to the writers and correspondents was, "When you leave this show you leave with no friends but this room." It just has to be that way, so that we didn't bow to external pressure. I never had to go to those parties, and sit at those tables, and make nice with those people. It always felt like, "If we have access to powerful people, great. If we don't, great. Who gives a fuck? Green screen's our friend." We can find a picture that resembles the place we're supposed to be and we'll still have fun. We were parasitic on the political-media economy, but we were not a part of it.

Washington is very similar to Los Angeles in this way. In their insularity, they don't realize that not everybody runs on their currency. So when I went and did the White House Correspondents' Dinner, in 1997, and they said, "Man, you better be careful, you saw what happened to Imus," I said, "Imus added, I think, fifty stations." "Yeah, but people in Washington were really mad at him."

"Yeah, but he doesn't give a fuck about that because he doesn't work here, and he's not running for reelection." They do not recognize that. They view their economy as paramount to everybody else's interests, when it's not. That's what they never understood about us, that we didn't actually run on that fuel.

JAMES DIXON

I used to get calls. I would get a lot of, "Could Jon come to my fund-raiser?" Jon, from day one, said, "I will never endorse a political candidate overtly for the show, or even behind the scenes."

Offers for commercials? All the time. Everything from American Express to Microsoft and Apple. Jon's never done one and wouldn't. So I used to kid around with him. I used to beg. "Jon, do my kids have to stay in public school? This is not right. One day's work. Come on, baby! I get a million dollars in commission, Jon. Just one."

HILLARY KUN

Now people, major politicians and stars, were coming to us volunteering to be guests on the show. But Jon still wanted a very different mix of people, people he cared about talking to. The ones that didn't go well were the celebrities who were just selling something. The worst was when Jennifer Love Hewitt came on to promote *Garfield*, the movie. I know Jon felt badly about how he treated her.

ELLIOTT KALAN

I had to escort Jennifer Love Hewitt after the interview, and opening the door for her to the studio, she had tears coming down her face as she walks out.

The show's ascent in 2004 brought new scrutiny and raised expectations. Even fans of the show, for instance, were underwhelmed by Stewart's softball questioning of Kerry. But that letdown was nothing compared to the disappointment on election night.

STEVE BODOW

It started with all these exit poll rumors that Kerry was going to take it. Then, by the end of the evening it hadn't gone that way at all. Yeah, we were just feeling crushed, because of the whipsaw as much as anything else.

MICHELE GANELESS

I have pictures from the 2004 *Daily Show* election night party. It was morose.

STEVE BODOW

We couldn't believe, from where we were sitting, that the country—or Ohio, which was really what mattered—was continuing to buy this bullshit, not just to buy it, but to embrace it.

It was also sad because it was a realization that we have to deal with these assholes for four more years, just on the level of making a show. It wasn't a casual affair so much anymore. It was more like sustained, genuine anger. We would still be looking to make things funny, but it was funny coming from a bit more concerted place of...*fuck*.

The Daily Show's *election night coverage ended at 11 p.m. on the East Coast, too early to make the results official. But Colbert and Stewart managed to capture the mood—while also being remarkably prescient about the near future, both the country's and their own.*

Jon Stewart: Stephen Colbert, it's been a long night...clearly we are gonna have to get off the air soon. Do you have any final thoughts?

Stephen Colbert: Yes, Jon. For years our country has been torn apart by politics that exploit our differences rather than celebrate our common values. But tomorrow morning, regardless of who wins this election, we'll be faced with an opportunity to come together as a nation. This is an opportunity we must reject.

Look at the facts. After decades of apathy, this election, filled with partisan rancor, marks the highest voter turnout since 1968, when our country was also bitterly divided. The biggest mistake we made back then? Quelling those street riots! They were just America's way of letting democracy know it cared.

It's too late to turn back. Ours is now an anger-based economy! I see a glorious tomorrow where hybrid vehicles run half on gasoline and half on seething hate! I call it rage-o-hol! Join me in the future, for the future belongs to the furious.

Jon Stewart: Very inspiring, Stephen.

Here's the final electoral college votes that we know right now. There it is. [*map shows the northeast voting for Kerry and the rest for Bush*] It looks very red, and there's some blue there at the top where many of us will most likely spend the next four years, I would imagine huddled together and, in fact, weeping.

It's been a great night, I hope you guys have had some fun. It's a great country. We love it.

JON STEWART

I don't think I was ever under the impression that what we were thinking was popular, or majority opinion, or anything else. It was more like I couldn't believe that this guy, Bush, could make this kind of a botch of a major initiative, the war, and still get reelected.

My favorite thing was Bill Russell calling to try and cheer me up. Bill Russell, the legendary Boston Celtics center. He's a gentleman, a real gentleman. In the sixties he stood up on issues when it was not easy.

Every now and again, he would call, and just chat. Said he was digging what we were doing, and don't get down, and keep on keeping on. Like he was giving a pep talk, a halftime talk from when he was an NBA coach.

ELLIOTT KALAN

The election night show in 2004, you could see Jon just being crushed by Bush being reelected, but even more than that, by all these anti-gay-marriage amendments and referendums that were being passed in different states. It was a really depressing night, and that hits me as a turning point in realizing, "Oh, there's a lot of people in this country who don't want it to move in the direction we do."

At work after that Jon was just like, "I don't want to do another show like that." From that point on I wonder if Jon felt a little bit more—not activist, because we were always very careful not to be too activist-y. It felt more like Jon started saying, "This show needs to make arguments rather than just point out absurdities. We need to have organized, coherent arguments." Which became something we did more and more often.

7

Do You Have the Balls?

Bush's second term supplied plenty of farce—from the Texas hunting trip where Cheney shot a friend in the face to the Baghdad press conference where the president dodged two shoes hurled by an irate Iraqi. But it wasn't necessary for The Daily Show *to become heavy-handedly "activist" in 2005. The administration's attempts to paper over serious tragedies and outrages with "info-ganda" handed* The Daily Show *the raw material to build stronger arguments.*

Overseas, the wars in Iraq and Afghanistan dragged bloodily on. The mainstream American news media had become much more skeptical in its coverage, but it was still in the middle of a massive transition, losing nearly one-third of its audience during the decade. In 2005, Peter Jennings, dying of cancer, left ABC after twenty-two years as its news anchor; Dan Rather, embroiled in a dispute over his reporting about Bush's National Guard service, departed the CBS anchor desk after twenty-four years.

But the most important changes weren't about ratings. They were about the contours of the political-media culture. With the breakdown in authority of traditional news sources came more sensationalizing and fractionalizing, and less watchdogging of politicians. Washington and cable news grew more polarized along left-right lines.

Stewart pushed in the opposite direction: not toward "on the one hand, on the other hand" objectivity, but toward keeping The Daily Show's *fake news firmly anchored in verifiable reality.*

This didn't just protect The Daily Show *against accusations that it was twisting the truth. Facts became a weapon as the Bush White House became more sophisticated in weaving a warped version of what was happening in Iraq or the American economy. "Stewart's series provided a psychic salve, especially during the worst parts of the past few elections and the run-up to the Iraq War,"* wrote New Yorker *TV critic Emily Nussbaum. "If you were driven nuts by the twenty-four-hour shouters, if you couldn't bear to watch any more flashing chyrons and Sam the Eagle gravitas, here was your catharsis. Like* Get Your War On, *David Rees's post-9/11 comic strip,* The Daily Show *became a gathering place for the disenchanted—a place that let viewers know they weren't crazy . . . Over time, [Stewart] became not merely a scourge of phonies but the nation's fact-checker."*

Research chief Adam Chodikoff read seven newspapers and a half-dozen websites a day, scoured the Congressional Record *and* Congressional Budget Office *reports, and assembled a list of trusted academic policy experts to consult, generating ideas for and vetting the accuracy of* Daily Show *segments.*

ADAM CHODIKOFF

My motto is, "Without credibility the jokes mean nothing." I want that on my tombstone.

BEN KARLIN

No amount of credit is too much credit to Adam Chodikoff. The guy has come up with more content and more ideas for content, with the way his crazy brain works, than anyone else at *The Daily Show*, with the possible exception of Jon.

ADAM CHODIKOFF

The Bush Administration was very aggressive about trying to create its own reality, and Jon was pushing back by creating this neat entity, a comedy show that had fact-based arguments. So when Bush appointed Paul Wolfowitz to head the World Bank, for instance, we found some of his most notorious quotes about Iraq—Wolfowitz pooh-poohing General [Eric] Shinseki's suggestion that we'd need hundreds of thousands of troops, and saying that Iraqi oil revenue would pay for reconstruction and relatively soon. It definitely showed how badly the administration screwed up, and Wolfowitz was now being rewarded for it! Another personal favorite, from later, was from Cheney's interview with Martha Raddatz—she mentioned how Americans were opposed to the war, and Cheney said you can't go by public opinion. And then I found a Cheney clip from earlier in the war where he's citing favorable Iraqi polls.

*   *   *

After The Daily Show's *morning meeting settled on a set of subjects for that night's show, Chodikoff would assemble stacks of background material for the producers and writers, including two new hires who arrived as the second term of the Bush era began.*

RACHEL AXLER, *writer, 2005–2008*

When I was hired the writing staff was all men, so when they interviewed me for a job, they asked me a lot of questions about how I'd handle being the only woman. But I think it was more about my comfort than about theirs. It wasn't them saying, "Oh my God! A person with different genitalia!"

Actually, the most memorable thing about the interview process was after I'd submitted two packets of material, D.J. and Ben called me to come in. I get there and they were eating lunch, and they both had these steak fries. And they stuck one in each nostril. So they each had sort of tusks of fries while they were talking to me. And I was like, "Yeah. This is the first challenge: 'Do not acknowledge the steak fries.'" It was really lovely, because that was kind of our goal on the show—ridiculousness central.

KEVIN BLEYER, *writer, 2005–2013*

I'd been doing this kind of work for almost a decade, first with Bill Maher on *Politically Incorrect* and then with Dennis Miller. But to be at *The Daily Show* at the time I was hired, in 2005, was a unique experience because of the currency it had in the national dialogue. And because Jon was the most hands-on of the three hosts, by far. He wasn't just the talent, he was the editor in chief. Jon was inventing something.

Stewart's work in progress would soon get a big technological boost. YouTube launched quietly in February 2005. Daily Show *clips were perfect for passing around on the web the day after they had aired, swelling the show's viewership beyond what was captured by traditional Nielsen ratings.*

More immediately transformative was The Daily Show's *move, in July 2005, two blocks south and one block west, to a studio at 733 Eleventh Avenue, conveniently located around the corner from Larry Flynt's Hustler Club. The office space, previously occupied by Emeril ("Bam!") Lagasse, Rachael Ray, and the Food Network, was nearly double the size of* The Daily Show's *previous home and was laid out newsroom style, with Stewart's exposed-brick private office at one end opening onto a floor of staff cubicles. The street-level studio was bigger, too, accommodating an audience of 216. Less happy was the set redesign: Cold and austere, it made Stewart look as if he were sitting inside a two-dimensional book.*

The awkward on-air look was a coincidental reflection of backstage tensions. As the show started jousting with a second Bush White House term, The Daily Show's *success and maturation bred a restlessness during what would turn out to be the middle years of Stewart's run as host. Funny and ambitious younger staffers were itching to contribute more than grunt labor. Veteran writers were looking to get paid more. A charming office romance entered a rough new chapter. And the show's second biggest star was eager to move on to a show of his own.*

ELLIOTT KALAN

That summer the show was moving from West Fifty-Fourth Street to West Fifty-Second, a much bigger, more modern studio. Ben said they wanted to expand what at the time was called postproduction. Now it's called studio production, and both names are totally incorrect. It's the department with the producers who collect the footage, work with the writers on getting the right material for the headline, then take the scripts and work with the editors who actually produce it.

At the time it was three guys. It was Rory, Lowitt, and Ari Fishman. And Ben said, "We want to do more with footage. We want to make that more the core of the show. We're going to need more people, so we'd like you and Jimmy Donn to join as associate segment producers."

The summer of 2005 included another milestone: The wedding of Jen Flanz and Rory Albanese, who'd both worked their way up from entry-level jobs to become not just valued senior producers but crucial elements in the internal culture of The Daily Show.

JEN FLANZ

In college at SUNY Binghamton I made a pact with myself: I will get a job in TV no matter what, because I am not going to law school. I really didn't know what *The Daily Show* was. I looked it up the night before my interview. They hired me as a production assistant in January 1998. I ran the scripts around.

RORY ALBANESE

I was just an upper-middle-class white kid from Long Island who didn't want to be a lawyer. And I was funny and I was too lazy to really do anything else.

Jen was one of the people who interviewed me for a job in 1999. She was in charge of the production assistants. We hit it off right away. We still hit it off.

JEN FLANZ

I had a boyfriend, so that is not why I hired him. He was in love with me. I was not in love with him, okay? I was supervising Rory, and we were friends for a long time. Once he got promoted into a studio production job, I was more okay with it.

We had the best wedding. Oh my God. Stephen Colbert still talks about the food. My parents know how to throw a good party. Elliott and Jimmy were there, Melkmann was there, Lowitt was there, Jo Honig, Dan Taberski, Thom Hinkle, Beth Shorr. Lewis Black pulled up in his tour bus.

RORY ALBANESE

Yes. It was badass. Lew rolls deep.

You start working at a place where everyone is twenty-three that becomes your group of friends. That becomes who you date, that becomes who you marry.

JEN FLANZ

Rob Fox and Beth Littleford got married way before us, while they worked at *The Daily Show*. Then Elise Terrell and Pat King got married. I was in their wedding.

RORY ALBANESE

The place was a family, and Jen and I were legally family. For a while.

Meanwhile, Stewart was wrestling with a different kind of family dynamic: how to continue his professional relationship with Colbert. They had been searching for new collaborative vehicles since 2002, when NBC gave the pair a development deal for a sitcom starring Colbert, with Stewart as executive producer. But nothing came of it. In late 2004, Colbert and Dixon met with Doug Herzog, Comedy Central's president, about signing a development deal and coming up with a spinoff show. The eventual, brilliant solution came about somewhat by accident.

But Colbert's exit turned out to be the first domino in a long, often difficult stretch that would roil and renew The Daily Show *during the next three years.*

JON STEWART

It became clear that we've got to find something else if we want to still be working together. So we tried a sitcom about his life in South Carolina. Stephen and I wrote that together and pitched it to CBS, and it didn't go because, apparently, Burt Reynolds had a reboot of *Evening Shade* or something. Who the hell knows?

CHRIS REGAN

Jon was, at some point, getting sick of being on camera all the time, and they were looking for easily producible, kind of refillable things to bump into commercials with. That's where "Jon Magazine" came about, and D.J. and I worked on one of them. I think that's an all-but-forgotten feature of the show.

But they were easy. It was a bunch of graphic stuff, and those would be about a minute and a half. Then, in 2004, there was an assignment to me and Bodow, "Do a minute of Stephen selling this book." It was just a parody of a Bill O'Reilly commercial, where O'Reilly was selling one of his silly books. It's just Stephen arching his eyebrows, turning to the camera, and asking the viewer if he or she had the balls to buy his book: "Do you have the balls? *Do you?*" And he says "balls" about nine times. That was the first time Colbert began to emerge as a conservative blowhard.

JON STEWART

The Colbert character that became the sensation, a high-status idiot who was driven by his own narcissism, that wasn't the character he usually played in the studio. It's something he would inhabit at times.

CHRIS REGAN

We also wrote, in that same batch, something that honestly I liked a little more, with Rob Corddry, called *Sunday Mosaic*, which was a parody of those Sunday morning public-affair programs. It was basically Corddry, in a dashiki, in a small African hat, trying in vain to interview leaders of the black community. It was never produced. They decided to go with *The Colbert Report* over Rob Corddry's *Sunday Mosaic*. It would be a very different world if they'd made a different decision. So, yeah, something that was produced to make things more convenient led to a whole other television show that ran for a decade.

JON STEWART

I think the idea was that we would try and develop him a show that came on after *The Daily Show*, and that we would use those promos as kind of a template.

Stephen would come by the old Busboy [Productions] office, on Forty-Sixth Street. We just sat in there and bullshitted—here's the character, here's some bits. You could tell in the room when an idea is working. You both feel like you want to stand up and start pacing around and throwing shit in.

STEPHEN COLBERT

The Daily Show started with a local TV news model, and in some ways almost like a local TV newsmagazine. The first pieces I did, they were like newsmagazine pieces, with Craig Kilborn as a small-market anchor almost. When Jon came in, it became the equivalent of a network or a cable network anchor show. That changed the role of the correspondent. Instead of pieces about Bigfoot, we were parodying more of the network—or at least the cable network news—self-importance.

That went on for years very successfully. Then we started thinking, "Gosh, the real model here, a new area to model—" and this is how the conversation started at *The Daily Show* "—is we don't have anybody doing a pundit show. We don't have the equivalent of an O'Reilly or a Hannity or a Chris Matthews or other people who hold forth with an opinion on either side of the spectrum." And so we started thinking about what that means and how that has nothing to do with facts. It has only to do with assurance, and really in some ways aggressiveness. That's what led to "truthiness." It was those conversations that we had on *The Daily Show*, which actually led to promos for a show that didn't exist. That we did as a joke called "*The Colbert Report*—it's French, bitch." The No Fact Zone came from these promos. We did a few of them and they were popular and people started asking, "When is that show starting?" We actually started making jokes: "A new show that the *New York Times* has called 'not real' or 'will never be on TV' or 'has already been canceled.' " Before we did the bit, Jon had to say to the audience, "This isn't real."

So that concept of emotion over fact started with us trying to figure out how to evolve my character.

JAMES DIXON

Colbert was skeptical, as we all were, whether it could be sustained. He's like, "I can't do this character four nights a week every week of the year. I can't do that." Jon told him, "You can do it and here's how you're going to do it."

JON STEWART

Stephen's concerns were, "How do I make this guy interesting, and in the long term, how do I keep people from utterly despising him?"

The reason I thought it was easily sustainable is that Stephen's interested in and knows about tons of shit. So I felt like he could always embody the argument as long as he was interested in the subject. The main thing with a character like that is he sets the agenda. He *feels* the news, and in many ways, he *is* the news. The character is interesting because Stephen is interesting, and the core of this character is not hateful.

DOUG HERZOG

Stephen's contract was up. He was definitely ready for something else, and so we gave him a development deal. I remember hearing the *Colbert Report* idea the first time and just trying to wrap my head around it.

JAMES DIXON

We had to fight Comedy Central to get a two-week commitment for it. Two weeks, basically as a trial. We had to push it hard.

JON STEWART

I remember sitting up on the roof of our building talking to Doug on the phone. Originally, Comedy Central said, "Well, we'll do a pilot." I said, "We're not doing a pilot. Back this thing." I knew what we had with Colbert, and I knew where the show was going.

Why was I on the roof? Because I was used to doing stuff on the roof, from the old days of smoking.

CHRIS REGAN

Like most things involving the *Daily Show* empire, I might've read about Stephen getting his own show in the paper.

STEVE BODOW

To be clear, nobody owed me anything. But it gets back to the environment, that management-writers divide that might've led to some of the mistrust between writers and Jon. Because it would've been easy to tell us something. Finding out about things having to do directly with where you work in the press is really unpleasant.

JON STEWART

Stephen's show took our old studio space. We brought in Allison Silverman, who had been at our show, and she started working with Stephen as head writer. Ben started going back and forth. He had a moped, and he was basically commuting between the two shows, *The Daily Show* on Fifty-Second and Eleventh Avenue and *The Colbert Report* on Fifty-Fourth and Tenth. Ben was helping to construct the machine that can deliver that character's point of view, day in and day out, because it had never been tried. The machine had to be built to spec, and so Ben's experience in that was invaluable.

DAVID JAVERBAUM

Stephen and I talked about what his show could be for months before he left, and you're looking at the person who Stephen wanted to run the show. They wouldn't let me go. It was flattering.

STEPHEN COLBERT

Jon said, "No, you can't have D.J." I didn't understand how important it was until I ran my own show, and then I went, "Oh my God, I was asking to take his head writer! That's crazy!" It's funny the things you don't know until you know them. One of them is how delicate the machine is that you're building in terms of your process and who fits what position. As soon as I knew the enormity of what I was asking I apologized to Jon.

BEN KARLIN

Did I want to leave *The Daily Show* and go to *The Colbert Report*? It was the new toy. Jon was more of a father figure and Stephen was more of a brother figure, you know. *The Colbert Report* was a new thing, and I felt a sense of ownership over it that I didn't feel over *The Daily Show*, just because I didn't create *The Daily Show*.

Colbert is—I don't even want to say one of the most, he's *the* most fundamentally decent man I've ever met. He's a delightful person to talk about pop culture with, and he'd nerd out about *Reign of Fire* and weird dragon movies. I was fascinated by his Catholicism and how he can reconcile being a progressive, liberal-minded guy on most social issues with a very dogmatic religion. And to hear him speak so comfortably, and eloquently, and knowledgeably about how he can hold both those things, I'll remember that more than any joke.

ALLISON SILVERMAN

Stephen felt very thankful to Jon. He would sometimes talk about how he liked the idea of being of service to Jon, which I think had a lot to do with his thoughts about faith. A lot of Stephen comes down to his very real and complicated feelings about faith. Stephen felt that he worked best when he was in service to an idea or a person.

Stephen was kind of sandwiched between Jon, who was our ultimate boss, and me, who was his most direct employee. I remember him saying that he felt like he was a tool in the hands of two tough Jews.

JAMES DIXON

From the first five fucking minutes of the show, when Stephen says, "I promise to *feel* the news at you," it was like a rocket ship on a pad. To their credit, Doug is nobody's fool. He knows his shit. He saw gold right away.

DOUG HERZOG

We just sort of put it on the air, and it was incredible. That thing came out baked. *Baked.* That's a credit to Stephen, that's a credit to Jon, that's also a credit to the guy who was producing *The Daily Show* at that point, Ben Karlin.

STEPHEN COLBERT

"Truthiness" came from examining the behavior of punditry when I was on *The Daily Show*. I played a correspondent who had an ego and an agenda that was mostly preservation of his own status. That goes hand in hand with punditry, because pundits have to have status or why would you listen to them? Status has to be protected at all costs and you can never be wrong. The way to never be wrong is to not worry about what the facts are but to really go with your gut and what you feel is correct, because you will always be correct if you can name your own reality, which is closely related to what Ron Suskind wrote about in *The One Percent Doctrine*. He interviewed someone who later turned out to be Karl Rove, who is not named in the *New York Times Magazine* article where this thing started. A person in the White House, the Bush Administration, who turned out to be Rove, said, "You people in the reality-based community"—as opposed to the people in the White House, who were basically going to create a new and better reality with their own will toward truth. I read that and I'm like, "That's at the heart of punditry as well, because it's opinion treated as fact."

Pundits, those people are advocates. As a matter of fact, the guys who protected us when we had our separate shows, Jon's security nickname was "Educator" and mine was "Advocate."

STEVE BODOW

The first year that Colbert's show won the writing Emmy, and *The Daily Show* didn't, instead of congratulating them, we sent the writers each a nice dime bag of pot. We were just hoping that this will kill their ambition and work ethic, so they got this big basket full of weed, which I'm sure they appreciated.

DAVID JAVERBAUM

I had no involvement with *The Colbert Report* except for two things. I wrote the Christmas special, and I would write the tosses between Jon and Stephen at the end of *The Daily Show*, which was one of my favorite things to do. There's one I like a lot where they played the alphabet game. [*Opens phone, plays video*]

> **Jon Stewart:** [*at* Daily Show *anchor desk*]...Stephen Colbert, *The Colbert Report*. Stephen.
> **Stephen Colbert:** [*in split-screen shot at* Colbert Report *anchor desk*] A little alphabet game?
> **Jon Stewart:** But you promised we were through with this.
> **Stephen Colbert:** Continue.
> **Jon Stewart:** Don't drag me into this, Stephen.
> **Stephen Colbert:** Excellent.
> **Jon Stewart:** For God sakes.

Stephen Colbert: God has nothing to do with it.

Jon Stewart: Ha-ha.

Stephen Colbert: I'm so glad you've chosen to—

Jon Stewart: Just stop.

Stephen Colbert: K.

Jon Stewart: Look...

Stephen Colbert: Maybe you're right. Maybe we should stop.

Jon Stewart: Now, Stephen—

Stephen Colbert: Obviously, you want to quit.

Jon Stewart: Please. I'm having a great time.

Stephen Colbert: Quitter.

Jon Stewart: Really, I want to see this through.

Stephen Colbert: Seriously?

Jon Stewart: Totally.

Stephen Colbert: Understand, you're stuck with X and Z.

Jon Stewart: Very challenging, I know, but I have an idea.

Stephen Colbert: What's your idea?

Jon Stewart: Xylophone.

Stephen Colbert: You're making no sense.

Jon Stewart: Zero sense.

The departures of Carell and Colbert had been expected, but that didn't mean Stewart had a clear sense of how to fill the two enormous holes in the correspondent lineup.

JON STEWART

Losing Carell and Colbert is not necessarily what changed the show. It might've been the beginning of the change, because we were still in some ways in that original paradigm. Carell and Colbert were so strong that I think we were looking to try and regain that: "Let's get two more of those two guys."

Bob Wiltfong, who was more in the Colbert blowhard mold, lasted a year and a half as a correspondent. Nate Corddry, Rob Corddry's brother, left for a role on Aaron Sorkin's Studio 60 after only seven months as a Daily Show correspondent. Demetri Martin made fitful appearances as the Senior Youth Correspondent before landing his own show on Comedy Central.

The unsettled casting stretch produced one big success: Jason Jones, Samantha Bee's husband, went from working on a trial, piece-by-piece basis to a prolific ten-year run as a full-time correspondent. It also produced one painful mismatch.

DAN BAKKEDAHL, correspondent, 2005–2007

They brought me to New York from Chicago in August of 2005. The night before my audition I sat in the audience and watched the show—Stephen Colbert's last *Daily Show*. So we all knew it was imminent, they were going to hire somebody and it was going to happen soon.

A week and a half later, before I'd even moved to New York, I flew out to Seattle to do my first field piece. They don't bring you in and go, "All right, what can we do to make you comfortable and happy and teach you how to do this job?" They just go, "Do it or don't. Live or die." It's trial by fire.

I came from an ensemble background, at Second City and ImprovOlympic, and *The Daily Show*, it's not an ensemble show. It's a group of individuals that occasionally work one-on-one with Jon. It was a very difficult adjustment, and the adjustment period was nonexistent.

My first field piece was about this guy in Seattle who had invented what he called "bum-vertising"—paying street people a tiny amount of money to wear signs for businesses. Jon came in to view the footage, and it wasn't what we had hoped it would be. They never are when you first look at them—they're always a little sloppy. Jon came in and said, "I got a couple notes," blah, blah, blah. And he turned to me and he said, "What do you think?" And I went, "Jesus, I don't know." Because I honestly didn't know.

And that was the wrong answer at *The Daily Show*. It's an award-winning show that's trying to keep up with itself every year, and to come in and go, "Gee, I don't know, what do *you* think?" as an answer is not helpful. And I think that that's where it started. I felt like Jon froze me out.

ELLIOTT KALAN

Dan is such a funny actor and comedian, but he suffered from the people above not knowing exactly how to harness his voice and his talents. The show was not yet used to having someone who was that different from the Carell-Colbert form. Once it was clear that people weren't quite sure how best to use him for the show, this kind of disillusionment set in on both sides.

DAN BAKKEDAHL

I think Jon was way too smart for my clever little passive-aggressive game of just sit by and watch it happen. Jon's attitude was, "Not around here you don't. Around here you chop wood, you carry water, or you go home."

Stewart himself was displaying that sense of urgency on camera more often. As the outside world became more infuriating and absurd, he was dropping the "anchor" persona and delivering unfiltered anger. In August 2005, when Hurricane Katrina devastated New Orleans, Stewart opened the show looking directly into the camera. In later years, the pile-up of national tragedies would leave Stewart drained, and his tragedy reaction monologues would mix rage with a poetic weariness. But in 2005, the tone of The Daily Show *still sloshed between grave and juvenile, and Stewart was still loose enough to weave in a couple of jokes of dubious taste as he ripped Bush's incompetent response to the Katrina crisis.*

Jon Stewart: [*at anchor desk*] The real question is, in the four years since 9/11, have the government's advancements, procedures, etc., made us safer, given us more comfort, that they will have a more effective response to catastrophic events? And I think it's very clear that the answer is, Oh shit, we're in trouble.

Now, for people who were saying, "Stop pointing fingers at the president, the left wing media—" No. Shut up. No. This is inarguably, *inarguably,* a failure of leadership from the top of the federal government. I don't know if you remember this—remember when Bill Clinton went out with Monica Lewinsky? That was inarguably a failure of judgment at the top. Democrats had to come out and risk losing credibility if they did not condemn Bill Clinton for this behavior. I believe the Republicans are in the same position right now. And I will say this—Hurricane Katrina is George Bush's Monica Lewinsky. The only difference is this: that tens of thousands of people weren't stranded in Monica Lewinsky's vagina. That is the only difference. Although, here's an interesting point: Her vagina, at the time, was also known as the Superdome. [*laughter and groans from audience*] Do you prefer the Big Easy? That's fine.

But that is my point. So please stop with the, "Well, people are carp-
ing on—" He didn't even stop his vacation for three days! I mean,
please, just shut up.

SARA TAKSLER, *from field researcher to senior producer, 2005–*
Katrina happened not long after I started working at *The Daily Show*, during a week the show was on vacation. There was a strong feeling of anger and
frustration—the government is treating New Orleans horribly, how do we
hold them accountable? People needed this cathartic voice, and Jon knocked
it out of the park on the first day back. And I remember thinking, "Okay, this
is why *The Daily Show* matters."

The Daily Show *returned to Katrina often, and while many of the segments mocked the political blame-shifting game, others showed a new atten-
tiveness to class and race divisions, two themes that would grow as the show
matured over the years—and that would put Stewart ahead of the media
culture curve.*

DAN BAKKEDAHL
During those two years at *The Daily Show* I sat in my office and read *Live
from New York*, the *Saturday Night Live* oral history, and as I read it I thought,
"Yeah, some day, man, we're all going to write a book. And we're going to
fucking tell the truth, and everybody's going to know!"

My last three field pieces, in 2007, I just said fuck it. One was outside
Mexico City where wealthy Mexicans would pay to have the experience of
crossing the border like poor Mexicans. And I truly had totally given up at
this point, so I wore a track suit for the piece instead of wearing a business
suit like we normally do. I just started taking chances, threw myself into it
entirely, and I think at that point I hit a stride.

Thankfully now I can look back and say I didn't know how to take my
balls out of my purse and just go for it. Do whatever you think is right, and
at least if you're trying and you're wrong, you will have failed on your own
terms. But instead I stayed in the middle and said, "Well, I don't want to disappoint them, but at the same time, I don't want to try, because if you try and
you fail, well, then you've got no one to blame but yourself."

I know for a fact my life would not be a third of what it is—my life wouldn't be a tenth of what it is—if it weren't for the experiences I had on *The Daily Show*. I learned so much about how to deal with adversity.

JON STEWART

We are as unimaginative as most people. When Carell and Colbert left, that was when it really was like, "Oh, we've got to change the way that we view the correspondents and how they interact with the world." And the Iraq War had a lot to do with that as well. Corddry and Helms and Bee, to their credit, were able to come in and create something different.

They could do anything. It was me—I had to get out of my comfort zone as far as what the correspondents' role was, what they mean to the show. I had to reimagine it in a way. The show still had a lot of the patina of, "We're an alt comedy. We're that alternative white-boy comedy." It was *Harvard Lampoon*, it was everything that late-night comedy had been, that had become the rage.

One of the things I learned from Garry Shandling when I was working on *Larry Sanders* was the difference between caricature and character. To give you an example, Hank is a complicated character on that show. He's the second banana. Now, you can caricature him. When you were stuck in a scene or you couldn't crack into a character, Hank would storm in and yell, "Cocksucker!" and then the lights would come down. Garry was showing us how not to take the easy way out. To look at how character would motivate the scene as opposed to caricature.

The way that applied at *The Daily Show* was in terms of shortcuts. The early years, we basically dried the well of looking askance. So later we gave the correspondents more leeway to be themselves, to drop the facade and to attack it from a position of, "Wow, what you just said was truly horrifying. How can you possibly, possibly think that?" as opposed to eyebrow up. So, you're moving them from caricature to character.

Now, there is truth in caricature, but it's not necessarily very finely calibrated. The simplest version of that is toward the very end of the run where I just made faces and grunted. But that was the thing that you were always fighting—not becoming a caricature of your method.

DAN BAKKEDAHL

No matter how much I might have been furious with Jon throughout the years for my own feelings of being "wronged," quote, unquote, I had to acknowledge the guy's a fucking genius. You'd show up at 9:30 in the morning and his car was already in the garage, and you'd be sitting there at 10:30 at night doing an edit, and he's walking down the hall to get in his car. The guy gave his life to that job.

Samantha Bee was becoming a stalwart, but the post-Carell-Colbert lineup was still in transition. Corddry and Helms were tiring of the correspondent pace, and were on the verge of leaving for other TV and movie roles. The show sometimes resorted to airing "Klassic Kolbert" clips to bolster episodes. It wasn't until a rare overseas road trip by Stewart that The Daily Show *stumbled upon the comic who would become the new era's defining correspondent—and who would eventually become Stewart's first choice as host heir.*

BEN KARLIN

In December 2005, Jon, D.J., and I were in London, doing this big live event for *America (The Book)* in the West End, and Ricky Gervais was going to help us out, because he was a big fan of the show. We were really looking to kind of expand the types of voices on the show and we asked him who he liked in the UK. Ricky told us about Andy Zaltzman and his partner, John Oliver.

JOHN OLIVER, *correspondent, 2006–2013*

I didn't know Ricky, had never met him. I've subsequently said thanks. He kind of shrugged and went, "Oh, yeah, maybe I did tell them about you."

The Daily Show wasn't on TV in England at the time. I used to watch it on the Internet. I absolutely loved it. But as a goal, somewhere I wanted to work? No. I'd not been to America, so it did not seem remotely plausible that I would ever come here and work on the dream show.

I was living in London, planning to go to the Edinburgh Festival and perform. That was how my summer was supposed to shake out, and then I hear that *The Daily Show* is looking for correspondents. I think I wrote something, I put it on tape, and expected that to be the last of that. Then I got invited over here for a day to audition. I never really thought this was going to end up in anything other than a free day trip to New York, which seemed good enough for me.

I checked in to the Hudson Hotel and the next day walked to the *Daily Show* office. I ate at Applebee's, thinking it was a kind of local diner, and then read a couple of chats in the studio with Jon. I remember being pretty over-whelmed just by meeting him in the flesh. It all seemed a bit like a dream. So then, afterward, Jill Katz spoke to me and said, "You should call your agent because you got the job."

I called my manager and he said, "Well, you need to sign a lease for some-where. Don't sign it longer than four weeks, because you'll get fired." That's a very English version of an inspiring coach's talk, you know: "Protect yourself against inevitable failure."

He is still my manager. Yeah. He is.

BEN KARLIN

You could see Oliver had a quick wit. But he also has that ability to deliver biting commentary with a little bit of a gleam in his eye so that it doesn't feel negative or dark. And he's able to find the humor through performance, which is very hard. So few people have it. Colbert obviously has it in spades, and Oliver just had it.

JOHN OLIVER

It happened really fast. I came to New York in July 2006, landed late on a Sunday night, then had gone to work at the show on a Monday, thinking it would be a slow day. Then straightaway, at 9 a.m., it was, "Here's the assign-ment." President Bush had been at a conference with Tony Blair, and there was a live mic situation, and Bush said, "Yo, Blair," and so we did a chat about that. I'm still jet-lagged, and it was crazy hot that summer, it's my first day in America, I'm on the show.

I didn't even have a suit of my own. I went to...where'd I go? It might've been Men's Wearhouse. I think Corddry had told me that you can get cheap suits at Men's Wearhouse. It was trousers and a jacket that didn't match. The *Daily Show* music started, then you hear the audience go, *whoa*. It was like a loud noise. I'm standing just to the side, waiting to go in front of the green screen, and my knees buckled a little bit. I thought, "Oh shit."

I went out, and did it, and it went by in a blur, and then I turned round to leave. And there was one audience member in the corner, whose eye I caught, and it was J. K. Rowling. So, I walked past her thinking, what the...there's no fucking way that's J. K. Rowling. This is on my first day on the show. It turns out Jon was interviewing her at Radio City that night for the latest Harry

Potter book, so she comes round afterward, saying, "Oh, well done," and I said, "I haven't been here before, this is my first day." So she hugged me.

And that's like being hugged by the queen, if you cared about the queen. I care about J. K. Rowling much more than I care about the queen. She hugged me, and I had round glasses, and she said, "You look like Harry," and then glided off. For a tired, jet-lagged, overwhelmed man, that was...I absolutely felt stoned.

I walked back to Stuy Town, where I sublet a place, and I remember lying down, thinking, "I don't really know what just...Is it like this every day there at *The Daily Show*? Someone like J. K. Rowling is sitting in that corner seat?" And of course, she was never there again, so it was like a vision.

My stuff's still in storage in England. Somewhere in South London. I have a kind of time capsule of a previous life in there. If there's ever a South London *Storage Wars*, do not bid on that locker. There is nothing of any value inside.

JIM MARGOLIS

When Oliver first showed up, we were told, by Ben, that Oliver doesn't want to do those pieces where you talk to real people: "He's not comfortable with that, he just wants to be in the studio."

And then he started doing field pieces, and he could not get enough. No one, no one, enjoyed field pieces more than him, and he enjoyed all of the miserable parts of it. Oliver's second piece, he participated in a Civil War reenactment.

JOHN OLIVER

It was supposed to be a field piece to do with America's relationship with war in some way. I'd interviewed some reenactors and then put on a uniform to participate. All that was supposed to happen was I would charge ahead and ruin everyone's reenactment. What I was going to do is run through the opposing army and just keep going into the woods.

And then I fell. I was wearing dress shoes—Men's Wearhouse! And it had been raining, so I slipped. I had this bayonet, and I perfectly face-planted.

JIM MARGOLIS

I got a call from Tim Greenberg, the producer of it, and he was in a panic. "Oliver fell, and his nose is bleeding. I think it's broken, I need to stop this." And I said, "Absolutely not. Keep rolling. Whatever you do, roll on it."

JOHN OLIVER

Jim's response was, "Did you get it on camera?" And Tim said, "Yeah." And Jim said, "Was it funny?" "Absolutely!" So, then, it became a whole other thing. We go to the hospital and roll on it. That's Greenberg driving me to the hospital in the segment. Little did I know, he was like Hitchcock. He always liked to put himself somewhere in the frame of his pictures.

I went to the hospital, and they sent the tapes back to the office, so by the time I got into the office, I could hear the echoes of laughter around, and people were going, "Look at this! There he goes again!" watching me fall.

Every reaction everyone had was exactly the one you want them to have, which is, "That looks funny, let's do more of that. Let's follow the fact that you've hurt yourself like an idiot and see where that takes us." I thought, "This is exactly where I belong."

Hiring a Brit was bad enough. What was truly radical for the pinko-liberal Daily Show *was bringing in a correspondent who'd been a loyal soldier in President Bush's regime-changing military.*

JON STEWART

I feel like an idiot even putting it this way. It's certainly banal and not insightful, but at the time, it was like, "Oh, yeah, give me somebody who can talk about the war, but maybe with different life experience than just from the *Lampoon*." It changed the way we viewed things.

ROB RIGGLE

I had joined the Marines after college, in 1990, but I always wanted to try comedy. In 2000 I was a captain and I was going to get out of the Corps, but they asked what it would take for me to stay in the Marines, and I said, If you can send me to Los Angeles or New York, I'll stay on active duty. They sent me to New York, and I did Marines during the day, comedy at night at the Upright Citizens Brigade, for three years.

Saturday Night Live was my first job in show business. Talk about jumping in the deep end. But that ended after one year, and I moved to LA. In the spring of 2006 I get a call saying, "Hey, they're doing auditions for *The Daily Show* and they want to see you."

JON STEWART

When Riggle first got to the show, he was concerned about the mechanics. He'd go down to practice on the prompter in the studio. He's not a show biz guy. He's like, "I want to be in this business, and I'll work to get good." I'm not sure Riggle realized how good he was. The key for Rob was just to figure out, "Hey, man, you're funny as fuck. Just relax. Be yourself."

ROB RIGGLE

What's the biggest difference between Jon and Lorne Michaels? Lorne, I'm eternally grateful to him because he gave me a chance. He gave me a job. My personal experience, Jon was more hands-on, and I was granted perhaps a little more time to grow and figure things out.

JOHN OLIVER

I shared an office with Riggle. I was hired as a writer as well as a correspondent, and I had pretty hostile deadlines. If Riggle walks into the office during one of those, you've got a big problem, because he is like a six-foot-two-inch baby, so he *will* have his attention.

ROB RIGGLE

I felt I was helping by doing comedy bits. Get the creative juices flowing. He may have felt differently, you know, being a wimp.

JOHN OLIVER

The Daily Show was very difficult for Rob to do because he was still a Marine reserve at that time, so sometimes it was a little difficult to have him talk about Iraq or Afghanistan because the president was still his commander in chief, and there was certain shit he can't say.

ROB RIGGLE

Was it awkward at times, being on *The Daily Show* as a Marine? No. It wasn't. It really wasn't. You can hate the war and not hate the warrior. That's one of the reasons I served—because I live in the best country, where you can stand up and say something. If there was a segment I thought was too heavy-handed, I would either try to work on the verbiage or not do it. Now, did I hear from other people in the military? Sure. "Why are you on a show that's against us?"

But Jon was great. He didn't surround himself with sycophants and pound the drum and say the most popular thing the loudest and let the crowd cheer him. He would bring on people from the other side and say, "Well, explain to me why we are doing this." He would be sincere to the point almost of a student or a teacher. He wanted to learn.

When the protesters in Berkeley started harassing the Marines and the recruiters there, Jon saw the foolishness of that and told me, "All right. Go do a story on this."

Jon Stewart: [*at anchor desk*] One of the downsides of having an all-volunteer military is that you need people to...volunteer. That's not usually a huge problem—you just have to ask nicely. But some people don't want to hear the question. Rob Riggle has more.

Rob Riggle: [*in video, wearing flak jacket, at antimilitary protest*] Yes, the Marines dared to rent office space and open a recruiting center in Berkeley, California. I headed to the front lines to get the story, not only as a reporter, but also as a veteran of the Marines. With this amoral force refusing to leave their strip mall desks, Berkeley enlisted its own fighting force: Code Pink.

Code Pink Protester: [*wearing pink feather boa and tiara*] It is our responsibility as the public to shut this station down, to shut this recruiting station down. It's very important to protect free speech, and so we clearly have the right to be here.

Rob Riggle: If only there were an organization that was sworn to defend that free speech.

Code Pink Protester: Wouldn't that be great?

JOHN OLIVER

It was an odd time at the show because Ed Helms was leaving that week when I arrived, and then Rob Corddry was leaving in three months. A time of odd flux.

ED HELMS

The degree to which *The Daily Show* changed my career can never be measured. It's like orders of magnitude. But while I was superproud of my work there and my ability to kind of fit into that process, I knew that I could do more, and I really wanted to do more.

And by that, I mean acting. That's why, about four years in, I really started looking. And eventually, a meeting with Greg Daniels at *The Office* sort of brought Andy Bernard to life, and that became my next step. I had eight episodes offered to me, which is two months of work. I was pretty sure that was going to be the run of Andy Bernard.

It surprised me a little that when I asked for two months off from *The Daily Show* to do *The Office*, that they said they weren't sure I could come back. It wasn't Jon.

As The Daily Show*'s popularity spawned opportunities for its on-camera talent, it also stirred backstage questions about whether the staff was being treated fairly.*

STEVE BODOW

It was a complicated year, 2006. Our show wasn't unionized, and as far as I know, no basic cable show was unionized at that time, but we had started to have a level of success that was commensurate with network shows, and had won a bunch of Emmys in a row, and we were aware that the *Daily Show* writers were getting paid a bunch less than our counterparts at LA.

Didn't have health insurance. We were getting a weekly fee for the forty-two weeks a year we were working. Our counterparts at these, in many cases, less successful shows were getting benefits and a lot more money.

And this was after we had won two or maybe three writing Emmys in a row. Someone on the staff knew this guy named Chris Albers, who was a Conan writer for many years and had just become the president of the Writers Guild [of America]. So, he knew the late-night scene very well and he was gung-ho about organizing the shows. The writers had little secret meetings over the course of a few months about whether to do this and how to do this.

Some of us wanted to approach Jon about it, and others said that if we did that, he would shut us down. And the union recommended, for various legal reasons and strategic reasons, that we organize ourselves first, have the union be our reps, and then present a more formal demand.

DAVID JAVERBAUM

I lost my shit, and I remember we had a meeting about it, and I said something to the writers like, "Fuck you guys." I was so angry, not at the unionization, but at the way it was handled. They're very high-handed, union people.

STEVE BODOW

In retrospect, we fucked up the communication on it. I was still pretty junior at the time. I was just sort of getting to know Jon. D.J. was the head writer. Ben was the producer. They found out about the whole thing because someone from Viacom called them and said, "We just got this letter, what's going on over there?"

JON STEWART

It felt like a betrayal of trust with the writers. But it was more just honestly a feeling of, "Wait—I'm management?" I viewed us as more of a team, or group, or whatever…and I shouldn't have. They had to protect themselves. I could've handled it much better, too. The writers unionizing was, for me a misunderstanding of emotion, and what my role should be, and what their role is. I needed to understand that they were doing what they had to do for their families just like everybody else, and it wasn't a personal thing, although I took it personally at the time.

STEVE BODOW

As the thing moved forward, Jon became our greatest ally. He came to see that unionizing was the right thing to do. But that took months.

RACHEL AXLER

I went in to talk with Jon about unionizing because I felt torn between my first boss and the staff, and I was kind of being told to choose a side. Jon was not at all angry. He just seemed very saddened by the whole ordeal.

But as I was talking, I burst into tears. This would have been a moment when, if someone hated women or was uncomfortable with feminine emotions, he probably would have freaked out. Jon did not freak out. He didn't even comment on it. He goes, "Would you like some water?" He gets me a bottle of water, and I immediately started laughing because I was so embarrassed.

And he says, "Yeah, my wife does this, too. The crying-laughing thing. What is that?" This is a very, very good man.

So, too, in many ways, is John McCain—which is probably why Stewart's feelings about the Arizona Republican were volatile and varied. The arc of their relationship tracked the evolution of The Daily Show's *satire from playful to disgusted. McCain had provided* The Daily Show *a huge boost in 1999 by inviting Steve Carell aboard the Straight Talk Express. The senator then became a frequent guest on the show, with Stewart praising McCain's willingness to go against Republican orthodoxy on campaign finance, environmental policy, and torture, and McCain's boldly explicit condemnation of "agents of intolerance," including Reverend Jerry Falwell.*

Then, in the run-up to a 2008 presidential bid, McCain seemed to be violating his own principles by pandering to the hard right, and Stewart called him on it—gently, and somewhat regretfully, but in a preview of how their previously nuanced dialogue would soon take a sharp turn downhill.

Jon Stewart: [*at anchor desk*] Has John McCain's Straight Talk Express been rerouted through Bullshittown? You know who we could ask—Senator John McCain!

I heard this crazy story that Senator John McCain is giving the commencement address at Jerry Falwell's university.

Senator John McCain: [*on split screen, live from Washington*] Well, before I bring on my two attorneys, I'd like to—

Jon Stewart: Don't, don't make me love you! Are you really going to Liberty and delivering the commencement?

Senator McCain: I'm going to try to give these young people the same message I give to colleges and universities across the country— serve a cause greater than your self-interest, public service is good, character is necessary. And I'm going to invite you down, because I want you sitting next to Reverend Falwell when I give it.

Jon Stewart: Is that so if the rapture happens during the speech, somebody could be there to clean up all the clothes?

Senator McCain: Exactly.

Jon Stewart: Senator, you're killing me here...Are you freaking out on us? Cause if you're freaking out and you're going into the crazy base world—are you going into crazy base world?

Senator McCain: [*smiling sardonically*] I'm afraid so.

Jon Stewart: We have great regard for you here, and I hope you know what you're doing. I trust that you do. When you see Falwell, do you feel nervous, do you have vomit in the back of your throat?

Senator McCain: No, but I'll give him your love.

Major changes kept rattling through the show during 2006. Javerbaum, the prolific and cuttingly sarcastic head writer, decided he would be leaving by the end of the year to write musicals; his chair would be filled by the more solicitous Bodow. Josh Lieb, who'd worked with Stewart on his MTV show before stints as a writer and producer at NewsRadio *and* The Simpsons, *came on board as a co–executive producer.*

On camera, Corddry and Helms, two products of the traditional improv pipeline, had been capably replaced by Oliver and Riggle, a literal foreigner and an experiential outsider. But Stewart wanted to further enlarge The Daily Show's *capacity to tell a range of stories. Larry Wilmore's motivation for joining the* Daily Show *cast was different: He wanted to train to host his own show someday.*

LARRY WILMORE, *contributor, 2006–2014*

I had run *The PJs* for Eddie Murphy in the late nineties, and then created *The Bernie Mac Show*, and got a lot of acclaim. Then at the end of the second season Fox fired me. So I worked writing on *The Office* and ran Whoopi Goldberg's show, but one of my plans was that ultimately I wanted to write a show for myself, or do a talk show. My managers suggested, "Well, what if you went on *The Daily Show*? That way you could get back in front of an audience."

Colbert and Corddry had left, Helms was leaving, they were overhauling the show. I met with Jon. We had a great talk—about sports. I left thinking, "Wait, am I going to do this show or not?"

The first piece, the rehearsal went very poorly. I felt as if the crew wasn't even looking at me—like, if you're working on a farm and you don't want to name the animals, because you might have to eat them at some point. We went out to do the taping and I was very nervous. I thought, "Oh man, if this dies like it did in rehearsal, I'm done." Right before we came back from commercial Jon put his hand on my arm and said, "Hey man, just look in the camera and just fucking give it to America." It was the best thing he could have told me.

> **Jon Stewart:** [*at anchor desk*] As the summer winds down, the fall election campaign is heating up. And recently the topic of race has entered into campaign news. For a closer look, please welcome our Black Correspondent, Larry Wilmore.
>
> **Larry Wilmore:** [*sitting across from Stewart—silently staring at the desk, then up at the ceiling, his expression a cross between pouty and angry*]
>
> **Jon Stewart:** Uhhh—Larry?
>
> **Larry Wilmore:** [*more silence*]
>
> **Jon Stewart:** Okaaay—please welcome our *Senior* Black Correspondent, Larry Wilmore. [*as the chyron adds the word* SENIOR *to Wilmore's title and Wilmore breaks into a smile*]

LARRY WILMORE

And that became our relationship on the show: I would make Jon squirm at these racial issues more than I would take a political position, conservative or liberal. We figured that out in the first chat: Let's scoop out what the real racial relationship is between us, and it gave us more fertile ground.

That same month, another large step in diversifying the Daily Show *lineup came about more by luck than by design.*

AASIF MANDVI, *correspondent, 2006–2015*

It was August, I'm jobless and sexless, and I had just found out that my ex had gotten engaged, and I was in that funk that all guys find themselves in where they go, "I just fucked up this great relationship and now she's engaged and I'm single and jobless. Where's my life going?" I was sitting on a stoop. I was literally in a stupor and on a stoop.

I was writing a letter to her sort of exorcising all these things I had never said, all that shit that you say to somebody after the fact when it doesn't really matter. And that's when my phone rang. It's my manager's assistant and he says, "*The Daily Show* is looking for a Middle Eastern guy and they want you to go down there." And I thought, "This is the best Homeland Security sting operation I have ever heard of."

Oh, they probably want me for some fucking brown bullshit. This is going to be either me with a fake beard yelling, "Death to America!" or with a turban sitting on a carpet pretending to fly. And it's going to be ninety seconds, I'm going to get a couple hundred bucks. So I said, "Tell *The Daily Show* to go fuck themselves."

STEVE BODOW

We'd written a chat for a Middle Eastern Correspondent. Except we didn't have one. So we called a casting agent.

AASIF MANDVI

My manager calls me back: "Go in there today by three o'clock. If you don't they're moving on." And it was one of those moments in life that I was like, all right, you know what, I'm going to fucking rally, and I'm going to go home and shit and shave, put on a suit and tie, and I'm going to go down there. And so I did. Maybe one of the best career moves I ever made. Probably the best career move I ever made.

There was Jon Stewart, who I had seen on TV many times, wearing his signature baseball cap and sweatshirt and jeans. I remember saying to Jon, "Do you want me to do an accent?" and he said, "No, no, no, we just want you." And that was really reassuring. I was like, I love you, Jon Stewart. Because so many times you got asked in those situations to really make it campy.

I got done, Jon turned to me, and he said, "That was great," and he put out his hand and he said, "Welcome to *The Daily Show*," and I was like, "What?" Because jobs don't ever happen like that. He says, "Do you have plans, because you're going to be on the show tonight?" Then we had to do contracts and I was like, "I haven't had any lunch."

The rehearsal was an hour later. I go out there and they want me to do it again in front of like producers and crew. I'm reading the teleprompter and looking out at the audience, and there's this dude sitting there with a baseball cap on next to a teenage kid in jeans and a shirt. I'm looking at him and I'm thinking, I know that guy. Then I realize it's fucking Bruce Springsteen. I come running backstage: "Why the fuck is Bruce Springsteen out there?" Our stage manager says, "Yeah, he just came by to visit, we don't know." I was like, "Does that happen all the time?"

STEVE BODOW

That first piece, Aasif fucking knocked it out of the park. It wasn't even something we were trying to do, but it was like, "Oh, this opens up a whole new avenue for the show."

ROB KUTNER, *writer, 2002–2009*

In the Carell and Colbert years, we were having fun with broader performances. It started to shift with Corddry, who brought a more sarcastic style. And then the hiring of Aasif really reflected the new, sharply satirical tone. We were mirroring the stridence of the Bush Administration.

As Bush's second term wore on, he gave The Daily Show *plenty to be strident about, besides the war. There was the brief, embarrassing Supreme Court nomination of presidential crony Harriet Miers; the firing of seven U.S. Attorneys by Attorney General Alberto Gonzales, to make room for the appointment of "loyal Bushies"; the indictment of Cheney aide I. Lewis "Scooter" Libby for lying about his role in the leaking of the identity of CIA covert agent Valerie Plame; and the revelation of ongoing warrantless wiretapping in the name of antiterrorism.*

All was not joyless, however: "The Dow hit 11,000 today, first time since 9/11," Stewart said in January 2006. "So I'm just gonna say this to the world— we're back, bitch. Is there any indicator of a society's health more important than its stock market. Oh-ho-ho . . . I guess all of them." And with the Democrats expected to regain control of Congress, things were looking up, for the country and for The Daily Show. *Right?*

8

Midwest Midterm Midtacular

Election years always stimulated the show, usually for the better. For 2006, Stewart was looking to beef up the ranks of "contributors"—the comedians who would appear every so often at the desk to offer mock commentary and joust with the host—beyond Lewis Black and Larry Wilmore. The real world was ever more daft: The Bush team had hired an ad executive to sell democracy to the Iraqis, and it had tried to dress up torture by calling it "enhanced interrogation," when not being openly contemptuous of critics. "They're living in the tropics," Vice President Dick Cheney said of the Guantánamo Bay prisoners. "They're well fed. They've got everything they could possibly want." So one addition to the cast was a man who didn't fit any traditional Daily Show category—but who had a highly developed sense of the absurd that fit the times.

JOHN HODGMAN

At that point I was already in my midthirties. I was heavier than I am now, and a weird guy, a man-baby with a lazy eye. It did not seem like an on-camera career was really likely. And yet as implausible as it was, Jon made that happen.

JON STEWART

Why did I want John Hodgman as a contributor? Because he's a fascinating character. A man of substance, a man of flair. You treat him as the bon vivant that he is. When he shows up, you like to have the property minibar with the right ice and the highball glasses he requires. He's a walking Algonquin round table.

JOHN HODGMAN

The Areas of My Expertise, my first book, had come out. I got a call after a poorly attended reading in San Francisco saying, "Come back east, because you're going to be on *The Daily Show*." As a guest.

That reading in San Francisco was attended by about fifteen people, and my book was, I think, number 16,000 on the Amazon list. Then I went to New York, did the show, flew overnight to Seattle. When I arrived in the morning the book was number seven on Amazon, and the bookstore had attracted 450 people.

Ben called me up that winter and asked me to think about what I might do on the show as a regular contributor. I realized that I could adapt this character that I had developed for the book into an all-purpose authoritative academic know-it-all.

One of the things I said to him was, "You know, you're constantly seeing on CNN or Fox or whatever, they'll call in an expert to illuminate some esoteric point, and I could be that expert. And the joke is, whatever it is, I am the expert."

> **Jon Stewart:** [*at anchor desk*] The U.S. Army has recently sponsored a civilian-only essay contest called "Countering Insurgency" to solicit ideas from the public on how best to defeat the Iraqi insurgency... Now, it just so happens that there is a *Daily Show* connection to the contest. One of the judges is our own resident expert, John Hodgman.
> John, isn't it unusual, and perhaps a tad ominous, that the government is turning to the general public for help with its military strategy?
>
> **John Hodgman:** Well, not really. The nation has been brainstorming this way for cash and valuable prizes since our beginning. Our national anthem? The result of a jingle contest. The decision to drop the atomic bomb? That wasn't Truman, but sweepstakes winner Penny Holcomb of Palm Beach. And for that she received a case of Lucky Strikes—and a lifetime supply of sadness.
>
> **Jon Stewart:** What would be an example of a good essay?
>
> **John Hodgman:** When it comes to writing an expository essay about counterinsurgent tactics, I'm of the old school. First you tell them

how you're going to kill them. Then you kill them. Then you tell them how you just killed them. That's why I like this idea I read from Jonathan Colton of Colchester, Connecticut. He thinks we should drop thousands of king cobras into Fallujah—each equipped with its own little parachute, of course. It's simple, direct, elegantly written. Not to mention the whole snake-sized parachute industry is going to get a huge boost out of it.

JOHN HODGMAN

There's no question that breaking a taboo elicits laughter, right? The truth about what was happening in Iraq, and what was happening in terms of media coverage in Iraq, had become so taboo that it had become funny. *The Daily Show* wasn't satire. All Jon was saying was the truth.

And particularly in the first half of the last decade the truth was hard to come by. Indeed, there was a lot of pressure to not say what was plain on its face. I mean, this was Ari what's-his-name telling Bill Maher, "Watch what you say." That if you didn't conform to the narrative you weren't an American. And this boiled the blood of everyone in this country who didn't feel part of the narrative.

For someone like Jon—and I think for a lot of people like him who are profoundly interested in the experiment of America, and the history and the culture of America—to have that essentially taken away just because you had some questions about this idiotic and loathsome war, well, it really made a lot of people feel utterly in exile.

The 2006 midterms motivated a weeklong trip to middle America, to Columbus, Ohio. The Buckeye State had basically decided the previous presidential election in favor of the incumbent, George W. Bush. That alone made it an intriguing backdrop for The Daily Show. *But the choice of a politically purple state, near the middle of the country, made metaphorical sense, too. Fox News and MSNBC played to audiences on the right and left wings. Stewart and* The Daily Show *were, more and more, becoming the voice of the quieter, busier, more rational middle of the political spectrum.*

Jon Stewart: [*at the anchor desk inside an auditorium at Ohio State University*] Why Ohio? Because this is *the* battleground state.

The 2004 election was decided right here. Oh, and by the way—
thanks. In fact, Ohio has always been on the country's political
pulse. In twenty-five of the last twenty-seven presidential elections, Ohio has voted with the winner. No other state even comes
close. Is it because Ohio's values mirror America's values? Or perhaps, were Ohioans sent here from the future?

The search for an answer was conducted in true Daily Show *fashion—on the
first night of the trip, correspondents Bakkedahl, Bee, and Jones reported from
in front of three different Applebee's locations, while Riggle claimed to have
located the "real" Ohio at a Bob Evans.*

*But the lessons about America's complicated heartland values were especially
vivid for* The Daily Show's *newest correspondent.*

JOHN OLIVER

I'd been in America three months. I went out ahead of the rest of the
show, to shoot a piece in Chillicothe, Ohio. That was the first time I've seen a
gun in the wild. We were at a diner, and a guy pulled up in a truck and there
was a rifle in the back, and I'm thinking, "Holy shit."

You don't see guns anywhere in England. No. In Chillicothe, the guy
absolutely refused to believe that I had never seen a gun before, and that I
had never fired one. He swore I was lying. He offered to let me shoot his gun
in the parking lot. I very much refused that offer. I'm thinking, "This cannot
be my first time, with some random farmer in Ohio. It's got to mean more
than this."

*Six years into the Bush Administration, the run of bad news was wearing on
nerves—in civilian life, of course, but also inside* The Daily Show, *where digest-
ing, in Stewart's words, "the shit taco" was what everyone did for a living.*

*Karlin had mellowed somewhat since his bruising first years as head writer,
but his hard-driving style as executive producer, a crucial factor in creating a
top-notch show four nights a week, had frayed some relationships.*

ELLIOTT KALAN

Ben was very much the executive producer the show needed at the time,
when he replaced Madeleine. But he was also a much brusquer person than it

would have been nice to have had. He gave Jimmy and me a real shot, recognizing us and moving us up. Outside the show he's always been supernice to me and very gracious and very helpful. Ben is like Shaft. He's a complicated man.

JEN FLANZ

Ben is creatively very intense, and he was also young. He was taking on a lot, managing people.

He was hard on me. Yeah. Absolutely. Yeah, there were days I cried. Ben and I had crazy fights. But we always made up. I would go back at Ben like an older brother. Every few months we'd have a blowout.

But Ben at a party is great, and he started "summer fun day" at the show. And I learned a lot from him. There were a lot of people Ben didn't like dealing with—and there are a lot of people that just didn't want to deal with Ben—so he came to me for a lot, which ended up giving me a lot of opportunity.

RORY ALBANESE

I don't think the show would have become what it did without Ben. He was integral in taking it from this little basic cable thing to a juggernaut. He didn't ever lose sight of the goal of making the show great.

I don't think Ben was ever a mean guy. Sometimes he was curt. But people who work in TV are entitled and they're babies.

ERIC DRYSDALE

It's funny, I was thinking about this. I remember leaving work and burning with hatred for Ben, but I don't remember why. Insofar as his job was to protect Jon, he did a great job. And I think that he did that at the cost of morale among the writers.

DAVID JAVERBAUM

Ben had weather, and sometimes the weather was worse.

BEN KARLIN

That stuff really was a function of the transition to Jon being the new host and me being the new head writer and how much that shook up the status quo. Once we got into a groove, around 2001, there were quite a few consecutive years where I felt good about my relationships with 95 percent of the staff—writers and otherwise. After that, any tension or bickering or "weather" was mainly over production issues—missed deadlines, lazy scripts, graphics that didn't work, field pieces that would never seem to come together despite so many hours put into them. Producing that show was a motherfucker and it could get the best of you. Sometimes it did, and there certainly were times I wish I handled it with more grace and civility. I'm sure there is a platonic ideal of the showrunner—one who is creatively vital, in full command of all aspects of production and also beloved by all their employees and coworkers. I wasn't it. Maybe Jason Katims? He seems like a great guy. For real.

Karlin and Stewart had remained an effective creative duo. But in 2010 the grind and conflicting ambitions severed that bond, too.

JIM MARGOLIS

Jon and Ben were developing movies and TV shows together, then something happened between them and all of a sudden it just all went black.

JON STEWART

Ben got married in Italy that spring, and Tracey and I had a baby, I don't know, a month before, so I didn't go to Ben's wedding, and I think that bothered him a little bit. Then he didn't come back from the wedding, and that bothered *me* a little bit. And he didn't call me. Ben called somebody else who delivered the message that he was going to be gone two more weeks, and I was like, "In what world are you allowed to do that?" Ben says, "Well, I thought that I'd earned it from all the things we've done." I was like, "You may have if you had said to me, 'I'm taking a month off.'"

This felt different. Basically he was ready to be his own boss, it was clear.

BEN KARLIN

We'd done the book, then I was executive-producing two shows and planning a wedding in another country, and I was ground down to a nub. I'm bike riding in Sardinia, and I'm like, "Why the fuck do I want to go back to New York right now?" I made an extremely poor decision, in the throes of a new marriage and love.

JEN FLANZ

The tensions between Jon and Ben had been growing over time. But when we went to Columbus for the midterms in October, you could really see it. I'd be going to check in with Ben, touch base about some of the visuals for the show, and be told, "Oh, he went out for a walk." I'm like, "Fuck, that's weird." Ben never went for a walk.

BEN KARLIN

I was excited to be in Ohio. We had LeBron James on the show. But it was just hard.

JON STEWART

Any time you travel, any kind of fragility or cracks in the process or in relationships is going to be amplified by the lack of sleep, by the stress of not knowing where the copier is. But I was digging Columbus. Why not put a little cheese on something? Very nice people, very accessible, and basically anything Alfredo. You can't go wrong with that.

I could see Ben was really angry, and it was bothering me. I'm thinking, "I don't want to feel like I have to convince somebody that this show is a great place to be," and in his mind I imagine it was, "I don't want to have to fucking listen to you."

BEN KARLIN

There was a lot of fatigue. We had launched *Colbert* and I was really wearing two hats. That brought a lot of added pressure. Jon was very adamant about not raiding the mothership for the satellite. As much as we all loved, supported, and wanted *Colbert* to be a hit—and Jon was the executive producer of *The Colbert Report*—Jon really wanted to keep as much of a separation of powers as possible with *The Daily Show*.

JON STEWART

Unfortunately at *The Daily Show*, ultimately there's always going to be a block to your creative input, or to your fulfillment, and it's going to be a Jon Stewart–sized block. You had Ben with a sense of mounting frustration over a role that he didn't necessarily want to continue to fulfill because he had grown beyond it, and you had my frustration at needing someone to fulfill a role that was really crucial at the show.

BEN KARLIN

I just loved working with Stephen. I love him as a man, as a friend, just as a person, and his show was really, really exciting. Jon was a standup for so many years and he was able to find the joy every day in going out and doing material on *The Daily Show*. As a nonperformer and as a writer, I didn't have that same joy. I kind of sadly needed something new, and Colbert was something new. So I was very conflicted about where I knew my loyalty should be and where my heart was.

JON STEWART

After we came back from Columbus, that final conversation in my office was very hard. It was very hard.

BEN KARLIN

Superpainful. For the seven-plus years of our collaboration we were pretty much in lockstep. It was an incredible ride. What makes Jon great is he's a savvy and smart businessman and he knows how to protect the things that are most important. He worked too hard and too long to build the show into what it was, and he kind of recognized something that maybe I couldn't see.

Given the history and the nature of our relationship, I was kind of thinking that it would be something that we would plot out over a period of several months. I remember Jon just saying, "No, I think it's better to just cut it clean." That was kind of, I don't want to say shocking, but it was definitely disappointing.

JON STEWART

I absolutely did consider Ben a friend, and still do. But beyond that I'm not particularly close—I'm close to my family, in general, and I have friends, and I'm close to them, but probably not in the traditional way that people assume friendships are like. I'm not a big hangout guy. When I say we're friends, we're friends, but it's not like we summer together, or we went out to dinner every week. I don't really do that with anybody.

STEPHEN COLBERT

Ben and I have remained friends. What's between Ben and Jon is between Ben and Jon.

JON STEWART

Ben was the master of the grand polarities. He could be really rough on people, and then he could be really generous with people, and you weren't quite sure where you were at. But you don't want that to take away from the fact that he was incredibly gifted, and an enormously crucial part of making the show what it was in those early years.

The suddenness of Karlin's departure, on top of Javerbaum's impending, voluntary exit, could have left a large vacuum in the show's day-to-day creative management. So Stewart moved aggressively to fill the hole before it could cause damage. What was a good short-term solution for The Daily Show, *though, ended up fracturing a long-running friendship.*

RORY ALBANESE

The change was shocking. D.J. was supposed to leave, and then all of a sudden Ben got fired and D.J. was staying. It was weird, and then it got very odd, because D.J. clearly didn't want to be there anymore. He was done, he was burnt. He had said, "I'm gonna do Broadway, I don't want to be here anymore." And now this guy's in charge.

BEN KARLIN

The writing staff had thrown him a going away roast, at Keens. Then it became clear I wasn't going to be coming back to the show. Jon reached out to D.J. and asked him to stay. D.J. told me that he wasn't taking the job, and then I came in to find out he had taken the job. Jon would have survived it no matter what because he's incredibly talented at this, but it was definitely the smart move. I didn't begrudge Jon for it at all. To lose your number one and your number two producer, without even a remotely clear number three, would have been really, really tough for a show like that.

D.J. was one of my oldest friends. I had known him since I was sixteen years old, and I had hired him at the *Onion* and I had hired him at *The Daily Show.* I fought for him to take over as head writer, and I had really done right by him. I don't have an ax to grind with D.J. I have a disappointment and a measure of heartbrokenness over how our relationship kind of came to an end.

DAVID JAVERBAUM

Ben never forgave me for that, and he thinks I was disloyal and thinks I handled it poorly, and I probably could've handled it better. Yeah, that was an awkward thing, and I don't like the fact that this person who was my best friend for many years and to whom I owe my career and I are so estranged.

The changes weren't limited to the lineup of writers, producers, and correspondents. The Daily Show *was, and always would be, at heart a comedy. But its humor darkened as the outside world continued to serve up bleak events: the ongoing disintegration of Iraq, the beginning of the subprime mortgage crisis, the Paul McCartney–Heather Mills split. The sharper focus on politics and media, and Stewart's greater control of the creative process, spurred tensions and changes in the* Daily Show *ranks.*

CHRIS REGAN

When I started on the show, there was a lot of pop culture stuff, a lot of celebrity stuff. After the 2000 election, after the 2004 election, we abandoned all that for hard news. We heard the dreaded "point of view" phrase bandied about all the time.

I didn't get into comedy to talk about one thing over, and over, and over again, that being American politics. So I was pretty over it, and I think they were pretty over me. I went to Jon and I told him I was burned out, and he said to me, "You're burned out? Walk in my shoes one of these days." It was the most candid he's ever been with me, just going on about how he's up all night, looking online, trying to find a new angle. "Am I a comedian anymore, am I a journalist?" He went on for about six or seven minutes, telling me about how he was having trouble keeping it fresh himself. In seven years, we had never had a conversation that candid.

And at the end I said, "Okay, good luck." I left *The Daily Show*. This was somewhere in 2006. Jon somehow found a way to keep it fresh for nine more years.

JON STEWART

We were feeling around for a new direction. The one thing I couldn't change was my brain. I'd given up drugs largely by that point and booze, mostly. So all I had left in my life was conversation. After Ben left, we brought in Josh Lieb and Dan Sterling and David Feldman as producers from the outside. It was about creating new nutrients, new avenues, new people to view things with a different eye, because the one thing I always felt confident in is my ability to recognize a good idea.

STEVE BODOW

That was a weird time. I had moved up to being head writer and took the job thinking that I was going to be working for Jon and for Ben, and then their falling-out occurred, and suddenly I was going to be working for D.J., who explicitly had expressed no interest in being a manager. There was nobody around who was senior at a producing level, so Jon brought on all these other people from the outside. That's not an experiment that's really been repeated.

Two of the new producers, Sterling and Feldman, had fairly brief runs— Sterling leaving to run Sarah Silverman's new show, and Feldman less amicably. The third, however, became a beloved and instrumental presence inside The Daily Show.

JOSH LIEB, *executive producer, 2006–2010*

I'd grown up as a kind of hippie kid in Columbia, South Carolina. I like the old *Mad* comics, and dialect humor—*The Education of H*y*m*a*n K*a*p*l*a*n*. Charles Dickens is my favorite comic author—the very human failings. As a kid I watched *Laugh-In* reruns any chance I could. And WLTX from 11:00 to midnight every night was *Sanford and Son* and *Andy Griffith* reruns. Then I'd gone to Harvard and written for the *Lampoon*.

In 1994 I applied for a job as a writer on the new *Jon Stewart Show*, on MTV. I was such a cocky little son of a bitch. When they offered me the job I told Jon that I'd only take it if I could sing "Suicide Is Painless" on a test show. And I have no idea where that came from. So there's a test show somewhere out there with me singing, my friend Brian Kelly playing ukulele, and we're in Army camo fatigues. It's awful. But anyhow I took the job, and it was great. Then I did four seasons as a writer and producer at *NewsRadio*, and one season at *The Simpsons*.

I was a completely LA guy. And I got a phone call one day in 2006 from my agent asking, "Would you be interested in going to work at *The Daily Show with Jon Stewart?*" It was bizarre to me to think of going back to New York. But a lot of it was that I would love working with Jon again.

And I will say this. When Jon took the *Daily Show* job, I thought that was the stupidest thing he could've done, right? I thought it was idiotic, and I said that very loudly to a lot of people. Because at that time *The Daily Show* was just this crappy little cable show. I didn't watch *The Daily Show* very much in Jon's first few years. But I knew by the time I came back that he had turned what was a good but standard show into a special show.

RORY ALBANESE

Working with Josh Lieb, those were some of the best years of my life. He'd show up to work and call me and say, "Hey, can you come down and bring me money for the cab?" Josh would be in the back of the cab, reading a newspaper, holding a mug of coffee—not a travel mug, a kitchen mug. I'd do the backstory: "Let me retrace your steps. You poured a cup of joe, grabbed your paper, no wallet, walked outside reading and drinking, hailed a taxi, pulled up to work and realized you didn't have any money, and called me?" The guy probably owes me a hundred bucks.

ELLIOTT KALAN

There's certain guys who see the matrix in comedy. D.J. is one. Josh is another, where you feel like they can go into bullet time. They see a joke— they see the construction of it completely. They know it backward and forward. And he was just so much fun to work with. I remember Josh pushing Snarf as Jon's cohost for a week. Half seriously.

JOSH LIEB

I wasn't half-joking! This was a real pitch! It was a joke based on the feeling that we were never as good as a network show. When you're on basic cable, no matter how successful you are you always feel like you're in the ghetto a bit. So the joke was Jon would finally have a sidekick, but that the only one Comedy Central could afford was Snarf, from the *ThunderCats* cartoon.

Like, how annoying would it have been for Jon Stewart to have to deal with Snarf as a sidekick? Like, "What do you think of Dick Cheney, Snarf?" "Dick Cheney! He's a jerk! Snarf, snarf! He makes me feel bad! Snarf, snarf!" It could have been huge. Could have been a spinoff.

I can't believe anyone remembers that but me. It makes me happy.

JON STEWART

Everyone needs a little Lieb in your life. He wasn't a prick, he wasn't cynical, he wasn't haughty, he was just smart and fun to be around. He's a guy who will put away three martinis at the Friars Club while wearing pants that match the weird wallpaper, but he also scours white supremacist websites to see how the interesting Jewish conspiracy theories came about. He's just so... Liebish.

RORY ALBANESE

There were always a lot of bits, running jokes, when Josh was around. There was an ongoing bit where Lieb was getting threatened by various people. You'd leave a note on his desk: "Josh, you've got a phone call, it's David Remnick and the message is 'I'm going to kill you.' Please return call."

JON STEWART

It was always from famous people, like Tony Danza sending really threatening letters to Josh, and they would just appear in places around the office.

Josh walked into a very difficult situation in that he was coming in at a position of responsibility without having been through the process of the show. Generally people were promoted from within there. We tried it maybe three times, to bring in outside people, and it's worked once, and that's Josh.

JOSH LIEB

I think my great utility at *The Daily Show* might have been in telling people, "Hey, this doesn't need to be changed. This is working." They didn't know how good they were.

The Daily Show didn't have any *Lampoon* writers, except for D.J. and me. We did tend to get more writers who had come out of the magazine world—Bodow, Daniel Radosh. Radosh and J. R. Havlan both had an incisiveness and sort of a mordancy. There's no place too dark for them to go. Rachel Axler, out of the playwriting world. Rachel, like Rich Blomquist, has a great insanity where the jokes would come from a place you could not have imagined. Sam Means had a bit of a gentle weirdness. Rory could give you any kind of joke but he could also give you the straight-ahead joke, the "Let's cut through the bullshit, what are we really talking about here?" joke that we frequently needed to end a piece.

The first big meeting of the day was all of the writers and producers going, "Did you see this? Did you hear about this?" I had a whole chain of people who didn't just find the obvious stuff in page A1, A3 of the *Times* stories. Tim Carvell would have watched *Fox & Friends* every morning for whatever goddamn reason. Nobody assigned him to it. He's a sociopath. Everybody, whether writers or researchers or second producers, had their eye on something and everybody was saying, "God, at 6:15 last night on *NBC Nightly News* you should have seen…" or, "At 5:15 this morning on MSNBC, you had to see it," and they would have the tape and bring it up.

Lieb's eccentric energy was welcome after Karlin's more muscular style. So, too, was the onset of a new, Bush-less presidential campaign season. By early 2007, a mere seventeen candidates had declared, a coalition of the ambitious including Mike Gravel, Mike Huckabee, John Edwards, Ron Paul, Evan Bayh, and Duncan Hunter, sparking one of The Daily Show's *most apt rubrics: "Indecision 2008: Clusterfuck to the White House."*

Jon Stewart: [at anchor desk] Let's start with the GOP, where the front-runners include a conservative, [shot of John McCain] a Mormon conservative, [Mitt Romney] an evangelical conservative, [Sam Brownback] and a New York liberal conservative. [Rudy Giuliani] My money's on the white guy.
Across the aisle, the Democrats are fielding a veritable rainbow coalition. A win for any of these candidates would make presidential history. Be it the first female president, [Hillary Clinton] the first African-American president, [Barack Obama] the first Latino president, [Bill Richardson] the first leprechaun president, [Dennis Kucinich] or the first mimbo! [John Edwards]

*   *   *

The overcrowded field for a wide-open job was a comedy blessing. Keeping up with the glut of material, though, was still incredibly labor-intensive, and finding the clips that would become famous was still a remarkably free-form process.

RAMIN HEDAYATI, *from studio production staffer to field producer,* **2007–**

At that time LexisNexis was our search tool, and you only had a couple blogs that were flagging big moments on cable news—Crooks and Liars, Media Matters. We had about thirteen, fourteen DVRs, and they would only hold about a week or two weeks' worth of footage. So if we wanted to save anything, we had to manually put a tape in, a big beta tape. Nothing was assigned. People liked certain shows. Jimmy Donn really liked to watch O'Reilly. I would DVR the nightly news, and *Special Report with Bret Baier*, and a couple morning shows. People always think, "Oh, you guys must just sit in front of Fox all the time," and it's not true. You see something and think, "Hey, I should bring this upstairs to the meeting."

ELLIOTT KALAN

I noticed that CNN went to the trouble to fact-check an *SNL* piece. And then Jon Kyl, the Arizona senator, was on CNN and said something wrong, and the reporter goes, "Well, we'll have to leave it there." So we looked for clips, and CNN did this routinely—they didn't fact-check their own guests, they just said, "We'll have to leave it there."

If you look at the entire show over Jon's run, and how it evolved, everything it did, from going after CNN to going after the Obama Administration, yes, we were against war and for good things. But the larger theme was truth and not abdicating responsibility for the words you use. And we did a segment about "CNN: Nobody leaves more things there."

RAMIN HEDAYATI

I produced it. I think Jon's joke was, "Don't leave it there. There is a terrible place to leave it! You're just starting to get into some substance! You have twenty-four hours. Hash it out! There's nowhere to go. There's nothing else to do."

What was cool was that when we would find a trend or some kind of contradiction, that was a victory. Now when something crazy happens on CNN, there are five blogs that flag it. Back then, it was either us or no one.

ANDERSON COOPER, journalist, CNN

I don't have any specific examples of stuff where I thought *The Daily Show* was unfair. There's definitely times I felt like CNN came under greater scrutiny than a lot of other folks who are out there. But criticism can be a healthy thing, and I think it's good to have someone mock you with some regularity. I can't tell you how many times I would be in a newsroom and I would see something on the air and then think, "Okay, well, that's going to be on *The Daily Show* tonight," like when I was interviewing Louie Gohmert and he just starts yelling at me.

I think Jon was able to get at some truths mainstream outlets don't. And I was envious of *The Daily Show*'s ability to find old videos and mine old statements where politicians contradict their current positions.

I also appreciated, during the Egyptian revolution, when I got punched around a bit, Jon played the video of the attack and said something very funny about, "If they harm one hair on his head..." It was not a great time where I was—I was hiding out in the hotel in Cairo—and someone texted it to me and made me laugh. It was a nice moment.

The Daily Show's *second-floor tape library was now deep with cross-referenced footage, and the show's graphics and editing software now allowed a five-minute segment to rapidly cut between multiple clips and over-the-shoulders. The process was often hectic, and depended on the talents of dozens of staffers, but Stewart kept close watch on all the moving parts.*

JOHN OLIVER

Jon's saying is, "If you take your foot off the throat of the show for a second, it will just get up and walk away." And that is true. Like, if you lose focus early in the morning, that lost focus will come back to bite you hard in a few hours, and by that point, the show may be irrecoverable, just because you weren't focused enough at nine in the morning.

We end up sounding evangelical in a certain way, talking about "the *Daily Show* process." You sound like you are trying to sell Scientology equipment. But Jon taught people to do a version of their job that the whole machine needs.

LAUREN SARVER MEANS, *from intern to writer, 2003–*

There was also a great evolution to the writing process, because when I first started working at the show as Ben Karlin's assistant in 2005, the writers would have their morning meeting and watch the clips. They'd write a pass of jokes without really a story line, just loose jokes off of sound bites. Turn them in. There would be a joke pick, and then D.J., the head writer at the time, would assemble them into a headline. There was very little room for collaboration with studio production. And as time went on, Jon started shaping studio production to be a huge generator of content, and ideas, and jokes for the show, but he'd want the writers to shape a story line. He wouldn't just want a page of jokes. He wanted them to tell a story, too.

The writers could have their hands on something and have ownership of it a lot more than just handing in your jokes and being done with it.

DANIEL RADOSH, *writer, 2009–*

So much of the flow of the day, for me, is just those kind of small, weird moments that you probably get at any office, but just the more extreme version of them in an office of comedy people. We would always end meetings with watching YouTube videos. Jason Ross would be like, "Okay, well, I found this video of a hunter and his girlfriend having sex on top of the body of a dead bear." We'd watch and then we'd say, "Okay, now, let's get back to writing!"

After the morning meeting you had a really tight deadline, an hour and fifteen minutes to turn in a script, often out of nothing. It was the most stressful part of the day for me. But I learned, early on, that it was not that important to Jon that the first draft script be perfect, because he would figure out how he wanted to say it, and it didn't matter, at all, even if I had the perfect way of saying it. Jon was going to say it the way he wanted to.

JUDD APATOW

When you're in charge and have the final say, you're constantly rejecting people's ideas, all day long, and it's tough to do that in a way that keeps people really encouraged and positive. When I was executive producer at *The Ben Stiller Show*, I used to sit in my office reading management books trying to understand where the dynamic was going wrong. Jon, at *The Daily Show*, set up the exchange of ideas so people felt supported and believed in enough that they could really knock things around productively.

JON STEWART

Garry Shandling taught me about intention. Intention is a really big thing at *The Daily Show.* We always want to know where's the intention, and now, let's find a path to that intention.

A lot of my day is finding the writers enough time to bring what's great about their writing to the process. You sort of come in and you go, "Here are my notes," and then you leave. The meetings with me did not last long, but hopefully they were edifying. Because I know at four o'clock, I'm going to need to go down there, rehearse the show, drink two espressos, take a handful of chocolate, and pace, and get it to as refined a place as it can be.

In early April 2007, Stewart made a major cosmetic refinement: The Daily Show *set that had been installed less than two years earlier was completely overhauled. "The old set, a lot of people had written in and said, the old set, oh, uh—sucked," Stewart said, smiling happily from in front of a warm blue world map, with a flashy news zipper and a spinning globe blinking overhead. "And as it turned out, you were right. So our experiment in postmodern, neorealist, Waiting-for-Godot-fake-news-show shit is over." The only design mistake was that the new set included the giant head of Brian Williams.*

The guest chair on the retooled set got a workout from presidential contenders. Senator Barack Obama's first in-studio conversation with Stewart wasn't terribly memorable, though his exit stuck with one Daily Show *segment producer.*

ELLIOTT KALAN

There was a line of people waiting to shake Obama's hand as he left, and when he got to me, I was eating a fun-size bag of Doritos and my hands were covered with orange crap. And I said, "Oh, I'm sorry, I have Dorito dust all over my hands." Obama very quickly said, "Well, how about one of these?" and he put his hand into a fist and we fist-bumped instead.

No, we did not blow it up. If he had played that, I think I would've lost a little respect for him: "All right, that's too far. We don't have that kind of relationship, Mr. Senator."

John McCain's April 2007 visit, however, was stormy. Three weeks earlier McCain, as part of a congressional delegation inspecting the progress of the troop surge in Iraq, had visited a market in Baghdad. Mike Pence, then a congressman, described the scene as being as safe as "a normal outdoor market in Indiana in the summertime"—while military helicopters hovered overhead and a hundred American soldiers in Humvees secured the perimeter. McCain, preparing another bid for the Republican presidential nomination, then made his eighth and most contentious visit to the Daily Show *studio, attempting to defend President Bush's floundering Iraq surge.*

SENATOR JOHN McCAIN

Jon and I had gotten along very well for many years, and then I went on one night and basically he just launched on Iraq and didn't let me respond.

> **Jon Stewart:** I'm just gonna walk through the talking points, and you tell me why they're right. "If we don't fight and defeat Al Qaeda in Iraq, they will follow us home."
>
> **Senator John McCain:** Sure.
>
> **Jon Stewart:** Now my position is—
>
> **Senator McCain:** Why don't you read what [Abu Musab al-] Zarqawi said and what bin Laden said. Go online, go on the Internet, they'll tell you that. I'm not saying it, they're saying it. Then I can refer you to their statements. Their statements.
>
> **Jon Stewart:** But also, their strategy is to trap America in a war that will bleed them of treasure and lives. That's also their statement, so you can go both ways on that. But my point is, Al Qaeda—
>
> **Senator McCain:** I know one way to go, and that is Al Qaeda has declared their dedication to the destruction of everything we care for and believe in. I know that for a fact. Do you know that for a fact?
>
> **Jon Stewart:** Whether we're in Iraq—I do know it for a fact.
>
> **Senator McCain:** Good. That's the first time we've agreed— thank you!
>
> **Jon Stewart:** That's not true! Here's the thing that I'm trying to say. When [the Bush Administration] attacks people who disagree with their policy, they attack them in that they don't understand that there's a real threat out there. The American people, or at least the ones that I get on the subway with, they know there's a real threat out there. They feel like Iraq lessened our ability to fight that threat.

Senator McCain: The war was terribly mismanaged. It was terribly mismanaged. We are where we are now. And the question is, can we give this strategy a chance? A chance to succeed with a great general.

Jon Stewart: If the architects that built a house without any doors or windows don't admit that that's the house they built, and continue to say, "No it's your fault for not being able to see into it," then I don't understand how we're supposed to move forward!

SENATOR JOHN McCAIN

I have debates with people every day on the issue of national security policy, but I just feel that it's appropriate for me to listen to their point of view. I just didn't think it was fair, that interview. I know Jon felt very strongly about Iraq, and I felt very strongly about it. One of my sons, a young marine, was fighting over there at the time.

JON STEWART

I remember the moment in that interview when I realized it was over between me and McCain. We were arguing about the war and he wasn't looking at me, he was looking here. [*points to middle of forehead*] And I realized, "Oh...so this conversation has ended and it's never going to pick up again."

SENATOR JOHN McCAIN

That interview obviously had a chilling effect on our relationship.

JON STEWART

It was a breaking point of his ability to tolerate me and of our ability to pretend that he hadn't been one of the architects and promoters of a grand catastrophe.

SENATOR JOHN McCAIN

After the terrorist attacks in Paris and California in 2015, yeah, I feel vindicated on what I said to Jon about why we needed to fight in Iraq. But I wish I wasn't. Lindsey Graham and I were over in Baghdad three weekends ago, and I can tell you the dominant influence right now in Baghdad is Iran, and that's not good. It's not good.

JON STEWART

I was disappointed in him. Fairly or unfairly, I felt that McCain was ignoring a reality for a political purpose. That interview was at the height of the anger over the mess that we had gotten ourselves into in Iraq, the cost that the country had paid, the cost that the Iraqis had paid. It was hard for me to see a guy who I respected for his ability to occasionally speak hard truths sit there and, in the parlance of that great truth teller Judge Judy, pee on my leg and tell me it was rain.

Perhaps I'm giving him more credit than he deserves, or believing something about him that is maybe not the case, but if McCain had not made political calculations in the way that he did with the war, I think he would have ended up in a better place in the 2008 election.

JOSH LIEB

People give Jon shit and claim he breeds cynicism. He's the opposite of cynical. He really cares. And people who watch his show care about politics. That's why you watch it, and that's why you're not watching a Yogi Bear cartoon.

And Jon created the least cynical place I've ever worked. There was a note in the *Daily Show* staff kitchen, something like, "Your mother doesn't work here…." And any other place I'd worked I would have written, "Fuck you." I've worked in some pretty rough little comedy places.

And I realized when I looked at this piece of paper it was dusty, and weathered, and barely hanging in there. It had been up there for a long time, and that nobody had written any graffiti on it, and that this was a nice place, and that I didn't need to be the asshole who came in and was immediately defacing things. I did deface some other things later. But *The Daily Show* was a very nice place. Which is part of why the writers strike was so painful.

9

Not *The Daily Show*

The August 2006 skirmishing over the Daily Show *writers joining the Writers Guild turned out to be minor compared to the hostilities during the winter of 2007–2008.* The Daily Show *was really a bit player in the issues and forces driving the strike: how television and movie writers should be paid for content distributed through new technologies, including DVDs and the Internet. (In one side battle, YouTube, whose creation had been propelled in part by the popularity of video clips of Stewart's* Crossfire *appearance, was fighting what would become a seven-year court war against Viacom,* The Daily Show's *corporate parent, over copyright infringement.)*

Twelve thousand Writers Guild members went on strike nationally. Yet the three-month walkout became a disproportionately emotional test at The Daily Show*—because of the business and political issues involved, but largely because of the personal bonds that existed between Stewart and the show's staff.*

STEVE BODOW

It was tense. All one hundred people in the building had always been working together, and now this was something where this group, the writers, is separate. It was unavoidable, and people intellectually knew that, but emotionally it's difficult. I was the fairly new head writer at the time, and that sucked.

JON STEWART

The strike, that felt like the worst time at the show. Definitely the low point of the whole thing.

I suddenly had ninety people, the staff that wasn't writers—and in a lot of ways were as vital to the show as the writers—that had nothing to do with

Staff writers J.R. Havlan and David Javerbaum with head writer Ben Karlin, "covering" *The Daily Show*'s first convention, the Republican National Convention, in Philadelphia, 2000. (Photo courtesy of Eric Drysdale)

Steve Carell sings, 2002. Karaoke nights continue to be a staple of the *Daily Show*'s off-camera staff culture. (Photo courtesy of Jen Flanz)

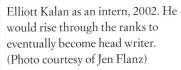

ELLIOTT KALAN

Elliott Kalan as an intern, 2002. He would rise through the ranks to eventually become head writer. (Photo courtesy of Jen Flanz)

ADAM LOWITT

Adam Lowitt as an intern in *The Daily Show*'s video clip department, 2002, when assembling the montages that became a *Daily Show* signature could take weeks. (Photo courtesy of Jen Flanz)

Rory Albanese and Lewis Black on a road trip to Myrtle Beach, South Carolina, 2003 or 2004. Black became Albanese's standup comedy mentor. (Photo courtesy of Jen Flanz)

Jon Stewart, field producer Jim Margolis, and Steve Carell at a *Daily Show* Emmys party, 2002. (Photo courtesy of Eric Drysdale)

Sound engineer Tim Lester and *Daily Show* co-creator Madeleine Smithberg, during the fateful 2002 midterms trip to Washington, D.C.. (Photo courtesy of Jen Flanz)

Director Chuck O'Neil, flanked by assistant directors Paul Pennolino and Andres Allen, at the Democratic National Convention in Boston, 2004. O'Neil and Pennolino left traditional TV journalism jobs at ABC to give *The Daily Show* a "newsier" look. Allen went on to become director of Larry Wilmore's *Nightly Show*. (Photo courtesy of Eric Drysdale)

Samantha Bee, Rob Corddry, and Ed Helms, in *The Daily Show* dressing room at the Democratic National Convention in Boston, 2004. (Photo courtesy of Eric Drysdale)

Executive producer Ben Karlin and head writer David Javerbaum at the producers' desk during the Democratic National Convention in Boston, 2004. (Photo courtesy of Kira Klang Hopf)

Writer Steve Bodow in front of a display at the 2004 Democratic National Convention in Boston featuring photos of soon-to-be-presidential nominee John Kerry and John Lennon. (Photo courtesy of Eric Drysdale)

A *Daily Show* poster at JFK Airport, welcoming Republican National Convention delegates to New York, 2004. (Photo courtesy of Kira Klang Hopf)

Writer Jo Miller and executive producer Rory Albanese backstage during the 2012 Democratic National Convention in Charlotte, North Carolina. (Photo courtesy of Jill Katz)

Beth Shorr—Stewart's assistant, the show's music and talent booker, and an ace crocheter—with Rob Corddry. (Photo courtesy of Jen Flanz)

Rob Corddry, Jon Stewart, Ed Helms, and Samantha Bee celebrate backstage after *The Daily Show*'s 2005 Emmys win. (Photo courtesy of Jen Flanz)

The infamous smoke-filled sushi boat is served at dinner the night before Jon Stewart hosted the 2008 Oscars. Clockwise: Stewart, J.R. Havlan, Kevin Bleyer, Rich Blomquist, Sam Means, Steve Bodow, David Javerbaum, Jason Ross, Rachel Axler, Rob Kutner. (Photo courtesy of J.R. Havlan)

Jon Stewart backstage, dressed in a fat suit for a bit about how much he'd eaten at the Jersey Shore during summer vacation and the supposed "filter" used to make NBC's Brian Williams look good, 2009. (Photo courtesy of Jody Morlock)

John Oliver and Wya[
Cenac with puppets c
themselves for a 2012
"This Week with Ge[
Snuffleupagus," abou
conservatives calling
PBS budget cuts.
(Photo courtesy of Jo[
Morlock)

Correspondent Michael Che
backstage with former president
Bill Clinton, a ten-time *Daily
Show* guest, in September 2014.
(Photo courtesy of Travon Free)

Stephen Colbert in Tennessee, after shooting his final *Daily Show* field piece, an unpleasant encounter with former congressman and *Dukes of Hazzard* star Ben "Cooter" Jones, 2005. (Photo courtesy of Jim Margolis)

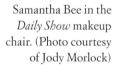

Samantha Bee in the *Daily Show* makeup chair. (Photo courtesy of Jody Morlock)

John Oliver in the *Daily Show* makeup chair. (Photo courtesy of Jody Morlock)

Jordan Klepper, dressed to arrest. (Photo courtesy of Jody Morlock)

Sister Jessica Williams, dressed to shame congressmen who'd voted against veterans' benefits, 2014. (Photo courtesy of Jody Morlock)

Former contributor Larry Wilmore and former correspondent Olivia Munn at the party following Stewart's final show, 2015. (Photo courtesy of Jody Morlock)

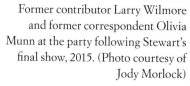

this fight and that could be out of work. Those people were really worried about their livelihoods as well, and I'm responsible for them.

We got to a point where Comedy Central stopped paying the nonwriting staff, and I went to Conan's office, and all the late-night hosts got together. The five families got together, and we all talked about pulling the shows. The other guys—Kimmel, Leno, Stephen—we talked to on the phone. Letterman was the linchpin. When he said he would do it, that was it. We all went off the air.

The Daily Show *went dark after its November 1, 2007, episode. Several months earlier, Stewart had agreed to follow up the best-selling* America *with* Earth (The Book). *Work on the new volume had barely begun, but the timing of the book deal turned out to be fortuitous.*

JOSH LIEB

I refused to take any producer credit during the strike. I went on strike because I'm in the Writers Guild and I think everything you do as a producer is writing. I wasn't happy to go on strike. I had to fucking break my lease. I had to move my family down to goddamned South fucking Carolina. I had a new baby.

Jon decided to give the writers their advances on *Earth (The Book)* the day we went on strike. We all went into the office of his manager and got our checks for our advances, which we all needed. I mean, put this in your fucking book. I needed that fucking money and there was no reason for Jon to give it to us then. Jon hadn't been given his money then, from the publisher, but Jon gave us our advances—out of his pocket, to keep us alive during the strike. The strike, certainly on our show, was at least more comfortable because Jon Stewart went out of pocket for hundreds of thousands of dollars to pay us our advances on this goddamned book that was a year away from being done.

STEVE BODOW

Jon and I were in communication. We knew that for whatever resentment there might have been, he was also really actually working on our behalf to resolve this thing, at least for *The Daily Show*, and so we weren't mad at him. We weren't mad at the people who worked in the building, certainly.

JOSH LIEB

Jon was put in an impossible position. We were on strike for a while and the crew and everybody was still getting paid. At some point, the network goes, "Okay. We're not going to pay the crew," and Jon is very much the guy that people think he is. It's going to bother him if Charlie the cameraman isn't getting a paycheck because, by the way, little Ivy League–educated writer isn't happy with his residuals.

CRAIG SPINNEY

I already respected the man, but this deepened it. All of us on the crew were home for two months and we still got paid. I don't know how Jon did it. I assume it was out of his pocket.

JON STEWART

It was a wrenching decision to go back on the air. I was miserable. But I couldn't keep paying them, you know? I paid as much as I could and I'd given the writers money as well, but there's only so much you can do.

David Letterman reached a deal with the union and went back on the air January 2. Conan O'Brien and Jay Leno came back that same night, but without their still-striking writers. Stewart's return on January 7, though, drew more controversy: How could a liberal icon break solidarity with the union strikers? In some ways it was a compliment, but one Stewart would have gladly done without.

When he went back on the air it was as the host of A Daily Show, *to further distance the bare-bones production from the real thing. The title change was hardly necessary. The only thing viewers needed to see was Stewart's doleful expression during the twenty-two writer-less episodes.*

What stayed hidden were the bitter feelings behind the scenes. The strike divided friends—not over the need to pay the writers fairly, but on whether their loyalties lay with Stewart, the show, or the cause, and over the best means to achieve an equitable end. Javerbaum and Lieb, for instance, friends since college, had both built their careers as writers, and were members of the Guild, but they were now producers at The Daily Show. *Javerbaum worked during the strike; Lieb didn't.*

DAVID JAVERBAUM

As a writer, I was technically on strike, but as a producer, I had to be there, at the show.

JOSH LIEB

If your union goes on strike, I don't care if you're Mahatma fucking Gandhi and it's the Union of United Hitlers of America, you go on strike. That's how unions work.

To everyone's relief, a settlement seemed to have been reached at the end of December. Only to have the rancor be heightened and extended.

STEVE BODOW

Letterman made a deal with the union and went back before everybody else did. Jon was able to get Viacom to agree to the same terms. Obviously, the *Daily Show* writers were fine with it. Jon worked hard on that, and he stuck his neck out—and the Guild wouldn't go for it. Letterman owned his show. Whereas Comedy Central owned *The Daily Show*. So, the Guild had a legal reason for being willing to do a carve-out with Letterman, a one-off show, but not with one of the main signatory companies, Comedy Central.

JON STEWART

That was an awful time, and I don't like being the bad guy, and I felt like the bad guy. I felt the writer staff looked at me like the bad guy, and that hurt a lot because I didn't feel like it was fair. I felt like I had really worked very hard to protect their interests and also protect the interests of the other people that worked on the show, and had done it and had lost not because Comedy Central was being ridiculous, but because the Guild decided for some reason to say no.

ROB KUTNER

I don't think it was about money for Jon. I think it was about control. The same creative instinct that drives him to go over every word in the script and redo it if necessary is why he wanted to have complete control of how the show works. He wanted to have *The Daily Show* be his thing from top to bottom. And also he felt that he was really taking care of everybody, that he was sort of the father figure.

JOSH LIEB

I think that's a false analysis. Jon is a naturally benevolent person, and it bothered Jon to be told you're not being fair to the writers.

STEVE BODOW

I remember walking up away from a picket event of some kind with Jason Ross and saying to him, "I don't know what it's going to be, but when we get back after this is settled, there's no way that things are going to be the same."

JON STEWART

I think some of the writers never forgave me. I think some of the staff never forgave the writers.

After the strike, there was a meeting at Busboy, my production company, with the writers and the producers to clear the air. And it took some clearing. You know, people were upset. Like, it was no *bueno*. Feelings were really raw. Honestly, I think we all felt betrayed by each other in a sort of a profound way. Where unfortunately everybody thought they were doing the right thing.

I gave them all money, the writers. And not one of them sent me even an acknowledgment. I remember when that came up in the meeting after the strike was settled. I was like, "Not even a word?" and one of the guys going, "Well, you know, we don't have your e-mail." *All right.*

JOSH LIEB

That was a rough meeting, and then we all went out and got drunk.

J. R. HAVLAN

The writers strike had a big effect on the show, beyond the personal stuff. A lot of the shows during the strike came through production. There was a lot more looking for a certain videotape, just to kind of bolster the show. Before the strike, we didn't lean on the video to drive the content. The content would drive the video. During the strike, the video started to drive the content because there supposedly was no written content.

When the writers came back, it seemed as if the producers thought, "This is working very well, actually. I like the way we're attacking the stories now." More power had been given to the production wing. Maybe out of some spite for the writers strike. But also, if you can just step away from how something affects you personally, you can say, "That's a pretty good idea."

STEVE BODOW

Two weeks after the strike ended, Jon was hosting the 2008 Oscars. He took the whole writing staff to LA. It was a pretty crazy trip, and just what we needed.

Stewart had hosted the Oscars once before, in 2006. That year he delivered a bunch of funny moments that poked at the self-seriousness of the awards ceremony. There was a written-on-the-spot joke about the winners of best song ("For those of you who are keeping score at home, I just want to make something very clear: Martin Scorsese, zero Oscars. Three 6 Mafia, one") and a laboriously preprepared montage of gay-ish cowboy clips from classic westerns like John Wayne's Red River *that played off the best picture nomination for* Brokeback Mountain. *Reviewers were not kind, however.* MEMO TO JON STEWART: KEEP YOUR "DAILY" JOB, *read the* Washington Post *headline. "It goes to prove that there's still a big, big difference between basic cable and big-time network television after all," critic Tom Shales wrote.*

So inside The Daily Show, *there was considerable ambivalence when Stewart was offered the 2008 job.*

DAVID JAVERBAUM

I remember thinking, "We probably shouldn't be doing this, because if your gig is deflating bullshit, then hosting the Oscars is inherently problematic."

Yeah, it was weird, the Oscars trips. It's always weird when talented writers are exposed to natural light. It's not a healthy environment for comedy writers. Comedy writers should grow hydroponically.

STEVE BODOW

The second time, in 2008, Jon went in with the attitude, "Let's do the show we want to. We hope they like it, but maybe we don't care if they like it."

RORY ALBANESE

That was the year with the saddest group of movies nominated for best picture. What was the oil one? "My Milkshake"? The Daniel Day-Lewis one. And it was *No Country for Old Men*. Every movie was dark and sad and dark and sad.

J. R. HAVLAN

We had written up a bit for Javier Bardem to open the show, as that character from *No Country*.

RORY ALBANESE

He agreed to do this whole bit with us, with Jon and him and the cow gun. They would do the coin flip and Jon would say, "And so I get to host the Oscars?" This was a big thing for us, and Bardem bailed on it.

J. R. HAVLAN

It was very last-minute, so we had to scramble. And as part of a sincere apology they sent a fruit basket. It was more like an edible arrangement. An edible arrangement is never *not* a joke. If you send an edible arrangement and it's not a joke, you should really up your game when it comes to gift giving or apologies.

RORY ALBANESE

We come into the writers' room one day and it looks like someone went to Associated and there's like nine pieces of cheese and it's sweaty and it's got toothpicks in it, and there's a card, "I'm so sorry I couldn't do the bit. Javier Bardem." Really cool, Javier. So that became a running gag the whole week.

During the Oscars broadcast, Stewart again landed some good lines ("Normally, when you see a black man or woman president, an asteroid is about to hit the Statue of Liberty"). Yet after the searing writers strike, the Oscars show itself became secondary to the chance it provided to repair relationships inside The Daily Show *and start fresh on "Indecision 2008."*

JON STEWART

On that Oscars trip, it's the Japanese dinner that's the classic story.

RORY ALBANESE

Oh, the sushi place. Well, Steve Bodow, who's a total foodie kind of guy—

STEVE BODOW

Right. So . . . it's not my fault. We're out at the Oscars. The night before the actual event, Jon decides he wants to take everybody out to dinner, which was great. We'd been working together real hard. It was going to be the first time when we'd all been out, since the strike, in any sort of celebratory way.

Jon knew that I was restaurant guy, and so he came to me and he said, "Where do you think we should go?" I was like, "What do you feel like eating?" And he said, "I don't know, maybe sushi. That's supposed to be good in LA, right?" I said, "Yeah, I think it is." And I had a friend who was an editor at *Bon Appétit* out there.

I think the restaurant was on Melrose. We get there, it's incredibly over-chic LA. It's all white leather banquettes, and rococo lighting, and it's a bunch of comedy writers from New York, and Jon in particular is very down-home, in his T-shirt and khakis and boots. We're all dressed like the writer slobs that we are.

DAVID JAVERBAUM

Even by comedy writer standards, Jon dressed disgustingly.

JEN FLANZ

Jon really likes to be comfortable. For his fiftieth birthday, we got him the same exact outfit that he wears every day. Khakis, gray T-shirt, and the boots, the whole thing. I call it his cartoon character outfit, because in a cartoon, the character wears the same thing every single day.

STEVE BODOW

The restaurant starts bringing food out, and it is the most haute silly parody of what fancy restaurant food could be, with portions all the size of thimbles, sushi and sashimi cut up into little tiny pieces, weird little vegetable stuffers. It's course, after course, after course.

JON STEWART

We were eating, like, garnishes.

RORY ALBANESE

Jon's style is to go to a hoagie place and eat a hero and go home. I used to have arguments with Jon about yellow mustard. Like, "How do you eat French's mustard?" He's like, "It's the best mustard!" and we go, "It's not even mustard! It's a yellow liquid! Mustard has to have grain in it. You're a Jew! Eat deli mustard!"

JON STEWART

It was like a show—a fish show. They bring out sea urchin delivered on a sloped plate. Here's how you eat it: You go down the slide with your fingers, grab the urchin, flip it twice, and just lick it.

STEVE BODOW

The capper is when the waiters bring, for everybody at once, these glass domes with smoke in them. You see the smoke swirling around, and maybe in there, somewhere, at the bottom, is a little bit of food. Maybe. And then the waiters all coordinate and they lift everyone's dome at the same time... it's tuna sashimi that has been smoking in hickory hay or something like that. You're supposed to inhale the smoke and then eat the sushi.

The room fills with all this smoke. Everyone's coughing and trying to find the little filaments of food that are in there.

JON STEWART

It really looked like memorabilia from a fire more than it did anything else. We laughed our balls off at that place.

J. R. HAVLAN

Everybody in our car was still hungry after the Japanese meal, so we went to an In-N-Out Burger drive-thru on our way back to the hotel.

STEVE BODOW

I wasn't in the In-N-Out car. I was too full of hay-smoked designer sushi and shame.

RORY ALBANESE

After the strike people were mad at Jon, people were mad at me probably, the producers were mad at the writers, the writers were mad at the producers. And that trip, it felt like all it took was Jon lifting that glass off the smoke, and we're laughing, and we're all good now, right?

Maybe not completely. But good timing once again came to The Daily Show's *aid.*

10

Indecision 2008—Clusterf@#k to the White House

The Daily Show *had come a long way from begging its way onto McCain's bus in 1999. Now an ad blared that Stewart had assembled "the best campaign team in the universe ever," headquartered it in "the* Daily Show *news-scraper: 117 stories, 73 situation rooms, 26 news tickers," and promised to deliver "you all the news stories—first...before it's even true."*

It was a joke, mocking the show's stature, and it wasn't. In 2008 the combination of talent, on and off camera; the gravity of the issues facing the country (a giant recession on top of the worsening Iraq morass); and the vivid cast of candidates (Barack Obama! Hillary Clinton! Dennis Kucinich! John McCain! Alan Keyes! Ron Paul! And introducing...Sarah Palin!) came together to produce twelve months of consistently extraordinary shows.

RORY ALBANESE

The hype that had been building about *The Daily Show*'s influence, *The Daily Show* being where young people get their news—I think that's why in 2008 we went with, "The Best Fucking News Team Ever" as the slogan. Let's stop pretending that no one watches the show, let's stop pretending that we can't do some great shit, and let's just own it. It was actually Jon saying, "Let's just go hard in the other way." Like, fuck CNN, fuck Fox, fuck MSNBC. We've got a skyscraper! We've got a news rocket! We have Riggle firing a machine gun!

JASON ROSS

Jon was really adamant about keeping up with the pace of the media that we were making fun of. So instead of being satisfied by sticking with some *Not Necessarily the News*–type format, he wanted to make sure that our graphics were just as good as Fox's graphics. We had planes flying. Anything on the screen could explode at any minute.

JOSH LIEB

There had been so much talk that when the Bush era ends that Jon's relevance is going to end, which was simply not true. We all knew that our job wasn't to make fun of one political party or a political person.

Indeed, after eight years of flaying Bush, Stewart and the staff relished the chance to defy expectations and challenge both sides. But even though most of the major candidates saw The Daily Show *as a key platform to sell themselves, Stewart and staff didn't overestimate the show's significance.*

RORY ALBANESE

Probably to me some of the most fun I ever had on the show was when we went against people's expectations. Because it was like, yeah, we're not just chumming the waters. Dick Cheney is like Darth Vader—we get it. Move on.

We went after Hillary in '08, during the primaries. The studio audience thinks Jon is our liberal guidepost through all things, and Jon would do a segment about what Hillary is doing wrong and the audience didn't know what to do. And there is a weird standup component to it. There's a Bill Hicks component to that where you're like, "Oh, you're going to leave? Then leave." And it feels kind of good sometimes to say stuff to people that they don't want to hear.

I'd go up to the desk to talk to Jon between acts, and we'd be like, "Man, these motherfuckers are so pissed. This is awesome!" We have a very left-wing audience and they'd be like, "This is not right. It's only funny when the jokes are about the guy we hate."

The problem is everyone thinks it's funny until it's something they care about. If you can't even look at yourself and laugh…It was really powerful for me to watch an audience deal with that, and who better to deliver that information than Jon Stewart? And after eight years of Bush, there was something very fun about going after the savior, going after Obama.

DAVID JAVERBAUM

You know, we had presidents on the show. We had all these different people. Didn't matter. We were always in the bubble and I think in a healthy way.

JASON REICH

The staff, we just wanted to go in and write jokes every day. It was trickier for Jon to constantly be asked, "Oh, do you think the show is important?" and having to do this song and dance about how we're just doing a dumb comedy show. Deep down Jon probably knew that the show was having an impact and was important in a cultural way, but that's a hard thing to speak to when you're the guy on camera.

JOSH LIEB

I don't know how much of what we did changed anybody's mind and I'm very leery of judging anything like that. But working with Jon, who had a voice in that conversation that year? No, it's exciting. You get spoiled in this business where words you say, words you write, get spoken to millions of people on a nightly basis, and repeated, and put on YouTube. So there's an echo chamber. But there are a lot of echo chambers out there.

Obama upset Clinton in the Iowa caucus, then Clinton rebounded by winning disputed primaries in Florida and Michigan. Super Tuesday tightened the race even more, just before Stewart and the writers headed out to the Oscars. On the Republican side, McCain had dispatched Mitt Romney, though Mike Huckabee hung around into the spring.

On June 3, Obama clinched the Democratic nomination. The Daily Show's *newest correspondent, Wyatt Cenac, made his debut that same night. The specific synchronicity was an accident. But the fact that* The Daily Show *hired its first black correspondent just as a major party was on its way to choosing its first black presidential nominee was not.*

JON STEWART

No, it wasn't coincidental, in the same way that Aasif's coming on board after 9/11 and Iraq wasn't coincidental. You are looking to mirror the issues that are at the core of the days' news. We started to realize that we didn't really have an ability to make fun of the Obama campaign, in the same way as me going to meet soldiers gave the show a greater ability to talk about the war. If your world does not include enough access to different people, and their world does not include enough access to you, you are speaking from ignorance. We didn't want to do that, and realized that we had been. So that was the impetus in hiring Wyatt. It was part of a process we weren't that good at—diversifying staff, changing patterns, finding new tributaries. The general thrust of the show was just trying to get it done every day, and the reforming of more macro processes took longer than it should have. That's me. I'll take the blame.

But even within that, I didn't realize the pressure it put on Wyatt. So even as we were growing and becoming more diverse, there were still blind spots.

Cenac came on as both a writer and a performer. Within days after arriving he had boarded a plane to Florida, where he bought a group of Jewish retirees the early bird special to explore whether race had anything to do with their opinions of Obama.

MILES KAHN, *field producer, 2006–2015*
I had pitched this to Jon, and it came from a very personal place because I'm Jewish and my grandparents live in Florida. It wasn't a story that I read somewhere. It was just like, I have a gut feeling that this is an issue: Obama is great, but I don't think he's going to get the old Jewish folks. And my grandfather's one of those guys who's not racist by any means, but just an old-school guy. I don't know if he has it in him to vote for a black guy.

So we got all these old Jews together, my grandma's friends, at the 3 G's Deli in Delray Beach. We offered them a free dinner. It was Wyatt's first field piece, and he didn't have to do much at all. He pretty much just sat at the table and let the Jews fight each other for a couple of hours on camera. We called the segment "Baruch Obama."

> **Wyatt Cenac:** [*seated at center of table, behind enormous corned beef sandwich*] I was sent down to talk about this election and see what we could do to bridge the gap between Jews and blacks—
> **Art:** I didn't know we had a problem between Jews and blacks!
> **Silvia:** A lot of Jewish white people here will not vote for a black man.

Art: Well, it's ridiculous.

Evelyn: Wyatt, I want to tell you something. All of a sudden there is Barack Hussein Obama—

Al: His first name is Barack! It's a Hebrew name!

Evelyn: *Hussein* is a Hebrew name?

Art: What is it relevant whether Obama's middle name is Hussein or Yankel? I couldn't care less!

Race and religion would prove to be rich veins of material during the 2008 campaign, with deft segments on everything from Reverend Jeremiah Wright to "terrorist fist jabs." The Daily Show was underequipped to tackle gender issues, however, even with Samantha Bee doing brilliant and prodigious work. New contributor Kristen Schaal, who made her debut in March 2008, came out of the New York–Los Angeles alternative comedy scene that prized off-kilter storytelling as much as punch lines, and her spacy delivery disguised an acute intelligence.

KRISTEN SCHAAL, *contributor, 2008–*

I'd auditioned twice to be a correspondent, but didn't make it past submitting a videotape. Then in 2008 I did a standup piece at this really cool show called Moonwork, on the Lower East Side. It was about Hillary Clinton running for the Democratic nomination, and she was steadily losing against Obama, and I was getting very frustrated because I was just so excited that she might win, and I felt if Hillary didn't win just the way things were going in our world, we probably wouldn't get another female president for, like, two hundred years. And Rich Blomquist, who I'd started dating, was writing for *The Daily Show.* Rich pitched it to Jon, who really liked it, and that became my first chat. I sort of did sleep my way in.

McCain, still irritated by his Iraq War argument with Stewart, made one appearance as a guest during the Republican primaries. But he turned down invitations after that, so The Daily Show *came up with an ornery felt stand-in senator.*

SENATOR JOHN McCAIN

I would've certainly gone back on his show after 2008. But the McCain puppet they created—that was so great.

CINDY McCAIN

Yeah, the puppet. I thought it was hysterical. It's the kind of joke that we enjoy. The puppet looked like John, too. They were making jokes about him, but in some ways you take it as flattery, that they would go to the trouble of making a McCain puppet.

But the time the show used a video of me to criticize John over his opposition to gays in the military? It was not fair and it was very uncomfortable, but that's also the nature of the beast. We're in public life, and so that comes with it, I guess. Of course I didn't like some of the things that Jon Stewart said, but Jon Stewart is very talented. I don't have to agree with everybody, but you know I enjoy him. Occasionally, yes, I'd like to throw my shoe at the television.

The 2008 campaign occupied much of The Daily Show's *attention, but Stewart didn't forget about the guy who was still in the White House. The show kept up its (ultimately unsuccessful) eight-year quest to persuade Bush himself to appear as a guest. In the meantime Stewart grilled several of the president's top advisors—and unveiled a furry red creature as a clever way to address one of the war on terror's most troubling excesses.*

DAVID JAVERBAUM

The Bush presidency had been a great thing for us in terms of building our brand awareness. Yeah. Honestly, if Al Gore had been elected president, who knows what our show would've done.

His final year in office, one character I came up with that I was very proud of is Gitmo. That was me. I just thought it sounded funny. Just the word "Gitmo." The word "Gitmo" sounds like "Elmo." That's all that it was. So I said, "We'll just have a character called Gitmo." It was just a pun. It's ridiculous. Everyone loves puns. Some people don't like the hacky puns. Some people like antipuns. But they're still puns.

Sesame Street gave us a puppet for that.

JEN FLANZ

They did not. He doesn't know what he's talking about. I made the puppet. I love D.J., but he didn't deal with making any of that stuff happen, which is hilarious. He'd just tell me, "We want this," and I'd be like, "Okay," and it shows up. We bought an Elmo at Toys"R"Us or something, we bought a beard, and we put a beard on it. If I didn't glue it myself, then Elise or Justin did it. We were a ragtag bunch. Jon would always say, "Don't make it look too good." I'm like, "Don't worry. We can't."

The junior high arts-and-crafts-class look of the prop served a larger purpose, too: Gitmo was a device that allowed The Daily Show *to express its agitation about torture without coming off as too strident.*

Jon Stewart: [*at anchor desk, with graphic reading* GUANTANAMO BAYWATCH *over his right shoulder*] Last week the Supreme Court ruled on a motion to let war on terror detainees held at Guantánamo Bay contest their imprisonment before a judge. It was a complicated ruling. Nuanced issues. I'm gonna hand this off to *Fox & Friends*.

Steve Doocy: [*in video clip, sitting on the* Fox & Friends *couch*] "So with the recent Supreme Court decision saying that the detainees down at Gitmo can wind up with habeas corpus, where they get legal rights and stuff like that—"

Jon Stewart: [*with off-the-shoulder graphic of important-looking musty book*] Legal rights and stuff. It's actually all been explained in Thomas Paine's famous, "A Treatise on the Rights of Man and Shit." So how is this decision playing among those most affected? For that we go live to Guantánamo Bay, Cuba, and our Senior Imprisoned Correspondent, Gitmo. [*split screen of tiny prison cell and red furry Muppet with bushy black beard*] You were just a cabdriver in Karachi when you were falsely accused by a reformer looking for reward money.

Gitmo: [*in squeaky voice and vaguely Arabic accent*] Yes. Snuff Al-Upagus will pay for this. He is brought to you by the letter *bullshit*!

Jon Stewart: Listen, Gitmo, wouldn't you want a chance to prove your innocence? Maybe go free?

Gitmo: Yes, yes. Gitmo go free. Gitmo go home, get back in taxi cab...fill it with C4, and drive it into east entrance of British embassy! [*bursts into squeaky ululations*]

Jon Stewart: Wait, Gitmo, you just said you weren't a terrorist!

Gitmo: When they caught Gitmo, Gitmo wasn't. But Gitmo is now!

*   *   *

Closing Guantánamo was one of the rare policy positions on which Obama and McCain agreed. Otherwise the general election matchup was full of policy contrasts and personal intrigue, pitting an iconoclastic Vietnam War hero against a charismatic young racial pioneer. So naturally The Daily Show *did everything possible to puncture sentimentality.*

JIM MARGOLIS

In August we were at Obama's acceptance speech at the DNC in Denver. Stu Miller and Oliver were doing a bit on the floor, and they got me to come with them.

JOHN OLIVER

Obama is speaking, and I'm pretty close to the front, crawling upon all fours down from the front to interview someone right near the podium. There's this older guy there, and I put the microphone in his face and ask him something, and I remember he put his hand on my shoulder and said, "Son, a lot of us have been waiting a long time for this moment. Please don't ruin it." I kind of... my heart shattered into a thousand pieces, and I started crawling, in defeat, back up the aisle, and all I could see was Smills [Stu Miller] and Margolis just saying, "Go back there, talk to him!" I go, "No, no, I will not do it. You have to leave me with one shred of humanity here!"

JIM MARGOLIS

I don't think either of us, Oliver and me, had ever felt worse. But Stu Miller was like, "No, no! We've got to ask all these questions!"

STU MILLER

It's an important historical moment not just for the people there but for the entire country. Fine. But it was a solid joke! And that was the only time we were going to get it! Oliver and Margolis refused to shoot it because they had some decency or something.

JIM MARGOLIS

None of that aired. But there was a segment on the convention floor where Oliver stands next to this great-looking woman. Maybe she was a delegate, I don't know. And John says something about Obama's speech being so moving and emotional. And then he leans over to kiss her. And she bolts. That was real.

JOHN OLIVER

All I remember after that is the cameraman saying, "What would you have done if she kissed you back?" I went, "That was never a problem. It was never going to happen. There was no world in which that was going to result in an uncomfortable, impromptu make-out session." If she had, it wouldn't have been in the piece. That's useless. What you need is the rejection, the humiliation. You need to feel the drop.

JOSH LIEB

He wanted to be rejected by her on camera for comedic effect. That to him is more of a sexual thrill. Getting a laugh is much more sexually thrilling to John Oliver than a kiss. I mean, he's a sick, sick man.

AASIF MANDVI

There were moments at the conventions, where we would realize the impact that the show was having, especially in the 2008 convention, when we were in Denver. I'd never experienced anything like this before. We got chased. By fans, by Democrats, which is worse than being chased by cops.

That same week, I was walking around with Oliver and Riggle and Jones. I'm the smallest guy. So there was Congressman [John] Murtha—big guy, eight feet tall, hands like fucking the Hulk, a Vietnam vet.

Oliver tells me, "Go up to Congressman Murtha and say to him, 'What does Congress hope to not accomplish in the following year?'" So I ran up to him, I stuck a microphone in his face and I said, "Congressman, can I ask you a question? What does Congress hope to not get accomplished in this upcoming year?" And he was pissed, like he was not even fucking playing. And I look around and Oliver, Riggle, and Jones are gone. They vaporized. I'm just standing there sweating. I thought Murtha was going to hit me.

The crazy thing about The Daily Show is that happens and your brain goes to two places: "Oh, shit, this is going to suck because this guy might fucking punch me right now." Then the other part of your brain goes, "If he punches me that's going to be awesome. I'm definitely getting on the show this week!"

*   *   *

Denver was the Democrats' show. But the Republicans succeeded in stealing some attention by announcing McCain's pick for vice president: Alaska governor Sarah Palin. The Daily Show would have plenty of fun with Palin's malapropisms and mangled syntax. What set the show apart, however, was that most of its jabs were aimed at the cynicism of McCain's choice, and at Palin's utter unpreparedness—notes that were struck right from the first Daily Show segment on Palin, hours after she was unveiled.

Jon Stewart: [*at DNC anchor desk*] The pick was a surprise, not least for Palin herself, who was asked about the job just a month ago.

Sarah Palin: [*in CNBC video clip*] "As for that VP talk all the time, I tell ya, I still can't answer that question until somebody answers for me—what is it exactly that the VP does every day?"

Jon Stewart: Oh, mostly you just sit around being prepared to become the most powerful person on earth.

Senior Female and Women's Issues Correspondent Samantha Bee joins us now with more on this stunning development. Obviously I know how moved you were by Senator Hillary Clinton's run for the presidency. How are you feeling now about this extraordinary moment?

Samantha Bee: [*sitting across desk from Stewart*] It's amazing, Jon. And as a proud vagina-American myself, I can tell you, I'll be voting for McCain in November.

Jon Stewart: That's it? You just vote for whoever has a—

Samantha Bee: A fun pouch.

Jon Stewart: Uh, the uh—

Samantha Bee: Love pita.

Jon Stewart: Right. But in many ways, Governor Palin is the ideological opposite of Senator Clinton.

Samantha Bee: Yes, but she's her gynecological twin. You see, the thing is, let me explain: They both have vaginas—

Jon Stewart: No, no, no, I understand. But Senator McCain is somebody who voted against equal pay for equal work—

Samantha Bee: [*her hands tracing circles in front of her chest*] Boobies!

Jon Stewart: I understand that. But both McCain and Palin believe *Roe v. Wade* should be overturned.

Samantha Bee: Ow, ow, ow, ow! Can you just stop overloading my lady brain? John McCain chose a woman who is almost completely unprepared for the job, and who disagrees with me on every core value I believe in. But I will be voting McCain in November, because he understands—women don't vote with the big head. They vote with the little hood.

Four days later The Daily Show *had shifted seven hundred miles east and north, to St. Paul, Minnesota, to catch the McCain and Palin act in person. The Republican convention was a clamorous event, from the crowd of protesters that engulfed* The Daily Show's *production trailer to the lightning bolt that struck a correspondent's love life to the ominous fatigue that was nagging a top producer.*

JOHN OLIVER

At the 2008 Republican convention, there was this one layer of the arena that we didn't have credentials for, and it's the only layer you wanted to shoot on because that's where all the top politicians and dignitaries were. So we found a back stairwell that we could get up, and sometimes we would hide our camera equipment with the catering equipment, because the caterers liked us. So, you've probably got a few hours until someone realizes you're not supposed to be here, or there will be a complaint from someone who you'd spoken to.

One day we were getting chased by security, we were about to get forcibly removed by them. I couldn't get arrested because I was on a visa, so I ran like a child who'd broken a window. Like a coward. Some military vets hid us in this room that they had to change in. One of them was this woman, Kate Norley.

JON STEWART

It takes a special woman to go, "Look at this frail, out of breath, scared, pasty man..."

JOHN OLIVER

Later I e-mailed her to say thank you, and also because she gave me her credential for the next day so we could shoot up there. I guess she was attracted to trouble. I guess that's the same instinct that drives you to join the army and go to war.

STU MILLER

That's a cute and romantic story. But we'd shot everything we needed, and I do remember distinctly making several trips to that floor with Oliver for not the clearest of reasons.

JOHN OLIVER

Then we spoke on the phone every day for months. Kate was working out of Walter Reed, in Washington, after doing tours in Iraq during the war as a medic. I didn't see her again until the next year. We got married in 2011.

But I don't recommend that as a dating technique. The RNC is the least romantic place on earth, that's for sure. The night I met Kate was the night of Sarah Palin's hockey-mom speech, and as a human being, I was at a pretty low ebb then.

JOSH LIEB

No, Sarah Palin did not seem like a gift. I remember when we were at the convention and she first came onstage, she was extremely impressive. We were all like, "Wow! Great choice, McCain. This is going to be an interesting race."

And the more she talked the worse she was, obviously, and the more her past came out. But every politician was a gift. Even if you were someone who Jon putatively agreed with politically—if you were Bill Clinton, you were a guy who got some intern to give him a blowjob. Everybody was worthy of making fun of.

In some ways, the ignorance was less troublesome than the hypocrisy. I thought Palin would be a terrible person to be vice president of the United States.

SENATOR JOHN McCAIN

I didn't see a lot of Jon's show in 2008, during the campaign. I was a little busy. But I was informed about what he was doing.

Oh, there was no doubt whose side he was on. Jon is not a raging liberal, but he's left of center, and a candidacy such as Barack Obama's was extremely attractive—hope and change, and on the heels of an economic collapse as well.

Listen, the one thing I have not only accepted, but understood well, and appreciated, is that Barack Obama was a candidate that really galvanized people—galvanized, to a large degree, Jon's base as well. So Jon was, I think, in tune with them.

One change in context that worked to The Daily Show's *advantage, if to the detriment of the citizenry, was the continuing convergence of cable and network news toward an info-opin-tainment muddle, with viewers choosing an ideological silo. The rise of the Internet only sped up that fragmentation. And it gave* The Daily Show's *hypocrisy-highlighting agenda even more relevance and credibility.*

DAVID JAVERBAUM

People would ask us, "Do you feel any moral obligation?" And journalistically, absolutely not. We tried to be fair, and just, and all those things for creative reasons, because creatively it's more challenging and more rewarding.

Creatively, it's more fulfilling to write jokes that are based on reality and are not cheap points and are not an endless series of "Bush is stupid, Clinton's horny" jokes. But it's not because it was any obligation to do it. We were on Comedy Central! Fox News is on Fox News. We do a better job of comedy than Fox News does with news. We lived up to our network's title better than Fox News does or CNN does.

That proficiency was on nearly nightly display when it came to dismantling Fox's tactics, particularly when it came to the "fair and balanced" network's efforts to prop up Palin. The Daily Show's *ability to find and match contradictory video clips was peaking.*

JIMMY DONN

At the 2008 Republican convention, our production offices were in some kind of music school in St. Paul. You'd sit with the writers late at night watching postconvention coverage, and we see Karl Rove talking about Sarah Palin's executive experience.

JUSTIN MELKMANN

The Republicans were trying to convince themselves that Sarah Palin was a viable candidate for vice president of the United States.

JIMMY DONN

We realize they're praising her for everything they'd criticized Obama for not being. And Jon would hang out, especially on the road at conventions, and he'd remember, "There's also an O'Reilly clip that fits." So we'd call back to the producers who were in New York to pull clips— "See what's out there from Dick Morris."

JUSTIN MELKMANN

Yeah, and you've got an army of PAs and interns who are putting transcripts into a database, so they're searching those and feeding us tape at the convention location.

JIMMY DONN

So by the next day we've got a great piece that really happened organically.

> **Jon Stewart:** [at anchor desk] The GOP's vice presidential nominee is earning rave reviews from at least one analyst with a head like a lump of unbaked bread dough.
>
> **Karl Rove:** [in Fox video clip] "She's a populist, she's an economic and a social conservative, she's a reformer. She's a former mayor of, I think, the second largest city in Alaska before she ran for governor."
>
> **Jon Stewart:** Karl Rove is impressed with her experience as mayor of a city with 9,000 people in it. I imagine he was equally impressed last month, when Tim Kaine, former mayor of Richmond, population 200,000, former lieutenant governor of Virginia, and now current Virginia governor, was on Barack Obama's VP short list.
>
> **Karl Rove:** [in Fox video clip from one month earlier] "He's been a governor for three years. He was mayor of the 105th largest city in America. And again, with all due respect to Richmond, Virginia, it's smaller than Chula Vista, California; Aurora, Colorado; Mesa or Gilbert, Arizona; North Las Vegas or Henderson, Nevada. So if he were to pick Governor Kaine, it would be an intensely political choice where he was saying, you know, 'I'm not really concerned with, Is this person ready to be the president of the United States?' "

Jon Stewart: Wow! Karl Rove is bitterly divided on this experience issue. Well, at least everyone can agree on the even more sensitive issue of Palin's pregnant teen daughter.

Bill O'Reilly: [on the Factor one day earlier] "Millions of American families are dealing with teenage pregnancy. And as long as society doesn't have to support the mother, father, or baby, it is a personal issue. It is true that some Americans will judge Governor Palin and her family. For the sake of her and her family, we hope things calm down."

Bill O'Reilly: [on the Factor from 2007] "On the pinhead front, sixteen-year-old Jamie Lynn Spears is pregnant. The sister of Britney says she is shocked. I bet. Here the blame falls primarily on the parents of the girl, who obviously have little control over her. Incredible pinhead."

Jon Stewart: See, what happens with opinions on teen pregnancy is that they gestate over a period of months. You pinhead!

Stewart's sympathies may have seemed clear to McCain and Fox. But he regularly found openings to skewer Obama (and to tease the Daily Show *studio audience about its reverence for the Democratic nominee: "You know, you're allowed to laugh at him"). Stewart poked fun at the treatment of Obama as not just a candidate but a messiah, and he eagerly pointed out the contradictions between the Democratic nominee's lofty rhetoric and his grubby compromises, as when Obama discarded a pledge to publicly finance his campaign.*

Jon Stewart: [at anchor desk] We're joined by Senior Electoral Regulations Correspondent Wyatt Cenac. How does Obama justify changing his position?

Wyatt Cenac: Jon, Obama struggled with this decision. He weighed the pros and cons. Considered every outcome. The many ways it might affect the election. Really, Candy Crowley said it best.

Candy Crowley: [in CNN video clip] "If you raised more than a quarter billion dollars in the primary season, would you limit yourself to $85 million in the fall campaign? Duh!"

Wyatt Cenac: I think it's pretty clear. Duh!

Jon Stewart: But is "duh" really the best argument to justify aban-
doning your principles?

Wyatt Cenac: He's raised a quarter of a billion dollars! He can buy all
new principles! And this time he can put rims and a dumbwaiter
on them.

Jon Stewart: He's on tape, Wyatt, promising his supporters that he's
for public financing!

Wyatt Cenac: Look, Jon, we all say things we don't mean just before
we get rich. "I like taking the subway." "The bleacher seats are
fine." "I love you." "It's an honor working here, Mr. Stewart."

Jon Stewart: Is that from the list?

Wyatt Cenac: [*after long pause*] I love you?

Jon Stewart: You cannot escape the fact that what Obama has done
seems somewhat hypocritical.

Wyatt Cenac: Don't think of this as a moral failure. Think of this as
pragmatism we can believe in.

RACHEL AXLER

My last day at the show was at the end of the 2008 Republican convention.
Why did I leave? I just didn't want the country to have a black president. *Sooo*
kidding!

I moved to LA to write for what they called the *Office* spin-off, which
became *Parks and Rec.* I went in to ask Jon to be let out of my contract, and
tell him why I wanted to leave. And he said, "This show was my dream. I
don't expect it to be anyone else's. It was wonderful to have you here." It was
not passive-aggressive. It was very, very real, and absolutely lovely.

*The confluence of a close, possibly-history-making election involving four
riveting characters—Obama had picked Delaware senator Joe Biden as his running mate—lifted* The Daily Show *to new ratings heights. Critical praise was on
the rise, too. "At a time when Fox, MSNBC and CNN routinely mix news and
entertainment, larding their 24-hour schedules with bloviation fests and mara-
thon coverage of sexual predators and dead celebrities, it's been* The Daily Show
*that has tenaciously tracked big, 'super depressing' issues like the cherry-picking
of prewar intelligence, the politicization of the Department of Justice, and the
efforts of the Bush White House to augment its executive power," Michiko*

Kakutani wrote in the New York Times. *"The Daily Show resonates not only because it is wickedly funny but also because its keen sense of the absurd is perfectly attuned to an era in which cognitive dissonance has become a national epidemic."*

The presidential campaign coverage ended on a fitting high note. For the first and only time, Stewart and Colbert did the hour-long live election night show— or, more formally, "Indecision 2008: America's Choice Live Election Special (A.K.A. The Final Endgame Go Time Alpha Action Lift-Off Decide-icidal Hungry Man's Extreme Raw Power Ultimate Voteslam Smackdown '08 No Mercy: Judgement Day '08)"—together from The Daily Show's studio.

DAVID JAVERBAUM

There were a lot of famous people in the audience. I came down before the show, and Robin Williams is sitting there just chatting people up very amiably. That was amazing.

AASIF MANDVI

Standing in the studio wings and hearing Jon announce that Barack Obama was the next president of the United States, in 2008...it was one of those incredible, sort of weird, surreal experiences of being on *The Daily Show*. This is a moment in time. Then going backstage and watching the rest of the show, from the monitor, standing next to Robin Williams and Billy Crystal. Robin Williams and Billy Crystal and I, we're watching *The Daily Show* together, backstage, at *The Daily Show*.

ROB KUTNER

The *Colbert* writers came over to watch the election results with us and brought this Crystal Head Vodka, some product Dan Aykroyd had been hawking, and so we were kind of getting drunk and enjoying the moment.

STEPHEN COLBERT

It was very emotional, when Jon announced that Obama had won. I think you'd have to have a heart of stone not to feel the significance of the moment. Thank God we had a script to do right away, because I can't talk without revealing my feelings. Afterward we all went to the writers' room and watched Obama's Grant Park speech. People were crying all over the place.

LARRY WILMORE

Oh, man. It was one of the most exciting nights ever, I think, besides the birth of my kids. Think about this: When I was a kid you couldn't even be a black quarterback. You couldn't lead a football team, let alone lead the nation. That's the world I grew up in, so I was almost reduced to tears. When Jon made the announcement we were all singing and everything and it was a moment that was beyond politics. It was just this moment that we knew something different had happened, and we did that bit on the show where I came out with the tape and started measuring Jon's desk, and Jon said, "What are you doing?" and I said, "Whatever I want."

I remember we all went out afterward. A big group of us, walking from bar to bar until about four in the morning just celebrating. It was amazing.

JOSH LIEB

After the show that night in Jon's office, Jon was watching with Tracey and my wife and I, watching Obama's victory speech and it was a great moment.

JON STEWART

Robin and Billy were there, but I remember mostly the faces of the crowd in Grant Park, and the disbelief and relief and joy and their feeling of shock. Chicago is a very segregated city still, and with the great migration from the South a lot of them are very close to the bad old days. For them to watch this happen, that's the thing I'll remember most. That and Lieb's fluorescent pants.

JOSH LIEB

Oh, there were plenty of drinks around. We hadn't intended like, "I'm going to be in Jon's office for the victory speech." But when it came up, it felt like, "Oh, this is a great place to be when this is happening. Okay. The country's finally turned a corner and good stuff can happen again."

11

In Cramer We Trust

The celebration was brief. Stewart's we've-got-a-show-to-do-tomorrow ethos meant a quick return to the grind. As 2009 began, the new and in some ways exhilarating challenge for The Daily Show *was proving the conventional critical wisdom wrong. For eight years* The Daily Show's *diet had featured an enormous serving of Bush Administration, with a side order of media, plus Democrats for dessert. Obama's victory would make Stewart and the show irrelevant—or so went the orthodox analysis.*

What it missed was that The Daily Show's *satire wasn't partisan, in the traditional meaning of the word. It was aimed at whoever held power or was peddling lies. The fact that Democrats were back in the White House certainly didn't mean there was a shortage of bad guys on the national stage. And, most immediately, the deification of Obama was ripe for deflation.*

JOHN OLIVER

Tony Blair was my first vote, and that turned out to be a bit of a disaster. There was such excitement with that first Blair victory because it was coming off the back of over a decade of conservative government, Thatcher and then John Major, and it felt like such a hopeful time. And then Blair went along on the invasion of Iraq. There were massive antiwar marches in England. I did march. I did.

That experience helped me to do those Obama Inauguration Day pieces on the Mall in Washington. There was a run, a section of unedited video, right at the moment of Obama's swearing in. This kind of annoyed people around us. They're cheering, I'm jumping up and down, saying, "Yes, now will this lead to inevitable disappointment? Of course it will! Does anyone know that yet? Of course not!" And you could feel people around us going, "Can you please just let us have this moment?"

There is something funny about that level of hope, because you know it's misplaced. Because you just think, "I recognize this hope and I know where this hope ends, and it's not where you want it to be. The best-case scenario is this hope gets compromised."

JOSH LIEB

We had prepared a joke for the show on election night, "Obama is accepting a double-decker shit sandwich." But I don't think any of us realized quite how big a shit sandwich it was.

The financial crisis had erupted during the late stages of the 2008 presidential campaign. Lehman Brothers filed for bankruptcy; AIG, the world's biggest insurance company, was on the brink until bailed out by the feds; the Dow Jones average was in the process of dropping more than 50 percent in less than two years, to a bottom of 6443; and Bush had backed an emergency $700 billion buyout of mortgage-backed securities and other distressed assets. In early 2009, Republicans were vehemently opposing Obama's stimulus plan—House minority leader John Boehner threw the bill on the ground—even as the damage was rippling through the economy with increasing force. Who was to blame for causing the financial meltdown—and who was really hurt by it—would become one of The Daily Show's *prime topics, and would lead to Stewart's most famous* Daily Show *confrontation.*

STEVE BODOW

It was March 12, 2009, and the country was freaking the fuck out.

That was the day Jim Cramer came on *The Daily Show*. But go back and look—that interview happened within five or six days of the very bottom of the biggest crash anybody alive had experienced. It was a disaster, and we didn't know at the time that it was the bottom—the experience was still free fall. It's hard to recapture that context and feeling all this time later.

JOSH LIEB

It was a rough time in America. But trying to recall that moment, it's like trying to watch footage of the Chicago cops beating up hippies in 1968. It's cute, but you don't feel like, "Oh, the whole world was falling down." And that's how it felt then. It felt like the whole world was falling down.

STEVE BODOW

Emotions were running very high. We were tense at the show, because we'd been preparing this assault for a few days. And we had Cramer nine ways to Sunday.

JOSH LIEB

Do you want to hear the backstory?

We'd done a piece the week before about these CNBC talking heads giving people financial advice, and then shitting on those people for taking their advice. There were a lot of people who'd lost a lot of their fucking money, and a lot of the value of their homes, and these CNBC guys hadn't lost anything. It was outrageous.

JON STEWART

Rick Santelli had gone on a rant about how homeowners who had taken these bad loans shouldn't get bailed out. It was interesting to see that on a network that has been traditionally soft on the people who designed that system and knew it would fail.

> **Jon Stewart:** [*at anchor desk*] Wall Street is mad as hell and they're not going to take it anymore! Unless by "it," you mean the two trillion in their own bailouts. That, they'll take.
> Rick Santelli believes in personal responsibility! Not rewarding the losers for missing all the warning signs. I mean, for God's sake, the guy works at CNBC! They're the best of the best! They're the only business network that has the information and experience that we need! So to all you dumb-ass homeowners out there who let your optimism and bad judgment blind you into accepting money that was offered to you from banks... get cable and educate yourselves!
> [*Video montage begins*]
> **Jim Cramer:** "Bear Stearns is fine! Do not take your money out! Bear Stearns is not in trouble!"
> **Graphic:** BEAR STEARNS WENT UNDER SIX DAYS LATER.

Financial Times **Reporter:** [*in CNBC interview*] "I would concur with Charlie. Lehman Brothers is no Bear Stearns. You can't compare Bear management with Lehman management."
Graphic: LEHMAN BROTHERS WENT UNDER THREE MONTHS LATER.

RORY ALBANESE

Santelli was supposed to come on our show, then he canceled.

ELLIOTT KALAN

The original piece about CNBC was written by Jason Ross and Tim Carvell. Jason was our go-to guy for financial stories, because he's the only one who really understood them. We did a headline where we showed how CNBC is essentially reporters cozying up to business.

JASON ROSS

I was almost as outraged as Jon about what was going on, and I could actually answer in a brief way what a credit default swap is. Tim was amazing in the research on those pieces. But it wasn't exactly difficult to find people with supposedly good reputations saying things on CNBC that only a few months later looked utterly ridiculous. We just happened to exist in a world where nobody was playing the clips from six months ago. And so we started doing it.

JOSH LIEB

Maybe on Wednesday or Thursday we do a piece about Jim Cramer misleading investors, and then on Monday he'd complained that we'd taken him out of context. At first it appeared he was right. So I was writing a response. Because we were always very good about saying we're wrong when we're wrong. Then Tim Carvell and Jason Ross came to me and said, "No, we were right." They said, "We were absolutely right. Let's show you the context."

And so we took it in to Jon. And he said, "That's great." And Carvell and Ross went off and wrote a new piece, probably with Adam Chodikoff giving them the research support.

Instead of the apology I'd been working on—not an apology, the clarification I'd been working on—that Monday we ended up having an even stronger comeback.

Jon Stewart: [*at anchor desk*] Well, we went back to the tape to listen.

Jim Cramer: [*in video clip*] "Bear Stearns is not in trouble!"

Jon Stewart: Jim Cramer, I apologize. That was out of context. Technically, you were correct. You weren't suggesting to *buy* Bear Stearns. That was something that you did five days earlier in your "buy or sell" segment.

Jim Cramer: "I believe in the Bear franchise. At 69 bucks I'm not giving up on the thing."

Jon Stewart: Of course, while Cramer wasn't giving up on Bear at 69, eleven days later, the stock market was more comfortable with it at . . . [*pauses, checks notes*] . . . 2! But it's all sort of equivocal. He's not saying literally, "I'm asking you to buy Bear Stearns." For that, you'd have to go back a full seven weeks before the stock completely collapsed.

Jim Cramer: "I'm asking people who are watching this video to buy Bear Stearns."

JOSH LIEB

And we had another one, and another one. And then Cramer demanded his moment.

So he came on that Thursday. And he's a smart guy. We were excited, like, "Okay, well, here's a real clash of the titans."

ADAM LOWITT

It had been on the cover of *USA Today*: STEWART VERSUS CRAMER. I pitched a joke that Jon used: "People staying in hotels are wondering why it's on the cover of their free paper."

That morning, Cramer went on Martha Stewart's show and there was a cooking segment where he was making light of the interview he was going to have with us that night. She asked Cramer, "Do you want to take out some of your anger on this piece of dough?" So the joke in our opening was "I think that guy has enough experience damaging people's bread." Cramer making light of what is really a gigantic fuck-up was the thing that enraged us. So we were going into the interview with that attitude.

ELLIOTT KALAN

Jim Cramer's work we found genuinely disgusting, especially that online interview where he was talking about fooling people and inflating companies. So we booked him on the show. We all thought Jim Cramer was going to try to defend himself.

JOSH LIEB

Cramer walked on and he immediately went into possum mode, or even like puppy mode. He laid down and exposed his belly and was like, "I'm sorry, I'm wrong, you got me."

JON STEWART

There was a sheepishness there that struck me as very disingenuous. I would also get annoyed at people who write polemics and come on the show and do the same thing. They would tell me, "Oh, you know, Democrats, Republicans, we're not that far off."

Really? Because you wrote here that they're responsible for skullfucking grandmothers, and that's the title of your book.

As Cramer went down the route of, "Yeah, boy, you're right, brother. I don't know. I'm trying, too," you're like, "Wait a minute…"

JOSH LIEB

I was sitting at the producers' desk on the studio floor with Rory Albanese, and I remember I was watching Jon. The normal human reaction when somebody goes, "I'm sorry," and exposes their belly is to go, "It's all right. Let's talk friendly stuff." Jon just sharpened his claws and went the fuck in on this guy. And I nearly hid under my desk.

That's why I can't be Jon Stewart. And that's what it took. He was genuinely angry on behalf of all the people who had lost a lot of money on Jim Cramer's shitty advice. And okay, you can't get mad if you take the advice of a guy on TV and then lose money based on it necessarily, but you can get mad if that guy or his colleagues then calls you stupid for taking that advice.

There was this really devastating, death-blow-type video clip we had of Cramer that Jon went to.

ADAM LOWITT

Do you know the term "roll 212"?

That was during the Cramer incident. If you're in act one, the "roll number" for a piece of tape is 100, 102, 104. It's all even numbers. After rehearsal, let's say we need to add another roll, then we'll have the 101, 103. So this was act two, when Jim Cramer came on.

When Jon is going into that interview, we are his henchmen, his support staff. We are his battalion, and he is our general. Before the Cramer interview, I remember walking down the hallway with Jon with a piece of paper—classic, like Aaron Sorkin–type shit, telling him, "Okay, roll 200 is this…" and talking to him at the desk, making sure that he knows which one to call for. I remember, "Roll 212 is the roll."

ROB KUTNER

It's very possible I found that clip out of a competitive spirit. The whole show is such a hive organism. We had ten TiVos running and the whole production department looking for stuff, and Tim Carvell, who's a bloodhound. So I think I was always trying to go deeper—looking on the web for clips.

ADAM LOWITT

Pat King had cut the roll, the you've-been-busted-in-a-lie piece of videotape that we'd found online from Cramer's Internet show at TheStreet.com.

PAT KING, *from intern to senior producer, 2005–2014*

That day was so nuts. I remember we got the roll numbers so late that Chuck didn't even have them and I had to stand behind letting him know which roll was which during taping.

JON STEWART

Oh, the video with Cramer talking about what appeared to be stock manipulation? Yeah. I was stunned. It's like watching a guy talking about, "So this is how we cheat." People outside of that system don't recognize how to an ordinary observer it really looks like gambling and cheating. It looks rigged. And generally there is a dismissive and arrogant attitude from the financial guys: "You don't understand, this is the fuel that makes the market go...clearly we're doing God's work." And I think ultimately it boils down to, actually, no, pretty much a lot of this is a shell game.

ADAM LOWITT

So afterward we go into the edit. Jon wasn't always in the edit, but he was for this. I think we all wanted to cut something, probably the moment that made Josh hide under his desk and me cover my face with my script. It was the dressing-down of another human being that you rarely see on TV. It was not, "You're an asshole." It was, "You're guilty of this thing."

So we're like, "Maybe we should cut that," and Jon is standing up and going, "No, fuck him, fuck him." You realized, there is no shading of what happened out there, and it was awesome.

JON STEWART

We'd spent a lot of time releasing steam over the CNNs of the world and the Foxes of the world, but very little over the financial analysts. So I think the level of missed opportunity that we felt, and their complicity in all that, was enormous. That's what gave the interview its foundational power. There was so much emotion around it at that time, not just because of the failing economy, but because of what we thought was the culpability of financial networks.

JASON ROSS

If there's anything *The Daily Show* was an antidote to, it was the culture of just talking on TV without any accountability.

STEVE BODOW

Cramer came on the show, and while not without sin, was forced to absorb an undue amount of radiation. It got uglier than even Jon had planned. That's the great thing about having a show every night. There's a lot you can't do, and there's a level of finesse we can rarely achieve, but what we get in return is the potential for immediacy. And when that hits, there's nothing that can compete.

JON STEWART

I didn't want the passion of it to overwhelm what I thought was most interesting about it. Because I thought there was something true and absolutely crucial about the conversation. It continues to persist to this day, a strange arrogance that they really didn't do anything wrong. It's just all, "Hey, man, this just kind of got away from us on this one." There's no other business that can do that with such impunity. It feels like there were two games being played and continue to be played, and one of them is being financed by the other one, that our larger investments of pensions and things like that are in some way financing this much riskier game, where even if they lose, they don't lose.

ADAM LOWITT

"Roll 212" became this thing, a code for, "Your career is over."

ELLIOTT KALAN

Not too long after that, Cramer just went back to doing what he'd been doing. It felt similar to election night 2004—there was a sense of, "Maybe we're helping the country change," and then it didn't change. A sense of, the best that we can do is point out stuff that is wrong. We can't expect to shame these people into getting better.

HALLIE HAGLUND, *from intern to writer, 2005–*

Jim Cramer had been on *Martha Stewart* that morning, and he had brought this pie to *The Daily Show*. I think it was a banana cream pie, although that might not be exactly right. And the interview went terribly, and afterward, in the crew area, the pie was just sitting there.

DANIEL RADOSH

It could not have stayed there long. I mean, the whole staff would be like, "Yeah, Cramer's a jerk, but we're going to eat the pie."

The fireworks with Cramer were one sign that the show was expanding its reach, looking beyond the standard targets of campaigns and the media to engage issues where politicians and policy were having an impact on ordinary lives. Stewart's intense criticism of Bush's misguided wars, for instance, morphed into a stinging, recurring criticism of the Obama Administration's inability to properly care for the wounded veterans of those wars.

Jon Stewart: [*at anchor desk*] Obviously, the big story tonight, the AIG bonuses. We also don't want to forget the smaller outrages, either. And we won't, with a new segment called, "That Can't Be Right."

You know veterans? The men and women who risk their lives defending our country? When they get injured, you know who foots the bill? You, the taxpayer! I know, it's incredibly...fair. Completely and totally fair.

So that's why it struck me as odd when I read that one of the money-saving proposals from the Obama Administration was to remove veterans with private insurance from the VA rolls.

So I guess what the government is saying is, if you still need a little rehab from when you got your leg blown off in Iraq, the government will cover you...unless your wife has a little COBRA from her previous substitute-teaching gig.

I've got some other ideas they might want to try out to save a little money: How about sponsored commendations? [*graphic of revised Medal of Honor*] For your service, I offer you the Frito-Lay Medal of Honor! Or how about this—[*graphic of tombstones and water slides*]—the Arlington National Cemetery and Water Park!

What the fuck are you guys thinking!?

The change in presidential administrations coincided with turnover in The Daily Show's *staff and cast. Some of the change was a result of longtimers, ready to do something new, moving on; some of it reflected Stewart's desire to diversify the talent base for a new political era.*

ROB KUTNER

After Obama was elected, it felt like the target changed in a way that was not as much fun. It had been so pure and clear with the Bush Administration. But let's be frank, most of us had voted for Obama, and in satire, you don't want to be on the side of power too much. Now, even though there was plenty to criticize, it still felt like we were supporting the guy in power. I'd been at

The Daily Show for six years at that point, my wife and I had a baby, which is kind of rough in Manhattan, and I heard about Conan's *Tonight Show* starting up in LA.

JO MILLER, *writer, 2009–2015*

I had wanted to write for *The Daily Show* since Lizz Winstead helped create it, and I even have a little note to myself from that time, when I was a PhD student in Medieval Jewish History at Cornell. I spent years teaching. I left academia and I did all kinds of technical jobs—Internet consulting for the government, a series of stupid jobs in real estate development, construction management, IT. I've been a waitress full-time in DC. And I just wrote comedy on the Internet for friends, and then helped Lizz with an Off-Broadway show for two years.

Steve Bodow and I had started an improv group together in college, and he reached out to me, in 2009, said, "We have an opening, we'd be very happy if some women applied." The only way to get more women on the staff is to get more women in the pool, so he did that, and of three hires that year, two were women, Hallie Haglund and me, and Daniel Radosh.

HALLIE HAGLUND

Jo's sense of humor can be pretty dark. One time in the writers' meeting, after one of the big shootings, Jo says, "God, why can't men just get eating disorders like us?"

DANIEL RADOSH

I was a print journalist, mostly freelance, writing for magazines, and I'd written humorous print stuff. I liked the politics of *The Daily Show*, both in terms of the fact that it took politics seriously and that it didn't just caricature politicians. I think David Kamp was the one who once said that *SNL* ruined political satire the moment that they turned Gerald Ford into the bumbling idiot, because then it was all about big personalities and silly stuff, and nobody ever really wanted to talk about the actual politics of it. Until Jon.

Sometime in 2007, Tim Carvell first told me there was an opening, and I applied for a writing position and didn't get it. Then, a couple years later, there was another opening, and I finally got in. I started working at the show when I was forty.

JO MILLER

Right after I started working at *The Daily Show*, in 2009, the news broke about Letterman and interns and stuff. The PA system comes on in the *Daily Show* office and it's Jon, apologizing to any interns he hasn't slept with. And I was like, "I *love* where I work!"

HALLIE HAGLUND

I was an intern at the show during my senior year at Yale. After I graduated they hired me as the receptionist. One of the great things about the show is that anyone can pitch story ideas. That was always Jon's thing—the best idea wins. It doesn't matter who it comes from. So I did that, and I did interviews of staff members and wrote little bios on the show's internal website. Then I was the writers, assistant for a couple of years before I applied to be a writer.

Haglund was one of the numerous staffers who worked their way up through the Daily Show *ranks, following in the paths of Jen Flanz and Rory Albanese. They had been central to the creation of* The Daily Show's *tight-knit office culture, and now the office "family" returned the favor by helping the two of them navigate a rocky personal and professional stretch.*

JOHN HODGMAN

Jen Flanz is a profoundly important force in the show. I think her elevation from production assistant to supervising producer to co-EP and then EP really reflected an acknowledgment that it's not all superstar comedy writers who do this. And Jen did it while surviving a lot of other stuff.

JEN FLANZ

Well, actually, it's funny, a kind of convention story. In 2008, we were in St. Paul and Denver and I just remember being so tired. But every time we had gone on the road I was so tired. After these, though, I just couldn't bounce back. Then there were other symptoms over the year. My legs were itchy. The doctors were like, "You're allergic to everything but cotton, wear cotton." They thought I had lupus. Finally, they're like, "You have had this for over a year and a half." Hodgkin's lymphoma.

And then the doctor says, "You're well into stage IV. It's in your bones. You're going to die." I was thirty-three.

I had the best life until I was thirty-three, and then things got hard. Me and Jesus. That's when I got sick, and that's when my marriage started to...

But the one constant was my family, and my job. I freaking love these people. Even the people I can't stand, I love. Every other Thursday, I had to go to chemo. I would take off that Thursday, and Elise Terrell and Dave Blog and everybody would split up my duties. Friday I'd come to work totally nauseous, not eating anything, on steroids. Then by Monday morning, back to normal enough, you know?

I remember being in a writers' meeting about two weeks into having it, or knowing I had it, and somebody making a cancer joke, and then the whole room getting really quiet. I was like, "Guys, come on, it's fine, I asked you to treat me normally, you know?" From there on, there were cancer jokes for the next few months.

I got my hair cut in a short bob, and all of a sudden it was falling out, but it wasn't really noticeable for a while. I remembered that Steve Carell had been using this powder called Toppik. It makes your hair look thicker. It's men's balding powder, so I bought it, and I'm like, "Okay, I don't think anybody can tell!"

Jon was amazing, but he used to yell at me: "God, can you please take a day off?" I'm like, "No. What am I going to do, sit at home and think about dying? I want to be here."

JOSH LIEB

You cannot tell the story of *The Daily Show* without telling the story of Jen and Rory. They're both enormously important parts of what made that show go. The personal part...life is weird, is all I can say.

Jen and Rory were having problems before she got sick. They put all that aside. Then, when she was well, that's when their marriage fell apart.

JEN FLANZ

Rory and I, there was a lot of fun there. But we fought a lot. The breakup didn't happen in a day. It was not easy, working together as your marriage is falling apart. And having cancer. Yeah. Yeah. But I was like, "I will be damned if you take my job. Take my marriage, go ahead, don't care." I mean, I did care. But I had worked way too fucking hard to get where I am in this business.

RORY ALBANESE

If I had to give someone of all the years of the show, from day one to now, the MVP award, hands down it's Jen. She's fast, she's quick. She gets the jokes but she's not necessarily a comedian. She can execute things. She is the guts and the heart and soul.

JEN FLANZ

I used to say to myself, in my head, "I think if I printed TEAM JEN shirts, there would be two people here not wearing them, but I'm not going to do that to him." I didn't want to be the one to get really ugly about it.

RORY ALBANESE

I don't think there would be too many TEAM RORY T-shirts sold. I'm not going to lie. I was on my own team for quite some time, as I should have been. Not everyone knows who they are at twenty-five, twenty-six. We were growing up while we worked there.

JOSH LIEB

Rory was the face of the creative side of the show, and Jen was the face of the production side. One was the person saying, "I need ten thousand more" and the other was the person saying, "I can only give you five." That negotiation happened every day. That was tough. But even when their relationship wasn't great, it didn't show up on the show.

LEWIS BLACK

I thought it was going to be tough, because it's marriage and, boy, let's inflame it with another three hundred things that might happen during the course of the day at work. It started out, "Boy, they own an elephant. And isn't that a great elephant?" And then eventually the elephant sits on your face.

JEN FLANZ

Yeah, it was definitely ugly, but you know what? You grow. Did I ever think I'd be a single girl, running around the city, in my forties, on Tinder? No, but I am, and I'm enjoying my life. Because I sat home for a year, crying, and then I was like, "I'm not going to be one of these sad, single divorced ladies."

Our dog, Parker? Rory and I share custody.

JOSH LIEB

Rory was indispensable not just as a writer and producer, but to the spirit of the place. For instance, he created O'Mallahans, the finest Irish Italian Jewish Greek pub in Hell's Kitchen, from whatever bottles were lying around Rory's cubicle. It was very nice at the end of a rough show to relax in O'Mallahan's.

JOHN HODGMAN

For about three months there was a regular hang in Rory's cubicle. O'Mallahan's, I think he called it, and it just started to be *Mad Men* up in there.

That was a very happy memory for me, telling John Oliver the difference between Scotch whiskey and Irish whiskey.

JOHN OLIVER

It was not about Scotch and Irish whiskey. I like single malt whiskey and Hodgman thinks I'm a philistine for not appreciating the art of blended whiskey. And I think you're taking a number of nice whiskies and then putting them together like a McFlurry and they become less than the sum of their parts.

I remember a very militant Hodgman, who becomes more articulate the drunker he is and even more convinced he's right. He'd say, "Try this," and it would be fine. But it's not as nice as a single malt scotch which tastes like it's been kind of sucked through peat and fire. That's like drinking a fireplace.

Hodgman tried, over one increasingly drunk evening, to convince me otherwise, and if anything I'm even more sure of my view of his bland disgusting malts because they vomited out of my mouth later that evening.

JOSH LIEB

Oliver, as we all know and the world knows now, he's a peasant. He knows nothing. He's a little child. It's a fancy accent to our ears, but the people in England, they know he's garbage.

JOHN OLIVER

That is both funny and a fact. Exactly. To American ears, it sounds like the accent of someone who's upstairs on *Downton Abbey*. This is a downstairs accent. But Josh is applying class tension that you shouldn't have as an American.

Josh's role in the mix of the show was a pretty big deal. That was a transitional time and he had a very different sensibility. He's an odd, eccentric guy and he's extremely funny in a very silly way and not necessarily a way that is easily or regularly translatable to *The Daily Show*. But I will say, the one time in ten that one of his ideas would make it through it would be a fantastic break of rhythm and style and tone.

JOSH LIEB

One thing I learned from Jon Stewart is that the most important thing in creating a show like this is exuding calm. Jon certainly has that ability, and Jimmy Fallon has it. You're going to put on a show that night and if it works or doesn't, whatever, you're doing another show tomorrow night and so big fucking deal.

We certainly needed that calm in 2010, when we didn't just do the show. We did *Earth (The Book)*. And a trip to DC for the midterms. And a rally for two hundred thousand people.

12

Oh, For Fox Sake

The past decade had transformed the American media industry. Corporate mergers and restructurings weakened the news divisions of ABC, CBS, and NBC. Newspapers and magazines were reeling as the information-wants-to-be-free Internet destroyed advertising revenues.

One of the few outlets to thrive in the chaotic new landscape was Fox News. It surged into the cable news network ratings lead in 2002 and, behind personalities like Bill O'Reilly, Sean Hannity, and Megyn Kelly, stayed there for more than a decade.

The Daily Show's *hand-to-hand combat with the fair-and-balanced cable network had been intensifying since the 2000 election, but in 2010 it ascended to levels both politically revealing and creatively surreal. O'Reilly, impish and pugnacious, had been an inspiration for Colbert's* Report *character; he had also been a* Daily Show *guest five times, beginning in 2001. In February 2010, Jon Stewart visited enemy headquarters for an hour-long interview on the* Factor. *He delivered probably the stiffest criticism of Fox News ever to appear on Fox News.*

Jon Stewart: Here's the brilliance of Fox News. What you have been able to do, you and Dr. Ailes, have been able to mainstream conservative talk radio.

Bill O'Reilly: Why wouldn't John McCain come on this program during the last campaign? Why did he dodge us and not come on if you—if we're in business to help the GOP? He wouldn't come in!

Jon Stewart: But you're not in business to help John McCain. He is not GOP enough for you. You're in business to help Sarah Palin.

Bill O'Reilly: Dick Cheney! Dick Cheney is to you Mr. Republican! Wouldn't come on the program!...I just gave you two examples you can't refute with your propaganda outlet!...John McCain running for president on the GOP side; Dick Cheney, Mr. GOP. Neither man would come in here because the questioning is too tough. So don't give me I'm a Republican shill. That's bull.

Jon Stewart: You have become the most reasonable voice on Fox...You have become in some ways the voice of sanity here, which, as I said, is like being the thinnest kid at fat camp. So let's just get that straight. Here is what Fox has done through their cyclonic, perpetual emotion machine that is a twenty-four-hour-a-day, seven-day-a-week—they've taken reasonable concerns about this president and this economy and turned it into a full-fledged panic attack about the next coming of Chairman Mao. Explain to me why that is the narrative of your network.

Some of the tougher exchanges, however, were cut before broadcast.

Jon Stewart: You've taken a cyclonic, narrative-driven news organization— a media arm of a political party, of a political wing, and you've sprinkled it, you've cut it, with a little bit of objectivity, a little bit of Chris Wallace asking a tough question...

Bill O'Reilly: You think that the Fox News Channel is set up solely to provide aid and comfort to the Republican Party and the conservative movement? Nothing else.

Jon Stewart: That's right. That's right. And to make some money.

That testy conversation, though, was tame compared to what came next, spontaneously and off camera. After Stewart left O'Reilly's studio, he was told that Fox News chairman Roger Ailes wanted to see him in Ailes's second-floor office.

JAMES DIXON

As soon as we walk in Ailes points at the inbox on the corner of his desk and says, "Hey, Jon. See that? You should put your paycheck in there." Jon says, "What?" And Ailes says, "Because you owe me money for making a career off of taking shots at us. You should be thanking me. You owe me."

JON STEWART

Actually, the first thing Ailes said was a casual pleasantry that read like a threat: "Hey, how you doing? How are your kids?" And he said their names. And I was just like, "They're...good. Why?" It was a very weird intimate pleasantry that sounded somewhat more ominous coming from him. Did he have a camera on my kids?

JAMES DIXON

It was contentious from the start and it just kept rolling. Two obviously brilliant political minds going at it. They weren't screaming, but their voices were raised.

JON STEWART

Yeah, it was heated. Ailes is saying, "You're a Communist asshole. You don't know what you're talking about." I'm saying, "You've mainstreamed this bile in a way that people can take without it blistering their skin. You found a way to insinuate it into polite society. Kudos to you for poisoning people while they don't even realize it."

JAMES DIXON

Jon's sitting in a chair in front of Ailes's desk, and I'm on a couch with Bill Shine, Fox's programming guy. The two of us, me and Shine, just looked at each other, like, "Holy shit." It was incredibly uncomfortable and fascinating—the two most influential media people on their sides of the spectrum going at it for probably a half hour.

JON STEWART

All my points were just that I get what he's trying to do. That there is nothing more cynical in this world than the slogan "Fair and Balanced." And I know that what he is doing is tactical and not journalistic.

What I came away with from the meeting was that the anger and resentment and victimization of that network is all broadcast out of the back of that guy's head, verbatim. His response to me is something like, "You have no idea how liberal these people are—the rest of the media, the world. They're steeped in it. They control everything. They indoctrinate the youth. The only people in this world that are persecuted are white males"—that kind of thing. The way that he views the world is how that network is programmed.

Ailes truly believes what he truly believes and I truly believe what I truly believe, and I don't think either one of us was going to soft-pedal that.

JAMES DIXON

I will say there was an immense amount of mutual respect, as contentious as it got. Rarely have I ever seen someone go toe-to-toe that effectively with Jon. Not that I agreed with what Ailes was saying.

JON STEWART

None of what's going on with Ailes and Fox now surprises me. They carried themselves like thugs.

In April, a Daily Show *segment juxtaposed clips of Fox pundits criticizing irresponsible overgeneralizations of the Tea Party with clips of Fox pundits making irresponsible overgeneralizations about the left. The piece ended with Stewart telling Fox and Bernard Goldberg, a former CBS reporter who had become a conservative media critic and Fox contributor, to "go fuck themselves." Goldberg responded in kind on O'Reilly's show, ripping Stewart for going easy on liberal* Daily Show *guests.*

This time Stewart didn't just answer with a few good lines from behind the desk, including, "I have not moved out of the comedians' box into the news box. The news box is moving toward me." There was also an appearance by the tuxedo-ed Toppington Von Monocle claiming to quote Catullus, in Latin ("I will sodomize you and face-fuck you"), to refute Goldberg's slagging of the Daily Show *audience as "unsophisticated." It was the over-the-top ending, though, that made this rebuke a classic: Stewart singing and shouting his scorn while backed up by a gospel choir and breaking into a dance that was part Jewish vaudevillian, part tent-show-revival preacher, to declare Fox "the lupus of news."*

BERNARD GOLDBERG, *journalist, author, Fox News commentator*

He started out, as I recall, saying something like, "Bernie, I don't want to fight with you." And then he used a black church choir for twelve minutes to tell me and Fox to go fuck ourselves, which I thought was hilarious. It raised my Q rating. I saved it on my DVR for years, and then I got a new DVR, and I almost wept that I had to give up that.

JON STEWART

The fuck-you choir? Yeah, that was my idea. A lot of those came from me being up at night.

BERNARD GOLDBERG

The idea that Jon Stewart is above it all, and he sees hypocrisy and goes after it in an even-handed way is ridiculous. He doesn't. He lets his ideology trump his intelligence, because if he didn't, he'd go after liberal hypocrisy with the same gusto that he does when he goes after conservative hypocrisy and stupidity.

At the very mention of the word "Fox," Jon's eyes would roll around in his head and he would foam at the mouth, and that's fine for a comedian, but it's not fine for a media critic. Jon would say, "But I'm not a media critic, I'm a comedian." Then fucking do jokes about horses that walk into bars and ask for a scotch and soda. I think Jon desperately wanted to sit at the grown-up table, so he did social commentary. No problem. But please, please, don't fall back on "I'm only a comedian" when you get caught saying something that is not fair or completely honest.

Is Fox fair and balanced? Well, I didn't come up with the slogan. Okay? But that's a pretty thin branch to go out on.

Goldberg, though, was mild-mannered compared to many on the right. It was a boom time for panic mongers, for the everything-is-bad-and-Obama-is-to-blamers, for the Eric Cantors and the Ted Cruzes and the Rush Limbaughs and the Laura Ingrahams. The apotheosis in conspiratorial thinking and performance style was a mercurial reformed alcoholic and Mormon convert with a gift for manic historical storytelling. At his peak in late 2009, Glenn Beck was averaging around three million viewers each night on his 5 p.m. Fox News show.

ELLIOTT KALAN

Glenn Beck seemed like he was this new thing on the scene, and he seemed very dangerous. And he provoked a big response from us.

STEVE BODOW

Beck at the time was the extreme expression of the crazy, paranoid stylings going on at Fox News in the aftermath of Obama's election. Beck was the best expresser of this histrionic drama which they created about how the country was being destroyed. It was just amazing and fascinating to watch because it was this long, sustained effort promoting a view of a reality that did not exist, but was still going out on the highest-rated news channels in the country every day, which is to say with some authority.

JO MILLER

What drew us to Beck was less the antics where he brings out food and stuff, although we did enjoy that. It was his alternate history, which always went all over the blackboard. He and a guy called David Barton, who is a regular on TheBlaze, concocted an alternative history of the United States. It was a coherent one, and it was compellingly articulated by this guy—and it's entirely false, and misleading, and insidious.

STEVE BODOW

And of course Beck is such a performer. Beck is emo. That level of drama is good for us, because our show is fundamentally about an emotional reaction to current events.

JON STEWART

The man is gold, and I mean gold at the level that gold was when Beck was touting it, not the level it is now. It's one thing when the content is unhinged. But when it's also delivered with such theater, that's when it becomes truly fun to build an entire program around. You can really chew it up.

STEVE BODOW

But none of us had planned for those segments to become the fifteen- or sixteen-minute arias that they became. Jon had done smaller flashes of a Beck impression at the desk. And then as Beck had gone along he started to get grander in the way he was producing his show, and would occasionally do these hour-long fucking episodes with his grand unified theory of how Woodrow Wilson had put fluoride in the water and that was making us all into Obama slaves or something. He would do it with blackboards and charts and props. I was like, "Okay, we should do this."

When we discovered that we had something huge instead of just big was the first time that Jon got on his feet and did it and surprised everybody, maybe including himself. It showed a range of Jon's performance that had not really been on view before.

The first time we did a big Beck piece—in November 2009—it played off Beck having his appendix removed.

JON STEWART

The difficulty with that type of thing is, how do you create it? The original, Beck, is so off the rails, it's difficult to embody it at a higher pitch than it already is. You have to find ways to emphasize the insanity of it without it just being a studied impression. So in that first one, we're talking about Hitler stealing Beck's organs to prevent him from speaking the truth.

ELLIOTT KALAN

The second Glenn Beck piece, "Conservative Libertarian," got huge. It was like an eighteen-minute bit.

Beck had been referring to progressivism as a cancer on democracy and a cancer on the Constitution. So Jon wanted to start the show with a cold open saying, "I just found out I have cancer," and then cut to the opening credits. We were like, "You can't do that!" He was going to give people heart attacks.

Glenn Beck: [*in video clip, dusting chalk from fingers after drawing progressive conspiracy time line on his blackboard*] "China is the goal. Why do you think there are so many Maoists hanging around the White House?"

Jon Stewart: You don't see it, do you? You still don't! Follow me, America! [*dashes and hops to his own blackboard, which shows large circles leading to a swastika and a hammer and sickle*] I'm going to show you something that is going to blow your mind! Why am I the only one who is saying it? Am I crazy or—okay. Look at the ovals of progressive folly! Look! Look! Look! Ovals, getting larger. And isn't it interesting that they go to China. It turns out that progressives advocating for government regulations on toxins in water and our children's toys turns us into China, the very country that has been putting toxins in water and our children's toys. It's so ingenious it almost doesn't make any sense whatsoever!

So, how do we get our country back? How do we stop the cancer from "progressing"? Do you see?

Glenn Beck: [*in video montage from his Fox show*] "Look back to our founders, because they left us messages." [*sticks drawings of Washington and Jefferson on his blackboard*] "This is an original document from Thomas Jefferson." [*holds up old-looking piece of paper*] " 'On the twenty-fourth day in the year of our lord, Christ, 1807.' Signed by Thomas Jefferson."

Jon Stewart: [*jumping and shouting and waving his arms*] Then Thomas Jefferson signed, "Year of our Lord Christ," licked the envelope, put a stamp on it, and gave it to one of his slaves to take for a couple of weeks to get it to Maryland!

ELLIOTT KALAN

The Glenn Beck pieces felt like Jon exploiting the possibilities of this forum in a way that we hadn't before. It's a little bit like . . . well, I was going to make a very labored Judas Priest analogy.

Judas Priest started out very bluesy and then got more operatic as time went on. Then in the '80s they were trying to bring in more synth-type sounds, and it didn't quite work. It was clear they were trying to break open their sound. They had these albums *Turbo* and *Ram It Down*—not so great. *Turbo* has one really good song.

But then they came back with an album called *Painkiller*, on which they said, "Okay. We can still sound like ourselves but we're going to bring in much faster, harder metal sounds, more like speed metal and death metal. It can still sound like us, but we can do a lot more with what we're doing." That's what it felt like with Jon and Glenn Beck: "I'm going to take these elements from other types of performance and I'm going to bring them to what we do and it's going to make our argument that much stronger."

We were not doing what *SNL* would do, but we were doing Jon impersonating a person rather than just commenting on them. And it was amazing considering most of Jon's impersonations are Jersey guy; other Jersey guy; French guy; very Jewish guy. So the Glenn Beck episodes were to us what *Painkiller* was to Judas Priest.

What a dumb analogy.

GLENN BECK, *Fox News host, 2009–2011*

I make fun of myself. So somebody else making fun, I took it as flattery.

If you're going to do what I do and you can't handle that, you're in the wrong business. The problem that I had, and one of the reasons why we moved out of New York, is Jon painted a picture of me that people took—and I'm not saying he was ever responsible for any of this—but some people took that and then made me into the absolute enemy. And we had an incident at a New York park where people were just vile to my children, my family, and to my wife.

I probably talked more about Gandhi and Martin Luther King than anybody on television in the last twenty years and I was always trying—and the media always missed it—but I was always trying to preach peace, peace, peace.

JON STEWART

To be honest I think one of my favorite Beck things ever wasn't even one of the big performance pieces. Beck has a big Walt Disney fetish and was going to create a town. Independence USA. He did a whole presentation about it— and it was all about the rules that were going to exist in this town. At Independence USA it was all about, "There won't be any backyards. Everything will face front because the people will have to be there, and there won't be any chain stores." And you're just like, "You do realize that that's state control over every aspect?" Stalin would blush at that kind of control over a community. In the name of freedom you're going to ban Applebee's. Okay.

I think that was one of the greatest pieces we did. It struck to just the heart of the contradiction of all these so-called constitutional-freedom fetishists who are, at heart, authoritarian. Who believe not in freedom and democracy—what they believe in is freedom and democracy for my idea.

GLENN BECK

There's nobody that you will find on the right, outside of people like Penn Jillette, that is a bigger freedom guy and libertarian. I am not a guy who wants the government to make any rules—except that I believe in the Constitution. I'm not a French libertarian. I am libertarian that bases everything on the Constitution. It's up to the people to decide, not to the federal government and, certainly, not up to nine people who sit on a court.

I live in a gated community right now. I can't put up a flagpole. Do I want a flagpole? Yes, but I bought in there knowing what the rules were. There's a reason why everybody loves to go to Disney—because it has real strict rules. Is that the way you run a country? No.

JON STEWART

When you listen to these guys on talk radio there's a relentlessness and an urgency and a call to action and it is all 24/7, "You are losing your country. It is being taken away from you by all these people and you can sit there and do nothing or you can listen to me."

I don't mind divisiveness. What I mind is divisiveness for its own purpose and without good, sound argument behind it. I don't mind conservatism, with argument, but when you listen to the radio, that's not conservatism. I don't know what that is. That's angry nativism.

GLENN BECK

Do I feel any responsibility for creating the conditions that led to [Donald] Trump? Oh, none whatsoever. That is the dark side that I warned about in 2008. If Barack Obama is elected and if he isn't everything he says he is, if he's a typical politician in the end, a gravy-stained guy who's just got a fat mouth is going to come out. I said to the left, "Please don't push the pendulum so far to the left because the pendulum always comes back and it's going to come right, and whether it's our side or your side, some fascist wannabe is going to grab it in times of strife."

I thought it was going to come from the left…I had no idea it would be Trump…He says, "I'm going to build a wall." If he doesn't build a wall, what do you think his supporters are going to do? How disenfranchised will they be? And then what comes after Donald Trump? Who then has to step up and say, "I'll fix it"? Good God, we're on this slope to hell.

JON STEWART

One of Fox's great accomplishments was to mainstream that truly out there, urgent, paranoid style of broadcasting and make it much more palatable. They took a little bit of the acid out of it, a little bit of the stridency, and they packaged it in a much more, "I'm just asking these questions" way. They packaged it in a much more nonconfrontational tone and mainstreamed it.

*   *   *

The Daily Show's *ability to package video material had been painstakingly honed over the years. The production department had stockpiled hundreds of hours of clips and grown more adept at logging the contents and accessing them to build montages. But the process still required a half-dozen researchers watching footage, and searches often needed to be supplemented by the prodigious memory of Adam Chodikoff. In 2010, though,* The Daily Show's *methods took a quantum leap forward.*

JUSTIN MELKMANN

We would have four producers standing in front of a wall of TiVos, trying to grab four separate things from Fox and CNN at the same time. And everyone's shutting off everyone else's TiVo with their separate remotes. It was ridiculous.

JILL KATZ, *executive in charge of production, 2006–*

When we were upgrading the taping from standard to high-def, one of the consultants said to me, "There's this piece of technology that looks really interesting for what you do." SnapStream was originally meant for the advertising industry, and it couldn't do what we wanted. Pat King, a *Daily Show* producer, was key in working with SnapStream to design what we needed in terms of search. It took months and months to get it right.

RAKESH AGRAWAL, *founder, SnapStream*

What we invented was a unit that connects to a company's computer servers. One of them can record up to ten television shows at a time. The recordings you make can be watched on the network, from any desktop inside an organization, by multiple people at the same time. But for *The Daily Show*, the point is not really about watching TV. We translated the TV audio into text, and made it possible to search inside shows.

ALISON CAMILLO

Say you need to find out who said, "good guy with a gun." Suddenly, instead of blindly searching through hours of clips, you can put in quotes, "good guy with a gun," and it pulls up the last ten different things on *Good Morning America*, the *Today* show, CNN, and you can just put them all in a little playlist.

JILL KATZ

It turned out to be an incredibly expensive investment, but I really saw this as a way of changing everything that we do and reducing so much of the legwork so we could spend more time being creative.

PAT KING

It absolutely changed the way we produce. It could take hours to find the clips we wanted, and then it used to take ten or twelve minutes to get a clip into an Avid editor. SnapStream cut our production time down by about 60 or 70 percent.

The technology had finally caught up with The Daily Show's *needs. Stewart, meanwhile, was intrigued with a very different experiment in altering the show's form and process—for a one-time-only extravaganza.*

JON STEWART

Beck started doing rallies, and I just thought that was a really funny idea. I can't remember what his was called. Something ridiculous. "Restoring Honor." He was going to gather people to restore something that hadn't been lost.

Glenn Beck had decided he was going to go down to Washington and hold a rally in front of the Lincoln Memorial, because he was so inspired by Martin Luther King that he was going to go down there and do it right where Martin Luther King did it. Sure. Such an analogous situation. Take a nonoppressed people and show the nonoppressed people they could use this area, too.

I was always looking to find other structures to fill. In many ways we are a Mexican restaurant that's run out of ideas. We take cheese, beans, and meat and wrap it this way. We'll call it a burrito. I got an idea: Why don't we fold it this way and call it a taco? So we're sort of using the same ingredients but finding new constructs you can sell it with, to give it new inspiration. So *America (The Book)* was that—how do you re-create the false authority of the show in written form? And I thought we could do the false authority in a live context.

So I called Stephen to see if he'd go in on it. He said, "Yeah. Let's get in trouble. Let's have fun."

*   *   *

A permit for the National Mall was reserved under the name of Craig Minassian, a media strategist who had worked for Bill Clinton in the White House and then at the Clinton Foundation.

JON STEWART

We sort of back-channeled the idea to see if it was feasible. For all the Parks Service knew, we could have been Girl Scouts.

The original idea was, we didn't want to do it on the steps of the Lincoln Memorial. We wanted to do it *on* the Lincoln Memorial. We wanted to do it flat out standing in Lincoln's lap.

RORY ALBANESE

The rally? I said, "Don't do this." I hated that idea so much. I feel like it stood against everything we thought—we never thought we were anything but a TV show. Why the fuck are we doing this? I appreciated the motivation behind it. I agree that we only listen to the two extremes, and it's a disservice to the country when most people are actually very reasonable. I just didn't like it.

JOSH LIEB

For several months, we said, "Don't do it. Don't do it." And then Jon said, "I'm going to do it." Stephen is great, and he's just as much of a lunatic as Jon is. Neither of these guys are people you want to play chicken with, because they'll beat you. They will fucking go all out.

The original notion was to stage dueling rallies, with Colbert leading "The March to Keep Fear Alive." Instead it was merged into a single event, "The Rally to Restore Sanity and/or Fear." What never changed was the intention that Stewart announced on The Daily Show, *to put on a pageant for noncrazy, non-book-and-flag-burning, nonscreaming America: "Not so much the Silent Majority as the Busy Majority." In other words, a plea for rationality in an increasingly irrational political and media landscape, a reminder that there's a distinction between "political" and "partisan." Plus Colbert in an Evel Knievel jumpsuit.*

JON STEWART

We'd never asked anything of the audience before, but now we're asking them to show up somewhere. One of the reasons it appealed to me was it had the scent of demagoguery. That's what you're playing with. You're playing with this idea of, "Let's go down there and get a bunch of people, but then not have them do anything." In essence the rally was, as the show was, the frustrated expression of impotent rage.

We didn't think it would be that hard to design a program, because obviously we were naïve and had no idea what we were doing.

Adding to the degree of difficulty was that The Daily Show *was preparing the rally at the same time that the show was in Washington as part of "Indecision 2010: Midterm Teapartyganza." Three nights before the big event on the Mall was a big event in the temporary studio: President Obama was the guest.*

CRAIG SPINNEY

The president, that dude, he came bouncing up the stairs like Fred Astaire, and just as he did the elevator doors opened and Jon came out doing his pre-show Robert De Niro in *Raging Bull* impersonation, throwing punches. The president says, "So, you're here to restore some sanity?" And Jon, still using his De Niro voice, says, "You bet we are!"

The interview turned out to be a prime demonstration of the merits of Stewart's conversation-instead-of-interrogation style. He wasn't "tough" on Obama by the standards of network TV sitdowns—grilling him about gaffes or the midterm horserace—and yet the eighteen-minute session was, in the evaluation of the president's top aides, the toughest one Obama endured that fall.

DANIEL RADOSH

Jo Miller and I worked on the prep for that, and we broke down, "What are the big foreign and domestic policy things we want to do?" We found all these specific things that we wanted to get him on.

And Jon looked at the notes, and he just starts laughing at the idea that this is going be the interview that he was going to do with President Obama. He says, "What we really want to do is create a narrative, and we're going to tell a little story. What's the big picture, rather than all the details that we can nail this person on?" And the interview Jon did ended up calling Obama on stuff better than asking about all the details.

Jon Stewart: You ran with such, if I may, "audacity." So much of what you said was, "Great leaders lead in a time of opportunity," "we're the ones we're looking for." Yet legislatively it has felt timid at times. I'm not even sure at times what you want out of a health-care bill.

President Barack Obama: Jon, I love your show, but this is something where, you know, I have a profound disagreement with you... This notion that health care was "timid": you've got thirty million people who are gonna get health insurance as a consequence of this... It gets discounted because the presumption is, "Well, we didn't get 100 percent of what we wanted, we got 90 percent of what we wanted, so let's focus on the 10 percent we didn't get as opposed to the 90 percent that we did." And right now there is a woman in New Hampshire who doesn't have to sell her house to get her cancer treatments because of that health-care bill. And she doesn't think it's inconsequential. She doesn't think it's "timid."

Jon Stewart: The suggestion was not that it's inconsequential or that it doesn't help—

President Obama: The suggestion was that it was "timid."

Jon Stewart: Timid. And I'll tell you what I mean... it's that you ran on the idea that this system needed basic reform—

President Obama: Yup.

Jon Stewart: It feels like some of the reforms that have passed, like health care, have been done in a very political manner that has papered over a foundation that is corrupt.

President Obama: That, I think, is fair... There are all kinds of things that happened during the course of these two years, in terms of process, that I'd like to see changed... If the point, Jon, is that overnight we did not transform the health-care system, that point is true.

Jon Stewart: [*laughs*] When you put it that way, it seems so petty!

President Obama: When we promised during the campaign, "Change you can believe in," it wasn't, "Change you can believe in in eighteen months." It was, "Change you can believe in, but you know what, we're gonna have to work for it."

The studio audience erupted in cheers and applause, and Stewart admitted, "It's a good point," but he'd elicited a fascinating amendation from Obama.

That Wednesday night, after shaking hands with the commander in chief, Stewart went back to frantically figuring out just what he and Colbert were going to do onstage for three hours on Saturday.

JON STEWART

No, I didn't sleep. Except when I took Xanax. Shuts it down pretty good. Pretty, pretty, pretty good. But no, I was a mess.

We were booking bands up until that last weekend. I had the dumb idea that I was going to be "Peace Train" because I'm representing sanity, and Stephen was going to be "Crazy Train," representing fear. We wanted it to be almost like a battle of the bands. And the O'Jays would settle it all with "Love Train." So most of our time went into trying to figure out how you get Cat Stevens, Ozzy Osbourne, and the O'Jays in one place.

JILL KATZ

We were told, "Call this guy, he's the manager of the O'Jays." So we call and the guy says, "Listen, can I call you back at five o'clock? I'll be done with my UPS route then." This is a couple days before the rally.

JON STEWART

The night before the rally, I remember working with Hillary Kun. We're trying to figure out how to send a jet to pick up a variety of O'Jays. For some reason I had this stupid idea that the O'Jays lived together in the O'Jay house. They all wore the same outfit every day. They did their moves at the breakfast nook. It was a little more complicated than that.

JILL KATZ

Security was a big deal. We were working with Gavin de Becker, who is great, and they wanted Jon and Stephen to wear bulletproof vests, because not everybody is a fan. But they weren't interested.

JON STEWART

Look, I've got a hard enough time singing. With a bulletproof vest on, my range is cut down. I'm an alto-tenor-soprano, so I'll lose that high C if I've got the vest. And at that time I was fat enough that I was well protected.

Stewart did indeed fill out his red, white, and blue fleece when he took the rally stage on Saturday, October 30. Otherwise he and Colbert were an excellent fit for the jittery moment in American politics—a moment very much in need of a few laughs and a dose of civility. The economy was still reeling from the financial meltdown, with unemployment at 9 percent. The growing belief that the system was rigged for the elites was stoking genuine populist anger on both the right and the left. There was plenty of contrived anger in the air, too, including the controversy over a "Ground Zero mosque," with a fringe Florida pastor grabbing TV time by threatening to burn a Koran.

In June, congressional Republicans, determined to obstruct Obama, had stalled an extension of unemployment benefits, and Democrats had passed Obamacare without a single GOP vote. The ripples of McCain's desperation move in 2008 of putting Palin on the ticket were becoming more visible: In the fall, the Tea Party wave was cresting, with candidates including Delaware's Christine "I'm not a witch" O'Donnell winning primaries. Democrats were bracing for a beating in the midterms and begging Stewart not to hold the rally three days before the vote, because they were worried it would distract campaign workers. Oh, and then there were the rumors flying around that the rally was really a launching pad for Stewart 2012.

MICHELE GANELESS

I remember the craziness of people saying, "Jon's going to announce he's running for office," and people so desperately wanting it to be serious and not satire.

JAMES PONIEWOZIK

Although *The Daily Show* had a definite political slant, there was also this element that developed that was simply about being a voice for comity. There was this old-fashioned streak in Stewart, which I think he shares with Obama in a way, where he misses this time where maybe there wasn't bipartisan consensus on everything, but at least there were spaces in the middle where people could meet and agree to disagree and get things done. And through the Obama years, it's important to note that this sometimes got the show in trouble, especially with the more strident part of the left. A lot of progressives really hated the Rally for Sanity. They wanted him to hold a rally that would try to influence people to vote for Democrats in the midterm, and that was not a role that he wanted to embrace.

JON STEWART

The momentum of the industries that surround politics and surround governments are so self-fulfilling and self-driving that they can't fathom the idea of going down and having fun and putting on a show. They immediately assume that there must be, for every single moment, something calculated as a political campaign, not as entertainment.

But for me, there's very little that's better than sitting in a trailer on the National Mall the morning of a rally, of the thing you've never done before, rehearsing with Questlove and the Roots and Ozzy and Cat Stevens and the O'Jays. You're saying to Cat Stevens, "Okay, so you're going to do 'Peace Train.' You're going to give me twelve measures." He says, "Twelve measures? Why? What do you mean?" "You're going to do twelve measures and then Ozzy's going to come in and cut you off." And Cat Stevens says, "But it's a beautiful song!" "I understand it's a beautiful song, but the bit is—" "Look, I flew in from Dubai!" "No, I get it. You'll get a chance to play." And then you explain to Ozzy that Stephen is the guy coming out of the Chilean Miner capsule wearing an Evel Knievel suit. All *right*.

CHUCK O'NEIL

The rally was probably the toughest show I ever directed, because it was three hours without a commercial break, and it was also 100 percent unrehearsed. Jon did not want any information getting out to the press that week we were down there doing the midterms. So even the night before we were to do it I hadn't seen any scripts. And then the script came in that morning, and it was so thick I didn't have time to go through it.

JUDY MCGRATH

That morning I was thinking what I think before most live events: Is anybody going to show up? And then to see that sea of people, to see Jon and

Stephen trading off on a stage like that and sort of capturing the zeitgeist of the country again—it really was just a sensational day in every way.

Some of it was so brilliant, and some of it was so wacky. I'm standing backstage with Sharon Osbourne and Cat Stevens and Jeff Tweedy? Even backstage, there was a feeling of, huh? It's not Woodstock, and it's not a convention. What the hell is this?

JIM MARGOLIS

It was a surreal thing to walk backstage at the rally. What sticks out is how much I was like a hobbit, in a burrow, next to Kareem Abdul-Jabbar. And also how little interest Kareem Abdul-Jabbar had in talking to me.

MICK FOLEY, *pro wrestler, author, recipient of Rally to Restore Sanity Medal of Reasonableness*

I know Jon meets a lot of people, but he probably doesn't meet them at Arlington National Cemetery. In 2009 Jon was being honored for the work he did with the USO. I'd been volunteering for the USO for several years, and Jon and I really bonded over a mutual friend, a young service member who'd been severely burned, named Rick Yarosh. I said "Jon, I just want you to know, I'm a big fan. But I'll be honest, I was a little hesitant to actually meet you because I was afraid you might be—" And then he filled in the blank: "—an asshole?" And I said, "Yeah, and I thought that might take away from my ability to enjoy the show." But I saw the way he interacted normally with the service members. He was looking for no special treatment whatsoever.

A few months later Jon had me on the show as "senior ass kicker," in a segment where I stuck up for a kid who was being bullied at school. And then Jon gave me a medal at the rally.

I mean, I wasn't around for Woodstock, but the rally felt like my Woodstock, you know? It was really a very peaceful time, no troubles, something I was very proud to be a part of. And it's always fun to see Kid Rock.

JON STEWART

It's hard not to react emotionally to this feeling of standing in front of the Capitol. It's incredible. The lawn in front of the Congress, and you're having a goofy rally and there's thousands of people there who are having a good time. People said to us, afterward, "Did that work out for you guys?" We're like,

"Hell, yes!" It was awesome. We had an amazing day. And then they're like, "Well, but you didn't increase Democratic voter turnout. You failed us." Oh, okay. I didn't know that.

STEPHEN COLBERT

There was the Rally to Restore Sanity and there was the March to Keep Fear Alive. To me, that wasn't just a fig leaf for both of our shows to be there. They were about two different things. You can ask Jon what the Rally to Restore Sanity was about, because I had no intention of restoring sanity. And I think I won.

What I was making fun of is the commoditizing of other people's fear. Using other people's fear for your own self-aggrandizement or your own enrichment and your own ego. Fear, anger—those are generally not your real feelings. They're a reaction to the other feelings you're having.

Did Jon and I try to point that out—the commodification of fear, the division into camps? Sure. That was a source of a lot of the satire. It was everywhere.

I don't want to speak for Jon about what the Rally to Restore Sanity was, but fear is the mind killer. I think Jon was encouraging people to calm down and think rather than feel all of the time.

Stewart's speech concluding the rally—corny as it may have been, with its imagery of cars peacefully merging to enter the Holland Tunnel—was a welcome, hopeful appeal to Americans' better nature, and a borderline-prophetic warning that things could get worse if sanity didn't make a stand.

JON STEWART

The rally was on a Saturday, after we'd done a week of shows in Washington. That was about as messy as I've gotten in terms of loading things up and having a deadline and being a little stressed out and then having to write that stupid thing the night before. That whole little soliloquy at the end of the rally.

You're always trying to balance the satire and the subtext and the pratfall with the sentiment. Sometimes it's completely in sync and you hit that sweet spot and other times it's overly sentimental or overly earnest or too ridiculous.

Afterward, some critics argued he'd missed the mark. "Stewart's rally," wrote Jamelle Bouie, Slate's chief political correspondent, "[made it seem] as if

Washington gridlock were a case of bad manners and not deep-seated ideological differences about government and its place in the world."

JON STEWART

I certainly understand how much of the problem is about ideology. But what got people so mad at us is that the rally didn't seem to have any real point other than "He says we've got to be nice to each other." That's not in any way what we were saying. The point, for us, was about, "If you're going to have an argument, have the actual argument. Be precise. Don't call people racist if it doesn't rise to that level of offense." Not "be nice," but if you are at the same level of outrage over everything, then I guess you're not really outraged about anything.

Salman Rushdie had a different, highly specific complaint. The Satanic Verses *author called Stewart, angry that the former Cat Stevens, who'd endorsed the fatwa against Rushdie, had been featured. Stewart, who had been unaware of Stevens's statements, apologized.*

JON STEWART

Death for blasphemy is kind of a nonstarter, especially at what you call your sanity rally. Should have known more about it earlier. Point Rushdie.

The more common effects and memories of the rally—even if it didn't immediately transform DC's partisan standoff—were stirringly hopeful, especially for many Daily Show *staffers.*

HALLIE HAGLUND

I just remember Jon walking offstage at the very end of the rally, after he delivered his speech, and a bunch of us were backstage, and he saw Tracey and just started crying. I think that he was so overwhelmed by that rally. It had a life of its own that surprised all of us.

ELISE TERRELL

I remember walking through Washington at eight o'clock at night, after the rally. Everyone had gone home, but all of the garbage cans were filled with signs that people had made and materials that they'd carried, and it felt like Times Square an hour after midnight on New Year's Eve. You still had the remnants of how amazing this thing had been, and how much it had meant to so many people. Our in-studio audience, when they come in, they sit down. They clap when they're supposed to clap. The rally was the one time that we really felt connected with our audience and with the country. As cheesy as that sounds.

Later I saw this video on YouTube, "Jump Rope with a Muslim." A Muslim woman had gone around the rally and made a video of herself jumping rope with different people. It was an incredible acknowledgment of what this rally meant. It was just so overwhelming.

STEPHEN COLBERT

I sincerely believe that while using fear and anger is still effective in politics, our country is increasingly sickened by it. I think that there's a diminishing return for that game. You had ten years plus of America quite naturally responding to the attacks of 9/11 through fear and anger. That manifested itself in a lot of different ways. I think people were happy to pick sides, like a sport, in a way. I don't think people are as happy about picking sides as they used to be.

JON STEWART

I went right from the rally to the airport and flew home because Halloween was the next day. We had to go trick-or-treating with the kids.

STEPHEN COLBERT

After the rally, Jon couldn't stay for the after party, but we took everybody to the Old Ebbitt Grill in DC, and I stood up on the fountain and the first thing I said was how proud I was to once again be working on *The Daily Show*. I love that show and I love him.

13

Worst Responders

The rally's achievements in comedy and civility were hard to quantify, but the event certainly helped boost the show's ratings. In October 2010, The Daily Show beat Letterman's and Leno's shows among the coveted 18-to-49-year-old viewers, the first time any late-night show other than those two network giants had won a month in more than a decade. The Rally also demonstrated Stewart's ability to deploy Daily Show fans on behalf of a cause. At the end of the year, he would spend some of that capital on behalf of some real heroes.

MICHELE GANELESS

South Park and *The Daily Show* built Comedy Central. With Jon, you have the highest-income audience, the most dedicated audience—and they're young guys, and nobody else can find young guys. The young guys have fled TV and they're playing video games. But *The Daily Show* became a magnet for advertisers and really the calling card of the network. Then we had Colbert come on, and Tosh come on, and Key and Peele, and Chappelle in the middle of all that.

But *The Daily Show* was the constant, was the bedrock, was the award winner, was the cultural touchstone, where every politician ultimately wanted to be. You cannot overstate its importance, particularly in that time. It's still important now, but in the years of 2000 to 2010, you cannot overstate the importance of *The Daily Show* to Comedy Central.

JUDY MCGRATH

The company had a great relationship with Jon, but he didn't hesitate to say what he thought internally, either. Once there was a *South Park* episode about the prophet Muhammad. We had a really hard debate in the office about what to do because we were nervous. I was getting calls from Homeland Security and NYPD, saying, "Don't do this." We didn't run the full episode the way they wanted to, and Jon really took us to task on his show for not being brave.

At the same time, The Daily Show *itself was becoming a target of increased scrutiny. Over the years it had been knocked for being too white and too male in its roster of correspondents and writers. The criticism peaked in a story published by the feminist website Jezebel and headlined* THE DAILY SHOW'S WOMAN PROBLEM. *It quoted former female staffers to build a case that the show was "a boys' club where women's contributions are often ignored and dismissed," and implied that the first female correspondent hired in seven years got a tryout because she was a hottie. Olivia Munn had made her* Daily Show *debut three weeks before the story appeared, delivering part of her first report as Senior Asian Correspondent in fluent Vietnamese.*

JO MILLER

The Daily Show, these rooms are full of women who make the show go every day. The executive producers, the producers, you don't see them on the camera so they don't exist. That's offensive as shit, to erase them and say they don't exist, and that they're not important, and that they don't make this workplace.

ALISON CAMILLO

I was walking to work down through Riverside Park, and that's when I started thinking about, "If I could write a letter back to Jezebel, what would I write?" Then I came in and talked to Jo Miller, and that's when we started putting the letter together. Thirty-one *Daily Show* women ended up signing it, and we put it on the show's website.

We must admit it is entertaining to be the subjects of such a vivid and dramatic narrative. However, while rampant sexism at a well-respected show makes for a great story, we want to make something very clear: the place you may have read about is not our office.

The Daily Show isn't a place where women quietly suffer on the sidelines as barely tolerated tokens. On the contrary: just like the men here, we're indispensable. We generate a significant portion of the show's creative content and the fact is, it wouldn't be the show that you love without us.

LAUREN SARVER MEANS

I've never, ever personally felt that my gender impeded my progress along the way. And the unsung hero of *The Daily Show* is Jen Flanz. She is an inspiration to every girl who's come up at the show. She's the superhero, rock star, best friend, big sister, prom queen of *The Daily Show*, and I think after Jon, she was the second most important in shaping the spirit of the show and what it felt like to work there.

JEN FLANZ

I just could not have been more angry. I sit in a room and throw out jokes with these guys every day, work on the visuals of the show. We have women on set with writer credits. Women field producers, women correspondents.

Is the late-night industry saturated with white men? Sure, yes, but that's because they all grew up watching shows and wanting to be in this for a long time. I didn't grow up watching late night. I didn't care, and maybe that's more on society than on women.

KRISTEN SCHAAL

I don't think *The Daily Show* hates women at all. I think the show loves women, and it wasn't doing anything different than any other show. Well, I will say that after the Jezebel article came out, I got on the show a lot more, so I am grateful about that. It was a good wakeup call.

JON STEWART

Within the shitstorm were some real nuggets. The Jezebel story articulated a very clear problem we had. But it wasn't because I didn't think women are funny. It was ignorance, more or less. Ignorance of a system that was designed to perpetuate a particular sense of humor and individual. Ignorance of what it took to actively subvert that system. Ignorance of what the value of that would be. The triple crown of ignorance. They didn't know we were in the process of changing those things, and we probably didn't change them fast enough.

The nerve that story struck was that it delved into the worst kind of criticism of the show, which is, "We know something about Jon Stewart's character that you don't. He's pretending to be something that he's not." That struck me as lazy. And I thought it was an implied criticism of Olivia Munn that was not fair, either, that we hadn't hired more women until we found someone hot. We hired her because we thought she was funny.

But the larger premise that we didn't do enough to find women writers and performers, that was justified.

STEVE BODOW

The fact is, when it comes to hiring writers, the show has had blind submissions for years. I know because I developed it, in about 2009 as head writer. And we've continued it, with adaptations, having chiefly to do with expanding the applicant pool. And for all the ink about how terribly skewed the writers' room supposedly was, under Jon we had the most even male-female split in late night. I'm not going to say the show has become a perfect place for women, but it certainly is a good place for women to work.

LIZZ WINSTEAD

The Daily Show is one of the hardest shows to execute well in the history of shows, because it requires a hybrid human being—take gender out of it— who eats, drinks, and breathes not just the news, but politics and history, that is funny and can write, and then can translate that funny into the tone and the voice of Jon. And there were just not a lot of people who gave two fucks about politics and who wanted to write. So when you ask yourself, "Why does *The Daily Show* not reflect the world at large?" it's like, the world at large doesn't like this shit! Why do you think our fucking country's falling apart?

STEVE BODOW

Jon underwent a bona fide evolution on some things over the years, with diversity being prime among them. It was something that he came to believe in deeply by the third quarter of his run, and by the fourth quarter, he'd put in place more mechanisms to make it happen. Especially on camera, he just came to see that having this diversity of people allows us to say a whole lot of things that we couldn't get at before, and once you get out of that defensive clutch from people telling you, "You're doing it wrong," and open up, instead, to what the possibilities might be if you look at it a different way, it could be really liberating, creatively juicing.

JON STEWART

I'd always looked at the metrics of hiring people wrong. They were about, "This guy can write nonsense jokes. This guy writes great one-liners." The metrics weren't about life experience, things that make the show healthy and fuller.

In the old days, when we were looking for correspondents, you would call a casting agent and say, "Who do you have?" And they would send you the same thirty improv people that they all sent everywhere, and a lot of them were really good, but they all tended to be of the same ilk. So we had to learn how to expand. That's probably one of the things we learned much deeper into the run, which was you have to be active in finding interesting talent outside of the general pipeline.

Daily Show producers became more aggressive in expanding the pool of applicants, circulating word to friends and colleagues to encourage a more diverse set of choices, but they also pushed agents for a wider list of possible correspondents and writers.

In the meantime, though, the show broke out of its routines in another provocative way, and this time it didn't just make headlines—it helped pass a law. The issue was health care for firefighters and other first responders who had become sick after working at Ground Zero in the days after the attack on the World Trade Center. It brought together several of The Daily Show's *major themes—the fecklessness of politicians, the misguided media focus on petty squabbles instead of policy impact, the twisted uses of "patriotism."*

The Zadroga bill, which would pay for 9/11 first responder medical treatment, was stalled by partisan maneuvering. Senate Republicans filibustered the bill—even as they passed a tax cut for the wealthy. So in mid-December, Stewart decided to become an overt advocate, something he'd avoided doing for eleven years.

JON STEWART

In 2001, the first responders were told, "No, the air is safe." Sure, why not? Why wouldn't it be safe—you're taking a thousand different chemicals and you're burning it at a high flame, and inhaling it, freebasing it?

In 2010 we had gotten wind of the fact that those guys had gone down to DC and almost been thrown out of Congress. That's originally what got our dander up. So it's on our radar and we're following a story line.

Congress was going to leave for Christmas, and [Mitch] McConnell had a friend who had retired from the Senate. Was it Judd Gregg? Yeah. And McConnell gave a crazy, emotional, literally tearful speech. His friend is leaving, and it's Christmas, I want to get out of here, and he's utterly ignoring these sick guys or treating them like a distraction, with the backdrop of the Republicans having waved the bloody flag many times.

ADAM CHODIKOFF

I assembled a list, going back to 2001, of congressmen who voted against Zadroga after praising the 9/11 responders. It was a long list.

JON STEWART

Lowitt and those guys in the video room, they're all on lockdown, looking for video that makes the connections. The point of the show is always, let's make connections. So what are our connections? "McConnell is superemotional. At the same time they're being really cold to the firefighters." Okay. Well, have the Republicans ever shown emotion about 9/11 previously, having nothing to do with these guys? Cut to all the speeches of the Republicans in tears.

It was one of those issues where normally we would come up with the workaround, the funny conceit. But with certain situations you just feel like you run out of fun to be had, and the most powerful thing to do would be to just go right at it. Doing a panel with the first responders, it felt like an unusual thing for us to do. I called up John Feal and was like, "Can you get me guys?"

JOHN FEAL, *Ground Zero demolition supervisor, head of Fealgood Foundation, charity group for first responders*

For eight years we'd been walking the halls of Congress fighting for Zadroga. Now it was about a week before the deadline and the bill was in trouble. Out of nowhere I get a call from Beth Shorr, Jon's assistant. I was a fan of the show, but I didn't know him at all. Jon got on the phone—he was eating a sandwich or something—and he's like, "Hey, John, you're going to come on my show tomorrow. We're going to make fun of Republicans, and we're going to get the bill passed." I was like, "Holy shit, Jon Stewart's calling me!"

I had to be in DC the next day. I had a meeting with Nancy Pelosi. So that whole day before I left for DC, I worked with Beth and I vetted four guys. A non-uniformed cop, a firefighter, a construction worker, a city transportation department guy. Yeah, it's probably the best thing I never did, going on that show.

JON STEWART

Those four guys were eloquent, real, angry, and still had a great sense of humor. They were human, and that's what the situation needed, their humanity. I think they felt relieved to be able to have their say. Those guys were tired, man. They were tired of fighting this.

Thank god Denis Leary was away shooting something, because my original idea was to have the firefighters on with Leary as the character from *Rescue Me*. And in the middle of it I was going to say to Leary, "Hey, dude, you know you're not actually a fireman, right?" That was because I was nervous, because we'd never done something like that, and I thought, "Okay, what can I do to inject humor into this?" Denis would've been funny, but it would've been the wrong tone.

I was in the green room beforehand, with Kenny Specht and John Devlin, who's just passed away, and Ken George and Chris Bowman, basically just to say, "Good to see you guys. On the show, we just want you to talk from the heart." Because sometimes people come on and they think, "Oh, okay, he's going to want us to be funny."

And I was ranting to them about, "These fucking congressmen, they just want to go home, they're talking about how nostalgic they are for Christmas and they can't bear another day away from Tennessee or Arizona…" And Kenny Specht said, "Oh, you know we always thought it was an honor to work on the holidays, to protect people's families."

And I told him, "Say that. That's how we're ending."

Stewart set the stage with a furious introduction entitled "Worst Responders" that castigated the Senate for misplaced priorities and Fox News for being beaten on the story by Al Jazeera. Then he introduced Specht, Devlin, Bowman, and George for a nine-minute conversation that was by turns painful and enraging. And highly effective.

GLEN CAPLIN, *senior communications director for U.S. congressman Anthony Weiner, 2005–2010, and U.S. senator Kirsten Gillibrand, 2010–2015*

Here's what happened. The New York *Daily News* had been like a dog with a bone on this issue for ten years. That kept the New York delegation's feet to the fire. They don't want to get beaten up by their hometown newspaper. And the first responders had made dozens of trips to DC. But it never became a national issue, even though there are first responders in the program from all fifty states. On the Senate side, Kirsten and Chuck Schumer had been working hard on Zadroga. On the House side, you had Carolyn Maloney, Jerry Nadler, and Peter King. But we're in late December and Republicans filibuster the bill. Jon Stewart did his show, and the next day Shep Smith, on Fox, goes nuts: "Jon Stewart is right! No one's covering this. It is shameful! This is a national thing."

Then Fox decides to give it the full Fox treatment. That put an enormous amount of pressure on the Republicans. And so they caved. We don't get there without the *Daily News*. We don't get there without all the hard work of Kirsten and the responders themselves. If you take one piece out of the Jenga puzzle, the whole thing falls down. But it doesn't happen unless *The Daily Show* flips the switch. And the important thing is Jon didn't just shame Congress, he shamed the media. Really important thing. The impact was massive.

JON STEWART

The problem would have been if the segment just made everybody go, "Yeah, I was thinking that, too." Which is fine. But for that feeling to effect something, it has to be because it's so weightless. Maybe this is a better analogy: It's Patrick Swayze in *Ghost*. Generally, *The Daily Show*, we're just in the subway, yelling at dead people. But if you really focus it just the right way, at the proper time, you can move a can, as long as that can is sort of near the edge of something. That's all that Zadroga was.

DENIS LEARY, *comedian, actor*

Kind of remarkable when you think about it. A show that can make you laugh that hard, and at the same time discuss political and social issues on a friendly level, an intellectual level, and on a level where it actually makes a difference. Kind of crazy.

JOSH LIEB

The show didn't seek out places to do good, but this was a particular time where people were getting fucked for doing what was right for the city and for the country. So we very happily said, "Hey, America, listen up."

It worked. Six days after the panel of first responders appeared on The Daily Show, *Congress hastily approved $4.3 billion to cover the cost of medical care for those sickened by the World Trade Center's toxic fumes and dust—with one devilish catch: The funding would expire in 2015.*

14

Anthony and Cleopenis

The end of an extraordinary, exhausting 2010 brought a major reshuffling of Daily Show *leadership. Lieb left, because he wanted more variety in his work life, and because he wanted to raise his kids in California (three years later Lieb would return to New York, taking "the only job better than the one I'd left," as showrunner for* The Tonight Show, *where Jimmy Fallon was the new host). Javerbaum departed for the second time, and for good this time, to write musicals (his exit, like those of other* Daily Show *writers, was celebrated with a roast at Keens Steakhouse, where Lieb and Jill Baum, Javerbaum's assistant, delivered the most witheringly funny shots). Steve Bodow, Jen Flanz, and Jim Margolis were named executive producers; Tim Carvell was promoted to head writer; and Pam DePace, who had the pivotal insight that* The Daily Show *should invest heavily in TiVos, was made a supervising producer.*

The host remained the same. But Stewart was changing, too. Ingesting the bilious flood of political news and regurgitating it as satire was growing tougher after twelve years. The show's tone became less ironic and more biting, never more so than when it jousted with Fox. "The Parent Company Trap," for example, dissected a Muslim-mongering discussion on Fox & Friends *about the Saudi money behind the proposed "Ground Zero mosque" without mentioning that Prince Al-Waleed bin Talal was the second-biggest shareholder in News Corporation, the parent company of Fox.*

Jon Stewart: [*at anchor desk*] If we want to cut off funding to the terror mosque, we must, together as a nation, stop watching Fox.
Fox tells us the terrible thing about this Kingdom Foundation is where they fund, and he's a very bad guy. But they never mentioned this

fella's name. And they never showed this fella's picture. And they certainly never mentioned that the fella they're talking about is part owner of their company. Did the gang at *Fox & Friends* genuinely not know the head of the Kingdom Foundation's name, and the fact that he is one of their part owners? Or were they purposely covering it up, because it did not help their fear-driven narrative? For more we're joined by Senior Media Analysts John Oliver and Wyatt Cenac.

John Oliver: [*wearing pale blue T-shirt with* TEAM STUPID *across the chest*] I'm going to go with they didn't know. Remember, things are hectic on the morning show. Plus Gretchen [Carlson] isn't there, and she's the only one who knows how to use Google.

Wyatt Cenac: [*wearing pale blue T-shirt with* TEAM EVIL *across the chest*] Look, I'll give you [Brian] Kilmeade and [Steve] Doocy. But do you know who Dan Senor and Dana Perino used to work for? George W. Bush! And do you know who George W. Bush used to hang with? Prince Al-Waleed bin Talal! That's some evil shit! That's a level of knowing obfuscation that can only come from having a heart of pure evil!

Domestic, congressional-grade evil didn't escape attention, with The Daily Show *pushing into a wider range of sensitive subjects. A Kristen Schaal chat skewered a House bill restricting abortion funding to victims of "forcible" rape.*

KRISTEN SCHAAL

I was the Senior Women's Issues Correspondent. The only subject that I was allowed to even talk about on the show was women's issues, so I felt 100 percent responsible for representing women, and sometimes that would frustrate me. Women's issues were sort of hard to get on the show, because they weren't often making big headlines. That "forcible rape" story was one I read about on my own in *Mother Jones*. Jon could tell it would make a good piece because I was so angry. That's the piece I'm always proudest of.

Jon Stewart: [*at anchor desk*] The bill seeks to undo a long-standing compromise that allows federal funding for abortion in extreme cases, like rape. Under the new bill, federal funding for abortions would be limited to cases resulting from what they call "forcible rape." Which could possibly exclude cases where women have been drugged or women with limited mental capacity, or statutory rape.

Kristen Schaal: [*sitting across from Stewart, grinning and raising her arms in triumph*] Hallelujah! It's about time! By proposing this legislation, Republicans are finally closing the glaring rape loophole in our health-care system. You'd be surprised how many drugged, underaged, or mentally handicapped young women have been gaming the system. Sorry, ladies—the free abortion ride is over!

Jon Stewart: [*dumbfounded*] Kristen, all rape, by definition, is forcible.

Kristen Schaal: Jon, I'm not comfortable with that word "all." In truth, there's a whole rainbow of rape covering a wide spectrum of gray areas. Like statutory rape. Something Whoopi Goldberg explained in the Roman Polanski case.

Whoopi Goldberg: [*in video clip from* The View] "He was not charged. I know it was not rape-rape."

Kristen Schaal: See? Plying a thirteen-year-old girl with Quaaludes, alcohol, and a famous penis isn't rape-rape. It's just rape-esque, and shouldn't be covered!
The important thing is, Congress is redefining rape to protect us from the worst kind of rape: money rape. That's forcible taking of taxpayers' money to pay for abortions. They have no say in the matter. They just have to lay back and take it while their bank accounts are violated over and over and over again!

Jon Stewart: [*spluttering*] How much money are we even talking about here?

Kristen Schaal: Well, in 2006 alone, federal funds helped pay for 191 abortions for victims of rape, incest, or when the health of the mother is at risk. So that works out to...[*pulls abacus out from under desk, slides beads*]...two-tenths of a penny per taxpayer.

The day after Schaal's piece appeared, the Republican sponsor of the bill, New Jersey congressman Chris Smith, changed the language, if not all of the substance, of the amendment.

It wasn't just the subject matter that was stretching—it was the actual show.

Thanks to the wonders of modern Internet technology, Stewart's third-act interviews could be allowed to ramble beyond the bounds of the nightly broadcast, with the extra material posted on Comedy Central's website. Guests soon took it as a badge of approval for Stewart to keep them overtime.

HILLARY KUN

Jon continually pushed to widen our range of guests, and to go after inaccessible people. The strangest one that's never worked out has got to be Paul Ryan. He says he's a fan of the show, but he's always refused to come on. I've gone to amazing lengths to try to make it happen. One of my relatives was going to be at the same wedding with Ryan in Wisconsin, so I had him make a pitch for us. Still didn't work.

We also spent a great deal of time trying to get Sarah Palin to be a guest. Tons of calls, e-mails. Jon may have even written her a letter.

JON STEWART

I didn't write her a letter. I cut out some letters from a magazine. Like a hostage note.

HILLARY KUN

On the other hand, a guest who I never expected to really get was Pervez Musharraf. He came on twice, the first time when he was in New York for the United Nations and he was the prime minister of Pakistan.

JON STEWART

That day was nuts. It was 2006 and Musharraf was fresh off of a couple of assassination attempts, and America was fresh off its paranoia overload. We had snipers up on the roof and AK-47s in the hallway and bomb-sniffing dogs in our building. It's always a relief to the staff that it's not drug-sniffing dogs. Nobody there had bombs, but man, would we have lost some people, had it been something else.

Musharraf got to wear a bulletproof vest and sit behind the Kevlar front during the interview. I was just out there. The security guys told me to duck in case anything happened.

Are you saying I should've read Musharraf's book, as much trouble as he was going through to get there, is that what you're saying?

HILLARY KUN

Jon always read the books. He's a freakishly fast reader.

JON STEWART

You want the interviews to have a point of view, even if that point of view is, "I can't believe I'm speaking to the guy." There was a certain level of astonishment that Musharraf was there.

So I was trying to defuse a very real question, which is, "Where is Osama bin Laden?" by offering Musharraf tea and Twinkies. You have to find some way to disarm natural suspicion, and also, the job of the show is to still present something mildly entertaining. If not funny, interesting. If not interesting, at least somewhat smart, and if not smart, weird.

Any time you're dealing with an autocrat, you generally take a slightly more wide-eyed approach, so that there's an understanding that you know what's going on, but there's also a nod to the fact that he's an authoritarian.

So the second time Musharraf was on, in 2011, after bin Laden had been killed, that's why I asked him, "Wasn't that weird, that bin Laden was in Pakistan all along?"

Do I worry that we humanize certain people? I don't think a decent shot on *The Daily Show* is going to necessarily raise Musharraf's rates in Pakistan.

Because Jim Cramer was beaten to a bloody pulp, the expectation became that anybody that came on would receive that beating and would roll over and show me their belly. It may be more satisfying for people to see someone strapped to a chair and be berated, but that's not a sustainable, revelatory, or interesting model. I think it's much more interesting to have an interview reveal itself of its own momentum and inertia.

AKBAR AHMED, professor of Islamic Studies, American University

After September 11 it had become fashionable to just associate, in a very lazy way, anything to do with violence with Muslim and call it Muslim terrorism, or Islamic terrorism. And I was wondering who is going to stand up and say, "Wait a minute, this is not how it is." I'm writing about Muslims in America, and I need to also understand larger society, and in that larger society, the media is very important. So, I see media like Fox and I say, "Okay, where's the counterpoint in American culture?"

Jon Stewart, almost single-handedly, changed the nature of the dialogue. He got guests like Musharraf. He, later on, got Malala [Yousafzai]. He had me, but he also had people like Aasif Mandvi and people like Hasan Minhaj. So people are seeing, "Well, these guys are just like us."

And it goes the other way, too. People are not looking at him, in the Muslim world, as a Jewish American, or even as an American. In Egypt, they're saying, "This is Jon Stewart. Look, he's reaching out to one of us."

Because of that respect, I think Jon should have challenged Musharraf more. Musharraf was selling one kind of Pakistan, which didn't exist. Appearing on *The Daily Show* did a lot of good for Musharraf. Jon allowed him to get away a bit too easily.

JON STEWART

I can't tell you how many times I was asked, "Why would you have that guy on the show?" Whether it was Musharraf or O'Reilly. My feeling is always, "Why would you not take an opportunity to find, within someone's humanity, some understanding of why they've done what they've done, or why you believe so differently from what they believe?" I think there's an instinct to want to two-dimensionalize people that have odious opinions, but maybe it's a little more complicated than that.

The Daily Show had special resonance for viewers in countries where democracy was in its infancy, or was still a dream. One Chinese fan took the risk of illegally downloading the show, then spent several hours each day subtitling episodes so they could be quietly disseminated on social media. She enjoyed the humor, but she envied the free speech. "We're not interested in your politics," Maggie Chen told journalist Anand Giridharadas. "We're interested in the style of the show, and the idea that you can use jokes to tell the truth."

The Middle East had been a significant Daily Show *subject for years, but the 2011 "Arab Spring" heightened Stewart's attention to the region. Little did he know that one of his biggest fans was right in the middle of the action.*

BASSEM YOUSSEF, *Egyptian political satirist*

In Egypt, there were very few TV channels from the outside world—the German channels, the Polish sex channels, and CNN International. And of course, CNN is boring, except that it carried the *Daily Show* "Global Edition." So, for me, Jon Stewart was not just another comedy show. He was basically my passage to American politics. And Jon was the best newsperson who ever covered the Gaza War. He was maybe the only person who stood against the oppressive actions of the Israeli government. Of course, they called him a self-hating Jew, but what he did was journalism. He didn't go so deep, because that's not his job, but he was fair about something that is totally untouchable in American popular culture.

I fantasized about having a show like Jon's in Egypt.

At the time, though, Youssef was a heart surgeon. During Egypt's eighteen-day revolution he treated wounded prodemocracy protesters in Cairo's Tahrir Square. Then he would go home and see Egypt's TV news wildly distorting the reality of what he'd just seen. So Youssef decided he would create his own satirical news show and upload it to YouTube. Three months and five million views later, Youssef was offered a weekly slot on an actual Egyptian TV channel, and with the help of puppets, mocking musical numbers, and Daily Show*–like graphics, the doctor-turned-comedian was making jokes about the Muslim Brotherhood, the strongman Hosni Mubarak, and his successor, President Mohamed Morsi, in a genuinely dangerous environment. The military-backed Egyptian government started cracking down on dissent.*

BASSEM YOUSSEF

There were some moments that were very scary, with thugs putting the theater under siege. But when I was summoned for questioning under Morsi, I was thinking, "If they put me in jail, I'm a hero—but I'm not going to have time to finish the episode."

He may have been a trained medical professional, but Youssef's show business instincts were sharp: He made sure to mention Stewart whenever he was interviewed.

BASSEM YOUSSEF

It worked—the first-ever English language article about me was called "The Jon Stewart of the Nile." By the time I came to New York in 2012, he had heard about me and asked me to be on the show.

Bassem Youssef: There are new charges coming up [against me]: "Propagating and promoting homosexuality and obscenity."

Jon Stewart: You know, we have a show like that. We call it *Glee*... Here's why you have my undying support and friendship. You are doing what I take for granted all the time—you are carving out the space for people to breathe and express themselves. It's incredibly admirable.

Bassem Youssef: The thing is, I get asked this so many times— "Aren't you afraid? Aren't you scared for your life?" And I tell them, "If I choose today to tone it down, if I choose today to shut up, tomorrow me and you and all of us will be forced to. And today what's considered a luxury will be taken away."

Jon Stewart: That's incredible. And here's the best part about it—for most satirists or comedians, they've been fired from every other job. You're a successful heart surgeon as well. Talk about somebody that really makes my mother angry—a successful heart surgeon who has decided to be a comedian?

The threats against Youssef grew more serious as his show grew more popular and as the aftermath of the Egyptian revolution turned chaotic, with violent clashes and a backlash from the military. Stewart stayed in contact with Youssef, asking whether more Daily Show *segments about him would help ensure his safety.*

BASSEM YOUSSEF

And I said, "Well, not really, because I don't want people to get the idea that I'm being supported by the United States." Because there was a story in Egypt that I am being trained by Jon Stewart, who is being recruited by the CIA to use satire against the country.

I know America has problems, but if taxpayer money is being spent to recruit Jon Stewart, things are worse than I realized.

It was a different kind of man of science who turned out to be one of The Daily Show's *most frequent and feisty visitors. The appearances by Neil deGrasse Tyson started out fairly conventional, usually centering on his newest book, but in 2012 they took an unusual turn.*

NEIL deGRASSE TYSON, *astrophysicist, director, Hayden Planetarium, American Museum of Natural History*

When I came on to talk about *Space Chronicles*, I needed a tennis serve to send back Jon's way if he got the better end of me in an exchange. But the interview was a lovefest, and I thought, "I've got to bring this up anyway." I waited until the very end, and I said, "Oh, by the way, the earth in your opening credits is spinning backward." He picked up the book with both hands, slammed it on the desk, and said, "Son of a bitch!" and then it fades to black.

Oh, yeah, we laughed about it when he went to commercial. But he never did change the rotation. I'm told by the *Daily Show* staff that when Jon takes questions from the audience, every single time someone asks, "When are you going to switch the earth?" So, it haunted him, surely, for the rest of the show.

That playful confrontation also encouraged the Daily Show *writers to make use of the theatrical Tyson as a character in ever more elaborate scripted bits—wearing a silk robe and bedroom slippers to dissect the magnitude of China's pollution problem, and using a flashlight and a spooky laugh as he allowed for the remote possibility of extraterrestrial undead in "Neil deGrasse Tyson, Buzzkill of Science."*

Jon Stewart: Space zombies! I knew it! You are afraid of space zombies!

Neil deGrasse Tyson: No, not at all. I'm afraid of *real* things. [*studio lights dim; Tyson shines flashlight on his own face as in a cheap horror movie*] Like how trillions of years from now, the irreversible increase in entropy in our asymptotic descent to absolute zero will leave the universe as nothing more than a cold, inert wasteland. Devoid of life, movement, and even the very concept of energy. *Bwwwahahaha!*

Jon Stewart: You're freaking everybody out, dude. Listen, you know I can just turn the lights back on? [*studio lights come up*]

Neil deGrasse Tyson: Oh, so you have the power to do that, but not make the globe in your opening credits turn the right way?

Jon Stewart: Motherfucking Tyson!

Between the jokes, Stewart always wanted Tyson's appearances to explore complex scientific concepts—which helped underscore The Daily Show's *defense of facts and reason. Tyson appreciated the underlying seriousness.*

NEIL deGRASSE TYSON

Jon was a guest on *StarTalk*, my radio show. I asked him, "What was your college major?" He said, "Oh, I majored in chemistry," and that he later switched because he realized that chemistry was hard. But I could still ask him the geek question: "What's your favorite element?" He said, "Carbon, because it's the slut of the periodic table, because it combines with everything." You don't make that joke unless you've thought about science and you embrace science.

That was a huge gift to late-night television. If I were the only scientist Jon interviewed, then I'd say, "Okay, he likes me," but since he had scientists on the show frequently, even scientists you've never heard of, that told me the interest is real.

Sometimes, though, even years of passion and preparation didn't pay off in the moment. Since 2003, Stewart and The Daily Show *had become experts in the political and military conduct of the war in Iraq, and the show had done dozens of segments lacerating Donald Rumsfeld, Bush's first secretary of defense and a chief architect of the war on terror. So in 2012, when the retired Rumsfeld came on as a guest to promote* Known and Unknown: A Memoir, *all the conditions appeared to be in place for a classic Stewart cross-examination, a chance to deliver some liberal righteousness directly to a pillar of the misguided conservative establishment.*

DONALD RUMSFELD, Bush Administration secretary of defense, 2001–2006

What's it called, Stewart's program?

JON STEWART

That was one of those things where people's expectation of wanting blood is not realistic. Right off the bat, I said to Rumsfeld, "When you guys sold that war..." And Rumsfeld said, "Well, presented our case." "Well, you sold it. You didn't present a case for war, like, here are the positives and here are the negatives. You presented the positives. That's what we call sales, actually."

That should have been the focus of the whole interview, because it was the crux of their deception. But I was so concerned with all the preparation we'd done that I blew past that gift Rumsfeld gave me at the beginning. I was not happy with it.

DONALD RUMSFELD

I enjoyed the interview. I told my wife, Joyce, after the program, that I think had we been in high school together we would have been friends. I mean that as a compliment.

Several months later at the memorial service for Betty Ford in Grand Rapids, after saying hello to the Ford family, President Bill Clinton made a beeline over to me, shook my hand, and said, "You went on the Jon Stewart program." I said, "Yes, I did." He said, "Good for you. I saw it and it was very good."

HALLIE HAGLUND

I worked on the preparation for the Rumsfeld interview, and that's definitely one that you wish Jon would've gone in harder. Ultimately, Rumsfeld is such a slithery guy that it probably would've been to no effect. But I think Jon was so tired by that point in his run.

RORY ALBANESE

I remember Jon feeling like he blew it. I remember saying to him afterward, "Look, dude, it's hard. You're sitting across from an old guy. You felt bad." Do I think he could have wrecked Donald Rumsfeld? Yes, I do. Jon was pretty soft on him. I don't know, man. You're going to pitch a shitty game sometimes.

It was far more common, though, for Stewart to challenge his right-of-center guests, many of whom treated the experience as a validation of their fair-mindedness and made multiple appearances on The Daily Show.

CHRIS WALLACE, *Fox News anchor*

For people like me, one, it was kind of fun to go on *The Daily Show*, and two, it was a little bit like being invited to the cool kids' table. It was a kind of a mark—"Hey, you're a player, you're somebody that Jon is sufficiently interested in that he wants to have you on his show."

I don't want to exaggerate the importance of Jon Stewart. Roger Ailes has never talked to me about going on Jon Stewart, nor do I know if he ever watched it. But I don't think my kids have ever been as impressed as when I did *The Daily Show*. They'd have a swag bag, you know. Not an Oscars swag bag but a little swag bag, and whether it was my kids or my producers, they would just go through it like raptors looking for the spoils.

Jon and I seemed to get along, and they invited me back a total of five times. So then Jon comes to DC and is a guest on my show. I was surprised at how touchy he was throughout that interview, because I saw it as trying, in my own way, to kind of do to him what he did to me and does to other people. I came away feeling that he dished it out better than he could take it.

The interview runs, and I remember I went to the *Huffington Post* and in red letters that were in a font only slightly smaller than you would announce World War Three, in quotes it said, "You're insane," which is what Jon said to me at one point.

And it became a much bigger deal than I thought it was going to be. Jon went on the air to kind of call me out and to sort of do a truth squad of the interview, and then I came back that Sunday and did a truth squad of his truth squad.

The second week, after I had done my thing, he called me, which I was surprised but pleased by, to basically say, "No hard feelings, this has gotten out of control, and I just want you to know this isn't personal." And I said the same thing back to him, and that was that.

Whether you agreed with Jon or not, I think that he was very much an idealist and really wanted the system to work well to help people in the ways that he thinks that government should help people. His show was done out of a spirit not of cynicism so much as frustration or dashed hopes. And that was actually one of the things I always liked about Jon's show, is that, yes, he mocked you, but it was mocking in a kind of disappointed way, like we should do better than that.

GLENN BECK

Why didn't I accept his invitation to go on the show? First of all, I grew up in an alcoholic family and I was the peacemaker in the family, and I hate conflict, believe it or not. I also am smart enough to know when I'm going to lose a fight. I'm going into Jon's house and whatever I would say, he would win. No thank you. He would've gone for the comedy, and you're not going to win when comedy is involved.

*   *   *

In January 2009, the Republicans, in a spasm of tent broadening, had chosen Michael Steele, a black, conservative former lieutenant governor of Maryland and a commentator on Fox News, as chairman of the Republican National Committee. Steele soon talked his way into a series of kooky controversies. The Daily Show, though, was eager to bring the unpredictable, independent-minded Steele on as a guest. When that failed, the show went to the felt in a segment called "Steele Crazy After All These Years," with Wyatt Cenac providing the voice of the jive-talking puppet.

MICHAEL STEELE, chairman, Republican National Committee, 2009–2011

I tuned in one night after an incredibly long day in a hotel somewhere in the Midwest and there was this blue thing called me. I was like, "What the hell is that?" It really struck me as this 1970s, Superfly, Shaft kind of period speak. I forget what I was being pilloried for, but I just remember being amused by the whole thing.

Real Michael Steele: [*in videoclip, at a fund-raiser*] "What you don't do is engage in a land war in Afghanistan. This is a war of Obama's choosing. This is not something the United States had actively prosecuted or wanted to engage in."

Jon Stewart: Okay! Forget about the fact that we'd been in Afghanistan since before Obama was even a gleam in the Senate's eye... This is the head of the Republican Party going against one of his party's core principles: blowing shit up in other countries... We go now to our good friend, Republican Michael Steele.

Puppet Michael Steele: [*wearing a bright yellow polo shirt and a chef's apron, voiced by Wyatt Cenac*] Fourth of July at the cribble, baby! I'm feeling the thrill of the grill, 'cause you know I likes to chill!

Jon Stewart: I must say I didn't expect you to be so upbeat. Your comments about Afghanistan are very controversial.

Puppet Michael Steele: I nailed it! I hibbled that bibble like a jibble on the dribble!

Jon Stewart: I'm not sure what that means, but people in your own party are blasting you. Here's Senator Lindsey Graham.

Lindsey Graham: [*in video clip, on* Face the Nation] "Dismayed, angry, upset. It was an uninformed, unnecessary, unwise, untimely comment."

Puppet Michael Steele: [*frowning, wounded, wiping eye*] Lindabale Grahibble?

MICHAEL STEELE

They said they did the puppet because I canceled an appearance. The request never came to my office. I wanted to do the show but the RNC communications shop was very nervous about it, because I was one of these guys who didn't stick to the script. They like you to go on TV and wear the uniform and say the words.

It was a comedy show, but Jon was asking a question that a lot of people, rank-and-file folks within the respective parties, ask themselves—why can't we compromise? You have the extremes animating and driving the discussion—Bernie Sanders and the progressives on the left, Ted Cruz or even more Donald Trump and Ben Carson on the right. It's a sort of standing-in-the-corner fight. Jon spoke to the frustration that the fight never ends. There is no room for actually starting to get things done.

Ultimately I did go on *The Daily Show* once I left the RNC. I got to confront the Muppet and Jon. Before the show Wyatt Cenac stopped by and we shook hands and he said, "It's a real honor to meet you. I've enjoyed playing you for the past two years."

I have the puppet. He has his own chair in my office. Sometimes I meet people and they're disappointed I don't speak like Puppet Mike Steele, you know, "That's how we do it on the street, lunch meat!"

SENATOR JOHN McCAIN

Jon and I had our disagreements. But look, when we focus on that one bad interview I had with Jon—I was so grateful later when he supported me on the issue of torture. That's far more important, frankly, than any real or imagined slight that I might've had from him. I was very grateful for that, because that's a seminal issue about what America's all about. It meant a lot to me, and he wasn't just talking about me. Jon was explaining to these young Americans why torture was such an important issue. That's what I really appreciated.

He is like Mark Twain or Will Rogers. He is a modern-day humorist of that genre, of that level.

Absolutely, I took the gift bag every time I was on the show. Absolutely. It was one of the nicest bribes I ever got.

JON STEWART

Puppet Mike Steele, Puppet John McCain, Gitmo. Oh, there's a lot of puppet subtext to *The Daily Show*.

No. I can explain all that pretty easily. You run out of ways to skin cats, and so all you can do is try puppets, try cartoons, try whatever you can get your hands on to make it a little different.

Democrats certainly weren't immune from prop humor and rough treatment. Stewart and the show had closely chronicled the battle over creating a new national health-insurance program. Three years after winning the legislative war, in October 2013, with great fanfare, the $800 million Obamacare website was finally launched . . . and immediately crashed.

STEVE BODOW

The website opened and it was so shitty. I came in the next day fuming. Jon came in and didn't see it at first— "I don't know, websites are hard, they'll get it right." I laid out all the reasons this was such a big problem, in policy and reputation and messaging, everything the White House was trying to fucking do. Within a couple of days we waded in; by the time the Sebelius thing came around, Jon was way angrier than me.   •

The stakes, and the ugly mood, were heightened by the tactics of Tea Party Republicans in Congress. Led by first-term Texas senator Ted Cruz, they had refused to fund the federal government in a bid to cripple Obamacare, halting food-safety inspections and closing national parks for sixteen days in October 2013. Or, as the attempted extortion was billed by The Daily Show, *"Shutstorm 2013."*

Six days into the ongoing website fiasco, Kathleen Sebelius, the secretary of Health and Human Services, arrived at the Daily Show *studio for a previously scheduled interview. "I anticipated taking a beating," she says. She was right, but Sebelius's tangled attempts to answer Stewart's questions were perceived as a public relations disaster.*

Jon Stewart: Nice to see you. We're going to do a challenge. [*reaches under desk, pulls out laptop, opens it as Sebelius gamely tries to maintain her smile*] I'm going to try and download every movie ever made—and you're going to try to sign up for Obamacare, and we'll see which happens first.

Let me tell you why it may seem I'm a little bit hard on this. For those of us who are somewhat believing that the opposition in Washington right now are crazy people, it is imperative that this government, the government that basically says the federal government has a role to play in people's lives, it feels like it's frustrating to have to defend something that is less than ideal, or is functioning at what seems to be a level of incompetence that is larger than what it should be... So this is a system that's been jerry-rigged to deal with the crazy people. By bending over to deal with the crazy people, we now face default. Has that taught a lesson?

KATHLEEN SEBELIUS, *Obama Administration secretary of Health and Human Services, 2009–2014*

I do remember very clearly leaving the stage feeling that there had been a bit of a mugging and not one that I understood. This tech-savvy administration having a major tech glitch—I own that and was accountable for that. But the line of questioning about the mandates and using our administrative authority to delay one and not delay the other was so sort of bizarre that I felt it was not only out of left field but it didn't make any sense. The part of the interview that was a bit baffling to me then, and still is, is the note on which it ended, with the suggestion that I might be lying to people.

I know Jon was always accused of having a biased presentation tilting way left, and of certainly being an ally to the president. So it is quite possible that this was to even the score. It's possible that he, like a number of people who we had engaged early on in the dialogue to be supportive of this effort, felt they had gone out on a limb and now we really screwed up and they had egg on their faces.

And by the way, I'm a huge fan of Jon Stewart. Always have been. Always will be. Got most of my news from him over the years when I just stopped watching news in Kansas. I watched him have a huge impact in 2010, with the 9/11 bill. We were pushing it from the inside. But he helped galvanize enough people to put enough pressure to really get that bill over the finish line.

JON STEWART

Congressional press secretaries used to come in and have meetings with us: "What do you think would be good for our client? How do you think they should approach a *Daily Show* interview?" And I would say, "Well, you could have them speak what they believe. Just have them stop being so managed, and cautious, and weird. Then maybe we'll have an honest conversation about an area we genuinely disagree on."

But that's not generally what occurs, and that's what I think bothered me about Secretary Sebelius in that interview. They're looking for safe harbor with high upside, not for anything real. We exist to expose the space between the press secretary and the politician.

Way back in January 1999, when Stewart was starting as host of The Daily Show, *Anthony Weiner was beginning his first term in Congress. The two had met in 1985, through mutual college friends, and gotten to know each other better in the early nineties, when Weiner dated a New York friend of Stewart's. Weiner attended standup shows to support Stewart; Stewart wrote a check to support Weiner's first run for New York's city council.*

ANTHONY WEINER, *former U.S. congressman, Democrat, New York, 1999–2011*

We were late-at-night-arguing-about-Israel kind of friends. Jon was smart and opinionated, funny, genuinely interested in politics, and we both had a wiseass Jewish guy sensibility.

JON STEWART

It's fun to get drunk and get in an argument with Anthony Weiner. But there is, I think, a real serious character flaw there: He has to be in the spotlight. When we would hang out and I would be funny, that's when he would generally pick a fight with me.

ANTHONY WEINER

When I ran for Congress, he did an event for me. But no, we didn't stay particularly close, and I wasn't crazy about what he was doing on the show, to be honest. The formula of educating the audience about an issue just enough to whack at it, like a form of tee ball—it seemed a little bit too easy and was accelerating the cynicism around politics. He might've had a serious point underneath it, but what he did, every night, was just basically portray politicians as buffoons, politicians as idiots, politicians as, you know, fools. It accelerated the downward spiral of young people kind of engaging in politics on a serious level. What Jon also served to do—probably correctly—was discredit other outlets who are trying to cover politics, like Fox News, MSNBC, and CNN.

I was in Congress during what I think we'll look back and see as kind of a transition time, when senior guys, working on issues, were supplanted by glib guys, working on TV, as the significant players in Washington. For better or worse, I'm a pretty good example—I care very deeply about issues, but I realized I could short-circuit twenty years of waiting around on the Energy and Commerce Committee by being good at talking about those issues on TV. The rise of split-screen television was happening during those ten, twelve years I was in Congress, and that also mirrored the time that Jon was making hay mocking the era of split-screen TV.

I never asked Jon to go on the show. I went on as a guest once, during the height of the health-care thing. I think that was in February 2010.

Jon Stewart: [after introducing Weiner and sitting behind desk] I've known Anthony for many years. We knew each other in the eighties, we used to go to the beach together. And I could—let's face facts—destroy your political career.

Congressman Anthony Weiner: That's funny. You know the concept of mutually assured destruction, Jon?

Jon Stewart: You believe you have pictures of me as well in compromising positions?

Congressman Weiner: Ohhh, I've got stuff.

JON STEWART
Turned out he did an excellent job of destroying his own career.

Slightly more than a year after Weiner's only appearance as a Daily Show *guest, the congressman tweeted a photo of his erect penis, somewhat disguised in a pair of gray undershorts, to a Seattle-area college student. At first Weiner denied the junk shot was his. Then he claimed his account may have been hacked.*

JASON ROSS

When the story first broke and it wasn't entirely clear if it was real or not, we played the clip of Weiner's nondenial in the morning meeting, where he said something like, "Well, there's lots of pictures out there." Jon immediately said, "Oh, I don't like that. This is not going to end well for him."

Stewart initially felt a bit conflicted, but holding back would have been comedic malpractice, and The Daily Show *quickly made the Weiner scandal a nightly highlight. There was an (animated) appearance by "News Angel Tom Brokaw," urging avoidance of juvenile gossip, and by "Comedy Devil Don Rickles," urging allegiance to laughs ("Comedians don't have friends! They have ex-wives and irritable bowel syndrome!"). An R. Kelly impersonator sang "Whip out the truth!" There were segments titled, "Distinguished Member of Congress," "Anthony and Cleopenis," "The Big Wang Theory," and "Circumcision 2011."*

As additional salacious Weiner texts appeared, life started imitating art—or at least imitating bad porn.

Jon Stewart: [*at anchor desk, next to over-the-shoulder head shot of Weiner captioned,* THE WANGOVER] One of the newly released texts did catch my eye. [*reading, as screenshot of Weiner texts appears*] Anthony Weiner: "Make me an offer I can't refuse." Lady in question: "To get us in the mood, first we watch back-to-back episodes of *The Daily Show* and *The Colbert Report*."
What mood are they going to get into?
Unfortunately, they continued: [*screenshot of woman's text*] "Or if this is not your thing, we can just get drunk and have mad, passionate sex!" Anthony Weiner: "Why choose? With me behind you, can't we both watch *The Daily Show*?"
[*Stewart fakes retching as the studio audience howls, then points at the camera in mock anger*] First of all . . . is this what you people are doing at home when our show is on? I mean, we spend all day writing and producing this thing! If it's just going to be background noise for your amorous—are you people fucking right now!? Hey, Chuck, hit the button that lets me see them! [*springs out of chair*] Oh, my God!

*   *   *

A week later, Weiner tearfully resigned—holding a press conference that Stewart and Oliver gleefully parodied with a bit involving a blender of margaritas. They even managed to keep laughing as Stewart dropped the prop and sliced his hand on broken glass.

ANTHONY WEINER

No, I didn't see a lot of the stuff he did about me at the time. I just had my head somewhere else. But I heard about a segment about me where Jon cut himself. So I called him to see if he was all right. Which, in retrospect, was kind of weird. I'm in free fall, he's pummeling me, and I'm calling him to see if he's all right. He might've called me another time and said some encouraging words— "Listen, you're going to weather this, it's always bad when you're in it," or something like that.

As the time has gone on, and more people have said to me, "Boy, your friend Jon can't be much of a friend, he was really killing you," you know, my view is, with everyone—reporters, colleagues, donors—you know, that I brought this all on myself. I'd never blame anyone else for how they reacted. Seriously, I mean, can you imagine a comedian not making fun of a guy named Weiner, who took pictures?

At one point Jon told me, "You can't confuse what we're making of you and what you really are," or something like that. "We have a piñata that we're whacking, but don't think it's you." That's easy to say, except I'm inside that piñata. I think that that is the way he gets through this. If you know someone who you're beating up on, I guess you have to objectify them rather than personify them.

JON STEWART

I told him, "We have created a character of Anthony Weiner and that's who's being dragged through this process, and while I'm sure you cannot take any solace in that separation, the level of vitriol and jokes is not necessarily commensurate with what happened, and for that I'm sorry."

JASON ROSS

Jon was conscientious about his willingness to destroy the life of practically anybody who really deserved it. He knew, to his credit, that he couldn't possibly go easy on Weiner.

LAUREN SARVER MEANS

I think the most valuable thing that Jon instilled in everyone on the staff was, "If it makes you uncomfortable, that's not necessarily an impediment to what you're trying to say."

So if we were working on a piece where we were confused about something, Jon would say, "Write that confusion into this piece. If you're upset about this, fall into whatever is keeping you from writing this."

JON STEWART

That's part of the challenge that keeps it exciting—making yourself uncomfortable.

15

The Amazing Racism

There was and is no more uncomfortable subject in American life than race. Stewart's run as host coincided with a period of remarkable progress—the first black American president, unprecedented ethnic diversity in major cities—and spasms of ugly backlash—bitter battles over immigration, the deaths of unarmed blacks at the hands of police, the demonization of Muslims as terrorists.

For Stewart, diversifying the Daily Show *staff and the cast wasn't primarily a matter of better reflecting modern American life—it gave him different ways to be funny, and more tools to address racial issues in more nuanced ways. So Larry Wilmore explained how he'd "rather we got casinos" than the twenty-eight days of platitudes that make up Black History Month. Aasif Mandvi traveled to Tennessee to interview opponents of a proposed mosque—or the "Community Center of Death," as* The Daily Show *framed the segment, with clips of mushroom cloud explosions and a talking skull straight from a horror movie.*

AASIF MANDVI

I'm not a Muslim who goes to the mosque or is praying and fasting during Ramadan. But I realized, through the *Daily Show* experience, that I had a dimension of experience to pitch that I really hadn't thought about before. I almost felt like it radicalized me. I started to realize that I was at a madrassa of comedy run mostly by Ivy League–educated Jews, and it started to feel like I was able to find a voice around being Muslim, around being South Asian, that I hadn't even realized was something I wanted to do. And it turned out to be very important to people, other American Muslims, to have a brown guy on *The Daily Show* represent them, to have a voice. Iraq was going on at that time, and people would thank me for talking about it.

One of the pieces I'm proudest of was in Tennessee, where there was opposition to building an Islamic cultural center. I was sitting across from this person who's basically telling me that one out of five Muslims are terrorists, and that there were terrorist training camps behind every mosque in America. Her misinformation about Islam, and the arrogance with which she spoke about this stuff, was hard to sit across from without getting genuinely angry.

But here's the crazy bananas part of it, an example of how much Stephen Colbert was correct when he said people get a lobotomy when you put a camera in front of them. Originally I said to her, "You know that I'm Muslim," and she said something benign like, "Yeah, I kind of figured you were." We had to stop tape for a couple of minutes to change camera batteries or something. Her husband was off to the side, and he fancied himself to be a standup comic. He said, "Honey, when he said to you, 'You know I'm Muslim,' you should've said, 'Nobody's perfect.'"

And she said, "Oh, that would've been really funny. I wish I had thought of that." Personally, I was incredibly offended, but then professionally, as a *Daily Show* guy, I was also, "That's gold. I don't need to be personally offended here, because she is going to basically die on her own sword."

So, we started rolling again. "You do know that I'm Muslim, right?" And she said, "Well, nobody's perfect." That's the one that we used.

But for all of the show's public, on-air grappling with race, it was a private, inside-the-office episode that illustrated just how thorny the topic remains. In June 2011, Congressman Anthony Weiner's first sexting scandal was consuming nearly all the media oxygen. After indulging in a week's worth of crotch shots himself, Stewart wanted to point out that there might be a few more important things going on in the world—oh, say, a secret U.S. bombing of Yemen. To illustrate the idea he spun a game show wheel, built by prop supervisor Justin Chabot, that was divided into serious topics. The wheel's pointer, in classic Daily Show style, was a ten-inch dildo. The rubber rod's final choice seemed harmless at the time.

ELLIOTT KALAN

This was during the Republican primaries, and the bit included a video clip of Herman Cain talking about how congressional bills were too long, and how when Cain became president they wouldn't be longer than three pages. And then Jon, at the desk, does an impression where he says, "I am Herman Cain, and I do not like to read."

JON STEWART

So I'd done the Herman Cain voice. And I'm not sure where it came from, but then there were people saying that I was a racist. It might have been amplified by my friends over at Fox. You know how they do the graphics in the lower third of the screen, we call it "the Cavuto," where they basically slander people and throw a question mark on the end of it: "Are Democrats terrorists?" So it was, "Jon Stewart, racist?" And they don't answer the question. They're just asking. "Your mother a whore? No disrespect intended."

And those moments, you don't take them lightly.

DANIEL RADOSH

Jon would usually come in fifteen minutes, twenty minutes after the morning meeting started. There were many times when Steve Bodow would say, before Jon arrived, "Okay, here's this thing that happened on Fox. Please don't mention it. Let's just see if Jon didn't catch it." And Jon would come in and say, "You see what they said on *Fox & Friends*?", and we'd be like, "Oh, here we go. I guess we're doing it."

STEVE BODOW

When people call Jon out personally, it gets his blood up and he wants to go back at them. I usually want us to not go back and revisit things. And have often been proven wrong. My first instinct is usually, let it go. But it's not my name getting dragged through the mud. If it's important to Jon, of course we should do it. Nine times out of ten, Jon's got a really great way of doing it.

JON STEWART

The morning meeting is where we make our bones, and that's the rawest part of the day. And I felt I wanted to make the case, because I found Fox's response to it so egregious. But it definitely probably had me off a little bit. When you're under that spotlight, it had some weight. So I'm probably not at the top of my game emotionally, and I certainly don't think I handled it well.

JEN FLANZ

What happened? In the morning meeting we'd been watching video of people saying Jon was being a racist. He's not a racist, so he was very upset about being called that, especially by Fox News.

DANIEL RADOSH

Even though Jon knew that this was a cynical game Fox was playing, he still took it personally, both on his own behalf and on behalf of the show. It was like, "We can't let them get away with that."

STEVE BODOW

He wanted to go back and prove, "No, I'm not racist—I'm an asshole to everybody." Here's the proof: a montage of the all-time stereotypical impressions he'd done. We were throwing that idea around the room in the morning.

JON STEWART

In the morning meeting there can be twenty-five or thirty people. There were quite a few people there.

RORY ALBANESE

You work with people every day, you get in a fight. Here's the thing you've got to remember: The conversations we're having in the *Daily Show* writers' room aren't about how many farts we can light. We're talking about real shit. So real opinions are going to rise. Hostilities are going to mount. I got in an argument with people about guns. I got into an argument with a bunch of the writers one time about voter ID laws. And one time with Jon about pink nail polish on boys. You're talking about passionate issues and not everyone agrees. Shit pops every now and then.

JON STEWART

My basic point was, I understand why Fox wishes to discredit our bits, and I would view it differently if we had approached it with any different methodology. If it hadn't been (A) clearly riffing off of a rhythm and piece of tape that we had. And (B) we thought this caricature is something that kind of stretched across every boundary.

So that was the general sense, to put together me being horrible like that to everybody. If you can't say that this was approached differently than it's been approached with other people, it's not racist. You're dealing with a horrible person who tends to do this to everybody.

STEVE BODOW

Jon might have said, "Does anybody have an opinion about this?" And Wyatt said, "Well, actually, I was in a hotel room and saw the bit and it made me kind of uncomfortable."

JON STEWART

I said this thing about the Herman Cain bit and, to my mind, out of nowhere someone raises their hand and goes, "Well, you are a little racist." It's conversational, but it felt like an attack. And so I respond defensively, which in the moment I do sometimes.

ZHUBIN PARANG, *writer, 2011–*

It seemed like Jon was genuinely surprised, one, that Wyatt had said that; two, that someone could've thought that about Jon, especially in the room; and three, that Wyatt didn't bring it up with Jon before.

STEVE BODOW

Wyatt says, "I'm not saying you're a racist, but the impression reminded me of *Amos 'n' Andy*, of Kingfish."

DANIEL RADOSH

And Jon fucking exploded.

JON STEWART

Wyatt started with, "It was Kingfish, and there's a certain thing…" I said, "What about Jewish caricature, that's different?" So we were going back and forth about that.

STEVE BODOW

So Jon turned his fire—not argumentatively right away, but making his case, the case he was going to make on TV, that, "I do this to everybody, it has nothing to do with race." And Wyatt is trying to make the case that, "I understand, but there's still a history of people who look like you using this kind of voice about people who look like me." It starts on an even keel but escalates pretty quickly, and Jon is getting angry.

HALLIE HAGLUND

It wasn't about Wyatt. I don't think Jon would've acted that way in another context, but he was feeling incredibly attacked. Fox had dug in on him for a week or more.

JO MILLER

I didn't think it was a very good impression. It did not, at the time, strike me as an *Amos 'n' Andy* type of voice. However, we're in a room with nineteen people, and when the only black guy says, "It sounded that way to me," whether you agree or disagree, he's the one who gets to say it. It took courage to stand up, as the only black guy in the room, and to say how it sounded to him.

JASON ROSS

I think Wyatt was probably in an incredibly hard spot. He could've swallowed his opinion, and that would've left him in a great deal of pain, and it would've left the show weaker for not having heard that point of view expressed by somebody who we love and respect.

J. R. HAVLAN

Wyatt had the freedom at *The Daily Show*, and the courage, to bring it up with Jon. I'm pretty sure Jon acknowledged Wyatt's feelings and interpretation of it and said, "You know, I get where you're coming from. Now, let's let it go." And Wyatt did not, and that's where the innocence that accompanies Wyatt's later retelling of the conversation doesn't match up with what happened. And I like Wyatt. Let me just put it this way: Jon got pissed off at Wyatt well after I would've gotten pissed off at Wyatt, if I was Jon.

JON STEWART

So the conversation gets a little more prickly, a little more prickly, then it gets heated, then I go, "Fuck this," which seeing now I think was interpreted as, "Fuck you, and I'm done with you," rather than "I'm done with this."

JEN FLANZ

Jon got up and started to walk out of the room. He said, "Fuck it, I'm done with this," and I believe, to this day, Wyatt thinks he said, "Fuck you, I'm done with you," and that is not what I heard. Jon started to walk back down the hallway, toward his office, and Wyatt followed him, and they yelled at each other all the way down the hallway, into Jon's office.

STEVE BODOW

There was definitely screaming and heat, and it continued, the argument, well into the morning in Jon's office. It upset some of the dogs.

JEN FLANZ

When Jon and Wyatt were yelling, the dogs were going crazy. They hated it. Parker loves Wyatt.

DANIEL RADOSH

I don't remember the dogs. The dogs went crazy for much less stuff, so . . .

JEN FLANZ

It kind of died down, and then an hour or so later—and this has never happened—Jon asked us to round everyone up and go to the writers' wing so he could apologize for losing his shit.

HALLIE HAGLUND

He cried.

DANIEL RADOSH

Yeah. He apologized and he apologized, and he said he had already apologized to Wyatt privately.

HALLIE HAGLUND

And he said he didn't want to give that impression that we weren't allowed to challenge him. But he was human, too, and he had this really emotional reaction.

JEN FLANZ

I don't think Wyatt was at the second meeting. I think he took a walk for a while that day. That whole day with Wyatt, he was so sad, and hurt. He's like, "Jon's done with me," and I was like, "No, he would fire you if he's done with you."

JOHN OLIVER

It was not a great day. Occasionally there would be a perfect-storm moment, frustrations from other days all building up to one thing, looking for a moment to come out, and that was probably one of those moments. But I don't get to sit as the jury on that one.

JEN FLANZ

Wyatt had been a really good friend to me always, and I understood why he felt really down, and that it is a weird thing to work in an office that's almost completely white.

I could say, as a woman, it's hard to work with a lot of men. There are points in time where it was like, "Wait, we work in an office with all white men. Let's start trying to diversify the staff." Wyatt was part of the evolution of the show.

RORY ALBANESE

Let me be clear. *The Daily Show* is probably one of the least diverse places you can possibly work, or at least it was. I mean, white dudes wrote the fucking thing for years. When I started working there it was a bunch of white guys sitting on chairs writing jokes white guy style. The executive producer originally was a woman and then the head writer was a woman, Lizz Winstead, but it was a boys' club like you'd never believe.

I think Wyatt was absolutely right to feel that that he was the one dude who represented black people in the whole building. I think Jon was really hard on him. But Jon has done that to me. He's done that to other people. You're calling a dude out in a meeting in front of all the other writers. He's your boss. He's obviously feeling sensitive about it. Probably not the best way to do it. I don't think either of them handled it properly, but I don't think Wyatt is a good dude.

JO MILLER

That was *the* uncomfortable moment in my six years there. The fact that it was such an exceptional incident in our writers' room tells you something.

LARRY WILMORE

I don't remember Jon going over the line in his impressions, going, "Well, yassuh. I believes…" I don't think he was doing that. I know what *Amos 'n' Andy* was, so I know exactly what that sounds like and I don't think Jon was doing that.

If you know Jon you know he would not have a malicious intent to do that type of thing. So I think at some point you have to give somebody the benefit of the doubt. He's done more offensive things about other races or ethnicities.

AASIF MANDVI

Look, as a minority myself, I can understand where Wyatt was coming from, in terms of probably feeling something and wanting to share it. I think he was the only African-American writer in that room, at that time, and so he probably did want to share something about how he felt and about how African-Americans might relate to this thing, you know?

I actually really liked Wyatt and still do. We had some really interesting conversations about life and about family. But he's kind of a dick at the buffet line, always grabbing for that fried chicken.

AL MADRIGAL, *correspondent, 2011–*

That blowup happened before I got to the show, but knowing Wyatt and Jon now, he probably just chose the wrong time to bring it up. I had similar shit happen. Rory Albanese wanted to put tequila in my hand and have me wearing a taco bandolier. And I said no, *gracias*. I just said it privately.

The correspondents were very white prior to Mandvi and Wyatt and Larry coming in. But yeah, it's comedy, man. Comedy has always been for white guys, and it's just now changing. I think Jon was aware of that and made a conscious effort to bring different people in.

HERMAN CAIN, *former CEO of Godfather's Pizza; candidate for the Republican presidential nomination, 2012*

The voice wasn't offensive to me. That was him being a satirist. Okay? I mean, I'm a learned man with a couple of degrees, so if I wasn't comfortable in my own reading skin then I would have been offended, but I'm comfortable in my own intellectual reading skin.

There is a line you can cross, and I've seen situations like that. What Jon

Stewart did, that didn't bother me, not at all. The fact that Jon Stewart con-
cluded you can't write a bill in three pages was offensive, because I happen to
believe you can write three-page-long bills.

JON STEWART

I did voices and caricatures that were way more over the top than Herman
Cain. But I also think, though, that in Wyatt's mind, this is a special circumstance. I personally as a Jewish guy disagree with that pretty wholeheartedly,
knowing the history of Jewish caricature.

If I can have anything to take away from the entire episode that could be
constructive in my mind, it's learning the pressure you put on people in that
situation, and to be cognizant of that. And I thought being cognizant of that
meant getting people's input, as opposed to how their input may be in some
ways shaped by the pressure and responsibilities they may feel as representing something. It's not enough to ask somebody's opinion. You also have to
understand the context and the atmosphere with which they're giving that
opinion, and the power dynamic that's involved. I think I did not take that
into consideration, partially because I think I was ignorant of that dynamic.
Because that's unfair, to ask somebody to represent a people. And it's a conversation I wish Wyatt and I had had a long time ago.

Cenac left The Daily Show *a little more than one year after the argument.
In between, Stewart and Cenac performed a number of* Daily Show *segments
about racism—segments that are even more remarkable in retrospect, given how
recent and raw their dispute had been at the time. For example, when stories
surfaced that the family of Rick Perry, the Republican presidential candidate,
had owned a Texas hunting camp referred to as "Niggerhead," the pair made a
larger point that was both funny and scalding in a piece called "The Amazing
Racism—Geographical Bigotry."*

Jon Stewart: [*at anchor desk*] For more now, we go to Wyatt Cenac,
coming to us live from Texas. Wyatt, I know that you grew up there.
It must be so hurtful to be reminded of the racial insensitivity that
has long marred the state.

Wyatt Cenac: [*in front of green-screen backdrop of two-lane road running beside a serene mountain lake*] Actually, Jon, I'm not in Texas.

I'm in *your* state. I'm standing in front of Nigger Lake, New York. The state even listed it on its website until recently.

Jon Stewart: Wow, Wyatt, that, uh, I guess it takes a while for name changes to go through.

Wyatt Cenac: How long do you need? You could call it anything. Cat Shit Lake. Fart Swallow Lake. The point is, everybody's rushing to condemn Texas. And sure, there's a lot of racist shit that goes on in Texas. But guess what? There's Niggerhead Rapids, Idaho. Niggerhead Point, Florida. Niggerhead Pond, Vermont. Niggerhead Creek, North Carolina—good fishing. Did you know there are over a hundred places that have been called Niggerhead in this country?

Jon Stewart: What does this say about America?

Wyatt Cenac: [*shouting*] It says there aren't enough black people making maps!

You know, it's not just about insulting black people...there's places like Chink's Peak, Dago Peak, Squaw Tit Mountain, Jap Road, Spook Woods, and Mexican Gulch.

Jon Stewart: Wow, this is embarrassing for America.

Wyatt Cenac: I disagree, Jon. While America may have a legacy of intolerance, it's also shown that it has the capacity to learn from its mistakes and transform those ugly feelings into expressions of our highest ideals...It reminds me of that song "America the Beautiful"—the lost verses.

[*sings*] Oh beautiful for rivers wide, and Strong-Like-Darky Creek / For Half-Breed Hill and Dago's Nose / The snow upon Chink's Peak! / America, America, God shed his grace on thee / And keep the blacks across the tracks / [*Stewart joins in*] From sea to shining sea!

The piece was funny, it was pointed, and it was awkward to perform, in ways that only Daily Show *insiders understood. Yet the blowup would stay a secret until three years later, when Cenac talked about it in a podcast interview with Marc Maron, with whom Stewart had long feuded. In the meantime,* The Daily Show *occupied itself with minor conflicts, like the one between the United States and Iran.*

16

Minarets of Menace

In June 2009, Jason Jones and field producer Tim Greenberg traveled to Tehran to have a little fun with the impending Iranian election. The three "Minarets of Menace" segments that resulted were remarkable achievements on their own—sending up the way American politicians demonized Iranians, providing an evocative glimpse of everyday life in the Islamic Republic, and crafting a moving reminder of the preciousness of democracy. But shortly after Jones left the country, the government brutally cracked down on protests and rigged the voting—and one of Jones's interview subjects, Newsweek *journalist Maziar Bahari, was tossed in prison, with his* Daily Show *appearance part of the "evidence" used to accuse him of being a spy.*

That unintended consequence was both tragic and farcical. It also transformed the lives of Maziar Bahari and Jon Stewart—and nearly put a premature end to Stewart's run at The Daily Show.

TIM GREENBERG

I think it was probably originally Asaf Kastner's idea for us to go to Iran. He's one of our best segment producers. And Jason Jones wanted to be the correspondent. Jason is fearless. His first piece, Jason volunteered to ride naked on a horse. And he loved the foreign stories.

KEVIN BLEYER

As Rachel Axler said, "You can't spell 'cojones' without 'Jones.'"

MILES KAHN

Jason is a tough cookie. If he sees any weakness, he will pounce. We were in Butte, Montana, doing a story about a toxic lake. Jason is supposed to kill his grandmother by pushing her into this lake. So I play the grandma and he puts me in a wheelchair, and we drive to this embankment and it's kind of steep and I'm scared as hell. He pushes me down and I'm just supposed to flatline into the lake. We didn't test it. I didn't know how deep it was.

It was so cold I lost my breath. I dried off and they put me in again. But it got in the piece.

Oh, here's a good drug story for you. Jason and I went to Denmark, to a place called Christiania, a little hippie commune that's mostly free from Danish law. It's basically just a squatter's commune in the middle of the city of Copenhagen, and you can smoke hash there. We interviewed the mayor of Christiania, this bearded weirdo, and the whole joke was that the mayor says to Jason, "Hey, you want to smoke?" And Jason will go, "Oh, no, no, no... Are the cameras off? Okay. Let's go get high!"

We go to a café in the middle of Christiania and Jason gets high on camera. I smoke a little bit and we get high. I don't think I've ever shot high before. We had an interview right after that with a Danish TV personality, sort of their Jon Stewart, and it was the most surreal interview, but Jason was so good.

DANIEL RADOSH

Jason usually played a real dick in field pieces. How much of that is him? Seventy-five percent?

TIM GREENBERG

I mean, not more than like 90 to 98 percent. Look, Jason is literally one of my best friends at the show and I expect we'll be friends long afterward. He's kind of a dick—

STU MILLER

Not really.

TIM GREENBERG

But kind of, but not really. It's kind of like a perma act. Let's put it that way. It's a permanent act. It's not who he is in his heart, but it's sort of a permanent act.

AASIF MANDVI

Not that Jones is necessarily a dick, although there's a part of him that is, in terms of his comic persona, you know? He felt the need to take his balls out at every single occasion that he could. I'm talking about in the office. I'm talking about wherever. He'd always just show everyone his balls.

SAMANTHA BEE

Jason did a piece once when our daughter Piper was a baby. He took her to a crowded bar. Because once everyone sees that you have a live human baby, then you can do anything you want with a doll baby. So then he strapped the Baby Björn and a fake baby to his chest and just drank, spilling beer all over the baby. At one point she slipped out, the doll slipped out onto the floor of the bar, and people screamed. Later in the piece he straps the Björn and the doll to his naked chest and dives into a pool. It's so funny. It's really funny.

Our children aren't that curious about what we do. They think all parents are on television. And Jason and I were like, "Piper, you've been on television." And she was like, "Oh, I want to see it." And we showed her that piece, but we weren't watching her reaction. She was standing behind us.

And Jason and I were completely self-satisfied in watching this funny piece together, just like, "It's so funny. We're the best." And we turned around, and Piper had tears streaming down her face, and she said, "Why did you try to kill me?" It was a big lesson. Children aren't that sarcastic.

We're looking at years of therapy.

TIM GREENBERG

Jason Jones at his house and the real Jason Jones with his family and friends is an utter sweetheart. In any other setting, he's generally a dick.

SAMANTHA BEE

I mean, Jason has been fucking with people since he was a child. He cannot not do it. He pretended to be stuck under a boulder on the Bruce Peninsula in Canada when he was like seven years old. He would pretend to be stuck under a boulder on the hike, and people would walk past him, he'd scream and ask for help, and people would rescue him.

JEN FLANZ

Sam is just like the sweetest, nicest...it's funny, because when you know them separately, you're like, "How are those two married?" He thinks she is so freaking funny. It works and it's awesome, and they clearly have a great relationship, but their personalities are so different. Jason likes to be the life of the party. Sam's a little bit just short of social anxiety.

SAMANTHA BEE

I did feel pretty confident that Jason would return from Iran. I was more afraid when he went to Russia, actually, because there's just so much violence, and Jason has a tendency to be so audacious.

You think I'm unafraid? Jason's completely unafraid. He'll say anything that tickles his fancy in the moment. And people will just put a sack over your head and disappear you in Russia these days.

But in Canada we don't actually talk about Iran like it's the devil's spawn. We know Iranian people, and they're really great. So I wasn't inherently afraid of Jason going to Iran.

TIM GREENBERG

When we were heading to Iran, the Viacom lawyers sat us down and told us about how there are certain rules based on not bribing foreign officials or something, about how you can't spend money in certain ways and everything has to be accounted for. Having shot foreign pieces before, like, this is close to impossible. So Jason and I are each traveling with $10,000 in cash to Iran, some in my backpack and some on my body, to pay off our fixer.

But in going to Iran, I think we were very naïve about what we were getting into. In Qom, a very holy city, we went to a square to play football, American-style football, with a bunch of kids. We filmed the bit and we thought it was relatively harmless. Our fixer said we have to leave. We're like, "Okay, good. We're done here." They're like, "No. We *have* to leave. You've been kicked out of the city." We're like, "Oh my God. That's pretty good. That's the first time we've ever been kicked out of a city."

RAMIN HEDAYATI

I grew up on Staten Island, but I'm half Iranian and I still have a lot of family there. For years I've heard from people who live in Iran about the despair they feel. So I'm really proud of the coverage the show did. Jason Jones and Tim Greenberg did it with heart and really humanized the country, showing that Iranian people are normal, something I've been trying to do my whole life.

My parents came in to *The Daily Show* and helped translate some of the inter-view footage. I think we paid them generously in salad bar–and-tilapia lunches.

SAMANTHA BEE

Jason traveled so much for the show, to all kinds of destinations. But the Iran trip changed him as a person, in a good way. It was very definitive for him.

Jason is the most underappreciated person who was ever on *The Daily Show*. So much of what Jason did was self-directed and self-taught, and his instincts are so correct about things, and his eye is so good. And I personally feel like he got lumped into "You're a white dude with dark hair. You're all kind of the same." But his work is really elevated. He did more field pieces than anybody has ever done on the show and has gotten the least amount of recognition, and I don't know why. I find it really upsetting.

TIM GREENBERG

The entire reason why we have a connection with Maziar Bahari is that when we were preparing for the trip we saw him talking to Ted Koppel or somebody. I was like "Yeah, that guy's a good interview." Had we not happened to watch that, and I had not happened to call him, Jon would have never made his movie.

In Tehran, Jones filmed a bit where he asked Iranians why they hate Americans. He also sat down in a café to talk with Newsweek *reporter Maziar Bahari. About two weeks after the interview Iranian police arrested Bahari and accused him of talk-ing with a "spy"—Jason Jones. Bahari was locked in the notorious Evin Prison for five months and forced to make a public "confession" to a variety of bogus charges.*

Bahari wrote a chilling and darkly funny memoir that recounted his prison ordeal and his family's tangled political history in Iran. Stewart bought the movie rights.

MAZIAR BAHARI, *journalist, author,* Then They Came for Me

I think the fact that *The Daily Show* was part of my imprisonment, part of my interrogation, that played a part in Jon being attracted to the story. But I don't think guilt had anything to do with him wanting to do the movie. Jon wanted to show what journalists are going through in order to get the story, in order to tell serious stories. He spends so much time on *The Daily Show* making fun of journalists for doing silly things, but that is because he believes good reporting is important.

DENIS LEARY

I can't remember what I was pushing, it was probably a Spider-Man movie, but we went backstage at *The Daily Show* and Jon said, "Lookit. I'm thinking of actually writing this script," and I said, "How are you going to find the time?" Because that's basically your weekends.

So I didn't really think much of it until after he said he'd actually written the thing, and when he said he was going to direct it. Everybody gets excited when they first think they're going to direct a movie or direct something, and then reality starts to set in as you get closer to the date and then you start doing it and it almost kills you.

J. J. ABRAMS, *director,* **Star Wars: The Force Awakens**

I had been a guest on *The Daily Show* a couple of times. Jon contacted me because he had written a script for *Rosewater* and he was looking for reactions. When I read scripts, I find myself having to do a lot of work in my head in terms of really understanding and seeing how moments are meant to play out, what the rhythm of it is, what the tone of it is, why I'm in a certain place.

When I read *Rosewater*, I felt like I was in wildly competent hands, and that the story and scenes and moments were playing out in a way that felt incredibly vibrant and specific and clear. It wasn't that there were shot descriptions or it was overwritten. It was more that it flowed in a way where I could see the movie as I was reading it.

No, Jon is not in *Star Wars*. I wish he'd come while we were shooting, but that never happened. I probably would have cast him as, like, a Jedi master's butler.

With the Rosewater *script shaping up in the spring of 2012, taking a break from* The Daily Show *to shoot the movie became part of Stewart's contract renewal bargaining with Comedy Central.*

JAMES DIXON

The toughest contract negotiation was the last one, with the film. None of them were ever that bad. All of them gave Jon nice raises along the way. He was at the top of the late-night pay scale. So at that point I was never going to haggle over a million or two dollars either way.

This time it wasn't about money at all. Jon was already making a great living. It was about getting him out for the film. Colbert's contract negotiation was going at the same time. We're all reasonable people. We're all friendly to one another. But it had some ugly moments.

DOUG HERZOG

I don't know what Jon will tell you, but I was like, "Dude, I don't want you to do the movie. I don't want you to leave the desk." And so there was a little push and pull over that.

JON STEWART

Yeah. There was a time when I quit.

My contract negotiations were fine. Only toward the end when I wanted to go do the movie did they get difficult. Once Philippe [Dauman, then-chairman of Viacom, the corporate parent of Comedy Central] got in, there was a bit of a change of atmosphere. Doug and Judy have a different ethos. I think Philippe is more…how should I put this charitably? Fiscally minded. One of the nice things about Doug, and Judy, and Michele is they try and balance the financial realities with a healthy respect for the creative process. I'm not so sure that's the case with Philippe.

With Stephen, that negotiation started first, and they got hard-line and weird. It was the first negotiation we had with Philippe in charge.

I mean, this was when Stephen was at his peak, coming off the Colbert Super PAC stuff, and their attitude was, "Yeah, no. We absolutely would like to continue the arrangement perhaps with maybe a small bump just to let him feel good about it." They were being shitty to Stephen, so he and I tied our boats together in the negotiations.

JAMES DIXON

Colbert's negotiation was a lot more acerbic. In our minds it was about respect.

JON STEWART

I don't think Philippe in any way saw what we do as special. As far as he was concerned the star is the real estate, and whether or not we are the ones who carved out that real estate and made it valuable is not important to him.

DOUG HERZOG

Philippe definitely leaned into this, and he definitely has a particular approach to negotiation, no matter who it is. We started negotiating with Colbert, it got a little testy, so we put that aside and went in with Jon. We thought we were at the goal line and then the movie came up.

JAMES DIXON

I know when it was, I'll tell you why. It was June 2012. I was at the fucking airport in New York leaving for London with my whole family, speaking to Stephen and he's saying, "I'm done, that's it." We did three days in London before we flew to Africa for our safari and I remember being on the street, whatever that famous shopping district is, and getting a call from Jon on my cell phone. I'm on with Colbert, I'm on with Jon, trying to conference through my office. So the whole thing crumbles, literally.

STEPHEN COLBERT

How close can you get to it all falling apart? I mean, Jon quit and we were a package. When that happened I was on the road taking my daughter to visit colleges. I got off the phone and she said, "Who was that?" I said, "Oh, I was just talking with Jon and Dixon. Well, I'm going to be home a lot more." She said, "What do you mean?" I said, "You know how we're in the middle of the contract negotiations? It hasn't worked out and so that's it. We'll end the show at Christmastime." She said, "That's crazy." We were at a restaurant in Philly. She said, "Our waitress who just came up, she doesn't know that your shows are ending in three months?" I said, "No. Nobody knows." "People are going to go crazy! It's going to be so bad." "Yeah, we'll do other things." My daughter said, "No, Dad, you don't understand!" I said, "Well, that's it."

JON STEWART

I didn't need a big bump in pay, I didn't need a big anything. But I wanted the summer of 2013 off. That was a difficult part because I had really set my feet on it. They came back and said, "Okay. You can have eight weeks, but we will fine you $500,000 a day if you go over."

So I said, "It sounds to me like you're not really letting me do it, by setting conditions that make it impossible." I don't think it was Doug's call. I think these decisions had Philippe written all over them.

DOUG HERZOG

We wanted Jon back behind the desk, and we were trying to find a way to incentivize that, because movie shoots have a tendency to run long.

JON STEWART

I remember it very clearly, standing out here at home in Jersey. I said, "James, call him back and say, 'Look, man, we've had a great run. Jon is going to do this movie, and we'll part as friends, and he won't renew.'"

So I quit.

DOUG HERZOG

It was a dark thirty-six hours for me. Sad, pissed off, confused—I was all of those. But my sense was it wasn't going to end that way. That we were going to figure this out.

JON STEWART

That weekend was like...you know, I said to Tracey, "Okay, it's over." I sort of kind of got used to it, like, "Oh, yeah, well, you know, it was great." Would've rather have gone out on my terms, timing-wise, but I really felt very passionately about getting this project done and I knew that I needed to get it done in a timely fashion.

And then Philippe called me a day later, while I was at a diner in Red Bank, and said, "Tell me about this movie. Why's it important to you?" So I had to tell him about it, and he said, "Let me see what I can do. Let me talk to them." Meanwhile, he was the one who had said draw the line.

JAMES DIXON

I get a call on Bond Street and it's Jon. "You're not going to believe it. I just got a call from Philippe."

So it all resets itself and we rejigger and we get both the deals done.

STEPHEN COLBERT

It was head-scratchy to me. Here's the crazy part of it: We went in and I said, "Okay, I'm ready to sign up for another four years. I'm willing to do the same terms. I'll guarantee through the 2016 election."

They said, "No, just two." Jon and I looked at each other, privately, like,

"What is going on?" Jon says, "I do not begin to understand what the benefit of their position is. How is this better for them that they have to do this again in two years?"

DOUG HERZOG

That's not my memory. I think Stephen wanted to go from four years to three, maybe to sync up with Jon's deal. And we ended up with two years.

JON STEWART

I think it was all part of Philippe's philosophy, the idea that there's a new sheriff in town. His sense that the artists aren't going to control us, we're going to control them. We weren't trying to control them. We were just trying to make a fair deal.

STEPHEN COLBERT

Thank God they said no to four years. All I know is that if they had taken our offer I would not have been available to take over for Dave. So all the people who think I planned it, I did not. I promise you this was not my idea.

JON STEWART

Ultimately I ended up paying Stephen a certain amount of money each year as a bump from my production fee. The penalty for going long on the movie got removed, but I ended up having to give up half my bonus, and there were ratings penalties—if *The Daily Show*'s ratings went down, I would owe them money. That's how bad it was with them.

DOUG HERZOG

The undertone of the conversation was that Jon was feeling a little restless, and that this will help him, right? He needs a break, and this will help him reenergize. In a perfect world I want him there every night, all right? I got a business to run, and these are every-night shows for a reason, and you want your guy there every night. So that was that.

In July, Comedy Central announced that Stewart and Colbert had agreed to two-year contract extensions. Nothing about the bitter negotiations leaked, however, and Stewart kept his movie plans quiet until early the next year. Yet even as he was spending nights and weekends hammering out a screenplay, Stewart and the show did some of their strongest work of the entire run.

Two new correspondents provided an infusion of energy. Al Madrigal, forty, had been living in Los Angeles but touring regularly as a standup comic. One night in Miami he got an e-mail from a stranger asking for a slot as an opening act. Madrigal said sure—"I was playing one of the worst clubs in Miami." Two years later that same stranger, Daily Show *producer Adam Lowitt, arranged for Madrigal to audition for Stewart, who hired him on the spot as Senior Latino Correspondent.*

AL MADRIGAL

I'd been in a sitcom with Rob Riggle, *Gary Unmarried*. I told Rob I'd gotten the gig at *The Daily Show*, and he mentioned having these handwritten notes from Colbert on how to do a field piece. Riggle transcribed them and e-mailed them to me, and I memorized those notes, because they're amazing.

Hey Al,

So I found Colbert's notes for me on things to think about when doing a field piece!

1) Burn Tape! Tape is cheap, keep talking and keep them talking...

2) Break up questions...Don't let them see where you're going.

3) Play the silence.

4) Match energy with subject.

5) Discover things in the moment! Be aware of when those "discoveries" happen.

6) Always be asking yourself... "What's my point of view on this subject?"

7) You have to think it's funny. Find a way to make that happen...

8) Get clear on 3–5 things you want your subject to say and don't leave until you get them.

9) Understand the real point...what's behind all this?

10) Character is key! Understand your P.O.V. on this issue and you will be able to react spontaneously in the moment.

That's it bro...These were the tips Stephen gave me when I started and they helped...I hope they help you!

All the best,

Riggle

AL MADRIGAL

My second field piece turned out to be one of the things of which I'm most proud. Steve Bodow's parents live in Tucson, and they flagged an article about an Arizona law banning ethnic studies in public schools. The law was being used to shut down this one Mexican-American studies class in Tucson, because they thought it taught hatred of the white man. So I interviewed this Tucson school board member and asked him, "So when you banned African-American studies, what did they say?"

Michael Hicks, Tucson school board member: Honestly, this law won't be applied to any of our other courses...the African-American studies program is still there. It's not teaching the resentment of a race or class of people.

Al Madrigal: I'm a black kid. Try to teach me about slavery without me feeling resentment toward white people. How did I end up here?

Michael Hicks: Slavery was a...hmm. Okay, the white man did bring over the Africans...

Al Madrigal: And what kind of jobs did we do?

Michael Hicks: The jobs that you guys did were basically slavery jobs.

Al Madrigal: So after we were freed, we got to vote?

Michael Hicks: Yes. Well, you didn't get to vote until later...We now have a black man as president. You know, Rosa Clark did not take out a gun and go onto a bus and hold up everybody.

AL MADRIGAL

There was a tremendous amount of press after the piece. It had an impact. It sort of ruined me for all normal comedy, because now all I want is to be part of something that's smart, silly, and has heart at the same time. Why can't everything have all three? It's really informed every single thing that I do since then.

The show had evolved so much by the time I got there. Jon wanted us to be passionate about what we were writing about and propose solutions as well—not just shit on something and walk away. Talk about what *should* be done.

Jessica Williams had studied improv and acted as a teenager in Los Angeles, then focused on college at Long Beach State, until a casting agent encouraged her to submit an audition tape to The Daily Show. *At twenty-two, Williams became easily the youngest correspondent* The Daily Show *had ever hired. She learned fast, in more ways than one.*

JESSICA WILLIAMS, *correspondent, 2012–2016*

I had watched the show some. I mean, I knew the show was that thing that my professors put on in a poli-sci class. They're like, "All right, we're going to watch this clip from *The Daily Show*. You guys remember Mark Twain? This is like his great-great-grandson. This is satire."

I was really terrified to try and hurry up and finish my exams, pick up everything, and move to New York City. John Oliver was really helpful, and Wyatt was like my silent sort of older brother, who introduced me to Brooklyn and took me out to cool spots, and Sam was this very beautiful, hilarious woman who would always give me really good advice. And Jon was always dancing around and acting like he threw his back out all the time, especially around me. He'd turn to me and be like, "You know, just don't get old." That helped, but I was so nervous.

I really appreciated the risk that Jon took on me, as a black woman. Because that hadn't really happened yet, a black woman in late night in any sort of capacity.

But the first few months were really tough. *The Daily Show*, it had been on for a while, and I think people can be very possessive of the show. When I first started, I got...you know just...you know the negative racial comments in my inbox. You do anything that ruffles a few feathers on the show, there's always going to be some racist dude ready to like call you a nigger, you know? I think a lot of it has to do with people just being really stupid. And people hadn't really seen a black correspondent on the show before. I think that was kind of jarring and surprising for people. So, their response was just to, you know, call me a nigger, I guess. At that time, it really bothered me a lot. Now, either I get it less or I just don't give a shit anymore.

As bumpy a beginning as it was for Williams personally, she and the rest of the correspondents were feasting on campaign material—in large part because, in the words of an "Indecision 2012" graphic, "Mitt Happened." As the campaign plunged into arguments about income inequality, The Daily Show *gleefully sprinted into the fray, turning what could have been dry economics lessons into civic-comic minisymphonies.*

17

World of Class Warfare

The former governor of Massachusetts and multimillionaire corporate-buyout consultant had to survive some stiff Republican primary competition, including Michele Bachmann, Newt Gingrich, and the two Ricks, Perry and Santorum. But Mitt Romney—or, in one of The Daily Show's *elaborations, "Willard Scott Mittington Romneysaurus"—triumphed. Romney's supposed gaffe, declaring that "corporations are people," turned out to be an apt preview of one part of his general election strategy—an appeal to conservatives and business elites. The other part was tarring Obama as an incompetent lefty socialist giving away what the "makers" had earned to the undeserving "takers." Occupy Wall Street and the Tea Party were stoking populism on the left and right, and the subprime mortgage crisis and Wall Street bailouts were still fresh. It all turned the 2012 presidential campaign into a fierce debate over the economy and privilege, and pushed* The Daily Show *toward starker takes on money and power.*

STEVE BODOW

I've always been really proud of our convention and road trip coverage. The sequence of 2012 debate coverage of Romney and Obama, and both of the conventions, but especially the Clint Eastwood Republican one, those had the combination we strive for—really fucking funny stuff and also some pinpoint insight.

ELLIOTT KALAN

The most enjoyable example of seeing something happen and saying, "Well, we know what we're doing tomorrow," was in the 2012 conventions.

We were in Tampa because the Republicans decided, for Lord knows what reasons, to hold the thing in Tampa in late August. It was disgusting.

Anyway, we were sitting in our offices watching the normal convention stuff and taking notes. The writers who were assigned to it would stay up until one or two in the morning writing material and then coming in the next morning to either finish it or just hand it in and it would get rewritten. But watching Clint Eastwood talk to an empty chair as if Barack Obama was there, and ramble on and be very jokey and abusive, it was so clear that this was not planned by anybody. The Romney campaign, there's no way they could have meant for this to happen. All of our mouths were open.

STEVE BODOW

To us, the Eastwood bit we did on the show was a statement not just about how the convention or how that campaign was going, but about what had been infecting the entire Republican Party since 2008. They have this fantasy version of the Obama presidency that they are incredibly upset about, but it's not real, and in fact, it's invisible. But that doesn't stop them from ranting about it. It's real to them.

The next month, Romney himself provided the material. A bartender working at a $50,000-per-plate fund-raising lunch in Florida recorded video of the plutocrat Republican presidential nominee claiming that 47 percent of the American public would vote for Obama because they were feeding at the government benefits trough.

JO MILLER

In the writers' room during meetings I was always knitting, and I got a reputation for saying the most dark, horrible things, but as long as I was knitting I could get away with them. Like when Romney was caught saying 47 percent of Americans will vote for the Democrats because they're moochers. I said something like, "Now he and his running mate will know what it feels like to carry a dead baby to term."

No, we did not do that joke on the show! But the 2012 campaign did bring together a lot of issues for us. We had a recurring bit called "World of Class Warfare," playing off the name of the game, but inspired largely by the business networks. Fox Business, they can get away with voicing the id of the right a little more than they could on main Fox. They used the word "moocher class" over and over, and proved it by saying that 97 percent of poor people had fridges...because poor people really deserve to be eating rotten food. This is not an impassioned and honest difference of opinion about trickle-down economics. This is just bullshit.

Those pieces, we surfed on a wave of pure rage. It may have peaked in one segment called "The Poor's Free Ride is Over." These guys on the business networks were talking about the half of the population who don't pay taxes. They cited the figures for the budget shortfall that needed to be made up by taxing the moochers.

And in rewrite, a half hour before the show, Jon did the math, on the back of a plate or something. He calculated that we would have to tax the poor 100 percent, take everything they own, their entire wealth, to make that number the business network guys wanted. That was when the piece was nailed, and it was all Jon.

Neil Cavuto: [*in video clip, from his Fox show* Your World] "Warren Buffett writing how the rich should pay more taxes but saying not a word about the half of American households that pay no income taxes at all."

Jon Stewart: [*at anchor desk*] So the solution to our economic problem isn't taxing the rich...Maybe Fox is right. Maybe the bottom 50 percent of Americans, while they already pay excise and payroll and Medicare taxes, do need to pay more. I mean, they can spare it. After all, they control 2.5 percent of our nation's wealth. [*pie chart graphic from* Business Insider *showing bottom 50 percent with tiny sliver*]

Robert Rector, Heritage Foundation: [*in video clip, being interviewed by Fox's Stuart Varney*] "When you look at the actual living conditions of the 43 million people that the census says are 'poor,' you see that in fact they have all these modern conveniences."

Stuart Varney: "Ninety-nine percent of 'em have a refrigerator."

Jon Stewart: You food-chilling motherfuckers! How dare you! I'm sure the 1 percent of those people who don't have refrigerators don't have them not because they don't have food, but because they're always ordering room service!...So you see, the problem with increasing the marginal tax rate on the rich and closing some corporate tax loopholes isn't that it engages in class warfare. It's that it's fighting on the wrong side of the war.

Neal Boortz: [*in video clip, on Fox Business Channel, standing in front of palm trees and luxury marina*] "It is all-out war on the productive class in our society for the benefit of the moocher class!"

Ann Coulter: [*in video clip, on Fox Business Channel, above graphic reading,* COULTER: DEMS WOULD BE DELIGHTED IF VIOLENT MOB AROSE HERE] "Welfare will create generations of utterly irresponsible animals."

Jon Stewart: Yeah! Fuck those people! [*over-the-shoulder photo appears, of elderly man sitting on a threadbare couch*] The poor!

JO MILLER

That was also the piece where Jon mentioned my name on the air, because I'd come up with a joke about the amount of money that Warren Buffett's cleaning lady pulls out of his drain, and there's a funny graphic for it, with a maid holding a big old hairball. It was a nice emotional break from the heaviness of the topic and the rage. Have I mentioned the rage?

Others at The Daily Show *may have dabbled in rage. For Lewis Black, it was a milieu, a metier, an art form, and a job description. After acting his way through the first two years under the Stewart regime, Black found a happy-unhappy groove, usually writing "Back in Black" with J. R. Havlan; in later years, Travon Free was also a valuable collaborator.*

LEWIS BLACK

Travon is young and he's black, which makes it interesting. And these kids really got my voice. They grew up listening to it.

TRAVON FREE, writer, 2012–2016

I listened to every album Lewis ever made probably five times a week as I walked around campus at Long Beach State. And so if you watch and listen to Lewis, he has a methodology to the way he constructs jokes before he gets to the part that makes him angry. I internalized the build and the structure of how he talks and how he thinks. So if you just told me an issue, I could pretty much figure out his point of view and then filter it, getting him to doing that thing everyone loves, which is when he shouts and points or does the really low tone, really angry thing. Mastering Lewis is understanding the heart of why someone's pissed off about something, or why something is stupid, or why something is crazy.

Black's segments could still be wildly funny tangents about, say, artisanal crystal meth or the need for a Trump 2012 presidential campaign ("This is what I've been waiting for my whole life, a president who's not afraid to tell the truth about being a lying asshole!"), but over the years many of Black's rants were vein-bulging exclamation points to The Daily Show's *main themes.*

Lewis Black: The presidential campaign is in full swing and every day brings another bland stump speech...

President Barack Obama: [*in video clip, at podium*] "Somebody invested in roads and bridges. If you've got a business, you didn't build that...The point is, we succeed because of our individual initiative, but also because we do things together."

Lewis Black: Most Americans hear that and they fall asleep. But not the Romney campaign!

[*Video clip of Romney ad begins, showing business owners watching clip of Obama saying, "You didn't build that"—but not the rest of Obama's statement*]

Businesswoman: "I can't believe he just said that!"

Lewis Black: I can't believe it, either—*because he didn't just say that!* Campaigns have finally arrived in the twenty-first century—they can produce bullshit at the same rate as actual bulls!

Rage, amazement, disgust, giddiness—the 2012 campaign didn't lack for emotional extremes and provocations. In September, Fox News's *flailing attempts to explain away the Romney 47 percent controversy spurred* The Daily Show *to scale the dizzying heights of "Bullshit Mountain."*

Kate Obenshain, Republican Strategist: [*in Fox interview montage*] "He wasn't criticizing them! He was saying that the American dream should be open to everybody."

Jon Stewart: [*at anchor desk*] "You're looking at and hearing the cynical, condescending, plutocratic words he was saying—not the aspirational, optimistic message he in retrospect should have been meaning!" It's like Romney jazz! It's the words you *don't* hear.

Sean Hannity: [*in video clip from his show*] "This is factually accurate, what Romney is saying."

Stuart Varney: [*in Fox News video clip*] "I think this will be seen as a *win* for Romney."

Jon Stewart: Let me sum up the message from Bullshit Mountain, if I may: This inartfully stated dirty liberal smear is a truthful expression of Mitt Romney's political philosophy—and it is a winner!

Sean Hannity: "Tonight, the GOP presidential nominee delivers one of his sharpest critiques yet of President Obama and the entitlement society that he enables."

Jon Stewart: This is the core of Bullshit Mountain. That somehow only since Obama, the half of Americans who love this country and work hard and are "good" have had the fruits of their labor seized and handed over to the half of this nation that is lazy and dependent and the opposite of good...Now in that 49 percent, Hannity is including those on Social Security and Medicare—or, as I like to call them, his audience. But perhaps Mr. Hannity is understating the problem. For there are many more of those on the government dole than even his 49 percent accounts for. Like those welfare queens at Exxon Mobil, AT&T, GE, the 250 corporations that from 2008 to 2010 got nearly a quarter trillion in federal tax subsidies...or the incredible tax breaks the government gives the investor class...Boy, I wish we had a poster boy for that element of the moochocracy. [*photo of Romney appears on screen next to Stewart*] Oh, right. In 2010, Governor Romney...got an absolutely fair tax break of four and a half million dollars...in moocher-class dependency terms, enough food stamps to feed Mr. Romney through the year 4870. By the way, that's no bullshit. That's the math.

The Romney campaign certainly took more shots from The Daily Show *than Obama did during "Indecision 2012." But the president didn't escape criticism, because Stewart cared more about Obama's first-term record than about the current horse race. And the White House cared that Stewart cared. First Lady Michelle Obama appeared as a* Daily Show *guest in May, followed by her husband in October, timed for when the campaign was coming down to the wire.*

DAG VEGA, *Obama Administration liaison to TV networks, 2009–2014*
The president sat down for interviews with Diane Sawyer, Brian Williams, and Scott Pelley, and afterward I remember we compared those three interviews with Jon's interview, and Jon's was the most policy driven of the four. The other three were much more focused on the political news of the day. His interview was tougher than the three network news anchors'.

> **Jon Stewart:** So you're the president now. Before, when you ran you had certain things you thought. I wonder if four years as president has in any way changed that. First is, we don't have to trade our values and ideals for our security.
>
> **President Barack Obama:** We don't.
>
> **Jon Stewart:** Do you still feel that way?
>
> **President Obama:** We don't. There's some things that we haven't gotten done. I still want to close Guantánamo, we haven't gotten that through Congress. One of the things we've got to do is put a legal architecture in place and we need congressional help to do that.
>
> **Jon Stewart:** I think people have been surprised to see the strength of the Bush-era warrantless wiretapping and those sorts of things not also be lessened.
>
> **President Obama:** The truth is actually that we've modified them and built a legal structure and safeguards in place that weren't there before on a whole range of issues. Now, they aren't really sexy issues.
>
> **Jon Stewart:** You don't know what I find sexy.

The president won a second term three weeks later, and he was soon being reminded about one issue that Stewart found enragingly irresistible, though hardly sexy.

Obama's Department of Veterans Affairs had a regulation limiting former soldiers to medical treatment within a forty-mile straight-line radius of their homes; after a Daily Show *segment ridiculing the red tape, the rule was changed to allow for driving distance. Then a cinematic two-part Samantha Bee field piece, in which she strapped on night-vision goggles and "raided" the Manhattan office of the VA, chronicled one vet's bureaucratic nightmare.*

SAMANTHA BEE

When you try to put false premises on things, you're just wringing comedy out of a dry cloth. I don't care for those pieces. I like a real story that means something to me or means something to other people. One great example was "Zero Dark 900,000." That was a story that came out of Miles Kahn's head, to conduct a search for an Iraq War vet's benefit claim form that was lost in the bureaucracy, and to shoot the piece like a movie.

I love VA stories. Not that I love the problems that the VA is having. I'm very interested in stories where people have sacrificed their entire lives, and they are getting the short end of the stick. It's fascinating, it's horrifying, it's unbelievable.

MILES KAHN

Eugene Manning, the Iraq vet we featured, got a call from the VA after that piece. It's sad that it took us shooting a two-part piece to get one person his benefits. But I'll take it. I'll take one guy, if that's what helped him.

There were bullshit internal politics at *The Daily Show* sometimes. But I got to write and direct things that were seen by millions of people, and that once in a while actually made a difference.

The Daily Show *didn't just shine a light on the hassles facing veterans. In 2013, with no fanfare, Stewart had producers Elise Terrell and Camille Hebert set up the Veteran Immersion Program: In six-week cycles, a total of seventy former soldiers got training in TV production, followed by job-placement assistance. Stewart and staff members helped the cause in other ways, too.*

JOE KLEIN, *journalist, author of* **Charlie Mike,** *about the vets who* *founded The Mission Continues*

I was with them on a service project, and we were fixing up a school in Brooklyn. I was painting, inside, and I went out to clear my head of the fumes, and there's Jon Stewart, raking. He has his kids with him. And I said, "Jon!

What the hell are you doing here?" He said, "Raking. And you're...painting." He did not draw any attention to himself. He didn't make a speech. He didn't have a photographer with him. He was willing to stand for selfies, but he just did his work and left, drove himself home. And I thought, what a total mensch.

Meanwhile, Stewart was racing to complete his Rosewater *script and cast the movie—a process so hectic that he wouldn't cast a key role, the movie's villain, until Stewart was in Amman, Jordan, two weeks before filming started.*

In June 2013, during a break in shooting the movie, Stewart traveled to Cairo and appeared on Bassem Youssef's show. The city was on edge. Two weeks later, millions of protesters took to the streets demonstrating against Morsi, who was then removed by a military coup. Youssef, his freedom and his show now at even greater risk, went to Amman and consulted with Stewart.

BASSEM YOUSSEF

After the thirtieth of June, I was scared to go back on the air, because now it's the military regime in charge. Jon said, "So quit. It's not worth it." And I said, "I can't. All of these people are depending on me." So he gave me the best advice ever. He told me to make fun of what you feel. If you're feeling scared, make fun of that. If you're feeling that you cannot talk about someone, make fun of that. So we did just that.

Months later the Egyptian government essentially forced his show off the air.

BASSEM YOUSSEF

Did I make a difference? Because I was trying to make a difference, and people were following me, but the masses of people who followed the show didn't do anything or raise a finger when the show was taken out. That's the power of oppression. So, at the end of the day, I left Egypt.

The consequences were significantly less severe, of course, but Stewart was highly interested in setting up a peaceful transition of power at The Daily Show. *So before leaving New York for the summer he placed his first choice of successor behind the desk for a test run.*

18

Whoop-De-Doo

John Oliver had many qualities to recommend him for the job as Daily Show *host: an outsider's curiosity about America, a distinctive writing voice, a performing fluency that enabled him to swing from screwball chimney sweep to indignant lecturer. He had also recently starred in one of* The Daily Show's *greatest field pieces, three segments that combined facts, fury, and embarrassing interviews to craft a devastating—yet funny—essay on the insanity of American gun politics.*

JOHN OLIVER

I had seen John Howard, the former Australian prime minister, on *Fareed Zakaria*, talking about an op-ed he'd written in the *New York Times*, about what he'd done to ban guns in the wake of the Port Arthur massacre, and I realized, "Oh, he sees this as a good legacy. He's spectacularly arrogant, as most politicians are, and concerned about what their legacy will be. Clearly he wants to talk about this, so he might speak to us." Howard was coming to Dallas. We had a chance to meet him there just for a one-on-one interview.

This was right after the shootings in Sandy Hook and the gun control legislation was collapsing in Congress. We were just going to explore the gun control idea in a sit-down interview with Howard, until Jon says, "Yeah, but you've got to see the consequences. You can't just talk about it in theory, you have to see it. There's a power in that."

And especially when we started uncovering the idea that some politicians had voted for this within Howard's Conservative Party and gone down for it, that was when Jon's ears went up and he went, "What are they doing now? Would they talk? Okay, you're going to need to go and speak to them."

The stage and the U.S. Capitol, the night before the Rally to Restore Sanity and/or Fear on the National Mall, Washington, D.C., 2010. (Photo courtesy of Jen Flanz)

Stephen Colbert gets his hair prepared to promote Fear, 2010. (Photo courtesy of Jody Morlock)

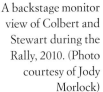

Executive producer Josh Lieb, backstage at the Rally to Restore Sanity and/or Fear, 2010. (Photo courtesy of Jody Morlock)

A backstage monitor view of Colbert and Stewart during the Rally, 2010. (Photo courtesy of Jody Morlock)

John Hodgman, dressed for a bit about Los Angeles Clippers owner Donald Sterling, backstage with Parker, head dog at *The Daily Show*, 2014. (Photo courtesy of Jen Flanz)

Production manager Pam DePace, Jon Stewart, executive in charge of production Jill Katz, executive producer Jen Flanz, production coordinator Elise Terrell, and production coordinator Kristen Everman inside a photo booth at the 2012 *Daily Show* holiday party. (Photo courtesy of Jen Flanz)

Daily Show staffers "kidnapped" field producer Jim Margolis and took him to Miami to celebrate his 2010 departure from the show. From left: Jason Jones, Tim Greenberg, Oren Brimer, Miles Kahn, Stu Miller, Jim Margolis. (Photo courtesy of Jen Flanz)

Correspondent Al Madrigal and executive producer Steve Bodow, dressed to attend the 2014 Emmys. (Photo courtesy of Jen Flanz)

Correspondents Jason Jones and Jessica Williams backstage after Jones's pants accidentally ripped onstage. (Photo courtesy of Jen Flanz)

Jon Stewart, preparing to take batting practice as part of *The Daily Show*'s 2015 field trip to Citi Field, home of the New York Mets. (Photo courtesy of Jen Flanz)

After the hard-won passage of the Zadroga Act extension in 2015, Stewart threw a dinner for World Trade Center first responders. To the right of Stewart, in the baseball hat, is John Feal, who led the lobbying effort in Washington. (Photo courtesy of John Feal)

Jon Stewart dancing in his final writers meeting as host. (Photo courtesy of Al Madrigal)

Jon Stewart in the rewrite room, revising the script projected on the wall. (Photo courtesy of Kira Klang Hopf)

Crispy rice cakes sent by Stephen Colbert to celebrate Stewart's final show as host. (Photo courtesy of Al Madrigal)

Correspondents Stephen Colbert, Ed Helms, Al Madrigal, Rob Riggle, and Aasif Mandvi backstage. (Photo courtesy of Al Madrigal)

Al Madrigal, Aasif Mandvi, and Hasan Minhaj, senior brown correspondents. (Photo courtesy of Al Madrigal)

Two decades of correspondents and contributors, preparing to rush the stage after Colbert's "Thank you, Jon Stewart" monologue. (Photo courtesy of Al Madrigal)

Jon Stewart hugging E Street Band guitarist Nils Lofgren as Bruce Springsteen looks on. (Photo courtesy of Jody Morlock)

Stewart passing the torch to Trevor Noah during the party on the *Intrepid*. (Photo courtesy of Kira Klang Hopf)

Jon Stewart, open for the catch one last time, just before taking the stage for his final *Daily Show* as host. (Photo courtesy of Jody Morlock)

Stewart, with Mighty Max Weinberg's drumsticks in hand, walks off *The Daily Show* stage for the final time as host. (Photo courtesy of Jody Morlock)

The team on that field piece starts reaching out to people in Australia. Brennan Shroff, the producer, and Asaf Kastner, who was the lead researcher on that, and then Tim Greenberg, who was overseeing the department. They're making calls and saying, "So yeah, where is this guy Rob Borbidge, who voted for gun control and lost his office, now? Is he happy to talk about it? Yes, he is. Okay. So we got him. Okay so now what we would want is a farmer who was against the ban at the time and now sees the value." Then it becomes something much bigger, and then you realize, "Oh, there's no way this is one piece, so it'll be two or three."

And then next thing you know you're on a flight to the other side of the world.

We were there in Australia six days, I think, and shot every day. The first day was shooting with John Howard. He was not thrilled. He's a humorless, arrogant politician, so he had no trust in what the point of view of the piece was going to be, and I had no interest in reassuring him. I didn't particularly like him in any other way other than that he did this one remarkable piece of legislation.

On the American side, we wanted to speak to a smart, articulate, Second Amendment guy.

Philip Van Cleave, President, Virginia Citizens Defense League: [The Australian gun ban] stopped one thing! That could also be a statistical anomaly.

John Oliver: Yeah—it was just their mass shootings disappeared.

Philip Van Cleave: But there were so few of them! Whoop-de-doo!

John Oliver: Whoop-de-doo?

Philip Van Cleave: Yes. Their shootings were rare anyhow.

John Oliver: In the eighteen years before the Port Arthur shootings, there were thirteen mass shootings [in Australia]. Almost one a year.

Philip Van Cleave: I was unaware they had that many.

John Oliver: Whoop-de-doo.

JOHN OLIVER

In his defense, Philip Van Cleave is at least intellectually consistent, so when you take him by the hand and you follow his logic down to, "Then we should have no drug laws whatsoever," he will own that. I find that much more admirable than I find the kind of snakey politicking of Jim Manley. I found him much more loathsome in that piece.

Jim Manley had been Senator Harry Reid's top guy. We weren't expecting much out of Manley. But there was a moment in that interview that felt like the culmination of all the things I've learnt on *The Daily Show*. I asked him, "What makes a politician successful?" and he says, "Getting reelected." At that point, from all the eight years beforehand, it's like time slows down in your head and you think, "I've got you." So then you say, "So, success would not be getting legislation passed?" And then Manley says, "Well, okay, if I were to rerun the tape..." And then he is right on the hook.

Sometimes, filming field pieces, it's hard not to lose your temper as a human being. I did, actually, with Jim Manley. I was just getting angry, which is not funny for anyone to watch. Instead, it's going to be funny watching Manley try and say, "No, this is a good thing we're doing. We'll do gun control one crumb at a time."

And the interesting thing with that piece was, if that is the view of anyone in favor of gun legislation—that you need to do it one crumb at a time—then you're absolutely playing into the paranoia that the government is coming to take your guns gradually. Whereas what Howard and [Deputy Prime Minister] Tim Fischer did in Australia was say, "Well, this is it. We're doing it once, we're not coming back." It's a much bolder move, and it worked.

Who was the person jumping around in the kangaroo suit during the Australian part of the piece, when I'm on walkabout? That's our fixer. We told him, "There's a suit in the back of the car. Get in it and hop around."

JON STEWART

I knew Oliver was going to kill it, hosting when I was away making *Rosewater*.

JOHN OLIVER

He always had a lot more confidence in me than I had. The summer is usually very, very quiet. So my main concern was for those sporadic moments where people are really looking for Jon, moments of real pain, if one of those major tragedies happened. I had no authority to talk. Then it happened, because of Trayvon Martin. I could really feel it in the warm-up with the audience that night. People were waiting to hear what Jon Stewart specifically had to say, and so I really put myself through the wringer with that show, and I think it worked out in the end. Less well than Jon would have done. But I don't think it was a shameful attempt.

John Oliver: [*at anchor desk*] We have Senior Black Correspondent Larry Wilmore with us. Larry, let's talk about race.

Larry Wilmore: [*across from Oliver*] Fuck you, Oliver.

John Oliver: Whoa! Larry! That's how you have a conversation about race?

Larry Wilmore: That's how everyone has a conversation about race...White people tend to look at race relations through rose-colored glasses. And black people resent the use of the word "colored" in that last sentence.

John Oliver: But hold on—couldn't it be that white people are more optimistic?

Larry Wilmore: Optimistic. Is that British for "delusional"?
The real outrage of the Trayvon Martin case is that an adult shot and killed a child and there were no consequences. Look, we don't know for sure what made George Zimmerman shoot an unarmed teenager. Maybe it was the racism in his head. Maybe it was the laws in his state. But it was definitely the gun in his hand.

John Oliver: So we should be having a conversation about guns?

Larry Wilmore: Fuck you, Oliver. Sorry, that's generally how these conversations start.

HALLIE HAGLUND

When Oliver hosted, we got so much on the show as writers. It felt like he trusted us, a lot, to do this stuff. And as talented and serious a guy as he was, he played on the *Daily Show* soccer team with us.

STEVE BODOW

It was tremendous fun with Oliver as host. I knew it would work, but not as well as it did. We had no way of foreseeing the amazing bunch of stories we got that summer.

JOHN OLIVER

Carlos Danger! It was not a quiet summer at all.

After quitting Congress in disgrace in 2011, Anthony Weiner had receded from public view, mostly. As he prepared a political comeback, though, part of his image rehabilitation effort was cooperating with a cover story for the New York Times Magazine, *in which Stewart was quoted saying that his old friend's offenses were hardly world-class crimes and that Weiner seemed to deserve a second chance.*

Through the spring and early summer of 2013, New York City voters seemed to agree: Weiner was at the top of the polls in the race for the Democratic mayoral nomination. Then, in July, new lurid online chats and photos surfaced, including some that occurred after Weiner had resigned from Congress and supposedly sworn off sexting strangers. To make it worse, or at least more ridiculous, Weiner had chosen "Carlos Danger" as his social media pseudonym. At the time, Stewart was overseas shooting Rosewater, *so Oliver gleefully did the* Daily Show *honors.*

JOHN OLIVER

Jon had taken some heat for not going in hard enough on Anthony Weiner the first time around, in 2011, because they'd been friends. It was probably easier for me to do jokes about Weiner, because there was no personal connective tissue between me and that story. So I could just enjoy it as a child.

> **John Oliver:** [*at anchor desk, next to high school photo of Jew-fro'd Weiner entitled,* WELCOME BACK, COCKER] He did it again! Although this time there are some awesome developments. He called himself— [*bad B-Western Spanish accent*]—*Carlos Danger!* Anthony Weiner's alter ego is a Bolivian action hero–slash–porn star.
>
> By the way, fun fact: "The campaign trail" is what Anthony Weiner calls that line of hair from his belly button to his pubes. [*disturbing photo of pasty-white belly with scraggly north–south line of hair*]

Weiner, though, kept campaigning well into the fall, even as the embarrassments erased his standing in the polls. Shortly after Stewart returned to The Daily Show, *the infamous mayoral candidate got into a shouting match with a Brooklyn Jewish pastry shop patron.*

Jon Stewart: [*at anchor desk*] Now look, Weiner's alienating some voters, but not his base! It's not like he's going into a kosher bakery on the high holy days of Rosh Hashanah and yelling at a guy in a yarmulke. [*pause; holds finger to fake earpiece*] Really? We have that tape as well?

Jewish Guy: [*in video clip, at pastry counter, confronting Weiner*] "Your behavior is deviant. It's not normal behavior."

Anthony Weiner: [*mouth stuffed with pastry, shouting and pointing a finger in Jewish guy's face*] "And you're perfect? You're gonna judge me?"

Jewish Guy: "I'm not running for office."

Anthony Weiner: "You know who judges me? You know who judges me?"

Jon Stewart: The voters of New York City? Everything that Weiner does just looks bad now. There's no reason for it! For God's sake, what are you yelling at this guy for? It's not like he insulted your wife! [*holds finger to fake earpiece*] Oh, really? Roll that tape.

Jewish Guy: [*as Weiner walks away*] "You're a real scumbag, Anthony. Married to an Arab."

Jon Stewart: Oh. Well, then, yeah. Fuck that guy. I didn't know that. Now, of course, this does raise an interesting possibility. What if everything Anthony Weiner's done actually makes sense if you look at it in a larger context? What if there is, for each of these incidents, one piece of information that makes each incident okay? Like, what if at the West Indian parade, he just didn't realize that his microphone had been set to "Jamaican accent Autotune"? Now you may say, "All right, fine. But what about that text message he sent to his nonwife lady where he said he wanted to, quote, 'fuck you so hard your tits almost hit you in the face'?" [*long pause; shrugs*] Maybe she had something on her face and he tried to get her attention by going like—[*pantomimes wiping off nose with his hand*]—but then he thought, "Oh, I know what could get that off!"

Nah, he's just a guy with self-control issues who never should have run for mayor.

ANTHONY WEINER

I mean, you know, Jon was more of a dick to me than he needed to be.

JON STEWART

I'm sure.

GLEN CAPLIN

I once asked Jon about Anthony. Jon feels—I'm trying to find the right words—burned by Anthony quite personally. Because when Anthony seemed to be putting things back together, Jon spoke on the record in that *New York Times Magazine* story about Anthony and Huma, and Jon was very gracious. Then more sexting stuff came out when Anthony was running for mayor. I think Jon feels like you don't ask someone to do that and then—you know, don't get me involved in your bullshit if you're still involved.

JON STEWART

My ambivalence about Anthony had been replaced by a genuine sense of, "Wow, you just don't give a fuck. This really is just about your ambition." He had called me after he resigned from Congress and asked me, "What do you think I should do with my life?" I told him, "I would disappear into the world of helping the people you said you wanted to help—no longer in the political arena, but in the real world." He says, "Yeah, yeah, yeah, I'll think about that." But he didn't do it.

On other fronts, Stewart's return was joyful: He got back just in time to see The Colbert Report *win a long-overdue first Emmy as Outstanding Variety Series—breaking* The Daily Show's *ten-year streak. The rest of the fall and winter was a blur, though. Stewart was editing* Rosewater *while hosting* The Daily Show, *and the exhaustion showed. Dark circles ringed his eyes; his voice grew scratchy; some nights, even Stewart's hair looked tired. He hadn't told Comedy Central yet, but he was growing certain that he'd be leaving* The Daily Show *at the end of his current contract.*

DOUG HERZOG

In 2013, Jon had ended up signing just a short two-year extension. And it was crystal-clear that there were only two scenarios. He was going to leave at the end of his contract, or he was going to consider staying through the 2016 election. We would have loved for him to stay till the election. But he was not signing a long-term contract.

JON STEWART

Shit bothered me too much, and there wasn't enough efficacy out of it anymore, catharsis-wise, to be worth that. Originally, it was really thrilling to have this platform, and I never took that platform for granted. But at a certain point you begin to feel like, well, now I'm just yelling the same shit. The cautionary tale for all comics is Lenny Bruce in the basement of the Hungry I with the court case transcript, onstage going, "This is what the judge said, you believe this shit?" You're always trying to tell yourself, I want to get out before I'm holding the litigation in my hand and yelling at the audience, "Where are you going? I'm getting to the good part where I get cross-examined!"

Stewart cared about the creative legacy of the show and he also wanted the changeover to be as smooth as possible, for the job security of current staffers and so that his successor wouldn't face the hostile reception that greeted Stewart when he replaced Kilborn. And he thought he'd found the perfect solution.

JOHN OLIVER

I remember Jon saying before he left to direct the movie, he said, "We'll talk when I get back about what you need to do next." And that was just horrible. That is horrifying to hear. You think, "Oh, am I being fired?"

JON STEWART

I knew I was going to be on my way out when I got back. And I knew Oliver couldn't just return to just being what he was.

I don't understand how the network let somebody take over the show without an agreement in principle. How do you not anticipate that it might be great? How shortsighted is it to let a guy stand in and not have him signed to a contract in the first place? I was talking to John the whole time, so I knew what they were saying to him, and I knew what they were saying to me. I think we were both a little stunned by the whole thing.

JOHN OLIVER

I guess they just didn't care. That's the only thing you can take away. There is nothing that would suggest that they cared.

DOUG HERZOG

I don't think that's true. Not having John Oliver signed was a giant oversight on everybody's part, including *The Daily Show.* Day in and day out, *The Daily Show* was responsible for these people. But Jon Stewart had a very long-standing tradition of never getting in the way of any of his talent. So if somebody gets an opportunity, he lets them go. With all due respect to Jon Stewart, those are decisions that are not necessarily run past Comedy Central.

JON STEWART

I'm not sure what *The Daily Show* was supposed to have done there. We weren't in charge of signing Oliver up to a hosting deal in case this thing took off. We didn't have the authority. At the time, I was focused on the movie, but Doug is right that I never said, "Hey, before Oliver hosts, what about signing him to a deal just in case somebody tries to poach him?" But that's relatively standard operating procedure in the business.

After Oliver's smash stand-in run, he and Stewart proposed that the arrangement be made more permanent, with Oliver taking over each summer.

JON STEWART

They were not willing to make John a reasonable deal, in terms of money. The HBO stuff came after all that other stuff had been exhausted with Comedy Central. So one day Oliver came into my office. And it was tearing him up a little bit, you know. He's an incredibly loyal fella. He felt like this place was his home, he loved the show, this is what he wanted to do.

JOHN OLIVER

There was no part of me that wanted to leave that show, other than a tiny part in my head which knew I had to. There was no part in me, and so I was clinging on to that thing. It ended up with Jon having to be kind of a momma bird pushing me out of the nest because I was so comfortable there. I was so happy. I felt I owed Jon everything.

JON STEWART

I said to him, "If you want to tell me what's being thrown around, and you want my advice, I'm happy to give it." He sat down and he said, "Well, you know, I'm being offered this at Showtime, and...and then there's really only this one that I've been thinking about." It was HBO once a week, and as soon as he said that I was like, "Okay. Well, let's think about this for a second. Yes, and take me with you."

JOHN OLIVER

He said you would be insane not to take that.

DOUG HERZOG

After John Oliver's first night as substitute host, it was clear that he could do this. But Jon Stewart's plans weren't clear. We offered Oliver a half-hour weekly show and so did HBO, and they wanted to pay him about twice as much as we did.

JAMES DIXON

As much as I like them at Comedy Central, and I don't want to cast aspersions on their abilities because they've been very good to me over the years—they're my friends—but let's face it. What they didn't do was prepare for succession. Probably over two or three million dollars they let John Oliver slip through their fingers.

DOUG HERZOG

Should we have paid the money? I don't know. And it would have changed things for Jon Stewart. Now there would have been somebody who we've designated as the Conan O'Brien to his Jay Leno. There was no timetable for Jon's departure at that point. After the difficulty of the 2012 negotiations, it got a little different. We have a great long relationship with Jon, but everybody got a little more guarded.

Shortsighted? You'd certainly be within your rights to say that. But that was the decision. And John Oliver chose one offer over the other.

JOHN OLIVER

My last day at *The Daily Show* was just brutal. I'm English. I'm dead inside. I don't have any echoes of feelings. What I have might be from ancestors centuries ago.

JO MILLER

The sendoff for Oliver... all day we just pretended that he was going to be in a regular chat, and we made him write it. And gave him notes and made him go rewrite his last fucking chat, and work on it all day long.

JOHN OLIVER

But it wasn't just a chat. It was an entire act one. It was a headline and chat and it was a perfectly executed prank. There was this whole charade in the morning meeting of "What about this queen thing?" And then I'd throw some ideas out there and it was "Okay, can you slam a headline and a chat together?" So we did it, and then we rewrote it. It was a fast, hard rewrite.

ELLIOTT KALAN

Every time he'd leave the writers' room we'd all burst out laughing, because we knew that during taping Jon was going to interrupt it in the middle and say farewell to Oliver.

JOHN OLIVER

During the taping, Jon was trying to make a nice joke out of the whole thing. I just couldn't handle it. I was in absolute pieces. I was kind of holding it together until he could see I was getting sad. I don't know if you can even hear it on the show, but Jon kind of said, "Are you okay?" And I just fell apart. Because that is basically reflective of my entire relationship with him taking care of me, making sure I was okay the whole time. That was when I cried.

Oliver wasn't the only one to move on before Stewart quit. Yet even those who left because they were burned out, or to seek new challenges, did so with some regret.

RORY ALBANESE

Look, I was there fifteen years when I left, and I told you the thing I'm most proud of is I put two espresso machines in a fucking staff kitchen. I wrote a lot of jokes for that show and I gave my fucking youth to that guy, and probably two hours' worth of decent standup. Guess what? I made that fucking choice. Nobody forced me to do it, and he treated everybody fairly.

There's plenty of people that have worked at that show over the years that could tell you things about Jon Stewart they don't like. They'll tell you he's a dick, he's a tyrant, he's mean. All of those things to me are coming from people who have very little perspective on reality and also very little perspective on how much value they provided to that place.

And at the end of it all, not only was it an incredible place to work, but we weren't making schlock. We were making something really good.

JAMES PONIEWOZIK

The Daily Show changed television, particularly because it advanced the late-night monologue into the post-broadcast-network era. Jon Stewart's own talent aside, and whatever specific comedy bits they did or arguments they made, the big important thing it showed was that there was a place where you could be successful doing comedy that had a strong point of view. Before *The Daily Show*, you can't overestimate how strongly ingrained was the idea that satire is what closes on Saturday night, that you could not be too strong or specific in a point of view. The change in the medium and the business and the growth of cable and smaller audiences influenced content, but *The Daily Show* pointed the way forward.

19

When Barry Met Silly

John Oliver's "replacement" as Daily Show *correspondent was a very different type: tall, blond, and middle-American Jordan Klepper. He'd come to New York after performing with Chicago's Second City.*

ELLIOTT KALAN

With Jordan you had this kind of manic strangeness behind a very bland facade—which is an insulting way to put it. Behind this super-nothing-special face that nobody would comment on—not good, not bad, just kind of fades into the background. That's better.

So the first chat that Jordan did was the one about Putin moving into Ukraine. It's Jordan's first day as a correspondent. He's getting increasingly flustered because he's making mistakes. He walks from the green screen to the desk and at one point he calls Jon "Dad."

JORDAN KLEPPER, *correspondent, 2014–*

That was the first joke I got on the show. I did it in the writers' room beforehand trying to figure out, "How much of this am I supposed to pitch in? How much are the writers in charge?" And it was such a communal place. We're riffing and ripping and running and I ended up calling Jon "Dad" accidentally. I played it in the room and Elliott says, "This is a fun bit." So we kept it.

What I also really remember from that day is standing in the wings as Jon did his preshow Q&A with the audience. Then "Born to Run" kicks in, as it did before every taping started. But Jon comes over to me before he goes behind the desk and says, "Hey, if you don't absolutely destroy it tonight, we'll leave you in a fucking ditch. Have a good show!" and walks back out. I felt like the tears started in my toes and built up. I was like, "Oh my God. This is a big moment for me right now. But I could destroy it."

ELLIOTT KALAN

Jordan, that was urine. Those were not tears.

JORDAN KLEPPER

That was a big night for me. The bit went well. I felt like a million bucks. I had friends who'd been on *SNL*, where you do a show and then you go and party with Paul McCartney. So I walked offstage and turned to people, saying, "Where do we go out? What do we do?" People are turning off the lights and they say, "Well, you do it again tomorrow." *The Daily Show*, you do a show and then you wake up at seven o'clock and you read the newspaper and you come up with something again.

The next new correspondent had grown up in a Lower East Side housing project. Michael Che was hired away from Saturday Night Live, *where he had been on the writing staff. In June, Che made his debut "from" Aleppo, Syria, "reporting" on the ruinous civil war and the rise of ISIS.*

Hiring distinctive new correspondents was one sign that Stewart didn't intend to coast his way to the finish. In July, Hillary Clinton came by for just her third visit, ostensibly to sell her new book about her years as secretary of state, Hard Choices, *but also to begin selling herself as Obama's successor. And Stewart found a sly way to mount the elephant in the room.*

> **Jon Stewart:** This [book] is, it's an incredibly, I think, complex and well-reasoned and eyewitness view to the history of those four years, and I think I speak for everyone when I say, no one cares, they just want to know if you're running for president.
> Let me ask you a question: Do you like commuting to work or do you like a home office?
>
> **Hillary Clinton:** You know, I've spent so many years commuting, I kind of prefer a home office. That's where I wrote my book, it was on the third floor of our house, so that worked.

Jon Stewart: Do you have a favorite shape for that home office? Would you like that office to have corners, or would you like it not to have corners?

Hillary Clinton: [*laughs*] You know, I think that the world is so complicated, the fewer corners you can have the better.

Having gotten Clinton to laugh, Stewart proceeded to make her squirm.

Jon Stewart: These talking heads, sitting around, picking out every little thing, making fun of it, it's just not right. [*looks archly at camera*]

Hillary Clinton: Could I say that I agree with you completely?

Jon Stewart: What was the one that caught you most off guard? Was it the "We were dead broke—"

Hillary Clinton: Well, you know that was an inartful use of words, obviously. You know, Bill and I have worked really hard and we've been successful and I'm really grateful for that. But what I worry about and I talk about this in the book is, I'm worried that other people and especially younger people are not going to have the same opportunities we did...

Jon Stewart: You know what was kind of awesome, it says to me you're running for president, how easily you pivoted from that to income inequality in America.

Then Stewart himself pivoted, from domestic to foreign affairs, with a wonkish question that produced an intriguingly political answer.

Jon Stewart: You see very small groups who are able to sow a great deal of destructive force, and is America—we are a large imperial power and the idea that we can exercise that power in the same manner, you know, what is our foreign policy anymore?

Hillary Clinton: You know, well, that's really why this book is something that I put my heart and soul into, because we can't practice our diplomacy and define our foreign policy as leaders talking to leaders anymore, because that's not the way the world works anymore, exactly as you said. People are empowered from the bottom up. What I found when I became secretary of state was that so many people in the world, especially young people, they had no memory of the United States liberating Europe and Asia, fighting the Nazis, the Cold War, you know, and winning. That was just ancient history. They didn't know the sacrifices they had made and the values that motivated us to do it.

We have not been telling our story very well. We do have a great story. We are not perfect by any means, but we do have a great story. About human freedom, human rights, human opportunity, and let's get back to telling it, to ourselves, first and foremost, and believing about ourselves and then taking it around the world. That's what we should be standing for.

JON STEWART

I thought that was nuts. Because the problem with America's story is it has to be told honestly. It's not that people haven't heard about it. Does she really think that America is a relatively obscure nation? You know we're not Liberia or the Marshall Islands. All we do is project our awesomeness.

I've always felt like what America has to do is act with integrity, and if somebody tells a different story, you can try and correct it, but more importantly, it's what you do, not what you say.

But all politicians are essentially salespeople. Some are more adept at concealing it. Others truly don't have the stomach for it and wear that part on their sleeve. I always get the sense Obama had a disdain for that part of the job. I still don't get the sense that he really likes anybody down there, in Washington. Hillary has the stomach for it, but more importantly has the ambition for it. And you'll stomach a lot when you've got the ambition.

She is very comfortable in the world of the establishment. So, the inauthenticity is not her affecting a drawl or not being a great campaigner. It's adopting a mantra that you know is not hers. Like, you don't give those speeches to Wall Street and then talk about how economic disparity is a terrible problem. The sense I get from Hillary is that she says, "Oh, they're liking this economic policy, so then I will stand and be Braveheart." I do think her passion is real and admirable with women's issues around the world. She's worked on that her whole life. But I think because she's been ensconced in the world of power and influence, when she takes the position of the champion of not that, it feels somewhat hollow.

*   *   *

Two days after Hillary Clinton's appearance came the chokehold death of Eric Garner, a black man, at the hands of a white New York police officer. It was, unfortunately, merely the first in a string of high-profile racial tragedies in 2015. Across sixteen years, The Daily Show had become adept at trying to make sense of madness through comedy. But often the weight of addressing a crisis fell directly and drainingly on Stewart. After Garner's death, he dropped the jokes for raw emotion, much as he had done after 9/11. Yet the years in between seemed to have sapped his optimism. "I honestly don't know what to say," Stewart told the audience after a grand jury brought no charges related to Garner's death. "If comedy is tragedy plus time, I need more fucking time. But I would really settle for less fucking tragedy."

LARRY WILMORE

I was in Los Angeles, working on *Black-ish*, where I was executive producer, when I heard about the police in New York killing Eric Garner with a chokehold. I remember thinking, "I have to leave and say something about this," and calling *The Daily Show*, and they were thinking the same thing.

It's always a collaboration between all of us. Usually the writers have an angle and I'll have a point of view as well, and we'll get on the phone and talk. When I come in the first thing I'll do is meet with Jon. "How do we really feel about this? What do you think, what do I think?" And we get that point of view down first, and then the comedy comes out of that. I came up with the idea that it wasn't the cops that were racist, it was the benefit of the doubt itself that was racist. Then you write toward that point of view.

I'm in the writers' meeting and somebody said, "Look, man, the only thing Garner was brandishing was his blackness," and I said, "Yes, that's it. That's what the piece is." That's the crystallizing line. Those lines come out of talking about it.

Jon Stewart: [*at anchor desk*] You really think police aren't as quick to choke out a white person as a black person?

Larry Wilmore: [*across from Stewart*] Well, let's compare. Eric Garner was unarmed, holding his hands up, and politely asking the cops to leave him alone. Here's a white guy in Michigan last month. [*video clip of rifle-toting angry guy*] Here he is threatening the cops with a rifle—oh, and now he's waving his dick at them! [*video clip of crotch-grabbing angry guy*] Oh, shit, they're gonna fuck him up bad! [*video clip of cops whispering in angry guy's ear*] Or...they're gonna sit and have a chat. You gotta be fucking kidding me! Jon, he was asking for a chokehold!

This guy could have shot his way out of Fallujah. The only thing Eric Garner was brandishing was his blackness.

JON STEWART

That August, Michael Brown gets shot in Ferguson, Missouri, by the police. The show was on vacation, but I'm always keeping up on things. At the time the ALS Bucket Challenge was big, and so on the plane back to New York I cooked up the Ferguson Protest Challenge, where I get maced and tear-gassed.

I watched the Fox coverage of Ferguson and their defensiveness about it and "maybe that cop felt threatened." I thought what they don't understand is, it's not just that these individuals live in a town where they feel the fragility of their safety with the authorities. It's a system, and I don't understand why we can't acknowledge that. I don't think people recognize how exhausting it is sometimes to be black.

So we also did a longer piece partly about how Fox was "outraged" that Ferguson was being cast in racial terms. And I talked about how we'd recently sent a producer, Stu Miller, who was dressed like a homeless elf with a week's worth of five o'clock shadow, and a correspondent, Michael Che, dressed in a tailored suit, out to do an interview—and how it was Che who got stopped by security. The point being, here's how ubiquitous racism and indignity is. To Michael, this wasn't "You're not going to fucking believe what happened." It came up in the course of the conversation about other things. That's what I meant in the piece when I said, "You're tired of hearing about racism? Imagine how fucking exhausting it is living it."

TRAVON FREE

There was an Andrea Tantaros clip, from Fox, where I think she says something to the effect of, "Why do we keep having to make everything about race?" And Jon and Jo Miller and I were talking about it in my office, and that line about how just being black in America is exhausting came out of the conversation.

It's sad I can't even tell you which shooting it was about. But I was just so fucking happy we got to that place. As an African-American, as a creative person, it felt really good to know that I was a part of something that millions of people would see and hear. As a civilian, you can feel so helpless. But because I knew Jon was a person who drove conversation, I felt like I contributed at least in some way to getting people closer to where I thought the conversation should be.

I spent a good portion of time talking to Jon directly about race, because he would come to my office. He cared about it a lot and wanted it to be done right.

Che was a Daily Show *correspondent for only four months, before jumping back to* SNL *to coanchor "Weekend Update." But it was long enough for him to star in a haunting segment called "Race/Off" that was stylistically reminiscent of Steve Carell's "escape" from Baghdad during* The Daily Show's *early days.*

MICHAEL CHE, *correspondent, 2014*

I was in San Jose, California, working on a field piece, and Jo Miller and Travon Free had written a piece about Ferguson and other police killings. A lot of them I hadn't even known about. So much had happened while we were on break. Everybody at the show was kind of licking their chops to do a piece saying, "What the F is going on?"

I took the red-eye back, and they sent me the script while I was on the plane. Got to New York, into a car, into wardrobe at *The Daily Show*, onto the set. That's one of the exciting things about *The Daily Show* that you miss out on at *SNL*—because it's daily, you get first crack at everything.

> **Jon Stewart:** [*at anchor desk*] We turn to Senior Missouri Correspondent Michael Che. Michael, what's the mood on the street right now in Ferguson?
>
> **Michael Che:** [*in front of green-screen photo of St. Louis Arch*] Beats me. I'm not there. There are too many white cops with itchy trigger fingers in Ferguson. I'm staying right here in St. Louis where it's safe.
>
> **Jon Stewart:** I'm pretty sure in St. Louis the police shot and killed a black gentleman three days after the Ferguson shooting.
>
> **Michael Che:** You mean like in a different St. Louis?
>
> **Jon Stewart:** No, I'm pretty sure it's the one in Missouri.
>
> **Michael Che:** That's . . . interesting.
>
> **Jon Stewart:** But this is good, because I can ask you about the St. Louis County Police and—
>
> [*Che reappears on-screen, standing on a beach*]

Jon Stewart: I'm sorry, Michael. Where are you?

Michael Che: [*cheerfully*] Jon, I'm as far away from the Shoot-Me State as you can get. Southern California! Nothing but sun, surfers, and palm trees—

Jon Stewart: Ummm...the LAPD recently shot an unarmed twenty-five-year-old black man to death.

[*Che "runs" down a highway as city welcome signs fly by—*CHARLOTTE, MACON, LITTLE ROCK, NEW ORLEANS, DAYTON—*and lists recent shootings as he does so; then Che reappears wearing a cheap plastic space helmet and "floating" weightlessly*]

Michael Che: Relax, Jon. I'm not even on Earth anymore. Nowhere safer for a black man than the infinite blackness of outer space.

[*Red lights flash; police siren howls*]

Police Voice: That's a pretty expensive-looking space helmet. You got a receipt for that thing?

JESSICA WILLIAMS

It seemed like there was a run of really high-profile racial incidents not long after I started at the show. I didn't feel exactly like I was representing black people, but being twenty-two and new, it was a lot of pressure. It means a lot to me to work on a show where we do dick jokes, but we could still make a point about Ferguson.

I did a stop-and-frisk bit that I really loved, when John Oliver was hosting, about how the cops should be in high crime districts like Wall Street. And do you remember the young black girl from McKinney, Texas? She and her friends were at the pool and the police officer totally jumped all over her and sat on her, and she was a fourteen-year-old girl in a bikini? Well, I did a piece where I had on full armor, with the bikini on top of it. I'm really proud of that bit. That was the first piece where I was like, "Oh damn, this feels good to do—and it feels important to do."

That fall, as Black Lives Matter protests filled U.S. streets and shopping malls, The Daily Show's exploration of racism broadened and intensified. A Jason Jones field piece generated controversy when a group of Washington Redskins fans claimed the show had tricked them into a confrontation with Native American activists angry about the team's nickname. Back in the studio, Bill

O'Reilly made a guest appearance to promote his latest bio-cidal book; Stewart spent twelve minutes trying to get O'Reilly to admit that white privilege exists.

Bill O'Reilly: If you want to say it's white privilege because whites didn't have it as bad as blacks, fine. But that's not what's happening here in contemporary society!

Jon Stewart: Yes it is!

Bill O'Reilly: No it's not! Yes, it's harder if you're a ghetto kid. Yes! But can you do it? Yes!

Jon Stewart: You can also win the hundred-yard dash on one leg!

Bill O'Reilly: Oh stop! Every fair person acknowledges—and I've said it many times on the *Factor*, the highest-rated cable news show in the world—

Jon Stewart: Somebody hasn't seen Megyn Kelly yet!

Bill O'Reilly: —that African-Americans have it harder!

Jon Stewart: So we've come to agreement. You admit that white privilege exists, and while it's not an excuse, it is a reality.

Bill O'Reilly: It doesn't exist to any extent where individuals are kept back because of their color, or promoted because of their color! Look, you and I are lucky guys. We made it, we worked hard. It's not 'cause we're white! [*turning to yell at a booing audience member*] Oh, you think I'm sitting here 'cause I'm white!? You moron! I'm sitting here because I'm obnoxious, not 'cause I'm white!

Jon Stewart: My point is this: Women face this, and minorities face this. They have to make strategic calculations in their lives that white guys never have to make. We never have to worry about walking down certain streets because somebody's gonna cat-call us.

Bill O'Reilly: What you're doing is promoting victimhood.

Jon Stewart: You know what I'll call it? And it's a word I think you'll understand: It's a factor.

Bill O'Reilly: I'll give you the "factor" business.

Jon Stewart: This was a historic moment. Your humility has moved me. You are like Pope Francis, that has taken the Catholic Church into an era of acceptance and humility. You, Bill O'Reilly, can lead the flock of the Fox fearful to a better place.

JON STEWART

Why was it so important to press him on white privilege? Because the community where O'Reilly grew up, that he's so proud of as being the roots of his virtue, is so steeped in systemic racism. Levittown was a whites-only community, and so much of its wealth was a GI bill creation. That experience was so crucial to his view of himself as a self-starter, and the work ethic that he learned. That's why I felt like it was imperative to at least have that argument.

Stewart's conversation with O'Reilly only touched on the subject briefly, but as issues like gender pay equity and violence against women became a larger part of the cultural dialogue, the increased number of female staffers helped The Daily Show *tackle those subjects with greater authenticity.*

ELLIOTT KALAN

Here's a big example of how the show's topics changed over the years but how important parts of the process didn't—writers collaborating and not being precious about their ideas, and Jon not giving into the temptation to just pump stuff out.

We had an idea to do a piece about campus sexual assault, for Jessica Williams. As head writer I assigned it to J. R. Havlan and Daniel Radosh, because they were free. Great writers, but what they came up with was not really the right perspective for this piece, and Jessica wasn't comfortable with it. Jon was decisive: "Okay. If you're not comfortable with this let's go with that feeling. We won't do this piece." We scrapped it the night we were supposed to shoot it.

JESSICA WILLIAMS

It didn't feel quite right. We didn't want to be making fun of the victims. Jon respected me enough to say, "Okay, go back and work on it." And it was getting down to the wire when the piece was supposed to run.

ELLIOTT KALAN

There are shows where the writers would have said, "We worked on these jokes for days. You have to do them. You're not going to do them?" But that wasn't the *Daily Show* style. So I went to Jo Miller and Lauren Sarver and asked them to get in a room with Sara Taksler, the producer, and Jessica, and think about different ways to do it.

SARA TAKSLER

I got teased, playfully, because I pitched a lot of stories about abortion and rape. The show, when I started, was more resistant to covering certain things, because the feeling was "We don't know how to make this funny." I think Jon always cared about these issues; I don't think his feelings changed. Part of it was you get bored covering the same stuff all the time. Women's issues were becoming more of a mainstream news story, which made it easier for us, if people are already talking about it. And as the show became more and more successful, there was a confidence that we can make anything funny. Any story that's important to tell, we can figure out a way to tell it.

LAUREN SARVER MEANS

There's usually a catharsis in whatever piece we do on the show, where we might try to find a solution for something, and in talking about this topic, we couldn't just stay focused on the campus stories themselves because it's actually a global cultural problem.

We're talking about rape, and we can't do a piece about how to get rid of rape. That's absurd. So we were all really upset and sharing our own experiences in college, and then that expanded just to feeling unsafe in New York and exchanging stories about walking to work and not feeling safe.

SARA TAKSLER

The conversation became about how women run this obstacle course in our daily lives and it's crazy to realize my brother or my boyfriend doesn't know about it.

LAUREN SARVER MEANS

We ended up with a piece where Jessica is talking about self-defense strategies for women, and Jordan Klepper is clueless.

SARA TAKSLER

What was awesome was that Jordan said, "I don't think I'm enough of a jerk in the piece. I need to be more ignorant."

LAUREN SARVER MEANS

It was Jessica who came up with the perfect line about men on the street saying they wanted to lick her back. I had wanted to pitch something more vulgar.

Jon Stewart: [*at anchor desk*] Clearly universities want their campuses safe. So Jordan Klepper and Jessica Williams have come up with some campus safety *dos* and *don'ts.*

Jordan Klepper: [*in preppy polo shirt with upturned collar, standing in front of green-screen photo of college dorm*] Okay, bros! Party commandment number one: Beer before liquor, never been sicker!

Jessica Williams: [*standing next to Klepper in sleeveless T-shirt and jeans*] Ladies, never lose sight of your drink! Ever! Don't be a doofie, watch out for the roofie!

Jordan Klepper: Um, bros before hos, and um, don't text your junk. Nowadays, potential employers will check your social media—

Jessica Williams: [*shoving Klepper aside*] That reminds me! If your crazy ex won't stop texting you pictures of his junk, save all of them! Also any angry voice mails, weepy voice mails, threatening tweets and Tumblr posts, and surveillance footage of him standing outside your window watching you sleep. Save it all! The college and the cops won't do anything, but maybe it will help you with your civil suit.

Jordan Klepper: Come on, Jessica. You're telling me women spend their whole day navigating an obstacle course of sexual menace?

Jessica Williams: Pretty much.

Jordan Klepper: Oh, wow. Shit. Sorry. But hey, men aren't all bad. [*proudly points to self*] Some of us are gentlemen!

Jessica Williams: Okay, thanks. I'll keep that in mind the next time a guy says he wants to lick my back when I'm walking to work at eight in the fucking morning.

College students comprised one of the most enthusiastic segments of The Daily Show's *audience throughout Stewart's time as host. Other viewers proved harder to reach, even as current events prompted not just more segments about racial issues, but some of* The Daily Show's *most memorable ones.*

LARRY WILMORE

Nobody at the barbershop ever knew what *The Daily Show* was. Well, I would say three black people at any given time watch *The Daily Show*, and if I'm watching it that reduces it down to two. In fact I was going to start an organization called One of the Three. I even did a bit on the show where I said, "Black people watching *The Daily Show*, the three of you need to listen to me very carefully," while I was convincing them it was time to let O.J. go, where he couldn't be a symbol of black anger.

JESSICA WILLIAMS

My experience has been a little different. I get a lot of beautiful, older, affluent, Alfre Woodard–type women saying, "Great job." And they also say, "That white boy Jon Stewart? He's a cutie!" *All* the time.

LARRY WILMORE

When I first came to the show the notion was that my character would be a black conservative commentator. I didn't want to do that, because for one thing I didn't want to suggest that conservatives were, by some reason, wrong just because they were conservatives. My nature is to be contrary, so I thought I would go against the grain of what you would expect from a black commentator. I like to think we weren't just preaching to the choir, that we surprised people sometimes.

Jon always deferred to me when I had an insight that he knew was genuine and was from my point of view. I would say, "Jon, I'm telling you the brothers don't care about this," or, "As a black person I would think this," and we always had that kind of relationship where he wanted to know what that was.

Early on, we were going to do something on Black History Month. The typical joke is that the black person is upset that February only has twenty-eight days and they feel robbed. I said, "Guys, I can't do that joke." I said, "I'll tell you my honest point of view on this is: Brothers are bored with the history." So then the piece became, what really would be valuable instead of a month of trivia, especially for four hundred years of slavery? Not twenty-eight days of trivia. I'd rather we got casinos.

One of The Daily Show*'s smallest demographics, however, was also one of its most attentive: official Washington and, in particular, beginning in 2009, the White House. They are very different men, of course: a soccer-playing Jewish comic from*

New Jersey; a basketball-playing Kansan-Kenyan Christian pol from Hawaii. Yet Stewart and Obama, born fifteen months apart, shared a wised-up, postmodern sensibility and a core optimism. And for all their basic agreement on liberal policy ideas, what they had most in common was a more fundamental conservatism: a desire for the country's politics to return to the mythical good old days of rational argument and functional, if messy, compromise.

DAVID AXELROD, *former senior advisor to President Barack Obama*

Jon played a role in the elections that I was involved with Obama, in 2008 and 2012. I'm sure we did viewership research at some point. There was a measurable number of people who said they got their news from *The Daily Show*, which probably would frighten Jon, but I remember in 2005 Obama did a remote into *The Daily Show* during the campaign. It was really a good hit, but Jon was ribbing him for being on this celebrity platform, and Obama said, "Yeah, Jon, I think the only person who's more overhyped than me is you." And Stewart almost fell off his chair. But those kinds of interactions were helpful to us, because we were galvanizing particularly young people. The *Daily Show* audience was sort of right down Broadway for us in terms of reaching people and defining Obama as a kind of new-generation candidate.

In the early part of our administration the progressives, and I consider Jon among them, didn't feel we were moving fast enough on different fronts or we were too willing to compromise. My first appearance on the show, in June 2010, basically Jon's message was, "You guys believe in government, so why don't you do it better? Because if you don't do it better, people won't believe in it." So it was an interesting conversation. For me, there was an element of, "Oh, yeah, well, why don't you come over here and do this, funny boy?" Because it's a lot harder than people think to get stuff done. But nonetheless, Jon's prodding was heard.

DAG VEGA

It was important for us to engage with Jon Stewart, because he was influential and the president wanted to get his point of view across. So we invited Jon to the White House twice, in 2011 and 2014.

JON STEWART

I think that nobody in government ever talks to you unless they have a reason. It is an agenda-driven life. And not to say that most lives are not

somewhat agenda driven, but not necessarily as relentlessly so as it is in politics. And so that aspect of them inviting me to the White House was not lost
on me.

The whole pomp and circumstance of it is crazy. I mean, you're going
to the White House. You go through a portico. You get searched. You go
through the gate. Somebody comes to meet you and takes you to the Roo-
sevelt Room. Like, it's crazy. You wait there, and then the Oval Office door
opens, and there is the president in the office that Nixon had his tape recorder
in, that Dolley Madison would bring the ice cream.

It feels like a movie set, unfortunately. I kept thinking Dave was going to
show up. I'd turn the corner and there'd be Charles Grodin in a little visor,
with a little calculator going, "He's with the president. Here's where we can
save some money." And you go in, and there's an attachment to the Oval
Office that's his office, and then beyond that is a little small dining room, and
you sit in that little dining room. And they bring you maybe the best salmon
you've ever eaten, and a salad, and a little dessert, and you try not to gawk.

Obama wanted to talk about whether or not I was making everyone in the
world cynical. And if I was, for me to stop doing it.

DAVID AXELROD

Where the president may have been zeroing in in those conversations was
that he was working pretty hard to get some significant progressive things
done, and for Jon to convey a sense that somehow he was less than serious
about it because it wasn't happening at the pace some people wanted is not
fair or realistic. If you're president and you can't get a public option even
though you want one, and the choice is no health-care bill or a health-care
bill, being called a dipshit for not getting a public option isn't very satisfying.
It does add to cynicism.

JON STEWART

We had a little disagreement over what the show represented. But that's
the first ten minutes, and then the next fifty minutes you get to have a really
interesting conversation about government and its function, and philosophy, and history, and media with the president. And you get to question him
about, "Why doesn't the VA work?"

Obama is emphatic and somewhat stentorian. It's intimidating. I can't tell you that it's not. He's the president of the United States. You figure there's a drone following somewhere.

DAVID AXELROD

Jon had a big megaphone. The thing about him was when he decided to deal with things directly—how 9/11 victims were treated, the condition of the Veterans Administration—because he is a comedian they almost had more impact, because it was sort of "I'm not even going to dress this shit up. I'm just going to lay it out here because it's so irksome and concerning to me." I say this affectionately—he was kind of a pain in the ass, which I think he wanted to be.

JON STEWART

I think a public service program is a really good idea—make college three years, pay for some of it, and give kids one year of public service. This is where the president and Axelrod would start yelling at me: "You can't get it through! Where's the money? You're an idiot!"

I'm not suggesting that the president is a magic unicorn. But if something is a priority, there are extraordinary levers of bully pulpit power he can bring to it.

I pocketed two boxes of M&M's with the presidential seal. You open it up and you really are expecting the best M&M's you've ever eaten in your life, and it's just fucking M&M's. You're like, "Well, these are the same M&M's I got at the train station." I thought president M&M's would somehow be like, I don't know, the chocolate on the outside and the candy on the inside, something different. But they're just M&M's. Pretty interesting.

Even as he was growing more certain that he was nearing the end of his run, Stewart kept tinkering with the process. Maybe it was his weariness with artifice in general, maybe it was a reflection of the baldly partisan times, but in Stewart's later years more Daily Show *pieces threw more direct punches.*

MILES KAHN

In the field department we used a formula, not on purpose, but it became sort of our default where we would lionize the villain and we'd villainize the hero. It was all done ironically, and it worked well.

But then Jon says, "Hey, this formula we've been doing for six, seven years, you don't always need to do it." It was a sea change. If you watched the last several years of Jon's show, you'll see there's a point where the correspondent drops the POV and just starts going after the interview subjects earnestly. A good example of that was a piece I did with Jason Jones about Google Glass. There is no irony in his reaction at all. His point of view was, "Are you fucking kidding me?" It's an amplified version of Jason, but it's him being angry and pissed off at these nerds wearing these ridiculous glasses and he calls them out on it the whole time, and it's such a satisfying piece. It's more satisfying than had Jason been like, "Wow, those glasses are great!" ironically. It would've taken the bite away from it.

In October 2014, the show spent a week in Austin, Texas—ostensibly to cover the midterm elections, but mostly because Austin is a fun town full of Daily Show *fans. Stewart hadn't yet told the staff he had decided to leave. But when he made a rare appearance at the* Daily Show *staff karaoke night, those who'd known him longest were thrilled to hang out with the boss outside the office, but were also suspicious that the end was near.*

JEN FLANZ

That was one of the best nights ever. Jon even talked about it on the show the next day. He did not get up and sing karaoke. He just watched all of us stupid people perform. He thought it was hilarious. I've never seen him just chill. But I think he knew he was leaving.

In November, Stewart hired his last correspondent: the rail-thin, pompadoured Hasan Minhaj. At twenty-nine, Minhaj was part of the generation of comedians that had grown up watching The Daily Show *most of their lives.*

HASAN MINHAJ, *correspondent, 2014–*

I'd been watching since I was five, six years old. Then, yeah, I was part of what Bill O'Reilly called *The Daily Show*'s slacker-stoner demographic. We would watch it at 11 in the college dorm room. The show had such a deep impact on us. It was this merging of comedy with intellectualism that none of my professors at UC Davis could seem to touch. It was like, oh, my history professor is trying to be funny—it's not working.

The dream was to work with Jon, because it would be like playing with

Michael Jordan, and because you get to do work that intrinsically moves the needle forward culturally in the national dialogue.

I'd shot a pilot for E!, but then Michael Che leaves *The Daily Show* to return to *Saturday Night Live* to do "Weekend Update." I get an e-mail from my manager, subject line, "Hey, do you want to audition for *The Daily Show*," with a question mark. Which is not a question mark e-mail. That's a statement e-mail. That's an exclamation point e-mail.

The Charlie Hebdo *terrorist attack occurred not long after Minhaj was hired, so he quickly got to participate in the type of* Daily Show *piece he'd always admired, one with both cultural and personal resonance. The takeoff point for the bit was a Rupert Murdoch tweet asserting that moderate Muslims "must be held responsible" for the acts of Islamic extremists. So Stewart convened a trio of "senior condemnologists" to try to out-blame one another.*

Jason Jones: I wholeheartedly condemn these acts and those responsible for them.

Jessica Williams: Yeah, and so do I. I definitely condemn them as well.

Hasan Minhaj: And Jon, yes, I, as a Muslim, of course, absolutely 100 percent, unequivocally condemn these actions.

Jason Jones: [*shaking head dismissively*] Uhhh...yeah. I gotta be honest. I just did not feel that last one, coming from him.

Jessica Williams: [*rolling eyes*] Yeah, I don't know, Hasan's wasn't as condemn-y as I'd like.

Jason Jones: You'd think it would be a little more shameful.

Jessica Williams: Right. Or denounce-ier.

Jon Stewart: [*earnest bordering on unctuous*] Look, maybe it's not necessary for each individual to have to own the worst actions of the people in their community. Maybe that's not necessary.

Hasan Minhaj: Oh, shit! Look who's trying to get out of this! [*pointing at Stewart*] Yeah, Mister Insider-Trading!

Jessica Williams: Mister Crash-the-Economy!

Jason Jones: Captain Bail-Me-Out!

Jon Stewart: I don't work in finance! Okay, okay! Actually, you know the last guy they nailed for insider trading was Raj Gupta.

Hasan Minhaj: [*indignant*] Oh, so I gotta *double*-apologize now?

HASAN MINHAJ

Evil terrorists have done this horrible thing. The backlash is that all brown people now have to pay, and that's a really, really awful thing to feel. Every time I turn on the news, every Facebook article I see, someone is asking, "Can you trust the brown guy next door?" And a lot of the media is involved in some level of scapegoating. But Jon, because he was a sensitive, critical thinker, comes up with a bit to humanize that experience, and do it in a satirical way. It meant a lot to me to be part of that piece.

ELLIOTT KALAN

At the end, when Jon was getting very tired, he would say, "You know what? Tomorrow let's just have fun. We're just going to have a fun day tomorrow." And we would be like, "Okay. We'll do something really silly on the show." And then that morning Jon would come in and say, "Did you see what Megyn Kelly did? We've got to get these guys." So we were like, "What happened to fun?" And he's like, "Well, this will be fun, too." It's a little bit like your dad saying, "Tomorrow we're going to Disney World." Then, "No. Your teeth are terrible. We need to go to the dentist—but it'll be fun! We'll have a fun time at the dentist!" Those shows would come out really well, but we'd all be like, "Awww. We were going to have fun today."

MICHELE GANELESS

Jon said, "You know when you're on the highway and you miss your exit, and you have to go around to get back to your exit? That's what I feel like I'm doing." That's how he described it to us when he was making the decision to leave. You knew he was tired. When he went to do the movie, we knew he had creative urges and creative ideas he wanted to pursue...and he'd been doing this for a long time.

DOUG HERZOG

There was a point, after Stephen left, where we have to know. So we started to sort of nudge him a little bit. Jon is very interested in the legacy of the show, what was going to happen to the staff. So he understood that his decision had a lot of impact for Comedy Central, a lot of impact for all these people.

He finally got back to us in November 2014: "Yeah, I think this is going to be it." I mean, you're like, "Holy fuck!" And then we were unable to do anything. We couldn't start looking for Jon's replacement, because Jon didn't want to announce it until after Stephen's last *Colbert Report* show, which was at the end of 2014, and until we launched *The Nightly Show with Larry Wilmore*, which was going to be in January 2015. So we just sat on the announcement for several months. Yeah, that was hard, especially when you're just panicked, like, "Who's going to be the next Jon Stewart?"

As Stewart was finalizing his decision to leave The Daily Show, *Oliver's new show,* Last Week Tonight, *was off to a smashing start on HBO. But Oliver's contract was for only one year. So Stewart called Oliver before the news of his exit broke, just in case Oliver would consider coming back to* The Daily Show.

JON STEWART

I always thought John had demonstrated an ability to run *The Daily Show* joyfully, to take it to another place, to make it interesting. So he would have been the most obvious choice for the health of the show and the health of the people who had already worked with him, were comfortable with him. And knowing that, when I did finally decide I was leaving, I reached out to him to tell him.

And we had a conversation. And the conversation was basically, "I think you would be amazing, but I cannot recommend that you do it. I cannot in good conscience. I would love for you to take over as the host of *The Daily Show*. As your friend, I cannot recommend it." Because he had done the thing that everyone strives to do, which is, to utilize your experience and your background and then take it to another place, and evolve it, and make it your own, and create a singular thing for your voice.

And he had done that, and he'd done it on HBO, which is maybe the greatest environment you do something on. I knew that it was a long shot.

His reaction was, "That's very flattering, but I can't. No, no, no, no, no, I'm not good at all. I'm a mushroom. I'm a mushroom underneath a log, underneath a pig's anus." But that's always John's reaction. He's a very humble guy, and genuinely so.

I think it ended up being a better situation for John, and *The Daily Show* has an opportunity now to grow with another person, and that's great, too. But it was absolutely Comedy Central's weirdness that facilitated any of that even being an issue.

*   *   *

Meanwhile, the December 2014 debut of The Daily Show's *newest contributor went largely unnoticed. Most American audiences had never heard of Trevor Noah, but he was a major comedy star on several other continents, and it had taken* Daily Show *producers nearly two years to get him onto the set.*

TREVOR NOAH, *contributor, 2014;* **The Daily Show** *host, 2015–*

I was in a great place. I really was. You're selling tickets around the world, people are coming out to see your shows, you're making a good living. That's the dream. I was in London and I got a call: "Jon Stewart wants to speak to you." He said, "I have a little show called *The Daily Show* and maybe you've heard of it." I said, "Of course I've heard of the show." And he said, "I saw your stuff and I'd love for you to come in, hang out, see if we could do something," and I said, "I'm sorry, but I don't have the time." I realize now how ludicrous it was to say that, but at that time I was too busy.

JEN FLANZ

In 2013 we were looking for correspondents and we were really interested in Trevor. Jon saw less than a minute of Trevor's *Letterman* set, and Jon says, "That guy's going to take my chair." I remember me, Tim Greenberg, Jocelyn Conn, Bodow, Lowitt, we were all in the room, and we were like, "Wait, is Jon leaving?"

JON STEWART

This was a long time ago. I saw a tape of Trevor, and I'd say within thirty seconds it was like, "Oh, that guy could do my job."

It was very clear he had a great deal of presence, a great deal of confidence, but also a really nice manner of thinking, of breaking down material in a way that was not rote, and it was unusual, and it was unique and thoughtful. And beyond that, the fact that if you put him in my clothes he somehow still looks like he should be in a magazine, whereas when you put me in my clothes I look like I should be selling oranges out on the highway.

That's what's annoying about him. Trevor can get laid in many different avenues, he doesn't need to be funny. I wouldn't be surprised if he can also play guitar.

Stewart's movie, Rosewater, *had its premiere in November 2014. After he was done with promotional appearances for the film, and Colbert had sung his way out of the* Report, *and the new year had passed, Stewart was ready to make his* Daily Show *farewell official.*

JEN FLANZ

It was a Friday in February. Jon told a few of us together that he was leaving. Me, Lowitt, Steve, Kahane was in there, Jill, Tim Greenberg. We were in a meeting in this glass room, and Jon's telling us, "Don't make a face, because everybody's going to be able to see you." My eyes are welling up. Jon just said, "I'm tired. I'm done, and I'm going to try and make sure you guys are all okay, and I told the network that the most important thing about this place is how it's run and the infrastructure and you guys."

Jon told the staff the next Tuesday.

JO MILLER

There's a thing called an all-hands meeting. And when it comes over the PA, "There will be an all-hands meeting in fifteen minutes in the studio," it's usually right before rehearsal, it's some big deal. Sometimes it's a cool announcement like Jon saying, "I decided to give everyone $1,000." Or it's a big thank-you to everyone for making a convention week happen. But all-hands meetings always make you think, "What's up?"

JEN FLANZ

It was dead quiet. People were crying. It was pretty emotional. Then it became really, really stressful for about a month and a half. People were freaking out that they were all going to lose jobs that they'd had for a very long time.

JO MILLER

Poor Hasan Minhaj. Oh my God, he looked like someone had just run over his whole family in front of him. He had just moved here and started on the show. And we were making jokes, and he had that it's-not-funny-guys face on.

HASAN MINHAJ

My heart just stung. Jessica was crying. For me, for three months it had been, "Hey, welcome to the team." Now it became a countdown to good-bye. No, dude, it wasn't because Jon realized he didn't want to work with me—I didn't make Dad leave the family. At least that's what Jon told me.

JO MILLER

I went over and drank with the field department in the field lounge. And I think the writers drank in the writers' lounge. But by this point a lot of the writers were newer and had just finally gotten their dream job a year, two years, three years before. So the writers' room was a bummer, and I didn't want to be there. Over in the field lounge things were a little more humorous, and the liquor was better.

The next day, in another sign of how far the media universe had shifted during his time as host, with a basic-cable satirist becoming more credible than a major-network news anchor, Stewart's departure "at a high point in his career" got equal, front-page New York Times *billing alongside NBC's decision to suspend* Nightly News *anchor Brian Williams for embellishing the facts of stories. Meanwhile, Comedy Central's search for Stewart's successor took on new urgency, and the speculation machine nominated tantalizing, if implausible, candidates.*

JON STEWART

Amy [Poehler] and Tina [Fey], and Chris [Rock] and Louis [C.K.]—if any one of those four had said, "Give me the reins," wow. That's amazing. But they were not my suggestions, because I never thought they would do it.

For selfish reasons I was hoping that it would be more of an in-house choice. Amy Schumer was someone who rose to mind immediately. She and I had pizza one night, just talking about her hosting *The Daily Show. Trainwreck* hadn't come out yet. But even at that point she had an enormously successful career, and purely for the purposes of *The Daily Show*, her career took off at the wrong time. Now it almost seems silly that we thought we could've gotten her.

DOUG HERZOG

Michele and I were sitting in Jon's office, just kind of shooting the shit, and I can't remember whether Jon said it or we said it: "By the way, I think Trevor can do this." So yeah, he was in the initial conversation.

TREVOR NOAH

Around the time Jon was making the announcement that he was leaving, I was meeting with the bosses at Comedy Central. We were just having a conversation about other things—life, plans, ideas, and so on. Did I think I would be in the running? No. No, no.

JEN FLANZ

I suggested Wyatt to the network, yeah. I think that the show needs somebody who has a fire in their belly and has a lot of things to talk about, and Wyatt does. I thought Key and Peele should do it, but they have other things they want to do.

JON STEWART

Someone like Amy, someone like Wyatt, someone like Trevor—someone that Comedy Central and the *Daily Show* staff really knew, then the transition would be a little easier. I'd be hard-pressed to think Jason Jones didn't think it should be him, and Sam, too. I don't think Sam would necessarily feel this way, but Jason would think like, "How come I'm not the guy that ever gets stuff?" And I don't begrudge him that.

TREVOR NOAH

I went to Jon and I said, "Hey, what are your thoughts on this? Do you know that they're considering me? I can't do this thing—or can I do this?" And he said, "There is no 'this thing,' that's what you have to understand. I'm doing my show. The host is what makes the show come alive. You have to make *your* show." But it was still very much up in the air, and I knew I was a wild card.

DOUG HERZOG

No one's smarter than Jon, no one knows the show better than Jon. Jon's track record for picking talent's pretty great. So that was a dialogue, and Trevor's was the second name that came up. At the end of the day the final vote was going to be Comedy Central's, because it had to be, right?

TREVOR NOAH

I'm sure Jon had a lot of weight in the choice. He doesn't like to hold that over a person, though. He's never made it, "Don't forget kid, I chose you!" He's like, "I recommended you." It's enough for me to know, and little enough for me to not overthink it.

Why would it bother me if John Oliver was his first choice? *My* first choice would be John Oliver. Well, everyone's first choice would have been Stephen Colbert. That makes complete sense. Then your second choice would be John Oliver. I'm not bothered by that, because—you do realize the Wachowski brothers' first choice for *The Matrix* was Will Smith? I've never struggled to enjoy that movie with Keanu Reeves. And had you told people it was between Will Smith and Keanu Reeves, before the movie came out, I'm pretty certain everyone would have voted for Will Smith. Sometimes you need to be in that position to get the thing. I think it was David Oyelowo who said he's told his agents, "Every script Denzel Washington turns down, give it to me." You can go, "Woe is me, I wasn't somebody's first choice." But I don't know if anyone has noticed how relationships in the world work. Most of us are not someone's first choice. But that doesn't mean we can't end up being the best choice.

The March 2015 announcement of Noah as the new host—he was in Dubai on a standup tour when Comedy Central called to offer him the job—provided some clarity and calm inside The Daily Show's *offices. The need to keep creating four shows a week was a welcome distraction from the impending regime change; the run of bad news in the world wasn't.*

JON STEWART

The same process that created the Wyatt argument moment created that Charleston moment on the show, which is, you come in raw, and you put it to the room. And you have enough respect and trust in the room that someone is going to be insightful or corrective.

This one, I came into the morning meeting and said, "I know that our process is, to take this feeling and transform it into something." It was sort of an apology to the room, saying, "Look, this can be a function of knowing I'm not going to be doing this much longer, but I don't have the energy to open a refinery today. I can't process the raw materials into rum. Cannot open the joke book on this one, unfortunately. I just got to do this on my own."

JEN FLANZ

With South Carolina, I was with him the whole day, because I was an EP by then. Jon's monologue, it never got written anywhere. He's just like, "I'm just going to go out there," and I remember being like, "What, really? Like, that seems like a bad idea." Me and Steve and Adam are looking at each other. He's going to go out there with no script, with no nothing? Seems crazy.

Indeed, the entire "script" that was loaded into the teleprompter was merely a short series of enigmatic phrases: "Once again," "Racism is wallpaper," "In a state where the Confederate flag still flies, streets named for generals that would keep black people slaves, and the white guy is mad." Stewart turned those notes into five minutes of eloquent, angry soliloquy. "I honestly have nothing other than just sadness," he told the audience, his tone both mournful and furious. "Once again, that we have to peer into the abyss of the depraved violence that we do to each other and the nexus of a just-gaping racial wound that will not heal yet we pretend doesn't exist."

JON STEWART

I also had Malala coming up as a guest that day, so I thought, who better to help in a time of this kind of uncertainty and unfortunate tragedy to just talk to? So the show basically was, I'm just going to set it up, and then we'll talk to Malala, and that's the show. And that's what we did.

The horror of the massacre itself was, of course, the main impetus. But Stewart's sermon added a fraction more clarity and attention, and less than a month after the shootings, South Carolina finally removed the secessionist's battle flag from a pole in front of the state capitol.

MICHAEL STEELE

I think Jon had a bigger voice on policy than a lot of people would give him credit for. After the church shooting in Charleston, when nine people were killed—Jon took the country by the collar and talked about it and about the Confederate flag. He grew from the guy that everyone laughed at to the guy that everyone listened to and would rally to his call.

JEN FLANZ

It got hard. People were putting a lot of pressure on him. Every time there was a national tragedy or global tragedy, it was like, "What's Jon Stewart going to say about this?"

ELLIOTT KALAN

After the Charleston shooting or on the day we covered the *Charlie Hebdo* thing—so much of it was in the moment, trying to figure out what to say. Jon became such a beacon in those moments. He's going to hate the word "beacon," but...

JUDD APATOW

It's hard to describe to people who don't do that type of work, but if you're going to write comedy about your opinion about the *Charlie Hebdo* massacre, you can't do it unless you really understand exactly what happened. We see the results, which is comedy, but when you have two hours with your staff talking about the different ways people hurt each other, that's depressing.

JON STEWART

I'm kind of relieved I don't have to say anything on TV about tragedies anymore.

As the next iteration of The Daily Show *was beginning to take shape, the current one had some unfinished business to attend to. Stewart had devoted hundreds of segments to the Iraq War, and what he saw as the media's complicity in the Bush Administration's selling of it. He had been scathing about a 2002 front-page* New York Times *"aluminum tubes" story, cowritten by Michael R. Gordon and Judith Miller, that laid out the White House case that Saddam Hussein was hell-bent on acquiring nuclear weapons. Gordon and Miller wrote, in what became an infamous turn of phrase, "The first sign of a 'smoking gun,' they argue, may be a mushroom cloud."*

Thirteen years, thousands of war deaths, and zero Iraqi weapons of mass destruction later, Miller came on The Daily Show *to promote her new book and try to explain that she hadn't been used by the Bush Administration.*

LEWIS BLACK

For a long time I think I was sort of Jon's anger translator, you know? I was the one on the show who's allowed to yell about shit. And then he started to yell more.

The days when I'd come into the office to do "Back in Black," I would never see Jon until the taping. But the day of the Judy Miller interview, he was showing up everywhere I was in the building. It was really interesting. He's pacing down hallways, talking to researchers and producers, literally going, "Is this that?" and, "Check on this fact," and "Make sure that cross-references…"

It was the angriest I'd ever seen him before going on, before doing an interview.

ADAM CHODIKOFF

Jon and I knew our stuff here. We'd hit that issue time and time again— the manipulation of the Iraq intel and of the media in the runup to the war, Miller's front-page story in the *Times* on Saddam supposedly having aluminum tubes to make nuclear weapons, and how Cheney was on TV the next day citing it as justification.

I'd read Miller's book and her explanation for that. Jon had great ideas for slicing through her with counterexamples. So, yeah, that was a really intense one, and it was toward the end of the Jon run. It felt sort of like the culmination of all we'd been doing on Iraq.

JUDITH MILLER, *former* **New York Times** *reporter,* **Fox News** *contributor*

Oh, I watched the show a lot. It changed nighttime television. It was a great contribution to helping get people, younger people in particular, interested in foreign affairs and domestic policy. I mean, it was an important contribution and Jon's a serious guy, which is why I was doubly disappointed, especially compared to Bill Maher, the interview I had there. I don't think Jon had read the book.

JON STEWART

No, I read the whole thing. It's amazing to me how many people she throws under a bus in that book and how little responsibility she takes for anything. She's not being honest with herself.

JUDITH MILLER

He wanted somebody who was going to say, "Oh, my, gosh, we were all wrong, wasn't this terrible, it was all our fault." And he wasn't going to get that, because that's not what my book is about. My book is about how these stories occurred and how intelligence reporting is done and how a narrative is formed and why we have to be careful about narratives.

I accept great responsibility for the fact that I was unable to do more to check out the reports that I got, but you're dealing with highly classified information here. I just think people don't understand what we do, but Stewart should've.

JON STEWART

She was a tool used by a group of people who said they were trying to sell a new product. So it's not that I didn't listen to her. It just sounds like hogwash when you look at the evidence. I can see how she was uncomfortable. I was uncomfortable, but she was spinning horseshit.

JUDITH MILLER

Do I think Jon contributed to the cynicism about politics? Oh, I don't think you can get *too* cynical about politics.

JON STEWART

There are people that I believe shouldn't like me, and if they did, I'd be sad. She shouldn't like me.

ADAM CHODIKOFF

Jon knew this was something big, the Judy Miller interview. This was like a final boulder.

The assessments of Stewart's Daily Show *legacy, pro and con, started pouring in. David Remnick, the Pulitzer Prize–winning writer turned editor in chief of the* New Yorker, *had a uniquely multifaceted experience of Stewart and* The Daily Show. *Remnick was a guest on the show three times, talking about everything from the intifada to his biography of Obama. But he also conducted public roundtables with Stewart and with ten* Daily Show *writers.*

As Stewart's hosting run neared its end, Remnick wrote a New Yorker *essay in which he connected Stewart's work to the performance tradition of Molly Picon, the great Yiddish theater actress, and with the media criticism of A. J. Liebling, who wrote for the* New Yorker *from 1935 to 1963.*

DAVID REMNICK, *editor in chief, the* **New Yorker**

I mentioned Picon because there is a huge element of Jewishness in Jon's comic voice, in his gestures, in his vocabulary. I'm not suggesting for a second that he's a Talmudic scholar or a Hasidic sage. But he has fluency in a tradition that's becoming increasingly attenuated in American culture.

And like Liebling, Stewart, with the help of his incredibly astute staff, was combining reporting with commentary, pointing a finger at stupidity and hollowness, and devising a creative hand grenade. All of it had political purpose and direction. It wasn't strictly ideological, although he's obviously left of center. And he was fearless, not in the sense that anybody was going to make him a political prisoner. But he punched up. He punched up, and the shots landed.

I don't think the world is any more absurd now than it's ever been, or more tragic, or more beautiful. But Jon took advantage of these new ways of seeing the world and took out his magic marker and drew circles around the idiocy. He set out to be a working comedian, and he ended up an invaluable patriot. He wants his country to be better, more decent, and to think harder.

JEFF ZUCKER, *NBC news and entertainment executive, 1992–2010; president, CNN, 2013–*

There were times where Jon was absolutely right to shine a spotlight on silly or stupid things that all organizations do, including ours, and there were times where he was being needlessly silly and ridiculous because it was funny but not that pertinent.

But right before he was leaving *The Daily Show*, I tried to hire Jon here at CNN, because I thought he had a keen, sharp, insightful, great political mind. Listen, I also tried to hire Jon to come to NBC, when I was running NBC Entertainment, to do a [five-night-a-week] strip show at eight o'clock back when—2001, 2002. They at least took the meeting and I had dinner with Jon, as opposed to this last time. I think they just thought because Jon had been making fun of CNN for so long that it wouldn't be a good home for him.

GLENN BECK

Did Jon have an effect? Are you kidding me? Huge effect. His effect on culture and politics will be felt in the next generation.

He was able to teach liberalism, progressivism, in a way that Edward Bernays would be thrilled. He had a point of view about people and parties and different philosophies. He made those points in a bite-size way that everybody wanted to eat, and they were eating it because they thought it was a chocolate chip cookie, but it was not just that, it had bodybuilding vitamins and minerals inside.

John Oliver's departure to HBO would prove to be an enormous missed opportunity for Comedy Central. But it was also a major step in spreading Stewart's greatest television legacy, the creation of what would become a comedy district on Manhattan's West Side, comprised of Colbert's Late Show, *Oliver's* Last Week Tonight, *and eventually Samantha Bee's* Full Frontal, *as well as* The Daily Show *with Trevor Noah. Stewart's influence could also be seen indirectly, in the "Closer Look" segments by Seth Meyers on NBC's* Late Night, *and in the way* Saturday Night Live's *"Weekend Update," with* Daily Show *alumnus Michael Che as one cohost, began using extended runs of jokes about a single subject.*

JUDD APATOW

News satire was always a floating idea in the comedy world, and people struggled to achieve it for a long time. There were shows like *Not Necessarily the News*; *The Wilton North Report* was a famous failure. Jon invented a form, just like Steve Allen did with *The Tonight Show*. People will take it and expand it and do different things with it, but Jon laid the groundwork. He's had a massive influence on how everyone talks about the news.

But inside the Daily Show *offices it was the series of staff farewells, and the impending big finale, that consumed the most emotional energy and tissues.*

ZHUBIN PARANG

The one thing I'm most proud of was Samantha Bee's last big segment, called "I Watch *The Five*." It was the result of my obsession with a Fox television show called *The Five*. Lauren and I would watch it, we would start imagining the show as a soap opera at large. The characters were all so well defined, and we started adding backstories and relationships to the characters—Andrea Tantaros, Dana Perino, Bob Beckel, Eric Bolling, and Kimberly Guilfoyle.

I eventually started writing e-mails to the *Daily Show* listserve—it's a pitch list that everybody in the show is on—about *The Five*. Some of the responses would be, "What the hell are you talking about?" and others would be—

LAUREN SARVER MEANS
Psychiatric referrals.

ZHUBIN PARANG
We would occasionally be in Central Park with our dogs—

LAUREN SARVER MEANS
And hope to see Dana Perino and her dog.

ZHUBIN PARANG
And hope to see her. Yeah. "Stalking" is a highly exaggerated term.

LAUREN SARVER MEANS
I would say it's a slanderous term.

ZHUBIN PARANG
I would say it's absolutely libel. Eventually Jon said, "Why don't we just put this on the air, this obsession, in this avant-garde style, with Samantha Bee doing it?"

Travon Free, who was one of the newer writers at the time, and Jimmy Donn and I rewatched as many episodes as we could. We put PAs on it, interns on it, to go through and find any patterns, and initially it was a twenty-minute segment that went into the backstories of every single character and how they interrelated.

TRAVON FREE
We worked on that for the better part of six months. It kept getting pushed back because of how complex it was to actually execute.

ZHUBIN PARANG
It went through twenty-five drafts, which is almost 1,000 percent more than any other draft in the show's history. Ultimately, the only story line that

made it through was the one that dealt with Greg Gutfeld and Dana Perino's torrid love affair and the other characters interacting with that.

TRAVON FREE

I can't remember a specific joke I wrote for it. The *Kill Bill*–style red-eye flare thing Sam does, I added that.

SAMANTHA BEE

At first I was really reluctant to do it. I just didn't understand how it would work. *The Daily Show* has a very, I don't want to say, rigid format, but it definitely has its patterns and its style. And it exploded the style of the show. Everyone said, "Okay, this is like a theater black box, and you're just going to be really dramatic." We rehearsed it a bunch of times, far more than we usually did things. And I was like, "Well, if I lay down here…" The camera people thought I was crazy. But I did it with a full heart, and then people did like it because it was so unusual. I was happy. I was very gratified. I gave Dana Perino my heart that day.

> **Samantha Bee:** [*standing on empty, dark stage to Stewart's left*] Jon, please don't compare *The Five* to other panel shows. *The Five* is so much more than just a panel show. It's life itself. It is…everything. Jon, perhaps you're unacquainted with my one-woman show inspired by *The Five*. I shall now perform it for you.
>
> Jon, *The Five* is the storyboard of the human condition. [*wearing black leggings and black turtleneck with the* THE FIVE *logo on her chest*] It's a story as old as time. A story of…love. One that rivals the works of a Shakespeare…or a Nicholas Sparks.
>
> It's a tale of a winsome blond ingenue, Dana Perino. [*prances and skips*] A young girl new to the city, with big dreams and a heart so pure she makes Mary Poppins look like a disgusting whorebag. [*montage of Perino saying things including, "There is a certain word that rhymes with 'truck,'" and "It's not because they're not having s-e-x"*].
>
> Now nobody falls for a good girl harder than a bad boy! [*puffs on lit cigarette as George Thorogood riff plays, followed by clips of Greg*

Gutfeld saying, "I was on Percocet for seven days, best week of my life," "I've been drinking since two," and "I gave three people hepatitis."]

A pill-popping afternoon drunk who is riddled with hepatitis? [*shrieks in delight*] There's gotta be a catch!

ZHUBIN PARANG

Samantha just completely killed it. It really defines the hallmark of our tenure of the show, I think.

LAUREN SARVER MEANS

I mean, it should be the subject of the entire book.

SAMANTHA BEE

You got to me, I'm crying. That show, it's a huge part of my life.

I was at *The Daily Show* for twelve years. Jason and I got deals for our own shows on TBS before Jon announced he was leaving. For both of us it was time to take ownership of our own projects.

When I left *The Daily Show* in April, they did a big good-bye piece. I begged everyone not to. I'm such a crier, as you can see. And I really ghost from parties. I don't like to say good-bye.

No, it was a really great moment. Because at the end, I think maybe I felt like we were peers. I felt less like Jon was my boss and more like we were in the same... I felt like all of that training... and I felt just ready to leave.

Off-campus outings built the staff bond at The Daily Show, *and over the years there'd been a wide variety: karaoke showdowns, a summer excursion to a Long Island winery, a "denim night" dance party. Stewart, being the boss, usually didn't participate. But the 2015* Daily Show *summer fun day was one he couldn't miss.*

JESSIE KANEVSKY, *from intern to executive assistant, 2004–*

We wanted it to be Jon's dream come true, and he's a diehard Mets fan. So we took over Citi Field for the day. I did most of the booking and arranging. We had batting practice on the field and all our names on the scoreboard, we're drinking beer. It was perfect—and I'm a Yankees fan.

Jon showed up with his glove. He's just very real. If he's angry that Trump ate pizza with a fork on camera, he's angry that Trump eats it with a fork off camera. He comes into the office like, "What the fuck is Trump thinking?" Jon actually doesn't curse. That's more me. But if he feels something off camera, he's going to put it out there and he's going to stand by it.

RAMIN HEDAYATI

One of my jobs when I worked in studio production was to collect material and bring it to the morning meeting. And one morning I noticed there was some footage of Donald Trump showing Sarah Palin around the city, and the place he took her was Famous Famiglia—which was the first strike against him. If there's literally nowhere else to go, you go to Famiglia. It's a convenience slice. Then there was footage of Trump with one slice on top of another slice. Which just creates a whole steam situation. The third thing, which was the most egregious offense, was eating the pizza with a fork.

I showed the Trump pizza footage to Rory, and I remember the two of us just shouting at each other. Like, "He can't eat the fucking pizza with a fork! What the fuck is this guy doing?"

And then Jon comes in to the meeting, and we show it to him, and it just kept escalating. The volume got louder and louder, where we're basically all doing the bit that Jon ended up doing on the show—that kind of visceral anger: "How could you? You offended me! You offended my family! You offend everything I stand for!" The energy of that bit really came out in the room that morning.

Everyone chipped in to create the seven-minute "Me Lover's Pizza with Crazy Broad," with head writer Steve Bodow's foodie tendencies really coming in handy this time. And for all the over-the-top laugh lines, the piece presciently explored Trump's phoniness, ending with a jab at how the reality-show star had been pandering to the Obama "birther" wackos.

Jon Stewart: [*after clip of Trump and Palin at Famous Famiglia*] Are you eating it with a fork!? *A fucking fork! Ah, Madonna! Noooo! La forketa da satanica!* [*guttural sounds of pain and disgust*] Ahhh! *El tool de diablo!* [*shouting now*] When you invite an important visitor to our house, our town, and you eat your pizza with a fucking fork right in front of us! You know what? Why don't you take a shit in

Fiorello LaGuardia's hat and feed it to Joe DiMaggio's crying ghost on Liberty Island, you son of a bitch!

RAMIN HEDAYATI

It became the first of the three big pizza rants—the other two were about Chicago deep dish, and then Mayor [Bill] de Blasio eating pizza with a fork. And they were funny and really silly. But they were also great illustrations of the show's process.

Jon was all about the passion. He always said, "We need to make sure we're channeling our emotions. What do we find joyous? What makes us have a strong emotional reaction? If something makes you angry, why? Bring that to the idea. If something's just purely fun, let's just have fun with it." He wants us to be writing to, and pitching to, that strong feeling. Plenty of times it's outrage about something serious. But we don't need to do the congressional takedown every night.

JIMMY DONN

Actually, my favorite *Daily Show* pizza story wasn't even something on the air. Justin Bieber was in the studio to do some bit, and he was hungry, and backstage he asked for Hawaiian pizza. And Rory Albanese just says, "No, that's not happening." Bieber's people must have been shocked. But pineapple and ham on a pizza?

It took a while for Trump to return fire, but when he did, it was in a flurry of tweets that were weirdly amusing at the time, but which turned out to uncannily foreshadow Trump's rise as Republican presidential candidate. A random Twitter user pleaded with the thin-skinned billionaire, "Please run for president, Jon Stewart would destroy you!" Trump responded, "I promise you that I'm much smarter than Jonathan Leibowitz—I mean Jon Stewart."

JON STEWART

There's this tweet saying, "If Stewart is above it all, why did he change his name?" At first we didn't realize it was actually Trump. We thought it was a parody account. But he kept going with it, tweeting, "Why run from who you are?" So that's when we decided to go back at him, saying Trump's real name was Fuckface Von Clownstick.

It's very easy to figure out Trump's ideology. He's not racist and sexist to this incredible degree. He's Trumpist. He views the world through the prism of, "How do they view Trump?" If you view Trump positively, you're good people. "Putin, hey, he likes the Trump, I like the Putin,"

That's all he is. His doctrine is the Trump Doctrine. If another country is nice to him, he will be nice to that country. If the country thinks he's an idiot, "Fuck them. That's a pussy country. They don't know shit about anything. That country changed its name from a Jewish name."

Stewart's rejoinder to a longer-running nemesis was a ten-minute segment called "Better Call Foul." On the surface, the bit was a tour-de-force response to Fox's most recent criticism of The Daily Show. *But it was also an emphatic restatement of purpose, and a display of how far* The Daily Show's *methods had evolved. The "Bush v. Bush" montage had been created in the stone tools days of 2003; now the show unleashed a Vine, "50 Fox Lies in 6 seconds." The segment also incorporated eternal* Daily Show *touches, including Stewart's cartoony,* Gone with the Wind–*ish affronted-foppish-Southern-gentleman voice. Most telling, though, was the rare on-camera cameo by Adam Chodikoff,* The Daily Show's *fact-checking secret weapon.*

Rich Lowry, Conservative Commentator: [*in* Fox News *clip*] "What he added to the political discourse was largely sarcasm, insults, and dishonest editing."

Howard Kurtz, Media Critic: [*in video clip, from* The Kelly File] "You know it's clearly selective editing of clips."

Megyn Kelly, Fox News Anchor: "And I can speak personally to a lot of the attacks that were levied on me, had no foothold in the facts."

Jon Stewart: [*at anchor desk*] The little game they play here is, "The only reason we look bad is that these guys are unfair liars." By the way, that sentiment is brought to you by Arby's pig anus and cheese. [*graphic reading* ARBY'S: PROOF JON STEWART CANNOT DESTROY A BRAND BY TELLING PEOPLE WHAT'S IN IT.]

My point is: We don't lie. We don't distort. We actually have a fella here who used every fiber of his being to prevent us from doing so. Moral bastard!

Adam Chodikoff: [*standing to the rear of Stewart's desk*] Jon? Actually my parents were married, so technically I'm not a bastard.

Jon Stewart: I know. It was a figure of—fine. I'll miss you, moral compass.

But the point is: On the right, they're pretending that our "truthfulness" is what's really important to them. Which, ironically, is not true. What matters to them is discrediting anything that they believe harms their side. That is their prime directive. And unlike Kirk, they fuckin' stick with it. They don't just drop the protocol any time they feel like humping a green girl in a unitard. [*video clip of Captain Kirk, pursuing a green girl in a unitard*]

And this, this, is their genius. Conservatives are not looking to make education more rigorous and informative, or science more empirical or verifiable, or voting more representative, or the government more efficient or effective. They just want all those things to reinforce their partisan, ideological, conservative viewpoint.

That jeremiad was the unofficial kickoff of a farewell tour. The coming months included plenty of quick-turnaround bits about a given day's news. But interspersed were "look backs" at The Daily Show's *greatest "questionable" graphics ("our new segment, 'Jon Stewart Looks at Kids' Junk'"), and Stewart's most extravagant "impressions" (turtle-talking Mitch McConnell, Redd Foxx–meets–Jerry Lewis Charlie Rangel). President Obama made one last appearance as a guest, as did a string of Stewart's comedian friends: Colin Quinn, Richard Lewis, Denis Leary, Louis C.K., and Amy Schumer. It was all, though, a warm-up act to August 6, 2015.*

20

A Man Who Was on TV

STEVE BODOW

Planning for Jon's final show started as far back as March, once we knew his out date. It was only in the last month or six weeks that we were really heavy into it, and we sort of divvied it up. My part of the show was to put together the first act, where all the correspondents would be coming back and they'd all be commenting on their time on the show, or their relationship with Jon. Once we knew it would be the same night as a Republican presidential debate, then we knew that's how we'll get into it.

NANCY WALLS CARELL

You know what? The show was August 6, right? And August 5 was our twentieth wedding anniversary. We combined that with a trip to New York. We wouldn't have missed that for anything.

JEN FLANZ

Rob Corddry was going to be on a family vacation in the woods somewhere. He was going to just send a pre-tape over. "I'm so sorry, I've made these plans already, I didn't know." And then, a few weeks later, he's like, "If you guys could help me get there, I will get there." We had to get him a helicopter to take him to an airport, but he came.

Olivia Munn came down from shooting like *X-Men*, Josh Gad came in from London from shooting a movie. Everyone wanted to be there. Helms was coming off a film set.

BETH LITTLEFORD

I was disappointed that I wasn't invited to the final show. I asked and they said, "Jon just wants people from his years." And I said, "But I *was* from his years." And they were like, "Well, people that he found." But he didn't find Carell. There was kind of no reason to have me—except that I did a hundred episodes and about fifteen half-hour specials. Jon is revered, and he deserves to be revered. So for me to say, "Oh, he was shitty to me in this way," it doesn't do me any good. It doesn't do anybody any good.

JON STEWART

Wyatt knew at that point that I had recommended him for the host job after I left, as one of the people that I thought could be really good. He's passionate, he's smart, he's funny. And so he wrote me a note explaining why he was noncommittal. I wrote him back, he wrote me back thanking me for that. I thought it was insightful, and cathartic, and helpful. And then the Maron thing developed.

JEN FLANZ

Two weeks before Jon's final show, Wyatt gives that podcast interview with Marc Maron where he talks about the argument with Jon over the Herman Cain impression. I was so mad that one of my last Fridays with Jon, where we were planning for the end of the run, I spent on the phone with the *New York Times*, dealing with press about the Wyatt thing. It was such an unnecessary thing.

RORY ALBANESE

Maron always wanted to know shit about Jon, and Jon wouldn't go on his podcast. I'm like, "Jon, just go on his fucking podcast. He was a dick to you in 1987—whatever!" I don't understand how Jon is still mad at Maron but not mad at Wyatt.

JON STEWART

At least Wyatt's coming from a good place. Maron, on the other hand...

TRAVON FREE

It's all relative to the person, and if Wyatt felt offended by the Herman Cain bit, he was totally valid in feeling that way. But I felt really bad for Jon—that this dude, who I knew, was being called a racist, because he's such a great guy.

RORY ALBANESE

I'm very protective of Jon, because Jon was very good to me and very good to everyone in that building for a very long time. He employed a lot of people and put a lot of kids through college. He kept a hundred-plus people working and even paid them out of his pocket during dark times and strikes and shit. So for him to be lambasted in the media as some racist, ignorant asshole to me is fucking absurd and unacceptable.

JON STEWART

Wyatt wrote me a note a few days after the Maron thing. Because I was sort of blindsided by it. We wrote a couple of notes back to each other and tried to, I guess, clear some air. But as I said to him in a note I wrote, "I would love you to be there because this show is a celebration of everybody that helped make it what it was, and you had a big role in that. You earned it." I very much wanted him to be there. That being said, if he was not comfortable with that I completely understand, and I would not feel slighted.

JEN FLANZ

Wyatt was very, very reluctant to do it. It took a lot of talking. We had a hard time in our friendship because of it. I think he couldn't separate me as a show producer and me as his friend.

TA-NEHISI COATES, *journalist; author,* Between the World and Me

I was a guest on the show the same day the Wyatt Cenac story had happened, where Jon caught some flak from Wyatt. It was a real coincidence. I didn't know about it before the taping. And I don't know if Jon had that in mind or what when we were taping the interview. I can't say that was why his questions were really, really probing. But Jon had clearly taken the time to read my book.

He's a great interviewer. I was nervous as hell, I'll tell you that. We ended up in this deeply philosophical place of, "Do you actually think it's possible to construct a system that's not one person stepping on another?"

When I heard about the Wyatt thing later, it didn't change my opinion of Jon. Not at all. There's this notion that when race or racism is any sort of factor between two people in an environment, that that necessarily means that the person is, like, a child molester. It must mean everything else about them is awful. I've seen some very, very good people, good, good people, people I'd leave my kid with, struggle with diversity.

The fact that the *Daily Show* cast got more diverse over the years, that's the thing that would happen to somebody that's struggling with it. I mean struggling in the best way.

I guess I considered him a force for good in terms of race, but I didn't really go to Jon Stewart for that, you know? I wasn't trying to get my black on watching *The Daily Show*. You know? I mean it was hilarious, but I also like *Seinfeld*.

It's really important that Jon Stewart was using his platform to talk about race, but it's probably more important for white people than for black people. If there was value in that, it probably was the value of telling other white people.

TREVOR NOAH

Jon is either not racist—because he passed the baton to me and gave me all the tools and the support necessary to do the show—or maybe he was just giving it to my white side.

Stewart's departure was the end of an era in a larger sense, too. He'd arrived at The Daily Show *when the state-of-the-art was three-quarter-inch VHS tape, and he was leaving with Snapchat ascendant. In between, Stewart and* The Daily Show *had eagerly incorporated new technology to speed its creative process, and Stewart wasn't averse to creating the occasional clickbait. But at heart he remained a throwback in his attitude toward social media.*

RORY ALBANESE

I'd say, "Dude, Twitter—we need to get in that game!" But when it came to a personal Twitter account, Jon would say, "Why? We have a TV show! I don't think anyone else needs to hear from me. They get to hear from me thirty minutes a day, four days a week." And he's right. But it was the last vestige of a show that's solely about the TV show. It just doesn't work that way anymore.

For the Daily Show *staff, Stewart's final few months were a blur. There were retrospective montages to assemble—of Stewart and correspondents breaking character and collapsing in giggles on the air; of Stewart, "a short, Jewish Susan Boyle," bursting into song. But many of the laughs were laced with anxiety about what was ahead and wistfulness about what was ending.*

ALISON CAMILLO

We were doing a joke having to do with *Toy Story*, the last one, *Toy Story 3*. We were saying it was a tearjerker, and Jon's like, "What made it a tearjerker?" So I was telling him the premise of the story: Andy goes off to college and leaves all of his toys behind. Jon says, "I don't get it, what's so sad?" And I was like, "Oh my God, you're Andy and we're your toys. Holy shit, you insensitive prick!"

JON STEWART

John Edwards came to a show near the end, during the last two, three months maybe. Sat in the audience. He came backstage very briefly to say hey, but we didn't talk much. I didn't sit down and ask, "So, what's your life like now?"

Does it show he had no hard feelings about the show making jokes about him? Maybe. I think it also indicates a person who feels isolated and removed from the life they once had and who is trying to reconnect with some of that.

HILLARY KUN

President Obama came on one last time. That was big. After that, Jon just mostly wanted to have his friends as guests, other comedians.

Obama's seven Daily Show *appearances traced an almost novelistic arc. His first appearance, as an Illinois senator in November 2005, was a part of the warm-up for his presidential run, and the two men seemed to be feeling each other out, trading playful jabs about who was more overhyped. The middle period, during Obama's White House years, was more contentious, with Stewart giving voice to the disappointments of the left and Obama arguing, defensively, for realism. The final interview, in July 2015, was a fitting combination of prickliness and wonkishness.*

Jon Stewart: You've got this deal with Iran worked out, you've got your fast-track authority. Are you feeling like seven years in—
President Barack Obama: I finally know what I'm doing?
Jon Stewart: Let me ask you a question about Iran. Whose team are we on in the Middle East? Because I know we're fighting with the Iraqis to defeat ISIS along with Iran, but in Yemen we're fighting Iran with Iraqis and Saudis.
President Obama: That's not quite right, but that's okay.

Jon Stewart: But whose team are we on? Who are we bombing?

President Obama: Right now we are going after ISIL and we've got a sixty-country coalition and that's our top priority. But with respect to Iran, this is an adversary. Anti-American, anti-Israel, anti-Semitic, they sponsor terrorist organizations like Hezbollah.

Jon Stewart: Sounds like a good partner for peace.

Appropriately, the last part of the twenty-one-minute, three-part conversation found Stewart and Obama united in an earnest desire for more common purpose in public life—perhaps, they fantasized, there could be a new national service initiative. Then the dialogue ended with a combination of unfortunate prescience and genuine affection.

President Obama: I guarantee you if people feel strongly about making sure Iran doesn't get a nuclear weapon without going to war, and that is expressed to Congress, then people will believe in that. And the same is true on every single issue. If people are engaged, eventually the political system responds, despite the money, despite the lobbyists, it still responds.

Jon Stewart: After seven years, is that the advice that you bequeath to future President Trump?

President Obama: Well, um, I'm sure the Republicans are enjoying Mr. Trump's dominance.

Jon Stewart: Anything that makes them look less crazy. Sir, thank you so much for stopping by. It was a pleasure to see you.

President Obama: You've been a great gift to our country.

DENIS LEARY

It's weird, dude, the level of fame that Jon has had, because he's not just another talk show host. It's like one of your best friends from when you were a young guy with nothing, he's this gigantic media icon. For my generation he was like our Oprah, you know? Our skinny little Jewish Oprah.

I don't think he's really changed, except he's got a ton of money and he does a lot of good with it, and he certainly can't walk down the street without getting his picture taken. But underneath it all, he's still really the same guy. Not a lot of airs going on. Well, he certainly looks way fucking old. But

I think even without the hit television show, he would have had that beaten down, middle-aged-Jewish-man look.

Oh, it was weird being one of the final guests. I usually get there an hour in advance and then we just spend like fifteen, twenty minutes kind of shitting on each other and catching up on the kids. But I could see that he was on the verge of tears. He really cared about the gig and the people who worked for him.

PAUL RUDD

Wow, I was in my twenties when I first started going on the show. So it was bittersweet but also exciting and gratifying to have been a part of the entirety of it, and to have Jon ask me to be one of the final guests.

I remember as a kid watching Carson and thinking, that's so cool that he's friends with these people and they just hang out and talk. I never saw the PR behind it. And then I became the Tony Randall of *The Daily Show*. I was on fourteen times in sixteen years.

In the green room there was a giant bowl of chocolate and candy for the guests, and then a Lucite box filled with games, like Hasbro games. You were free to play the games. You may have been free to *take* the games. I don't know if the games were one of the sponsors. But I would try to picture, I don't know, Malala or Jim Cramer playing Chutes and Ladders. Or Bill Clinton or Lewis Lapham.

The last time I was on, the week before Jon's final show, I didn't think anything through. I just said, "I love you, Jon Stewart" for everybody in the room. I mean, everyone was feeling that.

JEN FLANZ

The final day with Jon, it was a blur. There was crying during the day. I've been sitting in the room with Jon for so many years. He saw me go through a divorce and through cancer. I saw Beth Shorr during the day, and Beth is like stone. She doesn't get emotional, and her and Jon were a hilarious pair because she'd been his assistant for so long. They weren't looking at each other, but I saw her break down at one point. Beth lost her dad while she was at the show, a few years earlier, but Jon was kind of her dad and uncle. He's been there for her.

JON STEWART

I remember the moment Beth came in after sound check to tell me something...and we just kind of looked at each other, and she started bawling, and I started tearing. Because the people that you're the closest to, it's the hardest to talk to.

STEVE BODOW

Jon had some pretty clear ideas for how he wanted those first couple of moments to go on the final show, bringing people on, having it build up, and build up, and build up. We always knew that the last person to come on would be Stephen, who had been off TV for a long time at that point, and who also had a history of occasionally coming on *The Daily Show* to have these discussions with Jon while he was still at the *Report*. So, we had a broad sense of what this arc would be. Some of the correspondents would be at the desk with Jon, and others would be on a green-screen "remote." We had the montage of some of the politicians who had been targets over the years.

SENATOR JOHN McCAIN

Yeah, I said, "So long, jackass." I thought it was good. Was it heartfelt? It was fun.

STEVE BODOW

The weekend before the final show, I was culling the whole script, and I was just feeling like, everyone loves Jon and feels this great gratitude toward him, and he's not going to let that into his show, even though it's so much what everybody wants to say and so much what the audience would want to hear. So I e-mailed Stephen that weekend, and I said, "Look, this is missing something, and I think it's a moment of expressing something real to Jon, something that is not funny, necessarily. And I think that the show will not feel complete without it—not that night's one show, but the whole show, the Jon show."

And I said to Stephen, "I think you're the only person who can do this. I realize this isn't something that Jon is going to want until after it's happened, and so I'm not telling him. If you're into it, we'll work it out between you, me, Chuck O'Neil, and a couple other people who need to know."

Stephen says, "I think that's a good idea," and with one of his writers, they came up with a script by Tuesday or Wednesday.

On Thursday, the day of the final show, Stephen shows up and pulls me aside, before rehearsal, two hours before taping, and says, "I'm really not sure I should do this."

STEPHEN COLBERT

I didn't want to make Jon uncomfortable, and he meant so many things to so many people that I didn't want to step on anybody's toes. So I literally pulled Tracey, Jon's wife, into a room backstage that night and I said the whole thing, the speech, to her in one of the edit suites. I said, "What do you think?" Tracey said, "*Please* say it. Jon will squirm, but please say it."

LEWIS BLACK

Looking around at all the people that were there for the final Jon show, and me getting to see people I never get to see, like Riggle and Carell—that was really the joy of it. The other thing that really sticks out—everybody looks at the show and says, "Boy, that must have been a lot of fun." It's work. In the end, it's fun, it's fun work. But it's work. Part of us is, once we hit the stage, part of us is removed from that.

Maybe the others weren't. Maybe the others are more integrated human beings than I am. But for me, once you hit the stage, there was some sense of detachment. And it was very sad, you know? Something was coming to an end, and whenever something comes to an end, there's a sense of mortality. Which is never fun at a party.

SAMANTHA BEE

Jason and I were out of town shooting our show [*The Detour*] and Jason couldn't physically come back, because it would have shut down production and cost us the budget of an entire episode. So he was only able to tape something, but I flew back. It was a great reunion, the perfect send-off, really.

DAN BAKKEDAHL

I was completely fucking blown away to be invited for the final show. In fact, I thought it was one of those things where the police invite a bunch of wanted felons to get free gear, and then it turns out that they just arrest you. So I thought it might be Jon saying, "Hey, now that I got you back here, you fucking jerk, who's a coward?" So I said yes, because I thought, if nothing else I might have an opportunity to say, "Jon, I'm sorry."

And that's what happened. He came backstage, before rehearsal, and all the correspondents were standing back there. Jon came through one by one, shook hands, and gave a hug to each one of us and said, "Thank you." I said, "Thank you." He started to go, I held his hand for a second, he looked me in the eyes, and I said, "Really—thank you." And I considered that the best I could do in terms of the shit I had talked and the evil I had held in my heart for all those years.

ED HELMS

Most of us in entertainment don't stop and take stock of our accomplishments enough, because we're usually pretty scared about what's ahead, because it's an uncertain business. Jon's final show, to kind of be forced to confront the reality, it was really a gift.

Just overwhelming pride and gratitude. Being in the green room beforehand, and just seeing all these brilliant, hilarious people, and feeling like, "I cannot believe I'm part of this awesome legacy. This is so cool." It was one of those pinch-me moments.

AL MADRIGAL

Steve Carell is there. Vance DeGeneres. People I didn't come close to overlapping with at the show, but you feel this brotherhood. And you couldn't help but feel emotional about this guy, everything that Jon—it's meant so much to me. I was that standup comedian going from city to city where no one knew who I was, and now I'm "the comedian from *The Daily Show*." I was able to buy a nice house because I got cast in a sitcom.

JOHN OLIVER

I'd realized it in theory before, but standing backstage that night, it was just absolutely incredible to actually see the careers passing by like boxcars, and then thinking, "Oh shit, Jon did all of this for these people while creating the greatest political comedy show in the history of television."

JUDD APATOW

I remember, in the 2004 election, hoping that *The Daily Show* could have moved the needle more than it did. And I know Jon never thought it would, and that wasn't his intention. But I feel like it had enormous impact socially, on issues like gay marriage and how people look at racism, because *The Daily Show* mocked certain bad values and attitudes, and the new generation—at least in certain parts of the country—thought, "Oh, it would be ridiculous to act that way. Why would you ever not want gay people to get married?"

The Daily Show became a lens through which people looked at the news and the world that hadn't been there before, and it also trained people, in this complicated media age, how to read and listen and interpret everything they're being told.

SONIA SARAIYA, *TV critic*, Variety

Stewart and his show anticipated how we were going to be telling stories to ourselves, as social media has proliferated and video is widely available and anyone can add their commentary. *The Daily Show*'s style of commenting on the news is now how we comment on the news.

DAN BAKKEDAHL

I wonder if we could even dream of having someone like Bernie Sanders getting the kind of support he's getting if it weren't for *The Daily Show* and what it did in the fifteen-odd years that Jon was the host. That is not hyperbole. Jon exposed a generation of young people to politics. Nobody else was able to get them even interested. So any issues I might have had with my little hurt feelings, he had a much bigger job to do than keep little Dan Bakkedahl and his comedy career happy.

ELLIOTT KALAN

When Rob Corddry came back for the last Jon episode he walked by me in the hall and said, "I had a dream about you last night." And he keeps walking.

He finally came back and says, "I dreamed we were all here. We were all on the set. Jon was there. All the correspondents, and we were all ready to rehearse. Jon calls you over and says to you, 'Okay. What are we going to do? You've got to write something for us.'" Rob says, "I had an anxiety dream for you!" He was willing to have the anxiety dream that I didn't have so that I didn't have to have it.

JOHN HODGMAN

That night I said to Colbert, "I can't wait for *The Late Show* to start, because I am so glad that the rest of the world is going to get to see all of you." It was in the hallway between the crew lounge and the little antechamber right before you go in, right next to makeup, Jody Morlock's makeup place. Colbert said, "I can't believe I get to finally stop, it was just so hard." That was an amazing time.

AASIF MANDVI

It was far more emotional than we're used to being at *The Daily Show*. I walked into the studio at 2:30 that day, and Jon saw me and said, "Hey, you know, I'm so glad you're here," and turned around. I hadn't seen him in a long time, because I had been out on the West Coast. I said to him, "I just want to tell you before it gets really crazy, I just want to say"—and before I could even get into it, he was looking away from me and couldn't make eye contact. You didn't have those moments with Jon that often, but it was a real moment and it was kind of a moment that wasn't subverted by a joke. Jon is not very good at dealing with those kinds of things. I mean, that's why comedians do what they do, to sort of cope with that, you know? And people always wanted something from Jon. So there was an element of, he was talking to you, but there was a slight distance. He wasn't a hugger. He always seemed slightly distracted.

That night Jon says, "I'm not looking at you, I'm not looking at you, I'm not looking at you." Then I said, "But I just wanted to thank you."

MO ROCCA

The Daily Show was a place that was really fun, and certainly for me really formative, but it could also be really stressful. So there was a mix of feelings that a lot of people had about coming back, but they really did melt away as soon as I walked in.

BEN KARLIN

I had floated an e-mail to one of my friends at the show, Jen Flanz. "Hey, listen. I'm thinking about coming back for the last show, but I want to make sure it'll be cool with Jon." Then I wrote Jon kind of a jokey e-mail, and he immediately responded, and he was like, "I would absolutely love to have you there." It was absolutely incredible. I spent an hour and a half just walking around, sipping tequila, talking to everybody. So many people had come back, from so many different phases of the show. It was like taking time, which normally exists on kind of a line, and flattening it down to a point.

ADAM CHODIKOFF

As we were rehearsing the huge thing with all the correspondents, I went running in to the studio. There was a line in Jon's bullshit speech about the "Patriot Act" being the name because the " 'Are You Scared Enough to Let

Me Look at All Your E-mails Act' doesn't sell." I had contacted my Patriot Act expert, Ellen Nakashima at the *Washington Post*. I found her on vacation, in Hawaii, to check that the Patriot Act was about phone records, not e-mails. I was bullshit detecting the bullshit speech on the last day.

STEVE BODOW

The last thing to do, after rehearsal, was bring, in sequence, all of the people that were going to be in these bits back to that rewrite room and just go through rewriting it, punching up jokes. That was my favorite moment of the night, actually.

MO ROCCA

One of the things that was kind of remarkable is how into it Jon was up to the last second. I didn't expect that we were going to wing it on that last show. It had been pretty carefully scripted, as it needed to be. But I didn't expect note sessions. Somebody came out and said, "Mo and Vance, Jon needs you." We walked into the rewrite room and it was like a time machine. It was suddenly ten years before.

STEVE BODOW

Jon was sitting on the couch in that room, and it's literally a sequence of everyone who's ever been on the show coming in for two minutes, working on a joke, and leaving again.

It was fantastic. This parade of fucking legends. Lew Black, Carell, Kristen Schaal, there's Rob Riggle, Corddry, Helms, everybody. There's Wyatt. Jon and Wyatt, there's that whole weird thing between them, but they're cool in the rewrite and then it's all good, they're just joking about it, but then it's getting serious for a moment. It was like the whole experience of the show, over that fifteen years, collapsed into an hour. It was magic. And so, the last person to come in is Stephen.

He conspires to find a seat next to me. Jon gets distracted for a minute, and Stephen leans over and whispers to me. He says it in such a way that if Jon heard, it was still going to be okay: "I asked his wife about the thing. She thinks it should be a go." I said, "Well, that's all the answer we need." Stephen says, "So, let's do it?"

That was perfect, because Tracey knows Jon better than anybody, and what he might really want, and what he's capable of saying he wants. Plus, also, I think in the back of both my head and Stephen's was, if Jon is really pissed afterward, we can say, "Hey, Tracey said it was okay!"

STEPHEN COLBERT

Find somebody to throw under the bus—that's the first rule of show business.

NANCY WALLS CARELL

We spent a lot of time with people who were correspondents after us that we just met that day. It was really fun.

STEVE CARELL

We hadn't met most of these people, but there was a kinship. That we'd all gone through this exact same experience and...

NANCY WALLS CARELL

It was pretty amazing to be in a room with thirty other people who sort of shared your comic sensibilities, you know? I was definitely the dimmest bulb in that lamp. Well, beside both of the Corddrys. No.

KRISTEN SCHAAL

I remember they were miking me to go onstage, and seeing Trevor Noah standing across from me, just sort of shy and alone, waiting patiently to take the stage because he truly was the new guy, and he was about to own the whole show. That was interesting.

STEVE BODOW

We had the whole thing planned out right up until Colbert would come on, at the end, in that standing position where he would be behind Jon. It's that peculiar shot that Jon was always very fond of, because he likes to have both himself and the other person facing camera. It was just a way of sneaking someone on and then having them be able to play to the same camera with Jon in the foreground. There was also something about it that worked comedically, with the person behind very often delivering shots at Jon.

So we'd have Stephen back there, like, "Jon, aren't you forgetting about someone?"

After whatever the final joke that Stephen and Jon had written for that exchange, in the script it just said, "Come back to Jon," who said, "Thanks, everybody, so much, we'll be right back." So, I just told Chuck, the director, "When Jon says, 'We'll be right back,' just stay there and maybe widen out the frame a little, because Stephen's going to say some stuff."

We didn't put any of what Stephen was going to say in the script. He was off book with it.

Stephen Colbert: [*sitting to Stewart's right at the anchor desk*] Actually, Jon, we're not quite done.

Jon Stewart: [*rolling away from Colbert on his chair and nearly toppling off the riser*] Don't do this.

Stephen Colbert: [*rolling after Stewart and grabbing him by the arm*] No—you can't stop anyone, because they don't work for you anymore! Huge mistake!

Jon Stewart: Please don't do this.

Stephen Colbert: Here's the thing: You said to me and to many other people here years ago never to thank you, because we owe you nothing.

Jon Stewart: [*quietly*] That's right.

Stephen Colbert: It's one of the few times I've known you to be dead wrong...We owe you because we learned from you, by example, how to do a show with intention, with clarity. How to treat people with respect. You are infuriatingly good at your job, okay? [*Stewart covers his eyes, which appear to be filled with tears*] And all of us who were lucky enough to work with you—and you can edit this out later—for sixteen years are better at our jobs because we got to watch you do yours. And we are better people for having known you...Personally, I do not know how this son of a poor, Appalachian turd miner—I do not know what I would do if you hadn't brought me on this show. I'd be back in those hills, mining turds with Pappy!

Jon—and it's almost over—I know you are not asking for this, but on behalf of so many people whose lives you changed over the past sixteen years, thank you. And now, I believe your line—correct me if I'm wrong—is "We'll be right back."

STEVE BODOW

Stephen's incomparable. He landed it in exactly the perfect way and said what everybody wanted to say. What I didn't know was going to happen was everybody rushing the stage afterward. Stephen must've orchestrated that because he must've been starting to tell people, once Jon was onstage, like, "Hey, I'm going to do this thing."

JOHN OLIVER

There is a British person inside Jon. He is emotionally repressed in a classically British way. As a Jersey man I'm sure he would take that as a spectacular insult.

As Stephen is speaking, I was standing in the wings next to Carell and we were thinking we could rush the stage. It was interesting watching Carell, who knew Colbert's rhythms from so long back. He was kind of waiting to make sure that Colbert wasn't going somewhere that Carell was going to stamp on. It was like seeing a really old pair of improvisors. Having one say, "Wait, wait, wait, he's going somewhere with this. Now it's a crescendo. Hold on, hold on, not yet." It was amazing.

JON STEWART

When Stephen started with his thing, I mean, I think the first thing that goes through my head is, "Oh, fuck. You're going to do this. I had sort of thought that I was getting away a little scot-free here." But I kind of thought that if they were going to pull something, they weren't going to pull it then. I thought it would have to do with Bruce. Like at the end, after the band did "Born to Run," Bruce maybe was going to say, "Hey man, I just want to say..." and then he was going to call somebody. And they'd do like you do at a wedding. So I thought there might be some toasting at the end. So I was off guard.

But that's the people that worked there. They're sneaky bastards.

STEPHEN COLBERT

You probably can't hear it on TV, but we were all chanting, "Made him cry! Made him cry!" That's what we were yelling as we were jumping up and down: "Made him cry!"

*   *   *

A pretaped, Goodfellas-style tour of the Daily Show *offices gave the audience a glimpse of the inner workings of the show, and gave staffers a few seconds of well-deserved camera time. The segment also allowed Stewart a much-needed seven minutes to compose himself before delivering one last profane, seriously funny mission statement from behind the* Daily Show *desk.*

JON STEWART

"Bullshit is everywhere." I just thought it would be a nice way of undercutting the self-seriousness of that moment, but also in some ways trying to find something that maybe encapsulates what our ethos is. And I wanted to curse. It's hard not to curse. It's twenty-two minutes. I don't normally go that long without at least throwing something in there.

Harry Frankfurt was a guest years ago. *On Bullshit.* Yes, sir. And I love that book. I think probably George Carlin more than Frankfurt was the inspiration. But maybe Carlin with a hint of Frankfurt. A soupçon. If you were to say, "Who were the progenitors of the monologue?" it would be Carlin and Frankfurt.

Jon Stewart: Then there's the more pernicious bullshit...It comes in three flavors: Making bad things sound good..."Patriot Act." Because "Are You Scared Enough to Let Me Look at All Your Phone Records Act" doesn't sell...Number two: hiding bad things under mountains of bullshit. "Hey, a handful of billionaires can't buy our elections, right?" "Of course not. They can only pour unlimited, anonymous cash into a 501(c)(4) if 50 percent is devoted to 'issue education'"... And finally, my favorite: the bullshit of infinite possibility... "We cannot take action on climate change until everyone in the world agrees gay marriage vaccines won't cause our children to marry goats who are coming for our guns. Until then, I say we teach the controversy."

So I say to you, friends: The best defense against bullshit is vigilance. So if you smell something, say something.

STEVE BODOW

The first act had gone much heavier—longer—than we thought it was going to. The whole show was going much heavier. Michele Ganeless, the network president, was back there with us at the producers' desk, and we were just talking to her about "What can we cut?"

Jon wanted to cut that, the bullshit speech. He was feeling self-conscious about it. And everybody was like, "That's a bad idea! No, we can't do that!" But it was one of the ways to maybe solve the time problem.

We have this intense discussion backstage about it and figured out, okay, we'll do the band thing, and then we'll figure it out, okay? Okay.

So, we break, Jon goes this way, I turn around and it's fucking Bruce Springsteen and the E Street Band standing behind me.

JOHN HODGMAN

I may have a genetic malfunction that does not allow me to connect with Bruce Springsteen's work every time, but I have a very deep connection to "Born to Run," because that is the song I would hear if I was ever in the first act of the show. That meant I was present in the wings as Jon took questions from the audience. Jon said, "All right, let's go," and then "Born to Run" played until it was time to start the show. That was the way the show started every night, and now this was how the show was ending. And so it was not easy to keep it together, to hear "Born to Run" that way.

I don't know what other dumb song Bruce Springsteen played.

JON STEWART

After Bruce I was emotional again, but I think that's more a tribute to his music. He and I'd had lunch at a place down here, and we talked about it a little bit, and I wanted "Land of Hope and Dreams," and at first we were thinking acoustic, and then I just thought that was too melancholy. I wanted that last "Born to Run" riff to take everybody back into celebration mode. Let everybody have a moment, the last moment is us just celebrating with "Born to Run," celebrating an anthem of leaving. Celebrating an anthem together. There should be nothing melancholy about it. It should be a feeling of joyous and raucous celebration that we got to be on the air for sixteen years, we got to be in the conversation, all these things that we never thought we'd get. We got to work with people that we loved. I wanted that last moment to be one of just pure joy.

But when that was done, then I walked over to the kids, Nate and Maggie, they were just kind of staring at me like, "What do we do now?" That hit me.

*   *   *

No basic cable show was ever going to fundamentally change politics or news, and that was never The Daily Show's mission, anyway. But sixteen years later, judging by the 2016 presidential campaign, it appeared that depressingly little had improved. Democratic voters picked the stolid, establishment favorite as their presidential nominee, and the Republicans selected a candidate who was all vengeful, fear-mongering feelings. TV news coverage included extended, live footage of the imminent landing of Trump's plane.

And yet: Echoes of Stewart were all over the political-cultural landscape. The most obvious were his satirical heirs and assigns: Noah, Bee, Oliver, Colbert. But while Stewart alone was certainly not responsible, the ripples of his approach could also be seen in the Washington Post's annotation of every lie in a Trump speech; and in Fareed Zakaria, a nineteen-time Daily Show guest, saying in a live CNN interview that "this is the mode of a bullshit artist" when analyzing Trump's latest attempt to cover over his ignorance; and even in this exchange on MSNBC during the Republican convention:

Chris Matthews: I have a theory about being African-American.
Michael Che: Really? Tell me more.

Much had changed personally for Stewart, of course. In sixteen years, he had moved from a one-bedroom apartment on West Eleventh Street to an expansive condo in Tribeca to an even more expansive farm in New Jersey. He and Tracey McShane married and had a son and a daughter, who taught him, he said, "what joy looks like." But in essential ways Stewart was the same: He retained the capacity for fresh, genuine outrage, and he was determined to find new ways to spread comedy and sanity. Well, and get some sleep.

STEPHEN COLBERT

What drove Jon was being funny, but also being honest. Everything else came from that. The only benefit of fame is it allows you to work more.

JON STEWART

We were never cavalier about the twenty-two minutes of television we had. We might not have hit it every night. You can't. But I feel like we brought it every night.

21

Your Moment of Zen

His 2,614th and last episode as Daily Show *host was finished. Stewart traded his custom-made Armani suit for a T-shirt and khakis in his* Daily Show *office one more time. Buses took the correspondents and staff from the studio to a party on the flight deck of the USS* Intrepid, *where the war stories on this night were about two decades of field pieces.*

As a DJ spun hip-hop and fireworks exploded over the Hudson River, Stewart hugged Noah. During the previous month, as the old guy was getting ready to leave, the new guy had been frantically preparing for his debut, which would come just seven weeks after Stewart's finale. Now Stewart whispered in Noah's ear: "Thank you for never making me feel like the old furniture that was getting thrown out."

Many of Stewart's top staffers—including executive producers Steve Bodow, Jen Flanz, and Adam Lowitt—and his rank-and-file crew—including Chuck O'Neil, Kira Klang Hopf, and Adam Chodikoff—stayed, ready for the challenge of remaking The Daily Show *with Noah. Stewart, in his final months, had encouraged the holdover staff and the new boss to thrash out a show that followed Noah's vision, instead of asking themselves, "What Would Jon Do?"*

TREVOR NOAH

One day before he left, Jon called me into his office and he had a pair of shoes and he said, "What do you think of these shoes?" And I said, "Oh, they're good shoes." He said, "What size are you?" I said, "I'm a size eleven." He said, "I'm a size eight." And he said, "Will these fit you?" And I said, "No." And he said, "Don't let anyone ever tell you, you can't fill my shoes. You're not meant to fill them."

*   *   *

It was an important message in light of the fanfare surrounding Stewart's departure. Unlike Stewart in his first few years at The Daily Show, *Noah didn't have the luxury of experimenting in relative obscurity.*

TREVOR NOAH

Jon told me that when he was building the thing, no one was paying attention to him. For me, it's as if I'm renovating my house, but now I have neighbors watching, and there's permit restrictions, and there's zoning laws, and there's all of these things that didn't exist back then. So that is a big thing. But Jon also said, "Take solace in the fact that I also had to go through this with Craig Kilborn." There were people who thought Jon couldn't do it. I mean, people joked that Jon was the King of Failures. He had, what, six shows before *The Daily Show?*

The people who've gone on from *The Daily Show* to their own shows—they're not my competition. I'm only competing against half-black, half-white, African hosts. Barack Obama is my closer competition than anyone else. He could definitely do standup.

I guess my long-term vision of the show is to shift away from it being media criticism, have somewhat more of a global perspective, and move toward a more Juvenalian style of satire. More pointing out the folly on both sides. Jon's style was more Horatian. You see that with Sam Bee as well. Really polarizing, very end-of-the-world pessimistic. And I want to connect the show with a younger audience. Jon's audience was the oldest viewership on Comedy Central. Which is unsustainable.

Getting people to accept a different style or a different way of doing something, it has been harder than I thought it would be. Both the staff and the audience, yeah. I remember when people would say, "He smiles too much," or, "He's not angry enough." That's your style. Martin Luther King and Malcolm X had very different ways of tackling the same thing. You can't say one was right, one was wrong. You can say they were different.

I think compared to Jon, I'm more Martin Luther King. Jon went straight for the jugular. But he told me that as well: "Do you know how many years it took me to get angry?" It has to be genuine. You saw that with Jon around the stolen election and the Bush presidency. You saw that with the Charleston shooting. You saw that with 9/11.

*   *   *

Way back in 2001, that tragedy had first pointed The Daily Show's *comedy toward a new purpose and gravity. Now, both fittingly and infuriatingly, the long aftermath of the attack on the* World Trade Center *provided a coda that demonstrated what a powerful political and cultural force* The Daily Show *and its extended family had become, and it provided in some ways the real end of the Stewart* Daily Show *era.*

GLEN CAPLIN

In 2010, after Jon had done those shows applying pressure, Congress had passed the Zadroga bill, with health care for first responders. But the coverage expired after five years. So at the end of 2015 the fight was happening all over again.

The issue this time was whether it was going to be permanent or another five-year or ten-year bill. We strongly believed that there's no reason why these guys should have to go back to Congress ever again to beg for health care. Especially when there are similar programs that are all permanent, for black lung workers and nuclear workers. These guys shouldn't be treated differently. More than a hundred FDNY members have died of Ground Zero illnesses; another nine hundred are sick.

Stewart had been keeping busy: rubbing pig bellies on his wife's farm sanctuary in New Jersey, advising Colbert on taking over from Letterman at CBS, signing a deal for a new project of his own, a real-time animation show for HBO. He joined 16 Daily Show *writers, producers, and performers onstage in Los Angeles to collect the show's twenty-third Emmy Award. Oh, and Stewart got body-slammed by the WWE's Jon Cena at a wrestling match in Brooklyn. Unplugging from the* Daily Show *grind was physically transformative: Stewart's blood pressure dropped and the insomnia that had plagued him for years vanished.*

But as the end-of-the-year deadline for Congress to reauthorize the Zadroga health-care funding rapidly approached, the bill was stalled, with Democratic as well as Republican senators balking at the cost. So in mid-September Stewart and more than one hundred first responders went to Washington, walking the halls of Congress and holding a press conference outside the Capitol. Stewart and Ray Pfeifer, a retired New York firefighter who had spent eight months working at Ground Zero, also spoke to the weekly Senate Democratic Caucus lunch.

JON STEWART

Ray Pfeifer, truly one of those most gracious guys you'll ever meet. Stage IV cancer. His leg is basically a metal rod. He's having ministrokes because he has a lesion on his brain, and he's going down there to try and get these people to look him in the eye.

I have such a lowered bar of expectation, and they managed to crawl underneath it. They give you a lot of, "Yeah, we'll take a look at it." Take a look at what? It's a bill that expires in thirty days.

Through September and October prospects for a permanent renewal of the Zadroga bill appeared to improve. Stewart was wary, though, and prepared a backup plan in case Congress dithered. Caplin, now a private consultant, provided advice.

If necessary, he'd go back to Washington, but this time with a camera crew gathering footage for a field piece that would "name and shame" individual politicians. To exert maximum pressure, it would need to air near the end of the 2015 legislative session, but Stewart couldn't be sure of the date. And because he didn't want to interfere with Noah's early days as host of The Daily Show, *Stewart planned on running the Zadroga field piece on John Oliver's HBO show.*

GLEN CAPLIN

I didn't discuss this with Kirsten, but Jon told me, "Here's the thing, I'm going to do the bit on Oliver's show, but it's going to be very nasty and very personal and you need to know that. But I also need a deadline at which point the negotiation game is over and we need to do it. So you tell me when you guys are ready in Washington." He said he needed about a week to put something together.

That's the end of September. I kept holding him off, because it looked like Zadroga would be attached to the transportation bill, which would move during the first week of December.

JON STEWART

They were still trying to be tactful. I didn't know how effective I could be until they were ready to throw up their hands.

GLEN CAPLIN

Near the end of November, the bill starts to fall apart. I had Sunday, December 6, in my head as the date Jon could go on Oliver's show. So I'm getting ready to call Jon and tell him it's time to push the button. But first I fucking Googled John Oliver's show—and sure enough, his last show of the year was right before Thanksgiving. So I called Jon and said it's time to push the button—but Oliver's show is dark. He said, "No problem. I'll go on *The Daily Show*."

TREVOR NOAH

Jon called me and said, "Hey, I need a favor. I know this is a weird thing to ask, I don't even know how to ask it." He told me about the Zadroga thing being close to his heart. I was like, "Look, man, I haven't grown up in American culture, so all of the TV cultural things, I don't have. I don't have beefs with other shows. I don't have qualms with other networks. I don't have time for that. We're all working. You're still Jon Stewart. It's still *The Daily Show*. Come and hang out any time."

GLEN CAPLIN

Jon is a smart strategic thinker. He says, "The mistake Truman made was not dropping a nuke in the ocean first. Here's what we're going to do. I'll go down to Washington the week before we might need to run the bit, and I'll bring a camera crew. I'll tell people I'm doing a bit about Zadroga. That will be the warning." At that point, the transportation bill hadn't fallen apart completely yet. We were hoping Zadroga would get done in the transportation bill and that the show wouldn't be necessary.

JON STEWART

The first responders, they've got the stamina, the integrity, the heroism. All I have is a camera and an inherent sense of dickishness. And if that is what is needed right now, then that is what I will provide for them.

The threat of being embarrassed by Stewart on national TV seemed to have its intended effect. He and John Feal, the leader of a first responders advocacy group, encountered Ohio Republican senator Rob Portman in a hallway. Portman was one of thirty-four senators who had not signed on as a cosponsor of the Zadroga bill.

Jon Stewart: [*in voice-over, as he and the first responders, including Pfeifer in a wheelchair, make Portman squirm*] We finally caught up with Senator Rob Portman on his way from voting to make sure people on the terrorist watch list could still buy guns.

Senator Rob Portman: As I've said, we'll let folks know, as I have already, that I support it. The question is, let's find a way to pay for it.

John Feal: Listen, when you guys want to find money, you can find money. So that "pay for" stuff, it's really not reaching the litmus test with me. At all.

Jon Stewart: [*in voice-over*] That night, Senator Portman of Ohio signed on to the bill. So maybe shame does work.

GLEN CAPLIN

Jon sees Lindsey Graham in the hallway. He gives Lindsey his cell phone number. An hour later Lindsey called Jon and said, "I spoke to Mitch. We're going to get this done." [New Hampshire Republican senator] Kelly Ayotte calls Jon, same thing. But there's nothing in stone here. It's late and no one is saying how long, how much, and how it's getting paid for. Until it's done it's not done. So as late as Thursday night Jon was asking, "Do we have the show for Monday?"

Then the transportation bill fell apart. I called Jon on Friday and said, "Before I give you a whole explanation, let me just give you the headline: Unfortunately we have a show to do on Monday."

JON STEWART

McConnell would meet with the responders, as long as he didn't have to meet with me.

JOHN FEAL

McConnell sat down with five of us. The first words out of his mouth were, "You guys should feel good about yourselves. You're beating me up pretty good in the media." And I said, "Sir, you haven't seen anything. I think you're the world's biggest asshole." I said, "You took us off the transportation bill because of an oil deal that you didn't like. Shame on you for playing God with human life." So we went at it for about a half an hour.

JON STEWART

A couple of them I believe are actively evil.

I did meet with [Utah Republican senator] Mike Lee. I think something's wrong with him. We're talking about the attack, and the first responders are going around the room telling their stories. And one of the guys says, "No, I was in the South Tower when the North Tower collapsed," and Lee smiles and says, in that kind of voice that Diane Sawyer uses when she wants you to think she cares about something, "Oh, you must have some stories."

And you're like, "*Yeah, it's the story of how three thousand people got fucking pancaked.*" It was such a fucking weird nonhuman response that I thought, "We're fucked."

Yeah, it was bad, man. It's bad. They're bad people.

On Monday, December 7, four months after his final show as host, Stewart returned to The Daily Show *and sat in the guest chair. He was gray bearded and fifteen pounds lighter, but his indignation was vintage, with Stewart laying into McConnell for blocking the Zadroga bill.*

The field piece he'd shot during his second trip to Washington, with its scenes of congressional staffers ducking questions and Feal rebuking Portman, made for a sharp eight minutes of satire. But Stewart had also wanted to reassemble his 2010 panel of first responders for an in-studio discussion. The fact that it wasn't possible made the segment even more of a gut punch: Chris Bowman and Ken George were too sick to make an appearance. John Devlin had died of throat cancer. Only Kenny Specht, a former FDNY lieutenant suffering from thyroid cancer, was able to return, sitting next to Stewart and three empty chairs.

Kenny Specht: We were able to meet with Mitch McConnell last week, four of us. Boy, we got pats on the back and we were told by so many people how happy we should be that we got a chance to meet with an elected official in the United States. Mitch McConnell gave us his word that he's going to attach [Zadroga] to the omnibus bill and he's going to fully fund and permanently extend the Zadroga health-care act. That's what he told us. As this bill comes up this week, we're gonna keep him to his word. And this show is doing that.

Jon Stewart: We need your help...all politics are local. Kentucky, it's up to you. I would like you, right now, write Mitch McConnell a letter—

Trevor Noah: Jon, sorry to interrupt. No one really writes letters anymore.

Jon Stewart: A sharply worded editorial in your local paper would be—

Trevor Noah: Jon, people don't really read the newspaper...just tell the people to use social media.

Jon Stewart: Social media! Ooh! Great! Something catchy like this: "End the fuckery!"

But in the Daily Show *editing room afterward, Stewart was frustrated: Earlier that day, Donald Trump had declared that if elected president he would ban Muslims from entering the United States. Stewart knew that Trump's bigoted proposal would dominate mainstream news coverage for days. To keep up the pressure on Congress he would need to co-opt the prevailing infotainment trend: Three days after his surprise return to* The Daily Show, *Stewart crashed Colbert's* Late Show *monologue to deliver an earnest pitch for reauthorization of the Zadroga Act.*

Stephen Colbert: Jon, the media won't pay attention to anything at all unless you are Donald Trump!

Colbert plopped a garish blond wig on Stewart's head and rouged his cheeks orange with Cheetos.

Stephen Colbert: Bring da noise! Bring da Trump!

Jon Stewart: [*in his best thuggish New York white-guy accent*] Ay, lemme tell ya somethin', these 9/11 first responders are the most top-notch, first-class, diamond-encrusted heroes America can produce! Tweet at your congressman with the hashtag "worst responders"! Tell them Donald said pull up your big-boy pants and make America great again! Pass the Zadroga Act or I will glue Congress together, dip them in gold, and wear them around my friggin' neck!

*   *   *

The next day Politico broke the news, in a story headlined, MCCONNELL POISED
TO GIVE JON STEWART WHAT HE WANTS. *One week later, the bill passed: A $3.5 billion
reauthorization of medical care for seventy-two thousand known responders and
survivors of the September 11 attacks.*

GLEN CAPLIN

There was a lot of fuckery that went on until the very last minute, trying to cut the funding. Kirsten Gillibrand and her staff, plus Ben Chevat on
Carolyn Maloney's staff, they were relentless on the inside, fighting back. You
needed an outside game keeping up the pressure, too—that's John Feal, the
first responders, and the *Daily News*. But there's zero percent chance of this
bill happening without Jon Stewart going to DC.

JOHN FEAL

It was a combination of everything. We made three hundred trips to
Washington over twelve years. It was a lot of moving parts, and a lot of moving assholes in Congress. But it took a comedian to shed light on such a serious issue. Would the bill have passed without Jon Stewart? Probably. Don't
know. But I don't think I would've wanted to take that chance.

JON STEWART

In some ways the Zadroga thing was the subtext of the whole show, the
whole sixteen years. A bewilderment, a bewilderment over something which
seems obvious that was not being accomplished. The whole show was that:
"Does anyone else think this is fucking weird?" That's it. That's all the show
was.

I don't think that's a noble thing. But it's something. It's a shared moment.

Cast of Characters

Rory Albanese

Joined *The Daily Show* as a production assistant in 1999. Ran video research department before becoming a segment producer; promoted to executive producer in 2008. Showrunner at *The Nightly Show with Larry Wilmore*, 2015–2016. Credits/blames Lewis Black for inspiring him to become a standup. Extroverted and voluble. Family owns a second-generation Long Island toy distribution company.

Rachel Axler

Earned a master's degree in playwriting at UC San Diego. Moved home to New York and took a class called "Writing for *The Daily Show*" taught by J. R. Havlan. Learned well: was hired in 2005. Left in 2008 to become a writer on *Parks and Recreation*. Playwriting credits include *Archaeology* and *Smudge*. Heroes include Stephen Sondheim and Christopher Durang.

Stew Bailey

Segment producer for MTV's *The Jon Stewart Show*, field producer and executive producer for *The Daily Show*, executive producer for *Last Call with Carson Daly*. University of Kansas roommate of Paul Rudd.

Dan Bakkedahl

As a kid in Minnesota, loved *Saturday Night Live*. As an adult graduate of Florida State's theater program, moved to Chicago and joined Second City—but cried during an *SNL* audition (the tears were not part of the monologue). Hired at *The Daily Show* in August 2005, along with Nate Corddry and Jason

Jones. In a strip poker segment, the words "Exit Only," written by Bakke-dahl's wife in magic marker on his butt cheek, are inadvertently visible. Later costarred as Congressman Roger Furlong in HBO's *Veep*.

Samantha Bee

Born and semihappily raised in Toronto. As child, was either in school or in front of a television; over dinner every day watched Carol Burnett and *SCTV*, idolizing Catherine O'Hara. As teenager, had an unnerving propensity to steal cars. Thought she wanted to go to law school but instead became one of four cofounders of all-female Atomic Fireballs sketch troupe. Met Jason Jones when both were performing in live action anime children's theater production of *Sailor Moon*. Married Jones in 2001; has only recently recovered from trauma of *Sailor Moon* experience. Joined *The Daily Show* in 2003 and was longest-tenured correspondent, leaving in 2015 to create and star in *Full Frontal* on TBS. Mother of three. Takes no shit. Cries easily.

Jonathan Bines

Member of late-nineties New York sketch comedy group The Associates with Aasif Mandvi before becoming writer for *Turn Ben Stein On* and *The Man Show*. Joined the *Daily Show* writing staff in 2001. An accomplished cook, Bines cowrote with Mandvi the screenplay for the indie film *Today's Special*. Writer for *Jimmy Kimmel Live!* since 2003.

Lewis Black

Original and longest-running cast member of *The Daily Show*. Has been ACLU Celebrity Ambassador for Voting Rights, spokesman for Aruba Tourism Authority, and voice of Anger in *Inside Out*. Grammy Award winner. Accomplished playwright. Socialist.

Kevin Bleyer

Wrote for Bill Maher's *Politically Incorrect* and Dennis Miller's CNBC show; hired at *The Daily Show* in 2005. Through a friendship with White House economic advisor Austan Goolsbee, began contributing jokes to President Barack Obama's speeches, especially his appearances at the annual White House Correspondents' Dinner. Went to Iraq in 2007 along with Rob Riggle for *Daily Show*/USO visit to the troops. Later a speechwriter for New York City mayor Bill de Blasio.

Dave Blog

Worked as a production assistant at *The Jon Stewart Show*; hired by Madeleine Smithberg at *The Daily Show* before its debut in 1996, and pitched the idea for its first field piece, about a woman who channeled the spirit of her dead cat. During Stewart's early years as *Daily Show* host, made repeated half-naked on-air appearances, including in a very large diaper. Named the first (and apparently last) *Daily Show* "employee of the year" in 1999. Has been the show's primary graphics producer since 2002. Yes, Blog is his real last name.

Steve Bodow

Cofounder of Yale improv group Just Add Water and of New York theater company Elevator Repair Service. Ex–magazine journalist. Hired as a *Daily Show* staff writer in 2002. Became head writer in 2007 and executive producer in 2013. Brainy and blunt.

Alison Camillo

Was working at Outback Steakhouse in Virginia and came to New York to watch a *Daily Show* taping. Went to a computer lab that night, typed out a résumé, and landed an internship. That was in 1998. Receptionist; talent coordinator; segment supervisor; and, from 2006, coordinating field producer, where responsibilities included finding willing subjects for interviews, assigning correspondents, overseeing assembly of clips, and editing field-piece footage. In 2016, joined Sam Bee's *Full Frontal* as a producer.

Nancy Walls Carell

Went from Second City improv to *Saturday Night Live* for one season, then made *Daily Show* debut on December 7, 1999. Appeared as the "Money Bunny" in recurring "Dollars and 'Cents'" segment and as half of "We" in recurring "We Love Showbiz" segment, with husband Steve Carell. Played sex education counselor in *The 40-Year-Old Virgin*, directed by Judd Apatow.

Steve Carell

Grew up playing hockey, lacrosse, and the fife. Worked briefly as a Massachusetts mailman before moving to Chicago and joining Second City, where he met Stephen Colbert, with whom he would become half of the Ambiguously Gay Duo animated shorts for *Saturday Night Live*, and Nancy Walls, whom he would marry. First *Daily Show* appearance: February 11, 1999, in a field piece about a small town Nebraska snake expert. Went on to star in *The Office*. Oscar nominee as best actor for *Foxcatcher*.

Wyatt Cenac

Born in New York City, raised in Dallas, colleged at the University of North Carolina, wrote for *King of the Hill*. In 2008, at age thirty-two, hired by *The Daily Show* as a writer and correspondent; became Senior Meteorologist, Senior Debt Correspondent, Senior Political Image Consultant, the host of the hit game show "Rappers or Republicans," and the voice of Puppet Michael Steele. Left *The Daily Show* in 2014. Has recorded a live standup album and a standup special for Netflix, both named *Brooklyn*, and hosts a weekly standup showcase, Night Train, in Brooklyn.

Michael Che

Was writing for *Saturday Night Live* when hired as a *Daily Show* correspondent. Made nine appearances from June to September 2014, then rejoined *SNL*, this time as the first black cohost of "Weekend Update." Grew up on New York's Lower East Side, the youngest of seven children; came to comedy relatively late in life, at twenty-six.

Adam Chodikoff

Hired as a researcher at *The Daily Show* prior to its 1996 debut, his prodigious recall of obscure facts and contradictory political quotes, and his ability to draw connections between them, made "Chods" invaluable, particularly in preparing Stewart for contentious interviews of Bush Administration officials like Douglas Feith and Mitch Daniels. Dubbed "an investigative humorist" by the *Washington Post*. Tried to stump Stewart with baseball trivia questions. Duke graduate.

Glenn Clements

A product of the *Daily Show*–New Jersey–NYU pipeline. As a field producer, 2005–2008, traveled to China and Iraq for pieces featuring Rob Riggle, but also worked on great silly bits (Ed Helms in a Speedo, Jason Jones "drowning" his daughter). Later a segment producer for *The Late Late Show with James Corden*, and writer of an animated series starring Jones and Samantha Bee.

Stephen Colbert

Grew up in Charleston, South Carolina, the youngest of eleven children. Majored in theater at Northwestern University; studied improv under Del Close and joined Second City, where he was Steve Carell's understudy. Moved to New York and created *Exit 57* sketch show with Amy Sedaris and Paul Dinello. Hired as a *Daily Show* correspondent in 1997. Left in 2005 to launch *The Colbert Report*, where he won six Emmys and two Grammys. Author of the best-selling *I Am America (And So Can You!)*. Has testified before Congress and run for president. In 2015, succeeded David Letterman as host of CBS's *Late Show*. Can recite the *Lord of the Rings* trilogy from memory.

Kahane Corn Cooperman

A documentary filmmaker who had worked with Albert Maysles and Nick Broomfield, she was hired in 1996 for what she assumed would be a three-month job at a show with the provisional title "The Daily Planet." During the next eighteen years was a *Daily Show* field producer, media spokeswoman, human relations coordinator, and executive producer. Also found time, in 2005, to create *Making Dazed*, a documentary about *Dazed and Confused*, a movie in which she'd made a cameo appearance as a pregnant teen buying cigarettes and booze.

Rob Corddry

Toured for one year with the National Shakespeare Company. Member of sketch group Third Rail Comedy, so named "because we're dangerous!" Joined *The Daily Show* in 2002 and went on to become Senior Media Ethicist, Senior Middle East Correspondent, and Senior Anonymous Congressional Gay Public Restroom Sex Correspondent. Starred in *Hot Tub Time Machine*, cocreated the series *Childrens Hospital*, and costarred in HBO's *Ballers*. Older brother of *Daily Show* correspondent Nate Corddry.

James Dixon

Manager who began working with Jon Stewart in 1987. Other clients include Stephen Colbert, Carson Daly, Jimmy Kimmel, and Bill Simmons. Renowned for driving a tough but fair bargain and for his use of the phrase "baby doll."

Jimmy Donn

Joined *The Daily Show* as an intern in 2002, then was hired full-time as a production assistant. Teamed up with his friend Elliott Kalan to write and produce spec segments with correspondents Rob Corddry and Ed Helms, and was promoted to postproduction department. Has a keen eye and ear for CNN tropes and oddities—such as when the network played "Rock Me Like a Hurricane" to accompany a report on Katrina and New Orleans. With Rory Albanese, hosted a radio show parody called *Blue and Fish in the Morning* from an East Village storefront. Studio announcer for Trevor Noah's *Daily Show*.

Eric Drysdale

Started as *Daily Show* writer on the same day in 2000 as Allison Silverman. Veteran of New York's nineties downtown alternative-comedy scene. Moved to *The Colbert Report* in 2005 to, in Colbert's words, "infect" the new show's writers with Colbert's voice. Talented musician, 3-D photographer, and View-Master artist. Brother of actor and comedian Rebecca Drysdale.

Jen Flanz

Hired as a production assistant at *The Daily Show* in 1997. Worked her way up through the ranks, assembling graphics and props, wrangling correspondents and political convention logistics, and hiring dozens of staffers. Became an executive producer in 2011. Stylish and gregarious. Cancer survivor and unofficial *Daily Show* social director.

Travon Free

Grew up in Compton, California. A knee injury sidetracked his Long Beach State basketball career but prompted him to pursue comedy. A chance meeting with former *Daily Show* writer Rob Kutner at a Los Angeles standup show led to Free being hired as a *Daily Show* writer five months later, in October 2012. Left in 2016 to write for *Any Given Wednesday* on HBO.

Michele Ganeless

Executive at MTV when Stewart hosted *You Wrote It, You Watch It* and *The Jon Stewart Show*. Vice president of programming at Comedy Central when *The Daily Show* debuted in 1996; president of Comedy Central, 2004–2016.

Close friends with Stephen Colbert since they were students and waiters together at Northwestern.

Tim Greenberg

Was directing commercials and aspiring to become an indie filmmaker when he noticed an interesting comedy show job listing on a TV and film production website. Hired as field producer in 2006; first piece was called "Mini Kiss," about rival tribute bands featuring dwarf versions of Gene Simmons and company. Became head of field department in 2012 and executive producer in 2014. Frequent collaborator with Jason Jones, who wore "I'm with Jew" T-shirt while walking through Iran next to Greenberg.

Hallie Haglund

Was *Daily Show* intern during her senior year at Yale. Was then hired as *Daily Show* receptionist, and took the initiative to display her writing skills by creating short staff bios for the show's internal website. Spent two years as a researcher in the field department before being hired as a staff writer in 2010. Running inside joke: Elliott Kalan, her officemate, refers to her as "Midwest Hallie." Haglund, proud and annoyed, corrects him that she is from Colorado, which is definitely in the West.

J. R. Havlan

Standup comic and longest-tenured *Daily Show* writer, from 1996 to 2014. Creator and host of *Writers' Bloc* podcast. Husband of one of Ed Helms's cousins. Father of two. Head writer for *Black and White*, an A&E comedy series about race and culture.

Ramin Hedayati

Worked as a writers' assistant for Bill Maher's *Politically Incorrect* in Los Angeles, but wanted to move back closer to his Staten Island roots. Hired by *The Daily Show* in 2007 for the studio production staff. Spotted bogus crowd rally footage used by Sean Hannity; praised on air by Stewart, who brought out an elderly actor playing Hedayati to demonstrate the damage from watching too much Fox. Suggested Mystikal's "Danger" song as soundtrack to Anthony Weiner scandal segments. Supervised *Daily Show Podcast Without Jon Stewart*. Became a field producer in 2015.

Ed Helms
Grew up in Atlanta. Was on the swim team at Oberlin. Hired as *Daily Show* correspondent in 2002. Later created Andy Bernard on *The Office* and costarred in all three *Hangover* films. Gifted banjo player and irrepressible singer; has sat in with Mumford & Sons and performed at Bonnaroo as one-third of the Lonesome Trio.

Doug Herzog
President of Viacom's music and entertainment group. Former executive at MTV, USA Network, and Fox. Credited with bringing *South Park* to Comedy Central. Emerson College friend of Denis Leary.

John Hodgman
Earned literature degree from Yale; worked as literary agent; first work of his own literature, *The Areas of My Expertise*, got Hodgman on *The Daily Show* as a guest in 2005. Was hired as Daily Show's "Resident Expert" in 2006, enabling him to dismiss Stewart as "a boorish philistine." Those appearances led to Hodgman being cast as "PC" in a famous series of Apple TV ads. In later *Daily Show* years also played "the Deranged Millionaire," enabling Hodgman to bring Yale's a capella Whiffenpoofs on to sing his praises. Can grow an enviable array of facial hair.

Kira Klang Hopf
Hired as a production assistant in 1996. Not long afterward was on verge of taking a job with a new Maureen O'Boyle talk show. Was told by Craig Kilborn, "What are you, crazy? That show is not going to last even six weeks." He wasn't far off. Hopf stayed and is now in her second decade as *Daily Show* script supervisor. Gifted interpreter of cryptic last-minute rewrite instructions by Stewart, Noah, and the writing staff.

David Javerbaum
A product of northern New Jersey and the *Harvard Lampoon*, and a second-place finisher, by one dollar, on *Teen Jeopardy!* Hired for the *Daily Show* writing staff in 1999 by Ben Karlin, who had been a Jewish summer tour friend. Succeeded Karlin as head writer in 2002 and as executive producer in 2006. Major contributor to *America* and *Earth* (the books). Cowrote,

with Adam Schlesinger of Fountains of Wayne, eight original songs for the TV special *A Colbert Christmas* and, for the 2011 Tony Awards show, "Broadway: It's Not Just For Gays Anymore!" Knows God, with Whom he cowrote a Broadway play, a memoir, and tweets. Curly-haired and sharp-tongued. After leaving *The Daily Show*, was a producer on *The Late Late Show with James Corden* and cocreator of *Disjointed*, on Netflix.

Jason Jones

Was working steadily as an actor and comedian in Canada when his wife, Samantha Bee, was hired as a *Daily Show* correspondent. Two years later, in 2005, Jones himself joined the *Daily Show* team. First appearance was riding a horse, naked. His 131 field pieces broke the previous *Daily Show* record, 128, held by Stephen Colbert. Excelled in foreign adventures, including trips to Iran, India, Iceland, Denmark, and Russia, where he was threatened by Mikhail Gorbachev. In unfortunate accident, penis once became stuck in a cantaloupe. Left in 2015 to write and star in *The Detour*, on TBS.

Kent Jones

Wrote for *InStyle* and *People* before becoming member of original *Daily Show* writing staff, in 1996. Subsequently wrote and performed for Air America Radio, *The Marc Maron Show*, and *The Rachel Maddow Show*.

Miles Kahn

A self-described "film school nerd" who had been working in reality TV, where he often copied the style of *Daily Show* field pieces—good practice for when he was hired as a *Daily Show* field producer in 2006. Elaborate mini-action-movie segments he produced, with helicopters and stunt men, earned him the nickname "MKP," for "Miles Kahn Productions." Became an executive producer at Samantha Bee's *Full Frontal*.

Elliott Kalan

A 2002 *Daily Show* internship began his climb: production assistant, segment producer, staff writer, head writer. Made cameo on-air appearances playing a U.S. soldier in Iraq; Toppington Von Monocle; Doodle Von Taintstain; Steve Carell's butler; and throwing rose petals in front of Bill O'Reilly. Diminutive, high-spirited, and proudly nerdy; a serious Marvel Comics and Abraham

Lincoln buff. Cohost of the *Flophouse* podcast, which critiques flop movies. Head writer for new incarnation of *Mystery Science Theater 3000*.

Jessie Kanevsky

In 2004, wanted to intern at *Tough Crowd with Colin Quinn* but was redirected to *The Daily Show*. Became audience coordinator, handling ticket requests, chatting with excited fans waiting in line for taping, and accepting their gifts of oil-painting portraits of Stewart. Proud daughter of south Brooklyn and Daily Show Pizza Correspondent on podcast episode. Recommends L&B Spumoni Gardens of Bensonhurst.

Ben Karlin

Arrived at the University of Wisconsin thinking he wanted to become a journalist. Spent three years as a writer and editor at the *Onion*. Hired as *Daily Show* head writer in 1999; he was promoted to executive producer in 2003. Helped create *The Colbert Report*; later became a writer and producer of *Modern Family*. Editor of and contributor to the essay collection *Things I've Learned from Women Who've Dumped Me*. Round-faced and forcefully opinionated.

Jill Katz

Since 2006, *The Daily Show*'s executive in charge of production, handling, among other business responsibilities, budgets, contract negotiations, convention coverage logistics, and legal wrangles—for example, when a joke uses a piece of music or image without exactly, technically having permission. Knows to avoid the song "One Shining Moment," though it was a favorite of Stewart's.

Pat King

Senior producer who was instrumental in transition from laborious assembly of video montages to SnapStream era, allowing *The Daily Show* to rapidly knit together damning clips. Became supervising producer at *Full Frontal with Samantha Bee*.

Jordan Klepper

Second most famous product of Kalamazoo, Michigan, after Derek Jeter. Improv veteran of Second City in Chicago and Upright Citizens Brigade in New York. Spotted by *Daily Show* producers on web series *Engaged*, cowritten by and costarring his wife, Laura Grey. Debuted March 2014 as New Senior Caucasian Correspondent. Six feet four inches tall. Was paid perhaps Jon Stewart's ultimate compliment: "He's just as funny as a short guy."

Hillary Kun

Segment producer on *Politically Incorrect with Bill Maher* for eight years. Changed jobs and coasts in 2001 to help Stewart move *The Daily Show*'s guest interviews away from celebrities and toward politicians and authors. Married to standup comic Joe Bolster. Mother of twin boys.

Rob Kutner

Attended same Atlanta prep school as Ed Helms and Jo Miller. Wrote for *Dennis Miller Live* on HBO before being hired at *The Daily Show* in 2002. A leader, along with Steve Bodow, Tim Carvell, and Jason Ross, of the *Daily Show* writers during the strike. Left in 2009; later a writer and producer for Conan O'Brien on *The Tonight Show* and at TBS.

Matt Labov

Publicist; began working with Jon Stewart in 1994 and represented him until 2008. Other clients have included Judd Apatow, Sacha Baron Cohen, Rob Riggle, Will Ferrell, and Method Man. Started his own firm, Forefront Media, in 2010. Left-handed, as is Stewart.

Josh Lieb

Proud son of Columbia, South Carolina. A coeditor of *Harvard Lampoon*, 1993. Writer and/or producer for *Twisted Puppet Theater*, *The Jon Stewart Show*, *NewsRadio*, and *The Simpsons*. Joined *The Daily Show* in 2006 as a writer and producer. Author, *I Am a Genius of Unspeakable Evil and I Want to Be Your Class President*. As of 2014, showrunner of *The Tonight Show with Jimmy Fallon*. Death-penalty supporter, Second Amendment believer, snappy dresser.

Beth Littleford

Hired in 1996, the only original *Daily Show* correspondent to continue from the Kilborn era into the Stewart years. Her "Beth Littleford Interview" segment parodied puffy celebrity interviews, and included encounters with

Dionne Warwick, David Duke—who recommended Clorox to remove stains from white sheets—and an increasingly annoyed David Cassidy. Masturbated an Iowa boar for a field piece. Left in 2000 for a role on *Spin City*. Was married for nearly twenty years to former *Daily Show* producer Rob Fox.

Adam Lowitt

In 2002, while a senior at Florida State became the first full-time intern in *The Daily Show*'s postproduction department, was hired as a staff member right after college graduation, and helped pioneer the construction of video montages that became a *Daily Show* trademark. After years as a segment and supervising producer, became an executive producer in 2013. Performs as a standup; married to a writer of children's TV shows.

Al Madrigal

Mexican-Sicilian-American. Born on the Fourth of July. Grew up in San Francisco's poetically-named Inner Sunset neighborhood. Dropped out of college to work in family's human resources company, where his speciality was firing people. Rebelled against family desire that he take over the company to pursue a career in standup comedy. Hired as a *Daily Show* correspondent in 2011. Cofounder of All Things Comedy podcast network.

Aasif Mandvi

Born in Mumbai, grew up in northern England and Tampa, Florida. Award-winning actor who had appeared in plays by Tony Kushner and Tom Stoppard. Joined *The Daily Show* full-time in 2007; was Senior Muslim Correspondent, Senior Asian Correspondent, and Senior Foreign-Looking Correspondent. Nearly arrested for barging into offices of Idaho agribusiness while dressed as giant mutant fish for field piece about chemical dumping. Writer of a play, *Sakina's Restaurant*, and a memoir, *No Land's Man*.

Jim Margolis

Producer for *Frontline* and *60 Minutes*, with expertise in international terrorism, who joined *The Daily Show* as a field producer in 2001, one week before the 9/11 terrorist attacks. Credited with sharpening *Daily Show* field interviews and realistic look of field pieces. Became head of field department in

2006 and co–executive producer in 2011. Later teamed up with Rob Corddry on Adult Swim's *Newsreaders*.

Judy McGrath

Programming executive who helped launch and build MTV; an early and forceful champion of Jon Stewart. Rose to become chairwoman and CEO of MTV Networks, overseeing Comedy Central, among other channels, from 2004 to 2011. Now runs digital video company Astronauts Wanted and serves on board of directors of Amazon.

Lauren Sarver Means

Was a *Daily Show* intern while a film student at NYU. Hired, in 2005, as assistant to executive producer Ben Karlin. Worked as segment producer for four years, then became staff writer in 2012. Officemate and karaoke duet partner with Zhubin Parang. Nicknamed "Stone Cold Sarver" for her deadpan demeanor. Met husband Sam Means when he was *Daily Show* writer.

Justin Melkmann

Spent five years at ABC's *Good Morning America* before joining *The Daily Show*'s postproduction unit in 1997, rising to head of the department in 2013. Also a talented punk rock cartoonist and guitarist in the band World War IX.

Jo Miller

Motorcycle rider. Knitter. Was grad student in Medieval Jewish History. Helped found improv group at Yale with Steve Bodow, who invited Miller to apply for *Daily Show* writing job in 2009. Knit Jon Stewart a hat and scarf as a going-away present in 2015. Executive producer of *Full Frontal* with Samantha Bee.

Stu Miller

Spent three years as an associate producer at *48 Hours*, on CBS; hired at *The Daily Show* in 2003 as field pieces took on more of the tropes of "real" journalism. First field piece was a Rob Corddry report about a Jersey Shore boardwalk attraction—shooting paintballs at a guy dressed as Saddam Hussein. Thrived in improvised settings like political conventions. Known as

"Smills" to fellow *TDS* staffers. Left in 2016 to become executive producer at Bill Simmons's HBO show.

Hasan Minhaj

As college student, decided to try standup after watching Chris Rock special. Wrote a *Daily Show* audition piece that was inspired by Ben Affleck's argument with Bill Maher about discrimination against Muslims; in it, Minhaj boldly mocked Stewart's movie, *Rosewater*, while sitting across from Stewart. Was hired immediately. Debuted as correspondent in November 2014, defending mobility rights for pigs.

Trevor Noah

Grew up in the Soweto township of Johannesburg, the son of a white father and a black mother—a relationship that was illegal at the time. By the late 2000s had become an international standup comedy star. Was the first South African comic to appear on *The Tonight Show* and *The Late Show with David Letterman*. Joined *The Daily Show* in 2014 as a contributor and made two appearances before being named Jon Stewart's successor as host. Speaks eight languages. Author of a memoir, *Born a Crime*.

John Oliver

Grew up in a suburb of Birmingham, England, the son of two teachers. Attended University of Cambridge. Had appeared on British TV news satire show *Mock the Week* before joining *The Daily Show* in 2006. Hosted for eight weeks in the summer of 2013 while Stewart was directing the movie *Rosewater*. Creator and host of *Last Week Tonight* on HBO; hired former *Daily Show* head writer Tim Carvell as executive producer. Long-suffering fan of Liverpool FC.

Chuck O'Neil

Was working at *Good Morning America* in 2000 when a cameraman friend passed along a tip that *The Daily Show* was looking for a new director. O'Neil's background in network news and sports was indispensable as *The Daily Show* upgraded its coverage of live events, including conventions and election nights. Is the "Chuck" whom Stewart would call out to during a show asking for a video clip to roll.

Zhubin Parang

Was corporate lawyer by day and comedian by night. In 2007, met Hallie Haglund when they were partners on an improv team at Upright Citizens Brigade— "still one of the worst improv teams UCB has ever had," he says. In 2011, Haglund encouraged Parang to apply for an open *Daily Show* writing job. Promoted to head writer in 2015. Karaoke stalwart; ferociously proud Tennessee native. Head writer, *The Daily Show with Trevor Noah*.

Daniel Radosh

Reformed blogger and print journalist whose work has appeared in the *New Yorker, McSweeney's, Playboy,* and *Spy*. Father is a historian, antiwar activist, and former Communist Party member. Was, for a time, obsessed with the girl pop group Huckapoo. Author of *Rapture Ready! Adventures in the Parallel Universe of Christian Pop Culture*.

Chris Regan

A former advertising copywriter and standup comic, Regan was the first writer hired by Jon Stewart at *The Daily Show*. Creator of "Produce Pete with Steve Carell." Has also been a staff writer at *Family Guy* and coauthored a memoir, *Shatner Rules*, with William Shatner. Possibly big in South Korea, thanks to an acting appearance in a nineties foreign soap opera.

Jason Reich

A native of Long Island and a graduate of Cornell. Was hired as *The Daily Show*'s writers' assistant in 1999, two months after Stewart took over as host. Promoted to the writing staff in 2001. With Tim Carvell, wrote the judicial branch of government section for *America (The Book)*. Left *The Daily Show* in 2007; later worked with *Daily Show* alum Jim Margolis on *Newsreaders* and Samantha Bee on *Full Frontal*.

Rob Riggle

Big Rig. Studied theater and film at the University of Kansas, then spent twenty-three years in the Marine Corps, serving in Liberia, Kosovo, Albania, and Afghanistan, rising to the rank of lieutenant colonel in the reserves. While assigned to New York, joined Upright Citizens Brigade improv group. Spent one season as an *SNL* featured player; hired as a *Daily Show* correspondent in 2006. Returned to Afghanistan in 2007 to perform USO shows and shoot guns and *Daily Show* segments.

Mo Rocca

Italian-Colombian-American. Harvard graduate and Hasty Pudding presi- dent. Toured Southeast Asia in the cast of *Grease*; wrote and produced *Wishbone*, a PBS series about a dog who teaches kids about classical literature. Interest in obscure American presidents led to his hiring as *Daily Show* correspondent in 1998. After leaving *The Daily Show* in 2003 has been a regular contributor to CBS's *Sunday Morning* and is the host of *My Grandmother's Ravioli* on Cooking Channel.

Jason Ross

Was performing standup and writing for an Internet comedy site when he was hired as a *Daily Show* writer in 2002. Envied by nerdier *Daily Show* writers for his knowledge of guns, sports, and the financial industry, the last of which Ross put to extensive use during the show's 2008–2009 financial crisis segments. Proud of dressing John Oliver in a big foam suit for a "Schoolhouse Rock" parody segment. Left *The Daily Show* in 2013. Later a writer for Jimmy Fallon's *Tonight Show* and head writer for Bill Simmons's HBO show.

Kristen Schaal

Raised in rural Colorado, graduated from Northwestern, moved to New York to pursue a career in comedy. Played a stalker-fan in *Flight of the Conchords* and Hazel Wassername on *30 Rock*. Founding member of the Story Pirates, which adapts and performs stories and songs written by children. Married to former *Daily Show* writer Rich Blomquist, with whom she wrote *The Sexy Book of Sexy Sex*.

Allison Silverman

Hired in 2000 as *The Daily Show* beefed up its writing staff for the presidential campaign. Yale graduate; veteran of Chicago improv scene. Left in 2002 to join *Late Night with Conan O'Brien*, then became original executive producer of *The Colbert Report*. Silverman's legs doubled for Madonna's, with Colbert crawling between them, for a *Daily Show* segment about Madonna's wedding to Guy Ritchie.

Madeleine Smithberg

Talent coordinator for *Late Night with David Letterman*. Producer of *The Jon Stewart Show* on MTV. Cocreator and first executive producer of *The Daily Show*. Daughter of academics who later became psychoanalysts; mother of one son. *The Daily Show*'s "Moment of Zen" was inspired by Smithberg seeing her cat staring at the nature scenes that ended CBS's *Sunday Morning with Charles Kuralt*.

Craig Spinney

Has been stage manager since *The Daily Show* debuted in 1996. Responsible for coordinating all activity in the studio, from wrangling the talent and camera operators to the proper placement of props. Songwriter and guitarist. Son is a Marine Corps first lieutenant.

Sara Taksler

Like Jon Stewart, a proud native of central New Jersey. Hired in 2005 as a *Daily Show* field department researcher after working at *Tough Crowd with Colin Quinn*. Became a segment producer and senior producer. Has made two documentary films: *Twisted*, about professional balloon artists; and *Tickling Giants*, about Bassem Youssef's harrowing adventures in Egyptian political satire. Can talk backward.

Jessica Williams

Grew up in Los Angeles. Made her TV debut at sixteen, on Nickelodeon's *Just for Kicks*. At twenty-two, was juggling classes in improv at Upright Citizens Brigade with classes in English at Cal State Long Beach. Had to hurry up and finish college exams so she could move to New York to debut, in January 2012, as *The Daily Show*'s youngest correspondent. Left the show in 2016, ten months after Stewart, to develop her own project for Comedy Central. One of "2 Dope Queens," with Phoebe Robinson, who host a live comedy show and podcast.

Larry Wilmore

Grew up in Los Angeles as a self-described nerd, heavily interested in science fiction and magic tricks, before trying standup comedy in college. Wrote for sitcoms including *Sister, Sister* and *The Fresh Prince of Bel-Air*; created and/ or produced *The PJs* with Eddie Murphy, *The Bernie Mac Show*, and *Whoopi*.

Says his move from *The Office* to *The Daily Show* as Ed Helms went in the opposite direction was "a prisoner exchange." Younger brother, Marc, is a longtime writer and producer at *The Simpsons*. Triathlete. In 2015, took over the *Colbert Report* time slot as host of *The Nightly Show*.

Stacey Grenrock Woods

Had been a print journalist and the booker for LA's Viper Room club before spending five years as a *Daily Show* correspondent, from 1998 to 2003. Subsequently became longtime sex columnist for *Esquire*; wrote a memoir, *I, California*; and is a writer for *The Democracy Handbook*, a web and cable series starring Bassem Youssef.

Bassem Youssef

Was a cardiac surgeon in Cairo before being galvanized by the 2011 Arab Spring—and by *The Daily Show*—to create his own political satire program, which was initially shot in the laundry room of Youssef's apartment building and uploaded to YouTube. Its success led to the weekly *Al Bernameg* ("The Program") on Egyptian TV. Creator of American cable series *The Democracy Handbook* and author of *Revolution for Dummies: Laughing Through the Arab Spring*.

Acknowledgments

Maybe it's fate, maybe it's just the subway. This morning, with these acknowledgments unwritten and overdue, I stepped off the C train and standing there on the platform was a woman I hadn't seen in several years. Back in 1993, when we were colleagues at *New York* magazine, Rebecca Mead suggested I check out a smart and funny comedian friend of hers, Jon Stewart. So that's a pretty good place to start: Thanks, Rebecca.

She is just one of the many journalism colleagues whom I have had the honor to work with and learn from over the years. Joe Klein didn't just hire me as his assistant; he taught me how to be a reporter and how to tell a story, and he continues to be a friend and an inspiration. Peter Blauner, Peg Tyre, and Eric Pooley were and are exemplary role models. Matt Giles, Stephen J. Dubner, Bob Hardt, Mike Nitzky, Mark Jacobson, and Joanna Molloy have been standout comrades. Then there are the exceptional editors, whose help I could use right about now: John Homans, the late great Mark Giles, Jon Scher, Mike McCormick, Peter Herbst, Genevieve Smith, Michael Hirschorn, Ed Kosner, Kurt Andersen, Caroline Miller, and Adam Moss.

The Daily Show (The Book) would not exist if not for the hundreds of talented people who made (and make) *The Daily Show*. I wish I'd been able to reach every one of them during the sprint to write this book, but they all have my appreciation, especially the people quoted in these pages, and even a few of those who refused to be. I owe a particular debt to the staffers who made time to talk during the hectic transition to the show's new era.

Extra special thanks to Jen Flanz, Steve Bodow, Elliott Kalan, Jo Miller, Ed Helms, John Hodgman, Rory Albanese, Ben Karlin, Madeleine Smithberg, Josh Lieb, Lewis Black, Samantha Bee, Kahane Corn Cooperman, David

Javerbaum, Adam Lowitt, Adam Chodikoff, John Oliver, J. R. Havlan, and Stew Bailey, for fielding more than their share of questions with good humor and generosity.

For talking through a lunch, a gym workout, and two late-night car rides home, respectively, in between creating their own very funny daily shows, I am deeply grateful to Trevor Noah, Larry Wilmore, and Stephen Colbert.

For sharing their photographs in addition to their memories, huge thanks to: Alison Camillo, Kira Klang Hopf, Al Madrigal, Eric Drysdale, Miles Kahn, Jim Margolis, John Hodgman, Jill Katz, Travon Free, J. R. Havlan, Jody Morlock, Elise Terrell, Pat King, John Feal, and Jen Flanz.

Comedy Central's cooperation was indispensable. Doug Herzog, Michele Ganeless, Steve Albani, Renata Luczak, Lorne Mitchell, and Owen Miller, thanks for making it happen.

Working on this book showed me why James Dixon has such a distinguished and loyal client list: He's an honest, passionate advocate who is also tremendous fun. And thanks to Team Baby Doll, Dan Bodansky and Ben Taren, for handling key logistics.

Jamie Raab is not just Grand Central's savvy publisher but a deft and patient editor. A writer working on his tenth book would be lucky to have her guidance; this writer couldn't have completed his first without her incomparable clarity and calm.

Liz Connor, Nolen Strals, and Eric Baker came up with (many) terrific designs for the cover. Bob Castillo, Thomas Whatley, and Giraud Lorber produced a big book on a crazy deadline. Jimmy Franco spread the word. Cheryl Smith wrangled the audiobook version. Elizabeth Kulhanek was a swift and steady lieutenant. Elisa Rivlin kept us legal.

Stellar fact-checking: Thayer McClanahan.

Speedy and accurate interview transcription: CarolLee Kidd and CLK Transcription.

For the soundtrack: Bruce Springsteen and the E Street Band.

I collapse in gratitude—to borrow a phrase from the illustrious Jennifer Senior—for the wise counsel, in a wide variety of forms, dispensed by her, Bob Kolker, Megan Newman, Matthew Greenberg, Father Peter Colapietro, Dr. Nina K. Singer, and Walter Paller.

David Black is an outstanding agent in all the necessary, conventional ways. That he took my annoying calls while waiting for doctors' appointments, plied me with bourbon, and loaned me prime office space is above and beyond. His team at the David Black Agency, notably Jennifer Herrera, went out of its way to make a squatter feel at home. Sarah Paolantonio provided early and essential research assistance.

For friendship that years and miles can't dilute, Steve Etter, the Birddog. *Ahhhoooo!*

How do you thank your parents? Not enough, ever. Joan Serra and Bob Smith have been there for me on this and every other adventure. Liane Marooney, Barbara Jordan-Smith, Jason Smith, Sue Smith, David Brunicardi, and Caryn Marooney—your support has been as inexplicable as it has been invaluable. Tommy Fuller and Jim Marooney, you're with us still.

Thanks to Tracey Stewart for encouraging her then-boyfriend to host *The Daily Show*. Apologies to Nate and Maggie for taking up so much of your dad's time when he was allegedly retired.

Jon Stewart gave me enough hours of laughs and insights to fill a second book. Plus some pizza and a ride home. What I really owe him for, though, are the chance, the trust, and the freedom to tell this story. Thanks.

And as if that weren't wildly inadequate: There are three other people who deserve far more than words. Medals for putting up with me? Sure, but that's not new. Lila, Jack, and Lisa Marooney listened to my endless *Daily Show* anecdotes, offered sharp opinions on cover designs, and endured my fits of anxiety. They showed faith through unexpected setbacks; they kicked my ass when I needed it; they lifted my heart whether they were onstage, on the pitcher's mound, or on West Beach. Above all, and always, Lila, Jack, and Lisa supplied joy. May this book return it, even a little.

—Chris Smith, Brooklyn, September 12, 2016

Index

About the Authors

Chris Smith is a contributing editor at *New York*, where he has covered politics, sports, and entertainment. He lives with his son, daughter, and wife in Brooklyn.

Jon Stewart is a comedian, a writer, an actor, a producer, a director, a best-selling author, and a former host of *The Daily Show*. He lives with his wife and children in New Jersey.